D0282457

SCIENCE AND CULTURE SERIES
JOSEPH HUSSLEIN, S.J., PH.D., GENERAL EDITOR

THEY LIVED THE FAITH

MORENO

WARD

OZANAM

BROWNSON

Great Lay Leaders of Modern Times

DE MAISTRE

O'CONNELL

MONTALEMBERT

VEUILLOT

GÖRRES

WINDTHORST

THEY LIVED THE FAITH

THOMAS P. NEILL, PH.D.

THE BRUCE PUBLISHING COMPANY
MILWAUKEE

DE MUN

JARICOT

CORTÉS

TO THE MEMORY OF

REVEREND RAYMOND CORRIGAN, S.J.

(1889–1943), SCHOLAR, TEACHER, FRIEND,

WHO APPRECIATED THE ROLE OF THE LAYMAN

IN THE HISTORY OF THE CATHOLIC CHURCH.

PREFACE

Two considerations, above others, have prompted the writing of this book. The first is concerned with historical truth, the second with the work of Catholic laymen today.

In the first place, the ordinary history textbook covering the nineteenth century (1815–1914) tells of the industrial revolution, of great strides in material progress, of the advance of literacy and of universal suffrage, of a few short wars, and of Europe overcoming the whole world in the age of imperialism. It is a story which begins by ending the long Napoleonic wars and ends by beginning World War I. It is a story written around such men as Cavour and Bismarck, Darwin and Huxley, Schopenhauer and Nietzsche, Sherman and Von Moltke. It is a story devoted almost exclusively to material things, for the nineteenth century was an age of avowed materialism.

Such a story as this, which passes for a full and balanced account of the century, contains the names of only one or two of the men treated in the following pages. O'Connell is usually mentioned, because no one can tell the story of English and Irish history without telling of O'Connell's exploits. Montalembert and Windthorst might be mentioned, and, if the historian dwells on things social, Ozanam might receive a line or two.

One searches in vain, though, for such names as those of Görres, Donoso Cortés, De Maistre, or Veuillot. Even typical Church histories make little mention of these men. They dwell instead on the outstanding personalities of Pius IX and Leo XIII; of Gibbons, Manning, Newman, Dupanloup, and Von Ketteler. They tell of the Church's revitalized missionary activity and of such saints as Don Bosco and the Little Flower and the Curé of Ars. But they tend to overlook the outstanding work of such

Catholic lay leaders as are treated here. For that reason they fail to tell the full story or to render these Catholic laymen their due. It is to do something toward placing these laymen's names in the historical spotlight they deserve that this book is written.

Treatment is therefore given both to figures fairly well known to the American reader and to those on whom there is not more than a scattered article or two in the English language. O'Connell, for example, has been the subject of many biographies, whereas Donoso Cortés and Görres are unknown to the American and English reader. These two men are nevertheless as significant to the Church in the nineteenth century as O'Connell. Though less well known, they are important figures of the Catholic laity and are therefore put side by side here with the more renowned names in order to do them both justice.

There are still others, of course, who deserve inclusion in any full list of laymen who notably promoted the Church's welfare in the nineteenth century, men like Chateaubriand and La Tour du Pin in France, Mallinckrodt in Germany, William George Ward or Frederick Lucas in England. But it is necessary to stop somewhere — and the thirteen treated here are, in the author's opinion, more important than any who have been omitted. Other Catholic laymen were more famous figures in their respective fields, Louis Pasteur in biochemistry for example, but they do not stand out in the same way as do the men treated in this book — as lay defenders, namely, of the faith. The men we have selected were chosen because they considered Catholic Action a vocation, not an avocation.

In the second place, the study of these men can serve a useful purpose today. They serve both as inspiration and, to some extent, as models for Catholic laymen who want to promote the Church's cause on earth and thus mean to play their part in revitalizing a sadly sick society. Because this is an age when laymen are more important for the Church's welfare than formerly — as Pope Pius XI so insistently pointed out, and the present Holy Father frequently repeats — it is obvious that the example of outstanding laymen of the past century can prove especially useful and instructive at the present time.

And here the author wishes to make public his indebtedness especially to three persons in the writing of these chapters. First of all, he is particularly indebted to the late Reverend Raymond Corrigan, S.J., under whose guidance he first became interested in the Catholic lay leaders of the nineteenth century, and from whom he received valuable help and direction on this subject in years gone by. Had Father Corrigan lived, the author believes, he would himself have drawn together his various studies on this subject in the form of a book – a book which would have been incomparably more profound than this one. The author is also indebted to Professors Emerson Hynes, of St. John's University, and Charles T. Dougherty, of St. Louis University, for their patient reading of the manuscript and for their many invaluable suggestions. Their wide reading, balanced wisdom, and sense of style have done much to make these pages less burdensome reading than otherwise they would have been.

Thomas P. Neill

St. Louis University
February 1, 1950

CONTENTS

THEY LIVED THE FAITH

INTRODUCTION

Anyone not believing Christ's promise that He would remain with His Church for all time, must have thought in 1800 that it was inevitably doomed to quick and certain death. It is difficult indeed for us, who live in the twentieth century, to realize how weak and enervated, how senescent, how certainly doomed to death the Church must have appeared at the beginning of the nineteenth century. *Rigor mortis* was apparently setting in. The secular world waited impatiently for the final disintegration of the Church's body — as always happens when institutions have given up their spirit and begun to decay. On the surface, scanned from a purely secular viewpoint, there seemed good reason for so waiting. With the single exception of the Counter Reformation of the late sixteenth and early seventeenth centuries, the Church's history had been a story of steady decline since the late Middle Ages. That decline finally reached the point of death, it seemed, by the end of the eighteenth century.

The Church, indeed, had suffered from administrative anarchy, from moral decadence and consequent loss of prestige before the Protestant Revolt occurred in the sixteenth century. Administrative anarchy had been a major factor in promoting a deterioration that Rome was unable — and sometimes it seemed unwilling — to halt. When reform was accomplished later in the sixteenth century, the Protestant Revolt had permanently split up Europe religiously.

The result, indeed, was bad for all religions because the absolute ruler was able thenceforth to bargain with various religious groups and to protect that religion which buckled under and surrendered to him more and more of the functions formerly reserved to religious authorities. Thus in every country, Catholic as well as Protestant, the Church of the realm was identified popularly with the Old Regime until the French Revolution of 1789. French kings nominated and, for all effective purposes, chose the bishops of the Church. So it was in most of the other countries of Europe. The king enforced canon law, or refused to do so, as he saw fit; his permission had to be obtained before a papal letter could be read from the pulpits of the churches in his realm.

This interweaving of Church and State may not be a bad thing in the abstract, but in the concrete case of Europe in the eighteenth century it turned out badly for the Church. The rulers were not interested, by and large, in the religious welfare of their subjects. They looked upon the Church as a department of State, and religion as a means for keeping their subjects content. Thus, when the secular governments of the Old Regime were criticized by the new and revolutionary thinkers of the last half of the eighteenth century, the Church came under fire as part of the Old Regime. Revolutionary thought was bound, by the existing nature of things, to be anticlerical and even antireligious.

The trend of thought in the eighteenth century had been secularistic. At first deistic, then agnostic, and finally in some cases atheistic, the new thinkers tried to push God out of the world and far into the heavens where He could not interfere with the conduct of men here below. In turn they tried to push His representative, the Church, into the sacristy, confining its ministers to the administration of the sacraments and the preaching of sermons on "purely spiritual" matters. The rest of life, they held, belonged to Caesar or to the "sovereign people." So the revolutionary thought generated toward the end of the eighteenth century was ill-tempered as far as religion was concerned; the important, influential thinkers of the age were all anticlerical. Unfortunately, the Church could not produce men able to answer their arguments. Capable men were too busy administering their dioceses or – unfortunately – serving as diplomats or finance ministers in their various governments. So the Church suffered from the barrage of the age's "enlightened" thinkers without answering them effectively. We can say today, with the wisdom that more than a century of hindsight gives us, that when the Old Regime collapsed, the Church was almost bound to collapse too – save for the fact that the Church never dies when it apparently collapses, as does the State.

So when the French Revolution of 1789 swept across France and most of Europe with a fury and a power hitherto unknown in Europe, it directed its force against the Catholic Church in France as well as against the government of Louis XVI. It swept the Church as an organization out of the country, driving the clergy who were loyal to Rome into hiding in the rural areas or over the sea to America, and it set up in place of the Catholic Church a national organization controlled by the State, owned by the nation, loyal to the government alone. Frenchmen were given the choice of being good Catholics and suffering persecution, or being good citizens and obtaining economic and political preferment.

Thus France became a divided nation – which she continued to be all through the nineteenth century. The little people, peasants on the farms and villagers throughout the country, remained loyal to the Church, whereas the city people were loyal to the Revolution instead. When Napoleon came to power in November of 1799, he was astute enough to see that the breach between "the two Frances" must be healed. So he worked out an agreement with Pius VII whereby the Catholic Church was allowed to come out in the open again – but it was pretty much as a department of State, certainly not as an independent religious organization, that Catholicism was restored in France. Despite the many *Te Deums* and numerous parades, the Church in France was not a healthy institution in the early years of the nineteenth century. Its leaders did not have the intellectual acumen to meet the attacks of the Voltairean rationalists, nor did they have the spiritual *élan* to combat the secularized religion of nationalism generated by the French Revolution. The Church seemed to hang on grimly in France, standing only because of Napoleon's embrace – which was squeezing the very life out of the institution he was thought to protect. There was little reason for the French ambassador to Rome to change the opinion he had expressed to his government in 1799 when Pope Pius VI had died: "The late pope has just died; he will be the last of them." Another pope had been elected in Venice, it was true, but the secular observer must have thought that the cardinals were only postponing the Church's inevitable demise a bit longer.

When the colossal Napoleonic empire collapsed and the Bourbons returned to Paris, Catholicism was declared to be once again the established religion of the realm – as in the eighteenth century. This declaration did not give the Church in France new life or renewed vitality. If anything, it hurt the Church by associating it with the discredited émigrés and the gouty Bourbons, with things of the past against which the Revolution had been directed for so many years. Unfortunately, this association was encouraged by most of the bishops who thought a condition of normalcy had been re-established at long last; it was accepted by the remaining Jacobins and Liberals* who still agreed with Voltaire's famous dictum: "L'eglise, voilà l'ennemie!" And it was promoted by the government itself, which saw in a restored Catholicism a guarantee of social peace and political passivity. Judging from a purely worldly point of view, one could not hope for much from the Church in France in 1815.

Nor were conditions across the Rhine any better. There the Catholic Church had been terribly weakened by Napoleon's secularization of 1803, whereby he had confiscated Church properties – as the Revolution had already done in France, and as Napoleon himself had validated the French seizure in the Concordat of 1801 – in order to give them to petty German princes to bind them securely to himself. Thus he crippled the

* The terms "Liberal" and "Liberalism" are two of the most slippery in the English language. Their meaning changes constantly. In the greater part of the nineteenth century, however, "Liberal" had a fairly definite meaning, and "Liberalism" referred to a fairly definite set of beliefs.

Throughout this book we shall use "liberal" as an adjective opposed to "conservative" or "reactionary." We shall use "Liberal" and "Liberalism" to refer to the doctrine emanating from the French Revolution and associated with such thinkers as Constant and Guizot in France, Mazzini in Italy, Heinrich Heine in Germany. It has been well defined by Father Raymond Corrigan, S.J. (*The Church and the Nineteenth Century*) as "a many-sided system or doctrine advocating the emancipation of man from the supernatural, moral, and divine-positive order. . . . [It] asserts the absolute freedom of the individual in thought, worship, conscience, speech, writing, and action, thus denying all authority derived from God."

Liberalism on the continent, we might add, was a much more virulent and doctrinaire thing than it was in England and the United States.

Church in the Germanies. By robbing the Church of its formerly predominant role in charitable work and in education, he undermined Catholic influence on German life. By taking its properties, he reduced it to a beggar position in relation to the government. By these measures, moreover, he inadvertently took the first step in transforming intellectual leadership from Catholic southern Germany to the anti-Catholic, aggressive northern part.

Napoleon's blows at the Church in the Germanies, however, did less harm than did the dry rot which had been eating at its heart all through the latter eighteenth century. There still persisted the theory and practice, established by the Treaty of Westphalia in 1648 with the famous principle *cujus regio ejus religio,* that each petty prince should control religion within his realm in his own interests, as though it were a purely secular matter – the attitude which did at least something to justify Karl Marx's later jibe that religion was the opium of the people. This attitude, known as Josephism from its outstanding proponent, Joseph II of Austria, was almost universal in the early part of the nineteenth century.

Nor was such an attitude seriously opposed by German bishops at the beginning of the nineteenth century. Many of them were State-appointed nonentities. Hardly a one seemed as much interested in his position as shepherd of souls as he did in his personal worldly aggrandizement. Among these German bishops there had developed the virus of Febronianism, the theory that all bishops have power equal to the pope who through the course of time had arrogated to himself invalid powers and a false primacy in the Church. Sound reform in the Church must begin, these Febronian bishops held, by curtailing the authority of Rome and reducing it to its original and "pure" condition. Leadership in a rebirth of the Church in the Germanies would have to come from a few exceptional bishops and from outstanding laymen like Joseph Görres.

Even worse, perhaps, than Josephism and Febronianism was the deadening effect of the *Aufklärung* – a German brand of the Enlightenment – which would supplant supernatural religion with a natural one. Philosophy had almost succeeded in replacing faith; and now, as the century turned in the Germanies, science threatened to replace both philosophy and theology. There seemed no leaders within the sickly German Church intellectually able to oppose this tendency. For all these reasons, Cardinal Pacca, the Pope's secretary of state, reported sadly to Rome after his visitation to the Germanies: "The Church in Germany can be preserved only by a miracle."

Although France and Germany were not the whole of the Catholic world, nevertheless they were its heart in 1800, and it seemed that if the Church did not survive in these lands, it could not survive elsewhere. America was thoroughly Protestant, and the American Catholic Church depended in the early nineteenth century on the missionary zeal of Europe to keep it alive. The Church in Ireland was healthier than almost anywhere else — but Ireland was under the English heel and had, in name as in fact, lost its identity as a nation by the Act of Union of 1800. Catholics were proscribed from political life in Great Britain. Throughout the northern parts of Europe, those parts, incidentally, which had never been within the Roman Empire and which were to dominate European life throughout the nineteenth century, Catholicism was almost nonexistent. Spain and Portugal were decadent. Their day of power and glory had been in the sixteenth century; in the nineteenth they were utterly incapable of leadership in European affairs. As these countries fared, so it seemed their Latin-American colonies would also fare. Italy was still only a geographical expression in 1815, parts of it nominally independent and other parts incorporated into Austria. With its Papal States, moreover, the Church seemed more a political than a spiritual force in the Italian peninsula.

The future looked dark. Faith was needed at the beginning of the nineteenth century to believe that the Church could continue to exist at all. Both optimism and faith were needed to believe that its existence could be more than skeletal for generations to come.

* * *

The story of the Church in the nineteenth century is nevertheless a story of recovery, of revitalization and rejuvenation that equals, if it does not surpass, the Church's remarkable regeneration in the sixteenth century in the midst of the Protestant Revolt. It was a recovery which began slowly, almost apologetically, and then about the middle of the century gathered new confidence and new strength – so that Pius IX could venerate the Blessed Virgin, and at the same time defy a world that denied the existence of sin, by solemnly defining the Immaculate Conception. A decade later he could dare to issue the *Syllabus of Errors* bluntly condemning as erroneous and wrongful the most revered superstitions of the century. And a little more than five years later, the bishops of the Church, solemnly assembled in ecumenical council, declared this man, like his predecessors and his successors, infallible when he spoke *ex cathedra* on matters of faith or morals! If Pius IX tested the mettle of his Church by taking a defiant stand against the materialistic world of the mid-nineteenth century, Leo XIII enjoyed confidence enough and strength enough to employ sweet reasonableness and understanding condescension in his dealings with the world. For by his time, in the last quarter of the century, the Church was strong and healthy. It did not have to fear for its no longer delicate constitution; it need fear only the enemies outside its fold. Even outsiders respected the Church by the end of the century – because it had grown big and strong again and was an element no longer to be ignored by wise men. The ever old Church was fresh and young again.

The most remarkable thing about this rapid recovery of the Church is that it occurred when all the rest of the world was moving in the opposite direction. In an age of increasing irreligion and agnosticism, the Church gained in vitality and in numbers. In an age when the world moved in a secular direction, the Church moved successfully against the current by deepening its own spiritual life. Thus its history in the nineteenth century was unique. The general tendency of other religions was toward disintegration both of organization and of doctrine. Denominations continued to multiply and to grow smaller. Their pews became less crowded too. Their creeds, their codes, and their cults, generally speaking, decayed into pale reflections of their former selves. The creeds tended to evaporate, since it was held more and more through the century that no minister or no congregation had the right to tell an individual what to believe. He believed what he wanted to – and what he believed was no one's business but his own. The codes held on longer, but they generally lost their religious sanctions by the end of the nineteenth century. People were good because their neighbors were, or because it hurt business not to be good, or because it was difficult to be immoral without getting into trouble with the law. And the cult almost everywhere disintegrated into ice-cream meetings and hay rides.

Through the century, all dominant new trends of thought were antireligious. Liberalism was hostile to any kind of religious authority, and especially did it look upon Catholic thought as outmoded and harmful to "Progress." The world of the nineteenth century came to worship science and to extend its domain into the fields proper to philosophy and religion. As man learned more about nature, generally speaking, he cared less about God; as he gained control over the universe, he tended to lose moral control over himself. These trends of men's minds, as well as the direction taken by the state, are all summed up today by that general term "secularism." For the nineteenth century was a century which cut further and further away from God as it handed over to worldly agents more and more of the functions formerly and properly performed by religious organizations – such as education, the care of the sick, the maintenance of the poor, the raising of orphans, the setting up of social and business standards, and all those other functions of life which were pretty thoroughly secularized by the end of the century.

How, then, in the face of this general trend of secularism, is the historian to account for the Church's recovery through the nineteenth century? The full account would be a complicated story which could not be told in terms of purely natural forces alone. Mention would have to be made of the Holy Spirit, the sustaining power of the Catholic Church promised by Christ so that His Church would endure until the end of worldly time. No story of the Church's renewed energy in the nineteenth century would therefore be complete unless it took into account the Holy Spirit, working as a rule through human agencies. The historian, however, is required to tell the story of the Church – with its periods of decline and of revitalization – as exhaustively as he can on natural grounds alone. Economy of means demands that he have recourse to the supernatural, to the divine or the diabolical, only when natural means are clearly insufficient to explain the events he is recording and describing.

This rudimentary rule of history writing must be remembered as we tell the story of the part played by thirteen laymen in one of the Church's springtimes, the great revival of the nineteenth century. In this renewal of the Church's life, Catholic laymen played a role that has not been given due notice – and the burden of this book is to show the part they played in this great revival. As we follow these laymen and center our attention upon them, we shall naturally not concentrate on the work of the hierarchy, or the thousands and thousands of priests doing apostolic work in their parishes, or the nuns praying in their convents, or the millions of men and women promoting the health of the Mystical Body of Christ with their ministration of good works and prayers. Nor, as we have suggested, shall we attempt to discover the Holy Spirit at work breathing new life into the Church.

More particularly, a full account of the Church's revival in the nineteenth century would have to tell of the work of the popes, especially Pius IX and Leo XIII. It would have to give due consideration to such capable cardinals as Wiseman, Manning, and Newman in England; Hergenröther in Germany; Gibbons in America. It would have to tell of outstanding bishops, too, such as Von Ketteler and Droste-Vischering of Germany, Dupanloup of France, Ireland and Spalding of America. It would have to tell of canonized saints, such as the Little Flower and the Curé of Ars, Don Bosco and Klemens Maria Hofbauer – saints whose prayers and good works nourished the Church so splendidly with spiritual aliment throughout the century. Nor could the complete story omit such miraculous interventions in the course of human events such as the appearance of the Blessed Virgin at Lourdes. But we are interested here in outstanding Catholic laymen who were important as members of the Church in promoting its welfare throughout the world.

* * *

These are not merely men baptized into the Church who happened to achieve greatness in the world. They are more than that. They are men whose vocation in life was full-time Catholic Action. They are men whose primary work in life was apostolical, who achieved greatness standing side by side with the bishops of the Church, participating in their apostolate, crusading for the Church in various fields of action. Their's was the vocation of Catholic Action before that term had been formally defined by Pope Pius XI – for they participated in the work of the hierarchy, which is the pope's description of the "apostolate of Catholic Action." It is a vocation which the first of them in point of time, Joseph de Maistre, understood when he wrote of the need for laymen doing their part, because "every man is bound to bring a stone for the august edifice [of a revitalized Church]." Through this group of laymen who agreed with De Maistre that "men of the world . . . should number themselves among the defenders of the holiest of causes," the Holy Spirit worked to prepare this better age – religiously speaking – in which we live today.

These laymen in whom we are interested enjoyed certain advantages denied to the hierarchy and even to the lower clergy in the nineteenth century. For the layman could mix freely in the world; whereas in the anticlerical nineteenth century, the priest was pretty closely confined to his sacristy. Clerics had mingled in society in days gone by, and the result had been most unfortunate, because they were identified with the government they served and the society they helped form. They had been important government functionaries – and they had been discredited when their governments fell. They had formed public opinion – and their intelligence was discredited when an intellectual revolution overturned the old order of values. They had been influential as men of the world, not as priests – and too many of them neglected to function as men of God. The nineteenth century, consistently secularistic in all respects, limited God's ordained representative to the confines of his particular church; it allowed him to speak only from the pulpit and only on narrowly spiritual matters. He was not to be part of the world. Politics, economic and social questions, the matter of a living wage or right education, were not his affairs. This separation of the clergy from secular life was accomplished partly by laws – such as those in France and later in Germany denying clergy the right to teach, or those forbidding them to appear in public in clerical attire, or those which vested Church property in laymen's hands exclusively—and partly it was accomplished by the new secularist "climate of opinion." This is what De Maistre referred to when he said that people would not listen to a priest defending his faith because they believed he was only justifying his own position.

The clergy, then, were put in a spiritual pigeonhole and cut off from the world. There was a chasm between the Church and the society in which it lived in the nineteenth century—and it is the Catholic layman, more than anyone else, who was able to bridge that chasm. Frédéric Ozanam could trudge up back stairs to visit the sick in their garrets; O'Connell and Montalembert, De Mun and Windthorst could defend Church doctrine from the rostrum of their national legislatures; Orestes Brownson could argue out the truths of religion at the corner drugstore, taking on all comers; and Donoso Cortés could defend the Church by writing to editors of the leading Liberal journals of France and Spain. Thus the layman established a connection between the sacristy and the market place. The layman, then, was able to bring the truth into the dark corners of the world because he was not constantly confronted with hostile "out-of-bounds" signs that faced the clergy at every turn.

The layman enjoyed still another advantage. He could speak more freely than could his brother in holy orders. He could speak bluntly and flatly when he chose, without caution or even circumspection when it seemed advisable—as it always did with Louis Veuillot—for the outside world did not look upon him as the official representative of Rome, as it did on the bishop or the priest. The clergyman was forced to use extreme caution in uttering the lightest remark, since the world looked on his every pronouncement as the voice of the Church infallible. So whereas the clergyman had to be careful about his every utterance and consequently could not come to grips with issues on many occasions, the layman was able to speak openly and freely without fear of compromising his Church. His mistakes always could be disavowed easily as the mistakes of a fallible individual. And there are times when overstatement is the only way to get a truth across, times when a carefully worded statement of a doctrine sounds more like hedging than anything else.

Finally, it should be remembered that apologetics is not necessarily a function of the priesthood. Priests were busier in the nineteenth century with the care of souls than they had been for centuries — because of the dearth of vocations, another aspect of secular-mindedness — and thus they did not have time to devote to debating the truths of religion in the public arena, even if they were allowed to do so. So the layman found opportunities to serve his Church without fear of hurting it, opportunities not offered to his bishop or to his parish priest, opportunities which had not been offered to laymen in previous centuries. This was the kind of work envisioned by the author commemorating Brownson's death in the *American Catholic Quarterly Review,* when he wrote in 1876: "The sphere in which the educated layman can cooperate with the Church is daily widening, and the value of his cooperation is daily growing in importance." There were many Catholic laymen who took advantage of the opportunity offered them to perform the work of Catholic Action. There were many who enjoyed conspicuous success.

* * *

The history of the Church on earth, when looked at from the world's point of view, is the history of its adapting itself to changing political, social, economic, and intellectual conditions. Certainly this is true of the Church in the nineteenth century. A new world was in the making because of the French Revolution, the industrial revolution, and the revolution in men's minds. The old order was dead, and the Church had to accommodate itself to the new order so that it could carry on its divinely appointed mission of winning souls for Christ. But at the same time it had to preserve its essential characteristics. It had to change and still not change. Catholic lay leaders tended to group themselves into two camps, liberal and conservative, accordingly as they emphasized the need of change or the need of preserving the heritage of the past. Men like Ozanam and Montalembert and Görres emphasized the need for change, for they saw good in the new civilization. Others like Donoso Cortés, De Maistre, Veuillot emphasized the evil aspects of the century and counseled that the Church not compromise with evil. It remained for a convert and a cardinal, the brilliant Newman, to work out a solution to the apparent dichotomy of changing and not changing. And it remained for a layman, Wilfrid Ward, to present Newman's message to the world in popular fashion.

In this work of accommodation to the nineteenth-century secular world, Catholic laymen, as we have seen, enjoyed advantages over the clergy — and their most important work lay in working out these changes. In the first place, they helped the Church adjust itself to a new political arrangement by finding guarantees for its existence in the newly formulated bills of rights. Their job was to do what the clergy were no longer able to do: to obtain the rights of citizenship for themselves by removing all religious disabilities, as O'Connell tried to do for Irish and English Catholics; to have Catholics use their right to vote and to sit in the legislature and thus to protect the Church from its enemies and promote its interests in such fields as education and family life, as Montalembert tried to do in France; to form a party of Catholics in the country and the legislature, and so by strict party discipline to cooperate only with those who would allow the Church its freedom, as Windthorst did with signal success in Germany.

In the second place, Catholic laymen helped the Church adapt itself to a new social arrangement. The State tended to assume more and more social and charitable functions through the nineteenth century as it took over control of marriage and education, of hospitals and orphanages, of almshouses and care of the unemployed. Because laymen could wander through the slums and dig into the tenements, because they lived very much in the world and understood its problems, they could make closer contact with the poor than could the priest. Laymen could play a role in preserving the virtue of charity in a nineteenth century which threatened to smother the very spirit of charity and to replace it by the hollow substitute of philanthropy or State-directed welfare agencies. This work was accomplished with outstanding success by such a man as Frédéric Ozanam with his St. Vincent de Paul Society, by Pauline Jaricot with her Society for the Propagation of the

Faith, by Albert de Mun with his Workingmen's Clubs and a certain amount of wise social legislation which he obtained in the French legislature.

In the third place, Catholic laymen labored to effect an intellectual adjustment between the Church and the world of the nineteenth century. In a material way the world was accomplishing wonderful things as it uncovered the secrets of nature and solved the mysteries of the universe, as it harnessed the power and controlled the energy of the material world. Room had to be made in Catholic minds for these accomplishments. Priests did good work here – but they were exceptional priests, such as Abbot Mendel working with his plants in the monastery, or Father Lawrence Hengler, inventor of the horizontal pendulum used in seismographs. But laymen enjoyed an advantage in this field too, because they could more easily move in secular academic circles and they could mingle more freely with scientists of all faiths – or none. There are literally hundreds of outstanding Catholic scientists in the nineteenth century, men like Ampère in physics, Pasteur in biochemistry, St. George Mivart in biology, who showed that there is no real conflict between science and religion.

But that was only part – the minor part – of the problem. The century was blinded by its material success. It became infatuated with its own accomplishments. So the story of the Tower of Babel was repeated all over again, this time with distinctly modern variations. It was on the altar of Progress that the nineteenth century offered worship – and spiritual things were sacrificed to the idol of Material Progress. Sound progress in politics and economics, in biology and anthropology, in all fields of intellectual endeavor was compromised by the extravagant claims of enthusiasts in each field. Thus Liberal economists spoke with the "infallible authority of science" on matters of morality; anthropologists and geologists solemnly and gravely discussed the deepest theological problems, which they often did not even understand to be problems; political theorists spoke definitely about natural rights as though they were found in statute books somewhere.

The Catholic layman was confronted with the difficult task of winnowing the truth out of this welter of new ideas. He had to separate it from error lest it be lost by a blanket denial of everything new. This required not only a knowledge of the truth but also an understanding of the false doctrines which had to be assessed for their real worth. Here again the Catholic layman enjoyed a distinct advantage over the priest, for he rubbed elbows with the materialistic heretic, he knew the workings of his mind, and he was in a better position to extract the truth which is to be found at the core of every new trend of thought. This was the work of Joseph Görres and of Ozanam who saw a large measure of truth on the Liberal side, of Juan Donoso Cortés and Louis Veuillot who saw and condemned the evils of capitalism in terms as strong as Karl Marx, of Orestes Brownson who knew the Protestant mind and understood Protestant virtues as well as Protestant vices.

There was a host of Catholic laymen who helped make these adjustments for the Church throughout the nineteenth century. Many of them were obscure except in the locality in which they lived and did their work. Some, however, attracted attention through the Christian world because of the success that crowned their work. These are the individuals who deserve, by the norms of history writing, to be recorded in the story of man's past. We have selected from among this number a representative group whose collective biography should enable us to see the work accomplished by the Catholic laymen of the nineteenth century. These men are crusaders of the past century — to borrow Montalembert's expression — who in various ways and in different fields of activity carried on the fight for God and for His Church, men through whom the Holy Ghost worked to accomplish the Church's regeneration in the nineteenth century.

I.

POLITICAL ADJUSTMENT

The relationship of the Church to the State is a problem as old as human society. It is a problem, moreover, which never can be permanently solved, for as the State changes its form and content through history, so the problem of its relation to the Church assumes a new aspect. The temporarily satisfactory arrangement of medieval times was rendered obsolete by the Protestant Revolt of the sixteenth century and the concomitant appearance of the absolute state. For the Protestant Revolt shattered the religious unity of Europe and, wherever it succeeded, it led to the wholesale confiscation of Church property. Even more important in some ways, it drove the various churches of Europe – Catholic as well as Protestant – into the monarch's arms, where they sought protection from rival religions with a royally guaranteed monopoly of worship within each country.

One of the indirect results of the Protestant Revolt, then, was to promote State control of whatever religion was established in the realm. Churches everywhere, in Catholic and Protestant countries alike, tended more and more to become departments of State. After 1555, bishops were pretty much ordained bureaucrats. A none too happy arrangement had been worked out, whereby the Catholic Church in various countries submitted to the control of the monarch and in return received his protection. Sometimes the submission was nearly complete, as in Philip II's Spain and Joseph II's Austria, but usually the bishops retained independence in essential matters of faith and morals. Nevertheless, the hold of the State on the Church gradually tightened, largely through the king's right to nominate bishops in most countries, and also because of the general secularistic trend of thought and action through the eighteenth century.

All through Europe, in Catholic countries and in Protestant, the established churches of the eighteenth century were woven into the texture of the nation. The Church controlled education — having almost a monopoly of it. It owned much land which it used mostly for charitable, educational, and religious purposes. It registered births and it issued burial permits. It was record keeper as well as educator of the nation. Its clergy, who with the lawyers were the best educated class in the State, became secular as well as religious pastors of the people. They helped introduce new methods of agriculture, decide on vocations for young men, select husbands for the girls, diagnose and treat the baby's ills. They performed a thousand tasks, and their keep was provided not by voluntary contributions but by a tax — or tithe — collected as a rule by secular officials and handed over to the proper ecclesiastical authorities. High churchmen held top government positions — all too often — being even finance ministers and prime ministers, diplomats ordinary and extraordinary for Europe's most important monarchs. Church law was part of the law of the land. In short, the Catholic Church was an established institution in Catholic countries, as were Protestant churches in Protestant lands. It was a State institution, as well as a spiritual body, and any revolution directed against the government was almost bound to be directed against the established Church as well as against the established government.

The intellectual revolution of the eighteenth century found many weaknesses in this arrangement against which it could drive home its barbed attacks. So the French Revolution cut loose from this traditional arrangement. It struck at the clerical abuses of the Old Regime, and they were many, but it also struck at religion itself, just as it struck at the very essence of government. Because the Church was so intimately tied in with the Old Regime and suffered from its weaknesses, it too was dragged down when the old form of government fell. When the Revolution was over and the Bourbons returned to France, a natural reaction toward the established religion began in the first quarter of the nineteenth century, not only in France but through all European society. Leading Catholics, the bishops and the lay nobility of the Old Regime for the most part, took for granted that the Church-State relationship of the past should be re-established. They wanted to go back to that eighteenth-century arrangement whereby the Church would again become an established institution acting pretty much as a department of State.

Younger men who had grown up through the revolutionary years tended to look for a new arrangement that would be pointed toward the future instead of turned back on the past. Some of them believed the old society was dead. They therefore concluded that the Church must accept the new society, whether it liked it or not, and find a way to live in it. A *modus vivendi* must be worked out with nineteenth-century civilization, they believed, its good aspects accepted, its bad altered until they were acceptable. Others went further and maintained that the old arrangement had been vicious, for it had shackled the Church and put it so much under secular control that it ministered to Caesar rather than God. They were happy to discover *rigor mortis* in the old society and they unreservedly embraced the new civilization and the new freedom. Still others saw that neither arrangement was perfect, but they believed that a multichurch system in each state, with each denomination free to manage its own affairs, offered a chance for healthier and more substantial growth in the future than had been possible in the past. All three groups agreed, however, that a new relationship between the State and the Church had to be found. And they all agreed that it could not be found by trying to resurrect the dead past, as older bishops and nobles wanted to do.

What place could the Church find in nineteenth-century society? What guarantees could it discover on which to rest its secular foundations? What security could it establish so that it could build its churches and its seminaries, establish its convents, its monasteries, and its schools? If it were not to be the officially established religion, what arrangement could be worked out so that it might have a better assurance of life than the passing whim of the ministry in power? The answer offered by the younger Catholics was a political answer — and it was taken right out of the Revolution's mouth. Governments in the nineteenth-century world, they showed, either had constitutions or they were in the process of getting them. These constitutions included a list of rights which were guaranteed to all citizens, rights which the State had the duty of protecting and enforcing. Now in this list there was almost always included the right to follow one's conscience freely and to practice one's religion publicly.

Why not, these younger Catholics therefore asked, base the existence and the activity of the Church on these new constitutional guarantees? What more would be required in the new and free society? Was this not an arrangement which would free the Church from the antiquated and often embarrassing protection of the government? Would not the Church then stand firmly on its own feet? Such was the general line of reasoning taken by those Catholics who thought the new society acceptable and insisted that the Church must find its place within it. These were men who put great trust in a written constitution and in a bill of rights. They wanted Catholics to claim their constitutionally guaranteed right as citizens to practice their religion. They wanted them to form a political party which would use its power at the polls and in the legislature to protect the Church, to see that its freedom was not violated, that the State did not attack Catholic practices either by vicious laws or by adroitly inimical administrative procedures.

The advantages of such an arrangement seemed obvious. If we accept the suppositions of these Catholics, it is easy for us to see how they concluded that the Church would no longer be subjected to crippling interference by the government in ecclesiastical affairs, as was the case in days gone by. It is easy to see how they expected the Church to grow healthy in the environment of freedom, for it would be like the cripple who has thrown away his crutches to walk on his own feet. And had Christ not guaranteed that the Church would always walk?

But older members of the Church – especially the bishops who are almost automatically bound to be conservative because of their heavy material and spiritual responsibilities – were reluctant to accept this line of reasoning. And it is easy to understand their reluctance, for the more progressive Catholics wanted to give up a known position for one unknown. Those in power naturally preferred to keep the known position, with all its shortcomings, rather than take a leap in the dark by cutting the Church loose from the State on which it was accustomed to lean for support in the days before the French Revolution. Another and sounder reason for their suspicion was the strange lot of bedfellows with whom the revolutionary Catholics found themselves closeted. Those who advocated separation of Church and State, those who wanted the Church "to stand on its own feet," who insisted on freedom of religion and freedom of conscience, included those Liberals who wanted all those things as a step toward destroying the Church. They wanted the same arrangement as did the young, more progressive Catholics, but for a different reason. For they wanted to render the Church impotent, to deprive it of State support so that it would be too weak to defend itself against the onslaughts of Liberalism.

It is easy to understand, then, why, early in the nineteenth century, Catholics should have been divided among themselves on the relationship that should be established between Church and State. The old guard clung to old ways. Neo-Catholics, as Montalembert called his group, wanted to work out a new arrangement. There could be two such parties, both in good faith, because the question was one of prudence. The solution lay not in a dogma of faith or morals, but in the field of politics. And there was no infallible answer to this political question.

The advocates of a changed relationship between the Church and the State were almost bound, by the nature of things, to be laymen rather than clergy. For one reason, it was possible for the layman to venture out on thinner ice than could the cleric – because the layman could retreat after getting his feet wet. He could always change his shoes and go off in another direction, unless his pride pushed him straight into the deep water of destruction. But the clergyman, who always personifies the Church to the non-Catholic and speaks authoritatively for it, was bound to exercise greater caution, greater reserve. Moreover, the secularization of the age forbade the priest a place in political activity such as the layman could occupy. And the question was to be settled on the rostrum instead of in the pulpit — though the ultimate decision on these matters remained with Rome, and locally with the bishops.

The task of leading the way in this matter of adjusting the Church to a new political world consequently rested in large measure with Catholic laymen. Theirs was the job of working out a political solution backed by constitutional guarantees, implemented by good laws, secured by the formation of a Catholic party. This adjustment therefore involved what might be called "political Catholicism" to replace the "established Catholicism" of the eighteenth century. It is an adjustment which prevailed until after World War I, when the changing form of the State presented the question of Church-State relationships all over again in a new form. The Church of the twentieth century was in a stronger position to work out a new solution than it had been back in 1815 — and for this, Catholic laymen like O'Connell and Windthorst are at least partially responsible.

These men helped the Church adjust itself to the society of the nineteenth century, and we can see from our vantage point of time that adjustment of some kind was absolutely necessary. It was impossible for Catholics to oppose all things new and remain influential in modern society. It was impossible for them to revive the Old Regime of the eighteenth century. It was impossible, humanly speaking, for them to achieve a solution to this problem without entering the arena of politics and forcing their new adjustment on a reluctant secular world by pressure of the ballot. The problem was complex, perplexing, confusing. Its main outlines, however, can be seen in the careers of three outstanding Catholic laymen who entered the political arena to fight for the Church: O'Connell, who fought to get Catholics into Parliament; Montalembert, who fought to make Catholics vote as Catholics rather than as Royalists; Windthorst, who formed an effective Catholic party and maneuvered that party with supreme tactical skill to protect the Church and to ward off the attacks of the secular State. Light is thrown on the problem from a different angle in the career of García Moreno, for the famous president of Ecuador showed that a secular government constituted along Catholic lines could be as progressive and modern as the most advanced of Liberal governments.

1. Daniel O'Connell

Daniel O'Connell was an important man, both for what he dreamed of doing and for what he actually did. Living at the beginning of the century, in an Ireland that had been absorbed into Great Britain in 1800, he set about securing full civil and political rights for the Catholics of his native land. After a long period of unremitting political guerrilla warfare, O'Connell obtained for Catholics the right to sit in Parliament and to participate in the political life of Ireland, England, and Scotland, the nations which made up Great Britain. After this initial victory, O'Connell next carried on a long struggle to secure Irish independence and to ameliorate the condition of the Catholic Church in that Catholic land. Although he won some skirmishes in his parliamentary battles after 1829, he did not win his campaign. Thus his great lasting accomplishment, ostensibly, was leading the fight for the Catholic Emancipation Act of 1829.

But O'Connell's great importance in the revival of the Church in the nineteenth century probably lay in his becoming a legend. For the legend of O'Connell inspired Catholic leaders throughout the century in Ireland and France, in Spain and Italy, in Belgium and Germany. Among Catholics all over the world he became a model and an inspiration within his own lifetime, and in this respect he can be said to have accomplished more than he did as the living Irish leader from County Clare. Montalembert aspired to become the O'Connell of France, and admirers called Görres "the O'Connell of the Rhineland." Their ideal O'Connell was more like the figure described by Donoso Cortés than the man who lived in Ireland. "O'Connell is the angel of Ireland and the demon of England," Donoso wrote. "O'Connell is sublime like Demosthenes, impudent like Mirabeau, melancholy like Chateaubriand, tender like Petrarch, crude as a lackey, brutal as a savage, as prudent in Parliament as Ulysses in the camp of the Greeks, as impetuous, daring and audacious as Ajax demanding light from the heaven so that he might die in full day. In this rich nature there is something of the captain, something of the sergeant, of the king, and of the peasant. O'Connell is very much the savage and very much the civilized man; he is a fox and a lion at the same time; malicious and caustic as Goethe's Mephistopheles, he is innocent and candid as a baby. He is everything that makes up a nation — and a nation is made up of everything."

In Paris young Count Charles Montalembert had formed an even more glorious opinion of O'Connell than Donoso Cortés had formed in Madrid. Montalembert visited Ireland for the express purpose of sitting at his hero's feet in order to learn political wisdom from him and take lessons in how to form a Catholic party of France. But on close inspection Montalembert found his idol had feet of flesh and bone shod in muddy leather boots. O'Connell, he discovered, had very human shortcomings. He made very bad speeches. He was gruff. He seemed uninterested in young Frenchmen, or in France, or in the Church in France. He told Montalembert to go dance with the young people — and the romantic, idealistic young man returned to France disillusioned. But the French Count had found that as he receded from the flesh-and-blood O'Connell, his ideal Irish leader began to reappear. "I am deceived," he commented sadly on his visit to O'Connell's home. "This man is far from being the most interesting personage in Ireland. He has the appearance of a prosperous farmer." Nevertheless, when he met O'Connell in Rome almost twenty years later, he could address him sincerely in these words: "We are all your children, or rather your pupils. You are our master, our model, and our glorious teacher. Your glory is not only Irish, it is Catholic. Wherever Catholics begin to practice civic virtues and devote themselves to the conquest of civic rights, it is your work."

Montalembert was right when he made these remarks to an old man, who in a few weeks was to die. For here he was speaking of O'Connell the legend, the great Irish leader seen through a glass — as he was seen by Catholics everywhere in the nineteenth century. This is the O'Connell, the legendary figure who accomplished great things for the Church during his own lifetime and long after he was dead. This is the O'Connell who was more important than the man who fought doggedly and successfully to get Catholics into the British Parliament.

Catholics needed such a figure, and O'Connell's exploits on behalf of Ireland made him the logical choice to become the great legendary lay figure of the nineteenth century.

* * *

Wherever the English language is spoken by Irish tongues, the story of Ireland's sorry plight in the early nineteenth century is too well known to bear repeating here. Let us only call to mind a few salient points of that hard story in order to know better what Daniel O'Connell set out to do and to understand better the tremendous obstacles which loomed before him. When the Act of Union was passed in 1800 and Ireland was incorporated into Great Britain, the lot of Irish Catholics was not as severe as it had been twenty-five years before. For it was back in the latter half of the eighteenth century that Irish Catholics, and therefore the Irish nation of which they were nine tenths, had lost its pride and its life, its independence as a nation, almost its very soul.

Conditions had become so bad that even so English an Irishman as Edmund Burke spoke of the Irish Code as a machine "as well fitted for the oppression, impoverishment, and degradation of a people, and the debasement in them of human nature itself, as ever proceeded from the perverted ingenuity of man." Whereas English Catholics had managed to retain some degree of self-respect, and even a few of them to hold high social positions, in Ireland the Protestant oligarchy ruthlessly enforced the penal laws against Catholics to keep itself in control of a country where revolution smoldered in nine hearts out of ten. A Protestant Irish judge had rightly said in 1760 that the law did not recognize the existence of an Irish Catholic. By law he was excluded from the parliament at Dublin, from the professions, and from all civil and military offices; by law he was forbidden to lease land, to be an administrator or a guardian of property, or even to own a horse worth twenty-five dollars. Catholics were not allowed to vote or to possess firearms, to send their children to school at home or abroad, to observe Catholic holydays, or openly to practice their religion.

There is a good legend that in these days St. Patrick, St. Brigid, and the others continually agitated before the Great

White Throne. And a series of relief acts passed in the last quarter of the eighteenth century seems to bear witness to the truth of this legend, for by 1793 many proprietary and civil disabilities had been removed from Irish Catholics' shoulders. As a result of these acts, Irish Catholics could go to their own schools, they could own land, and they could enter most of the professions. Most important, many Irish peasants were given the right to vote. Irish lads could even enroll in the seminary at Maynooth to become priests and go out among their people again as religious and political leaders.

These improvements came partly because the Protestant parliament of Dublin saw how fruitless repressive legislation had been, and partly because there were many among the Irish Protestant oligarchy who were genuinely desirous of bettering their Catholic neighbors' lot. More immediately, relief came because of agitation by such men as John Keogh and Wolfe Tone. But then came the French Revolution in 1789 and with it the intoxicating wine of liberty, equality, and fraternity—wine which drove the more impetuous Irishmen to demand their full rights as human beings and as Irish citizens, wine which brewed up spirits and ghosts of revolution to haunt men of property and make them fear conceding to the slightest demand of the people. In the last decade of the eighteenth century, therefore, repressive legislation descended on Ireland again in the form of an Arms Act, an Insurrection Act, an Indemnity Act, and an act suspending the habeas corpus. These measures led to the rebellion of 1798, a rebellion which was put down with much bloodshed and which seemed to throw Irishmen back twenty-five years in their struggle for political and civil rights.

When the rebellion ended, Ireland's leaders were mostly dead or exiled or in prison. The English government used this rebellion of 1798 as an excuse for pushing through the Act of Union in 1800. Members of the Irish parliament were bribed a million pounds to commit political suicide; peerages, Anglican bishoprics, civil-service jobs, and positions in the army and navy were all passed out to those who would vote for the Union. So the Irish parliament ended its existence, and one hundred seats in the British Parliament were allotted to Irish constituencies. Ireland seemed sick at heart in 1800. For years the most energetic of her manhood had been spent uselessly in rebellion, or they had been drained off to see service in the French, Spanish, or Austrian armies, or else they had wandered to other lands, even to England, where they might live like human beings. Those who remained at home were apathetic. They seemed to have surrendered at last, to have given up the long and losing fight for once and for all.

Nevertheless, Henry Grattan, indomitable Protestant fighter for Catholic emancipation in Ireland, could come from his sick-bed to tell Parliament in the debate on the Act of Union: "I do not give up the country. I see her in a swoon, but she is not dead; though in her tomb she lies helpless and motionless, still there is on her lips a spirit of life, and on her cheek a glow of beauty." The "spirit of life" was still in Irish hearts, but it had burned so low that few besides Grattan could feel it there.

* * *

Two years earlier one who still felt that spirit of life, Daniel O'Connell, had been admitted to the bar, and by 1800 he was ready to enter the political life of his country. He was determined to fan that dying spirit of life to flame again, to gain for Irish Catholics the right to sit in parliament and thus to make their own laws and to protect their inalienable rights themselves instead of leaving them at the suffrance of an English Parliament. That was his first objective. His second was to have the Act of Union repealed, and thus win for Irishmen the right to have their own parliament to make their own laws and manage their own affairs.

O'Connell was ideally suited to lead his Catholic followers in their long struggle for emancipation. He was born at the right time, in 1775, for he was old enough to remember the old penal laws and young enough to profit by their abolition. He was old enough to learn his alphabet at an illegal hedge-school and his catechism from a priest who had been prosecuted for saying Mass, but he was young enough to benefit from the new laws which tolerated Catholic schools in Ireland. He was old enough to have to go abroad to study law, but young enough to be admitted to the bar and openly retain his faith. As a young lawyer, moreover, O'Connell was technically equipped to lead his countrymen in a protracted struggle against the English government, for he had learned how to break the spirit of the law and frustrate its purpose, and still to observe its letter. And men are imprisoned, organizations are suppressed, movements are stopped not for violating the spirit of a law but for breaking its technically worded letter. This was a matter of crucial importance, as Louis Veuillot saw so clearly in 1875, when he was called upon to help celebrate the centenary of O'Connell's birth. "To obey always and always to be fighting those whom you obey, remaining forever in revolt and always within the law . . . this is the law of the catacombs which the great Irishman has recovered for us Catholics."

Most of all, Daniel O'Connell was ideally suited by temperament for the role that Providence had assigned to him. He loved a good fight. He was boisterous and voluble, long-winded and contentious. Thus he came to be known to the English as "the Agitator," as he was later known to the Irish as their "Liberator." But there is something more to O'Connell than being an agitator or a liberator, something more than a boisterous leader who eventually won his struggle for emancipation simply because the English could not put up with him any longer. There is something more to O'Connell than the rough-and-tumble fighter he was. Daniel O'Connell's best asset was his ability to keep his agitation peaceful and within the law – a tremendous accomplishment for one trying to lead several million Irishmen in a struggle against their English oppressors. O'Connell was unique in having such influence over single individuals and over masses that he could not only arouse them to fever pitch but also keep them under control. O'Connell was unique in being able to keep his agitation bloodless, in holding it on a high plane and not allowing it to degenerate into one of those futile "battles of Widow MacCormack's cabbage patch" which was almost always the end result of past agitation for improvement of the Irishman's lot.

Ireland's past sufferings had made O'Connell conclude that no political change was worth a drop of human blood. He had seen too much of it spilled in 1798, and he had too high a regard for human life and human dignity to achieve his objective by the short cut of spilling more blood. His supreme achievement was not so much in leading Ireland to emancipation, but in leading her there without bloodshed or violence. His greatest struggle was not to wrest emancipation for Catholics from the English Parliament, but to keep his Catholic followers from breaking Protestant policemen's heads. His greatest victory was not in getting his Catholic countrymen into Parliament, but in keeping them always under control. His peaceful revolution thus stands in striking contrast to the long and bloody French Revolution of the same age.

O'Connell is unique for his time, moreover, in making his fight a democratic struggle. For he led what were then called "the lowest classes" – the forty-shilling freeholders – to the polls to win his battle. He did not follow the custom of the time and rely on the "better classes" to win his long struggle. In this respect he was a pioneer in winning his battle "by pulling out the vote." Daniel O'Connell was a robust, fiery man who was strong enough to resist the temptation of fighting for the sheer joy of battle, who was strong enough to control his own inflammable nature most of the time and the impetuosity of his followers all of the time so as to attain the object for which he was fighting. In this sense he was not only a wise man but also a shrewd political strategist. He was a good and a modern politician.

* * *

O'Connell based his agitation on the belief that Irishmen, as human persons and citizens of Great Britain, were entitled to the same political privileges as the English. He further believed, as he showed time and time again in his speeches, that no man's political privileges or civil rights should suffer because of his religious beliefs. This was a general, theoretical way of saying that Catholics should have equal rights with Anglicans, that one should not have to pay legally for being true to the faith of his fathers. This right which he claimed for his Catholic followers he would readily grant to members of other religions, because he no more believed in persecution by attrition, as the English had for centuries persecuted the Irish Catholics, than his contemporaries believed in bloody persecution. "Nothing can be more opposed to the spirit of our Saviour," he once said, "than to persecute for errors in religious belief. Nothing can be more exquisitely absurd. Persecution may make a hypocrite, but it will not make a convert."

The Irish Liberator insisted at all times that he was a loyal British subject — as loyal as the promoters of the Glorious Revolution who overthrew the Stuarts and secured for British citizens their Bill of Rights. As a loyal subject of the Crown, O'Connell maintained, he was only asking for his rights, for the opportunity to be an active, loyal, interested citizen who performed the duties imposed upon him by the English political system. This, indeed, is what made him so annoying to the English government and so dangerous, for he demanded only what was "cricket," what the English looked upon as their reasonable, hard-won rights. Though this was all he asked for, he never stopped asking, petitioning, agitating. In this sense, O'Connell can be said to be one of the first real democrats in modern history, for he maintained that all persons had a right to participate in government, be their religion what it may.

His immediate political aims were likewise democratic. His first objective, we have seen, was emancipation, whereby Catholics would be admitted to Parliament and to other political, civil, and military offices within the State, an aim which no sincere supporter of democratic government can fail to endorse. His second objective was to keep up perpetual agitation until the Act of Union was repealed and Ireland was given back her own parliament in order to manage her own local affairs. Early in the nineteenth century, before the coming of railroad and telegraph and consequent political centralization, local control of local affairs was considered an essential point of free government. Even today it is thought the wisest course to follow wherever practicable, as our respect for the American town meeting indicates. O'Connell's demand for self-government was based on the sound principle that the Irish people knew their problems better than did the English Parliament, and through their representatives they were better able to govern themselves than was a group in London who understood so poorly the Irish system of landholding, the Irish ecclesiastical arrangement, and most of all the Irish heart and mind. These things, O'Connell rightly maintained, only Irishmen understood.

As a third objective, he dreamed of the day when the

Anglican church would be disestablished in Ireland. This again was a matter of democracy and of justice, for though only one Irishman in ten was Anglican, still all ten had to pay for the upkeep of the established Anglican church in Ireland. Through the tithe system they had to support four archbishoprics, eighteen bishoprics, and thousands of parishes, most of which were sinecures for the incumbents supported largely by the impoverished Irish peasant. To disestablish the Anglican church would throw the burden for maintaining it on Anglicans alone, and the Irish Catholics would be free to support the Church of their own choosing.

These, then, were O'Connell's aims – all democratic and all progressive in nature. He hoped to achieve them by methods no less democratic. He insisted vehemently that peaceful agitation was the only proper way to achieve emancipation, repeal, and disestablishment. "Agitate, agitate, agitate," he told the National Political Union of Dublin. "Let our agitation be peaceable, legal, constitutional; but let it also be persevering, continuous, determined." It was easy for O'Connell to stir his countrymen to agitate, but it was difficult for him to keep them peaceable, or legal, or constitutional. Some of the younger Irishmen were reported to have taken oaths "to fight knee-deep in Orange blood for the restoration and continuation of the long-promised liberty to the Catholic Church." It was against this sort of romantic, Byronesque crusading, so endearing to young spirits, that O'Connell had to fight. And it was a hard fight, for he had to keep these young firebrands loyal to his cause while denying them that pleasure of "fighting knee-deep in Orange blood."

Agitation was only one of O'Connell's weapons. He also made use of mass meetings, always impressive things wherever it is believed that individual human beings are each of some account. Through these meetings he demonstrated graphically that the masses of the Irish nation supported his demands, that he was right when he asserted that only a tiny minority of the Irish gentry were satisfied with the compromise of 1793 and the union of 1800. O'Connell loved mass meetings, and he was at his best when addressing thousands. Democracy or demagoguery, call it what you will, for the line dividing the two is thin indeed, O'Connell appealed to the masses and they loyally supported his demands. He was their voice, and he therefore spoke for millions when he made his demands of emancipation, repeal, and disestablishment.

O'Connell also made use of that very English device, the petition. Time and again, over the objections of more conservative Irish leaders, O'Connell managed to have huge petitions presented to the king and to Parliament. No single petition achieved its requested result. But cumulatively they acted like steadily dripping water through the ages — they wore the rough edges off Parliament's resistance to emancipation so that by 1829 a large majority had come to favor some form of it or another. The right of petition was a prized English right, and though a petition usually seemed unavailing when it was offered, nevertheless it was a traditional method Anglo-Saxons had employed for moving their government to popular action. It was a method whereby Englishmen had made their will known to their representatives — which is the essence of democracy.

Finally, O'Connell hoped to force the election to Parliament of more and more Irish members who favored emancipation and even repeal and disestablishment. He therefore had to get out the forty-shilling freeholder, who had been enfranchised in 1793, and lead him to vote independently — a difficult thing indeed in a day when there was no secret ballot and when a peasant who did not vote as his lord directed was evicted from his home. Despite this seemingly insuperable obstacle, O'Connell put his faith in the little man and requested of him heroic action such as only a leader with assurance in the rightness of his cause, faith in himself, and trust in his followers could demand. It was democratic action, this getting out the little man and forcing his nose to count for as much as his lord's nose, it was democratic action to the heroic extreme that O'Connell advocated. He was one of the first men in modern times to see the power of numbers. He had faith enough in himself as a popular leader to put his trust in the little man of Ireland, and his faith did not go unrewarded.

Perhaps O'Connell should not be credited with so much vision in the power of numbers, however, or with so much faith in the Irish masses. He was driven to rely on them because the men of property in Ireland were content to let sleeping dogs lie. They opposed agitation of any kind, for in the past it had always led to bloodshed and bloodshed to reprisals. They had come a long way since the dark days of the eighteenth century, these better fixed Irishmen believed, and they were anxious to enjoy the fruit of these gains. So they wanted no part of O'Connell's program. For quite some time, neither did many of the bishops. Naturally conservative, as bishops almost always are because of their responsibilities as administrators of fixed properties, the Irish bishops were willing to accept compromises instead of following O'Connell's precept of "agitate, agitate, agitate." Not until the issues were clearly drawn and the alternative of victory or defeat definitely offered, not until there was good chance of success did the bishops back O'Connell against the propertied laymen in Ireland who opposed him as a demogogue and an agitator. O'Connell could not rely on support from the "better people" of Ireland. Circumstances, therefore, forced him to rely on the little men of Ireland who were large only in the aggregate. And it turned out to be a happy turn of circumstance, for O'Connell was at his best in appealing to masses of men.

* * *

The future Liberator's first political struggle was against the older Irish politicians who had done good work in getting the worst features of the eighteenth-century Irish Code remitted. Most important of these men was John Keogh, the Dublin merchant who insisted on maintaining a "dignified silence" in these first years of the nineteenth century. By "dignified silence" Keogh meant refraining from petitions and from any kind of agitation. O'Connell's arguments for a mass petition prevailed over Keogh's objections, and a huge petition was presented to William Pitt when the latter returned to office in 1804. Again in 1807 O'Connell triumphed over the moderates, when another petition was sent to Parliament. It was done again in 1808. O'Connell's repeated victories on the question of the petition gradually forced Keogh into political retirement. By 1810 Daniel O'Connell clearly had assumed leadership of the Irish cause.

Early in the struggle, however, the Irish forces divided on a question of tremendous importance – the "veto." This veto, or "securities" as it was sometimes called, was a string which Pitt had attached to the concession of Irish emancipation many years before to mollify the opponents of the measure. It would have given the English government a negative control over the pope's selection of bishops in Ireland, for the government could have annulled papal appointments to high Church offices on political grounds. The veto had been accepted in principle by the Irish bishops in 1799 and again in 1808. From the very beginning, however, O'Connell stood flatly against the veto and in no uncertain terms he condemned the "vetoists" as those who would sacrifice anything for religious toleration.

For a time O'Connell stood almost alone against the "securities men." Nor is this surprising. It seemed such a reasonable arrangement. It gave the English government merely the power to refuse to ratify papal appointments. It did not go nearly so far as arrangements in certain continental countries, such as France and Spain, where the government nominated the bishops and the pope had to accept or refuse these nominees. In return for this concession, moreover, supporters of the veto had been given to understand that provision would be made for supporting the Catholic clergy in Ireland. It seemed reasonable to Irishmen of the time, then, that such a typical English compromise should be worked out. But O'Connell saw that it meant the surrender of ecclesiastical independence – and for that reason he stood flatly against the veto.

Opposed to him were the other important lay leaders of Ireland, Henry Grattan, Lord Fingal, and especially the great orator Richard Sheil. More important than this lay opposition, Rome itself seemed on the vetoist side, for Monsignor Quarantotti, who was in charge of affairs in Rome after the Pope had been imprisoned by Napoleon, exhorted the Irish bishops to accept the compromise. O'Connell came close to rebellion against Rome on this political question in 1814 when, for a second time, Monsignor Quarantotti urged the bishops to accept the veto. So indignant was O'Connell at this time that he bellowed out in a public meeting: "I would as soon take my politics from Constantinople as from Rome."

By the summer of 1815, O'Connell had made headway against the veto. At that time a committee was sent to London with a petition containing O'Connell's "no securities" clause. But the victory was not yet completely won, and until 1823 it seemed that the veto question had so seriously split Irishmen that nothing could be obtained from the English Parliament. O'Connell was condemned by almost all the important Irish laymen for his refusal to compromise. He gradually won the support of the Irish bishops, however, younger men now who agreed with O'Connell's tactics in the struggle for emancipation. And O'Connell consistently had the support of the little men of Ireland, the poorer classes whom he had enlisted under his banner in the early years of the struggle.

These were dark days from 1814 until 1823, and they were made darker still by two or three embarrassing situations into which O'Connell's fiery temper led him, situations which proved wonderful opportunities for his enemies to discredit him. One of these was the Magee trial. John Magee, editor of the Catholic *Dublin Evening Post,* had been indicted for libeling the Duke of Richmond, viceroy of Ireland. O'Connell defended Magee, but in the course of a four-hour speech he forgot his client's case to launch into a tirade against the English government's administration of justice in Ireland. In this tirade, as the English historian Davis so cautiously puts it, "he showed more spirit than prudence," with the result that Magee received an unusually severe sentence of a year in prison and a fine of about $5,000. O'Connell contritely paid the fine, but Magee spent the year in jail. Moreover, as a result of the trial the Catholic press was silenced, and in 1814 the Catholic Board that had been organizing meetings and preparing petitions was banned. For four hours O'Connell had allowed his impetuous nature to lead him astray. He was a political demagogue instead of a lawyer – and both Magee and emancipation paid for O'Connell's tirade.

A second embarrassing situation developed when O'Connell killed a man in a duel – though this time the Liberator could probably have avoided the duel only by losing face as a leader of the Irish people. In a speech in 1815, O'Connell referred to "the beggarly corporation [the city government] of Dublin," a reference that sounded like any one of a thousand others he had made. But this time a man named D'Esterre, who was a member of the Dublin corporation, took offense at the charge and walked the streets of Dublin, horsewhip in hand, looking for O'Connell. The Liberator kept out of sight as long as he could, but when he was publicly challenged by D'Esterre to a duel, he felt obligated to accept the challenge because he was suspected of having backed down from similar challenges in the past.

Irish bookies of 1815 must have given long odds on D'Esterre, because, a slight man, he presented a small target — and he had the reputation of being an excellent shot. O'Connell, on the other hand, not only had no repute as a marksman, but he presented a burly, rotund target. To everyone's amazement, O'Connell won the duel by killing D'Esterre. He regretted the affair for the rest of his life. He offered to settle half his fortune on D'Esterre's widow, and though she refused the offer, he did provide a pension which was paid for the next thirty years to her daughter. Shortly after this duel, Robert Peel challenged O'Connell to another — but this challenge and the resulting events took on the air of burlesque instead of tragedy. Mrs. O'Connell had her husband arrested under a peace bond. After much talk on both sides Peel withdrew his challenge, and O'Connell made a resolution never, under any circumstances, to fight another duel.

These were dark days, and O'Connell was blamed by many for the delay in obtaining emancipation. His opposition to the veto compromise was assailed as uniting Protestants in England and Ireland solidly against emancipation. He was charged with trying to build himself up as a leader by refusing a reasonable settlement. These attacks caused O'Connell to style himself "the best abused man in the world." Grattan, Plunkett, Sheil, and the others used forceful language indeed to denounce "the leader," but O'Connell was prudent enough this time to hold his temper and to concentrate on keeping the Catholic Board alive through these days. He showed surprising tenacity and surprising restraint through this period of his career, tenacity and restraint which paid off after 1823.

* * *

That year was perhaps the low point of the struggle for Catholic emancipation. "At the beginning of 1823," Sheil tells us, "an entire cessation of Catholic meetings had taken place. We sat down like galley-slaves in a calm." But the calm was not to last long. For a new and successful phase of the struggle began in the spring of that year when O'Connell and Sheil agreed to join forces in organizing a wider movement for emancipation which would bring the message to millions. Sheil changed his stand on the veto by joining O'Connell's opposition to it. Then they organized the famous Catholic Association. To keep within the letter of the law, they announced that the association was formed to promote religious education and to answer charges leveled against Roman Catholics—objects which were not proscribed by any law. The association's real purpose, however, was to form a gigantic organization covering all of Ireland and directed by the priest in every parish. Its real purpose was to petition and agitate for emancipation. Anyone, Catholic or Protestant, was eligible to join. Meetings were public. Membership lists and minutes of the meetings were available to anyone who cared to inspect them.

The most annoying function of the Catholic Association, as far as the English Government was concerned, was its leveling a tax upon its members, the "Catholic Rent," which was a penny a month or a shilling a year. The Association grew astoundingly until it threatened, by its very force of numbers, to overawe every other authority in the land. At its meetings every public question and every grievance against the government was publicly debated. It followed, almost mockingly, the procedure of the House of Commons, and even though the government could find nothing seditious in its meetings, still it took alarm and looked for ways and means to dissolve the powerful Catholic Association. Lord Liverpool, prime minister of the British government at the time, accused the Association of "evading and nullifying the law of the land" by levying an unauthorized tax upon the Irish people. It was, he said in effect, not at all cricket to organize a lawful democratic association which financed itself and presented a united front for emancipation. "If Catholic claims were to be granted," he insisted, "they ought to be granted on their own merits and not to the demands of such associations acting in such manner." Thus, the prime minister went on record as opposed to political pressure from his citizens.

Early in 1825, Henry Goulburn introduced a bill forbidding organizations such as the Catholic Association to be in session over fourteen days, to collect money, or to have permanent executive committees. This bill was clearly directed against O'Connell's Catholic Association. But it missed its mark, for no sooner did it become law than a new Catholic association was formed to take the place of the one proscribed by Goulburn's bill. The new association supposedly was organized to promote the education of Catholic children, to advance science, to improve agriculture and commerce, and to pursue charitable and religious purposes. The Catholic Rent continued to be collected "for the purposes of the Association so far as not prohibited by law." Thus Liverpool's complaint about O'Connell's evading the law could still be made – but O'Connell was still within the letter of the law, so he could not very well be arrested. He and Sheil went on a victorious tour of southern and western Ireland to address wildly enthusiastic audiences, who applauded them as much, perhaps, for flaunting the English government with their new Catholic association as for carrying on the fight for emancipation.

Political accidents, more than anything else, brought about a series of events between 1826 and 1829 which culminated in the long-fought-for Catholic emancipation in the latter year. Briefly, this is the way events moved. Since Parliament had been dissolved in 1825, a general election had to be held the following year. O'Connell and his Catholic Association decided to try their strength at the polls by attacking the Protestant stronghold of Waterford. This constituency had long been regarded by the Beresford family as their private property, and in the election of 1826 the Marquis of Waterford decided to have his brother, Lord George Beresford, elected. He spared neither money nor energy to have him returned by a large majority, as had long been the custom, for the forty-shilling freeholders either did not vote at all or else they voted as directed by their lord.

The Catholic Association felt strong enough to challenge the Beresfords, so it put up the liberal Protestant, Villiers Stuart, as its candidate with O'Connell as campaign manager. O'Connell toured the county and saw to it that the priests brought out the vote of their parishes. So intense was the excitement that four thousand soldiers were stationed in the neighborhood in case election riots should break out. The election, of course, was conducted according to the open hustings system, whereby the polls were kept open at a central place in the county for about two weeks. Each voter had to come to the polls sometime during the hustings to announce his vote openly.

Parish by parish the forty-shilling freeholders came to Waterford to cast their votes against their lord's brother. The peaceful order in which the peasants proceeded was almost as disconcerting to the Beresfords as the way in which they voted. As a political maneuver, O'Connell was himself nominated for the office, so that he could speak at the hustings. For two hours he orated, and then he withdrew in favor of Villiers Stuart. From the moment the first parish contingents arrived the outcome was never in doubt, and on the fifth day of voting Lord Beresford conceded the election to Stuart and withdrew from the race. The count then stood a little better than two to one in the latter's favor — an overwhelming victory for the Catholic Association, the successful use of a new device to win emancipation.

Other candidates presented by the Association won elections at Louth, Westmeath, Monaghan, and Armagh. Thus the English government saw that Catholic emancipation could not long be postponed. The forty-shilling freeholders had at last come out in numbers — for the first time since they had been given the vote in 1793 — and their votes would be sufficient to put a bloc of Irish representatives into Parliament holding the balance of power between Whigs and Tories, ready to fall in with whichever party gave them emancipation.

The final test came in the famous Clare election of 1828. In a reshuffling of the British ministry, the Board of Trade was offered to Vesey Fitzgerald, representative from Clare. This necessitated his re-election; but because he had been popular and because his family was influential in Clare, it never occurred to the ministry that his election would be contested. The ministers had overlooked the fact that the Association was opposed to Fitzgerald because he had voted for the Goulburn Act in 1825 and that it would not pass up this chance to defeat him. The ministers were therefore surprised to hear that the election would be contested, and they were amazed to learn that O'Connell himself was to run against Fitzgerald. Because no Catholic from Ireland had been elected to Parliament since the Glorious Revolution of 1688, O'Connell's announcement that he was a candidate for election to Parliament was a bombshell in British politics.

This turned out to be one of the decisive elections of Irish history. Certainly it was one of the most colorful. On the first day of the polling, parish priests marched into Ennis with their flocks, each forty-shilling freeholder with a green emblem on his person. Eligible voters came almost to a man. In such numbers did they come that reliable witnesses estimated almost 50,000 persons were in the little town of Ennis during the election. The rest of the county, indeed, took on the look of a deserted country until after the votes were counted. Again, as at Waterford two years before, though the campaigning was lively, still perfect order was maintained. Priests urged their parishioners to vote the "right way," and sometimes persuasion was strong enough for us to call it moral intimidation. Protestant landlords used economic intimidation by threatening to evict any tenant who voted "the wrong way." Fitzgerald's friends tried to engage O'Connell's orators in duels, but though dynamite was in the streets of Ennis that week, dynamite enough to blow up not only Clare but Ireland itself, nevertheless perfect order was maintained and no explosion took place.

The peasants voted almost to a man for O'Connell, as the men of property voted almost unanimously against him. And because there were so many more poor people in Clare than there were men of substance, Fitzgerald withdrew before the last day of the hustings. When the votes were counted, it was found that O'Connell was easily the winner. The sheriff therefore signed the return, adding a note that the victor openly proclaimed himself a Catholic. O'Connell made no attempt to take his seat in Parliament because as a Catholic he could not take the required oath of office, but the Association planned to put up Catholics for every seat at the next general election and to require from its candidates a pledge that they would oppose the ministry on every vote until emancipation was granted.

The English government was in a dilemma – from which there was no reasonable escape except to grant emancipation. The government feared revolution in Ireland, so intoxicated were the Irish with their new successes. Consequently, seven thousand soldiers were sent over to maintain order. But amazingly, no serious trouble occurred. Nothing could be done now to stop the Association and the forty-shilling freeholders from electing Catholic after Catholic, unless Parliament were to have recourse to repressive legislation again. But the day of repressive legislation had passed. By 1828 a good majority in Parliament favored emancipation, and the only question was whether the Tory ministry should present the bill or whether it should resign and allow a Whig ministry to assume responsibility for Catholic emancipation.

Late in 1828 and early in 1829, Wellington and Peel, two of O'Connell's strongest opponents, prepared the emancipation bill that circumstances and O'Connell had forced upon them. After long discussions, Peel and Wellington agreed to drop the hated veto clause; but as a preliminary to emancipation, Peel insisted on the passage of a law dissolving the New Catholic Association. This compromise O'Connell condemned fiercely, but it passed nonetheless. A compromise to which he agreed — and this was perhaps his worst mistake — was the disfranchisement of the forty-shilling freeholders, the little people of Ireland whose votes had brought the matter of emancipation to a head, those people whose willingness to risk eviction was the principal ammunition in O'Connell's guns when he went out to meet his political enemies.

The Emancipation Bill easily passed both houses in 1829, and it was reluctantly signed by George IV on April 13. The king is supposed to have remarked bitterly as he put his royal signature under the law: "The Duke of Wellington is king of England, O'Connell is king of Ireland, and I suppose I am only the dean of Windsor." Nor was the king so wrong.

The Catholic Emancipation Law — which, it should be remembered, bestowed benefits on Catholics in England as well as in Ireland — provided that Catholics could once again become members of Parliament, both of the House of Lords and the House of Commons. A new oath, which Catholics could conscientiously take, was to be framed. Catholics also were allowed to vote in city elections and to hold office in the corporations, or city governments, and they became eligible for most civil and military offices in the realm. Attached to the law, incidentally, was a clause directed against O'Connell personally, a requirement that anyone elected before the passage of the bill had to take the oath of office in force at the time of his election. As a result, O'Connell had to go back to Clare, stand for re-election, and come back to Parliament to take his seat.

Certain civil and political disabilities still remained for Catholics to agitate against in the future. But the most important of them had been removed by the act of 1829. And for this act O'Connell was largely, though far from solely responsible. Emancipation would have come had there been no O'Connell, since the theological arguments against it had long since disappeared. It was becoming expedient for the English government to remove Catholic disabilities. O'Connell is therefore not so important for having obtained emancipation as for the method by which he obtained it. He made it a trial of strength between the Irish Electorate and the English Parliament, between himself as representative of the people, as agitator for their rights, and the constituted government of England. The Irish Electorate and the agitator won. Because of the way O'Connell had drawn the lines of the campaign, it was a democratic victory instead of the expeditious settlement the other Irish leaders would have made it.

* * *

O'Connell had won his first battle. But another remained, a bigger battle and a harder one to win. For this was a battle to be fought in Parliament for the removal of the remaining Catholic disabilities, and members of Parliament are by their very nature immune to the demagogic oratory which O'Connell used to stir up the masses of poor men in his native Ireland. O'Connell took his seat in Parliament, nevertheless, determined to accomplish two main things. First, he would lead the fight to repeal the Act of Union and to set Ireland free; second, he would obtain a new relationship between Church and State in Ireland by getting the Anglican Church disestablished.

These were the things for which he fought until his death in 1847. His fight was to be relentless — but it was to be unsuccessful. For Ireland did not obtain her freedom until this century, and the Anglican Church was not disestablished until long after O'Connell's death. O'Connell was unsuccessful because he was not fighting his own kind of battle, as he had done back in Ireland to win emancipation. Successful as an agitator, as a mass leader, as an opponent of the government, the Liberator found the odds too great against him to enjoy success in Parliament. O'Connell was a better guerrilla fighter in the battle of politics than he was a party regular. And the obstacles he faced were humanly insuperable. He was a party of one at first. The English Catholics treated him with contempt; the Irish representatives, by and large, did not think as he did, and certainly they refused to accept his leadership. Most of the Irish representatives were still Protestant, and they were almost to a man in favor of the Union. In time he had six close followers, all relatives, and a bloc of about thirty-five more who could be counted on to support him.

O'Connell was not the man temperamentally to engage in party politics and to organize a disciplined group behind himself. He never mastered the art of welding individuals into a unit — for even in Parliament O'Connell continued to be the great orator speaking to the masses, the "leader" of the people. The only trouble is that the masses did not vote in Parliament, nor did the members there accept leadership as did the masses in Ireland. Finally, O'Connell's position was weakened by the disfranchisement of the forty-shilling freeholder to whom he owed his first victory and his place in Parliament. O'Connell the leader did not have to be listened to seriously when the people he led no longer voted, for he was no longer Ireland's voice. He was just another representative of just another constituency. By agreeing to this measure depriving his followers of the vote, O'Connell had therefore hurt his future career as a member of Parliament. He carried on the fight for almost two decades, nonetheless, and in that time he came to win the respect of the House of Commons, even though he did not win a majority of their votes for either repeal or disestablishment.

O'Connell went into Parliament a radical — as compared with his contemporaries. His radical stand on questions of democracy was first shown in debate on the great Reform Bill of 1832. This bill was urged by the industrial and commercial class of England, the millionaire class, who were anxious to wrest control of the government from the landed proprietors. It was a small step in the direction of democracy, inasmuch as it aimed to increase the electorate slightly and to equalize the electoral districts, then so absurdly arranged in England. During debate on the bill, O'Connell made one of his long speeches – three hours this time – in which he promised to vote for the bill. But he objected that it did not go far enough, and he tried to amend it to grant universal male suffrage and vote by secret ballot. These were truly "radical" suggestions in 1832, as the *Annual Register* indicated by saying that O'Connell's proposals were based on "this simple, but mad proposition, that every man who pays a tax, or is liable to serve in the militia, is entitled to have a voice in the representation." O'Connell was several generations ahead of respectable European opinion in his thinking on democracy. Only thirteen out of more than three hundred members of Commons present voted for his proposals.

About 1833, O'Connell seems to have grown more conservative in his opinions and his action. Maybe it was just advancing age. O'Connell had been a typical youthful reformer; as a typical older man now, he was preoccupied with holding to present gains and not risking change. Moreover, O'Connell always did have a strong conservative streak in his nature, and his earlier activity seemed radical only by comparison with the ultra-conservatives he opposed. Those conservatives had largely died off by 1835, and younger "radicals" like Feargus O'Connor and the Chartists had come along behind O'Connell. Compared to these younger men, O'Connell took on a conservative coloring – though he did not change his views fundamentally.

From year to year he postponed introducing his bill for repeal of the Act of Union. Pressure from Ireland grew stronger. O'Connell was taunted with having agitated so noisily outside Parliament for repeal but with doing nothing to introduce a bill for it. Younger Irishmen demanded that such a bill be introduced so that the subject could be discussed in Parliament and the Irish arguments against the Union presented. Reluctantly O'Connell yielded. In 1834 he introduced his Bill for Repeal with a five-hour speech. The speech was listened to attentively – but after a week of debate the bill was defeated by 523 votes to 38.

For the next decade O'Connell the Agitator became O'Connell the Compromiser. He compromised on the question of disestablishing the Anglican Church. Instead of disestablishment he obtained a reduction of the tithe, and thus the burden of supporting the established church was lightened for Irish Catholics. He compromised his whole program for repeal by promising after 1835 that he would support the Whigs if they would govern Ireland kindly and wisely. He had decided to abandon his struggle for repeal in order to work for piecemeal reform of various Irish grievances – and in so doing he alienated his Irish followers. Ironically, these days when O'Connell obtained many things for Ireland – reduction of the tithe, reform of city government, partial extension of the franchise – his popularity declined. For the old O'Connell was no longer the flaming agitator, the great leader whom people admired more for the fight he fought than for the prizes he won. The old O'Connell was more the parliamentary manipulator who was seeking and obtaining the possible, piece by piece, bit by bit, ever securing a little more relief.

There was one last phase to O'Connell's long life of fighting. After 1840, disillusioned with the never fully realized promises of the Whig party, O'Connell decided to come out for repeal again. He did so by fighting for it on his home grounds, outside of Parliament, appealing to the masses, as in his younger days, making speeches to rouse these masses, agitating, always agitating. In 1840 his famous Repeal Association was established, and at the age of sixty-five O'Connell invigorated it with the fire and enthusiasm of his younger days. "Let the Irish rally with me for repeal," he told them. "My struggle has begun. I will terminate it only in death or repeal." Death rather than repeal terminated the Liberator's activity in this movement. But until death came it seemed more like the days of O'Connell's youth again. Monster meetings were held all over Ireland. O'Connell roused the people, but again he cautioned them to agitate peacefully.

He could not satisfy the new generation among his followers, the Young Ireland group, who could not abide O'Connell's insistence on peaceful agitation. Their "direct-action" methods and their radicalism stirred up fears in the old man, so that in the last years of his life he advocated a compromise arrangement whereby a legislature in Ireland would be established to have control over domestic affairs, while the Irish would continue to send representatives to the British Parliament to legislate on imperial affairs. Such a compromise, of course, satisfied no one, neither those who held the Act of Union sacred, nor those who wanted complete repeal.

In justice to O'Connell, it must be said that though he became conservative in the last fifteen years of his life, still his aims did not vary. He changed his tactics, not his objectives. As a member of Parliament, as an older man, as one who has grown politically wise, he had concluded that more could be obtained in the long run by compromise than by agitation. Each gain would be small, much less than he wanted, but added together they would constitute sound progress for Ireland. So though his tactics changed, his objective always remained the welfare of the Irish people.

After 1845, O'Connell and Ireland grew ill and weak together. Age and sickness were sapping the Liberator's strength; at the same time famine and poverty enervated Ireland. In February of 1846, O'Connell called Parliament's attention to the state of famine and disease in his native land, and he prayed Commons to pass relief measures for the stricken country. In his last appearance before the House he spoke for two hours in a whisper scarcely audible ten feet away. Disraeli observes of the Liberator's last speech that "it was a performance in dumb show; a feeble old man muttering before a table; but respect for the great Parliamentary personage kept all as orderly as if the fortunes of a party hung upon his rhetoric."

* * *

O'Connell is important, of course, for bringing emancipation to the Catholics of Ireland and England. But he is more important for having roused the Irish people from their deathlike apathy to a realization of their political power. He was the first to see the potentialities of numbers, of the little people of Ireland who had for so many centuries been despised and neglected, who did not themselves know how to use the vote that had almost accidentally been given to them in 1793, until the Agitator showed them what tremendous power it was in their hands. In doing this O'Connell was ahead of his time. He fought against vested interests, political and religious, and in his fight he showed how the common people could protect themselves from these interests.

O'Connell, then, won the first round of adjusting the Church to the modern lay state of the nineteenth century, inasmuch as he won the right for Catholics to sit in Parliament as makers of the law of the land. In that position they were to carry on the task of protecting the Church and adjusting it to modern society by wise and prudent legislation. More than that, O'Connell pointed the way to Catholics of other countries by indicating what political techniques they might use in trying to protect the Church through the suffrage and the parliament of each country.

He is important, however, not so much for his victory as for his struggle, not so much for what he won as for the inspiring battle he fought to win it, and the example he gave to Catholics throughout the world. It was, Louis Veuillot said fifty years later, "the first ostensible triumph of Christ in this century, secured by the wisdom and fidelity of a single man." Even without O'Connell, Ireland would soon have obtained emancipation. But without O'Connell, Ireland would never have been quite the same country. Irish hopes through the rest of the century would not have been so optimistic, Irish spirits so lofty, or Irish heads held so high. The sun of circumstance, it would seem, cast a longer shadow for O'Connell down the road of history than his stature deserved. For, as we suggested earlier in this chapter, O'Connell became greater and more important as a legend than he had been in the flesh.

It was because of the fight he fought and the conditions under which he fought it that O'Connell became so important. His struggle against almost insuperable odds in the Britain of his day stamps him as a man among men, one who, in Louis Veuillot's words, "was selected to plant in the whole Church a spirit of invincible hope and of unconquerable liberty." Pope Pius IX, a fighter of stature himself, described O'Connell as "the champion of the Church, the father of his country and the glory of the Christian world." Long after Pius IX died, long after O'Connell was in his grave, the Liberator continued to play an important role in Ireland's fight for freedom.

2. Count Charles Montalembert

Charles Forbes Montalembert, born of an English mother and a French nobleman, aspired to be the Daniel O'Connell of France. He fought a fight similar to O'Connell's, but he conducted it on a loftier plane than did his Irish model. Where O'Connell tended to be a demagogue who fired his listeners with anger and resentment, Montalembert was a polished orator who thrilled his audience with lofty motivation. O'Connell was a bludgeon in the battle, Montalembert a glinting rapier. O'Connell was a rugged Irishman who, though a gentleman at heart, had the crudities and the rough ways of his Irish and English contemporaries — and they were a rough lot. Montalembert, on the other hand, was a perfect gentleman at all times — a gentleman in his soul and in his mind, in his conduct and his manners.

Montalembert and O'Connell fought the same campaign of winning a place for Catholics in nineteenth-century politics and in this way protecting the Church on constitutional and legal grounds. Both fought almost alone, and both had to overcome their fellow Catholics and even their bishops before they could attack the real enemy. O'Connell had fought to get Catholics into Parliament. Montalembert found his Catholic associates in the Chamber of Deputies and the Chamber of Peers, but he had to rouse them to a sense of their Catholicity and to a consciousness that they could accept the new order of things and adopt it to their needs. Montalembert's struggle was deeper and more fundamental than the battle O'Connell carried on in Ireland and in London. Montalembert tried to accomplish a revolution not only in France but throughout the Catholic world, for he sought to detach the Church from the eighteenth-century system of State domination and to reconcile it with the new order of things in the nineteenth century. He tried to make Catholics accept the new liberty and the new democracy, use them to further the Church's interests and thus regenerate modern society. It was too much for one man or even for one generation of men to accomplish. But Montalembert planned the lines of campaign for the century's struggle. He recognized the forces at work, he saw which redoubts had to be taken, which garrisons must be held. But he could not convince others of his vision, and consequently did not succeed in selling his crusade to the Frenchmen of his age as Peter the Hermit had sold the First Crusade to their ancestors eight centuries before.

* * *

Comte Charles Montalembert came by his crusading zeal rightly. His forebears had been in the great crusading armies of the Middle Ages, and his more recent ancestors had been outstanding warriors fighting beside French kings in modern times. His grandfather had been expelled from France as a noble during the Revolution. His father had seen service with the English in India, and after the Restoration he entered the French diplomatic service. Charles was born in London, in 1810, and was left there to be raised by his English grandfather while his parents tried to take root in Napoleonic France. From his mother, Charles acquired a love of the English political system, and from his father he inherited the Montalembert love of defending good causes. Where his ancestors had used the sword, he used his tongue and his pen. "I am the first of my blood," he tells us with mingled pride and regret, "who has fought only with the pen. But my pen has become a sword, which has served with honor in the desperate struggle between truth and falsehood."

In a speech which is reported to have thrilled the peers of France, he rallied his Catholic followers and threw down a challenge to the self-styled Liberals in words which echoed through France for the rest of his lifetime. "Are we [Catholics]," he demanded, "to acknowledge ourselves such bastards that we must give up our reason to rationalism, deliver our conscience to the University, our dignity and our freedom into the hands of lawmakers whose hatred for the freedom of the Church is equalled only by their profound ignorance of her rights and her doctrines? . . . We will not be slaves in the midst of a free people. We are the successors of the martyrs, and we do not tremble before the successors of Julian the Apostate. We are the sons of the Crusaders, and we will never retreat before the sons of Voltaire!"

Montalembert spent his lifetime fighting against "the sons of

Voltaire." But as a young man he did not seem to enjoy the battle unless he was fighting for a lost cause. He constituted himself the "public prosecutor of oppression," and he defended the oppressed everywhere. His clients were the Irish, oppressed by England, the Poles abused by Russia, and the Greeks maltreated by Turkey. He spoke frequently and thrillingly in defense of the Christians of Syria, of the remaining slaves in the French Empire, and time and time again in defense of the Polish people. Although he constantly opposed the Orleanist monarchy while it was in power in France, as soon as it was expelled by the Revolution of 1848 and its property confiscated, Montalembert became an Orleanist. He seemed, indeed, to overlook the faults of the victim and the virtues of the tyrant and to become a special pleader for any person or any cause that he thought was not given fair play throughout his lifetime. He saw all things in black and white. Oppression was evil – so the persecutor was evil and the victim was good. In this respect Montalembert was a product of his romantic age.

Montalembert was an orator without equal in the France of his time. Because the French have always respected literary and oratorical ability and because they readily recognize a master before them, Montalembert could make statements and hurl accusations in the House of Peers which no other man could have uttered without being called to order. The noted critic Sainte-Beuve observed of him that "he could develop without interruption those absolute theories which from another mouth would have made the Chamber shiver, but which pleased them from his." Another observer tells us how, in the same House of Peers, Montalembert could "disturb with the accents of an impassioned voice the decent calm, the elegant reserve, and the polite conventionality of their habitual discussions as he vindicated, in the name of new generations, the rights and interests of that religion which was said to have no partisans but old men and no life but in the past."

Like most orators, Montalembert was to some extent a victim of his own eloquence. His ardor ran away with him, carried him into positions he could not defend, made him say things he never really meant to say. He was full of vehemence and indignation, full of fire and spirit, so much so that he frequently alarmed even his most ardent supporters. With his irony and his repartee he overwhelmed his opponents rather than succeeded in persuading or convincing them. He was brilliant and exhilarating, as even his opponents conceded. He was overwhelmed with congratulations after his speeches and on at least a few occasions he created such excitement that the Chamber had to prorogue its sitting for the day when he finished his speech.

Often enough Montalembert got himself into trouble because of his eloquence, together with the rhetorical rather than analytical habit of thinking which it engenders in the orator. He insisted that he spoke not as a theologian but as a politician – but even the politician must have his facts and his conclusions right if he wants them to stand up under attack. Because he was a crusader with his pen and his tongue, Montalembert made mistakes – serious ones – but he always had the humility to admit he had been wrong and to start over on the right track. He backed Louis Napoleon's *coup d'état* setting up the Second Empire, for example, because he thought that if anyone were attacked by such vicious opponents as Louis Napoleon was "there must be something good about him." This is the thinking of an orator and debater, a dangerous simplification of complex issues.

As a boy of twenty he enthusiastically backed the brash young Catholic paper *L'Avenir* for he saw in it the salvation of society. But when it was condemned by the pope, young Montalembert submitted as unhesitatingly as though he were a soldier receiving a command from his general. He opposed the declaration of papal infallibility, which was not made until shortly after his death, but he insisted on his deathbed that if it were defined as an article of faith he would submit. And he added, for the sake of those who looked on in disbelief: "It is simple enough; there is nothing extraordinary in it." This humility saved Montalembert from the fate of his friend Lamennais, or that of the German theologian Döllinger, or the several other crusaders of the Church who rebelled when their teachings were condemned after they wandered into error. Nobleman though he was, Montalembert was at heart an humble man – which was his salvation.

* * *

Charles Montalembert was a precocious boy. Though his attendance at school was irregular, he always had large collections of books at hand. He went to school in England for a few years, when he was still a little child; then he wandered around Europe with his parents for several years; finally he went to Paris at the age of fourteen to complete his education. By the time he reached his seventeenth birthday he revealed a penetrating mind filled with information. He was deadly serious, as all boys of seventeen are – deeply concerned with effecting a revolution in his own mind and then in Christian society, as few boys of seventeen are. It can be maintained, with very little exaggeration, that by the time he was seventeen young Montalembert had arrived at all the basic ideas with which he was to wrestle for the rest of his life.

His dilemma was a serious one – for a boy seventeen or a man seventy who lived in the first half of the nineteenth century. It was the problem of reconciling the Catholic religion with the new society created by the French Revolution. The two were fundamentally hostile, and history had shown conclusively that a person had to choose between the ideals of the Revolution and the Catholic faith. Those who claimed to be Liberal rejected God, and those who claimed to be Catholic might in their confusion reject liberty, equality, and all the ideas of the Revolution, good or bad. Montalembert took upon himself the job of reconciling the two. "God and liberty," he wrote shortly before his seventeenth birthday, "these are the two motive-powers of my existence. To reconcile these two perfections shall be the aim of my life."

His job, therefore, was to show that the Church was not hostile to true liberty, that one could be both Catholic and liberal. But impetuous and romantic youngster that he was in the heyday of Romanticism, he would go further than that. He would show that there was no liberty without the Church. "Would it not be a grand thing," he wrote to a fellow student, "to show that the Church is the mother of liberty?" It would require a real revolution to do this in the face of the stand taken by the bishops of France, as well as by the nobility who were in danger of being Catholic mainly because the Bourbons were Catholic and the Revolution was not. Young Charles demanded that these bishops and nobles and peasants reverse their age-old policy of alliance between the throne and the altar. He demanded that they disassociate themselves from the Old Regime, that they accept all the progress of the Revolution, that they enter into the new society and mold it so that there would be room in it for the Church to live and breathe and accomplish its mission.

He therefore advised one of his young friends to get into the new society and lead it, "to master it, to direct it in the good way, to show that religious faith is not a power that holds back." When this great revolution is accomplished, Montalembert believed, both modern society and the Church will be better off. For the Church will be free from the old entangling alliances with kings who appoint bishops, who dominate the teaching in the seminaries, who make the Church a department of State and a prop for the throne. From these connections the young French nobleman wished to free the Church so that it could grow healthy and strong in the full sunlight of liberty.

These ideas sounded daring, perhaps heretical, in 1827 when young Charles Montalembert first put them down on paper. That is why he had to spend most of his time and use most of his energy trying to convince his fellow Catholics of their soundness. In his youth he stated them brashly, absolutely, without restraint or safeguards. But his experience in the two French Revolutions of 1830 and 1848 disillusioned him somewhat about the fineness of one of his goals – liberty. He came to realize that his program was an ideal which could probably never be fully realized on this earth, that at best it could only be approached more and more closely as time went on and people of the Christian world learned how to use their liberty without abusing it and turning it against the other of his goals – God.

In the last speech of his life, made in 1863 after long years of retirement from political activity and after protracted meditation on this basic problem, Montalembert still held the ideas he had wrestled with before his seventeenth birthday. "The future of modern society," he told his four-thousand listeners, "depends on two problems – to correct democracy by liberty, to conciliate Catholicism with democracy. . . . Catholics must give up the vain hope of seeing a rule of privilege again revived, or an absolute monarchy favorable to Catholicism. . . . It is necessary to protest clearly, boldly, publicly, on all occasions against all thought of a return to anything which will irritate or disquiet modern society." Montalembert died a few years after making this famous speech on "A Free Church in a Free State." But the problem did not die. Montalembert had not solved it – but he made valiant efforts to do so, and he pointed out many lines of action that have been followed since his death in 1870 in attempting to reconcile the Church with liberty and with democracy.

* * *

His first effort, made before he was twenty-one, took on an almost comic light-opera air when he and his new friend Lacordaire opened a school in Paris with the express purpose of getting arrested for challenging the State's monopoly of education. Before he met Lacordaire, however, young Montalembert visited the land he had taken under his protection when he was only a boy. For several years he had wanted to visit Ireland. He wanted to talk with his hero, O'Connell, to learn the secrets of his trade, to see this wonderful Catholic people whose cause he had already adopted and whose history he had decided to write for the world.

He set out for Ireland just a few days before the July Revolution of 1830 started in the streets of Paris. In London he heard of the Bourbon king's flight, and he hailed the news as a "sublime victory" for the people. He hurried back to Paris so that he could take part in this glorious adventure, but his father hustled him out of the country again and off to Ireland for his long-postponed visit. Young Montalembert had pictured in his imagination an Ireland such as did not exist on this hard earth of reality. The Ireland he imagined was a miniature France, where all Irishmen were polished eighteenth-century French noblemen, where an abundance of grace and of flowering Catholicism was superadded to the natural culture of France.

Rude indeed was his shock, then, on finding Irishmen in the flesh and blood. Especially disappointing was his visit to O'Connell's estate in Clare. This terribly serious young French peer found himself ushered into a household of boisterous, fun-loving, noisy people who disappointed him with their lightheaded merriment and their rough good humor. O'Connell himself did little more than nod to his young visitor and then shunt him off with the young folks. The twenty-five who sat down to dinner impressed Montalembert as a disagreeable, boisterous, frivolous group who had not yet gone through the final stages of civilization. Later he went to hear O'Connell make one of his famous speeches, hoping to find the Irish leader take on new stature on the platform. Here again he was sorely disappointed. He thought O'Connell's talk quite common – with only an occasional gleam of eloquence. He found that the crowd applauded O'Connell's commonplace remarks, while his occasional significant statements apparently went right over their heads.

So the young Frenchman was disillusioned in this visit to O'Connell and in the political astuteness of the Irish people. But he was not disappointed in Ireland. For the people of Ireland, especially the men, had the faith. Montalembert was impressed by seeing men flock to Church as women did in France; he was moved to see a whole village pour out of its houses on a Sunday morning and fill the streets leading to the Church. At least part of his dream was realized – and Montalembert left Ireland deeply impressed, as a young man of twenty is wont to be.

He returned to Paris to meet two men who had developed ideas quite similar to his on the Church's place in modern society. These men were Lamennais, a gifted and eloquent priest who at fifty had reached the height of his power and influence in 1830, an independent thinker who loved liberty and God, and who thought he had discovered the formula for reconciling the two. The other was a young man, not yet thirty, Lacordaire, who had become a priest after his conversion from the paganism he had adopted in the schools of France. Lacordaire and Lamennais had started a little Catholic paper *L'Avenir* "to claim for the Church her part in the liberties acquired by the country." They advertized it as a work "at once Catholic and national, from which might be expected the enfranchisement of religion, the reconciliation of differing minds, and, in consequence, the renewal of society."

Lamennais had also organized a "Society for the Defense of Religious Liberty," with *L'Avenir* its official journal. The whole movement was a daring, romantic thing such as would appeal to a young man in this age of Lord Byron and Victor Hugo. Especially did it appeal to Montalembert, for *L'Avenir* was a modern Catholic Don Quixote jousting against anyone, big or little, who violated Catholic rights and liberties. It carried stories on such items as that of a prefect who forced a priest to bury an infidel in his Church; it defended such causes as that of the Poles' "holy revolt" from Russia. Such a journal was bound to violate the rigid press restrictions of the day, and in the second month of its existence *L'Avenir* was seized for two articles Lacordaire had written. Montalembert had met the young priest just that month. His "persecution" by the government almost automatically put Montalembert by his side, and from that time on he and Lacordaire became closely associated in various crusading adventures on behalf of the Church in France.

The first of these adventures took place the following May, when the two young men dramatically violated the law forbidding private individuals to conduct school in France.

The *L'Avenir* group was convinced that the country could never be made Catholic again, nor could the Church even draw a deep breath in France, unless the State monopoly on education were broken. They maintained, further, that the monopoly was contrary to the constitution accepted by the country in 1814. They were anxious to break the monopoly because it was under the control of the University and, as one contemporary put it, in the French secondary schools "the Deity was an unsuccessful candidate for the privilege of existence."

Lacordaire and Montalembert, joined by a third associate, De Coux, therefore brought the issue to trial by opening a school in Paris. Twelve children came to it, and before these twelve children Lacordaire and a Paris policeman enacted a seriocomic drama, the policeman telling the children to go home, Lacordaire commanding them to stay. Teacher prevailed over policemen, so Lacordaire and his associates were arrested. Before their case came up for trial, Montalembert's father died and young Charles became a peer of the realm – a wonderful thing for the publicity of their cause, for Montalembert could demand to be heard in the Chamber of Peers. He did. Lacordaire, himself a lawyer, prepared their defense, but it was Montalembert who attracted attention by speaking eloquently to his peers, and though they were somewhat amused and somewhat bored, they were also impressed with this youthful vehemence shown for freedom of education and for the Church. The three young men were found guilty, of course, but they were given only a gentle reprimand and the smallest fine possible, one hundred francs. Legally they were defeated, but morally they had won a great triumph, for they had advertized their cause to the whole nation and they had placed the issue of freedom of education squarely before the people of France.

Young Montalembert went on one more crusade before he settled down to mature work. And once again it resulted in failure – for this time the three editors of *L'Avenir* were rebuffed by their leader and chief teacher in Rome, and one of them, Lamennais, deserted the cause to carry on his battle alone, outside of the army of the faithful and not accepted in the ranks of the world. The *L'Avenir* episode belongs properly to the tragic story of Lamennais's career rather than to the life of Montalembert, for the young French nobleman merely tagged along as a faithful follower of the stronger Lamennais until the latter broke from the Church.

It is sufficient for us to note the bare outlines of this lost crusade. Through 1831, *L'Avenir* encountered as strong resistance within ecclesiastical circles in France as it did among the followers of Voltaire. It was a brash journal, imprudent and daring, and it came to absolute conclusions on the necessity of separation of Church and State, on freedom of conscience, and on other such political-religious questions which must always be judged in the background of a particular environment and pronounced on as prudential rather than absolute conclusions. It had the audacity of trying to commit the Church and the papacy to a revolutionary relationship with secular governments, to accept an entirely new place in society. And it looked upon the revolutionary arrangement as an ideal rather than as a necessary concession to modern society. That is why Lacordaire could say later, "We appeared to the clergy, to the government, to all parties, like a parcel of children, without ancestors and without posterity."

The children decided to appeal to their Father in Rome to ask not only his permission to carry on their campaign but even his endorsement of their aims and their methods. It was too much to expect – but they were trusting and naïve children, and the idea of going to Rome seemed so brilliant and so romantic, so sure of triumphant success, that without thinking twice they announced the temporary stoppage of *L'Avenir* until the Pope had endorsed it, and left for the Eternal City to obtain this endorsement. Eternal, timeless Rome swallowed up these up-to-the-minute Frenchmen from Paris. It smothered them with its vastness in the realm of time and of space. It seemed that Rome reckoned in centuries, and not in hours, as did Paris; it seemed that Rome had never heard of these three Frenchmen, at least the two younger ones, and what was worse it did not care whether they existed or not. After a long wait they obtained an interview with Pope Gregory XVI. They had been told to draw up a formal account of their aims and their intentions, but in their audience with the Pope they heard him talk only of small things – Montalembert's mother, Lamennais's brother, a picture of Michelangelo – and then he bade them good-by. Later they received a letter telling them that a decision would be rendered when the proper time had arrived.

From the very beginning, the Pope had been advised by such persons as Cardinal Lambruschini that it would be unwise to endorse *L'Avenir's* program, for to do so would be to approve of the excesses of Liberalism and to put the Church in the anomalous position of committing intellectual suicide. Lacordaire was the first to see the handwriting on the Vatican wall. He advised humility and submission to Lamennais, but the latter, to whom the adventure had come to mean everything, announced that he would stay in Rome until he had received the Pope's decision. Lacordaire went back to France, and Lamennais stayed in Rome. So too did Montalembert, who was as much interested in the historical sites of Rome and in friends he had made there as he was in the *L'Avenir* case. Like Lacordaire, he repeatedly counseled submission to his older friend, and finally in July he talked him into going to Germany with himself and some traveling companions. They went to Munich to observe the great work being done by the new "Munich School" and to listen to the renowned Joseph Görres.

At Munich they met Lacordaire, and there the three editors of *L'Avenir* received the encyclical *Mirari vos* condemning certain points of their program. French bishops had sent to Rome a list of Lamennais's errors, which a pontifical commission had studied carefully and from which it had selected certain errors for condemnation. None of the editors was mentioned by name, but there was no doubt *L'Avenir's* program was anathematized. The Pope refused to accept absolute freedom of speech and press as being good in itself, nor would he endorse freedom of opinion in the full and unrestricted way in which Lamennais advocated it. These were things which the Church might permit, but it could not approve them as being good in the abstract and therefore the aim of Catholics everywhere and at all times – as *L'Avenir* maintained. Most important of all, *Mirari vos* condemned the absolute separation of Church and State advocated by Lamennais as being an ideal which the Church should endorse as more than a *modus vivendi.*

All three editors accepted the condemnation of *Mirari vos.* Lamennais quickly wrote his letter of submission, but his spirit did not bend, as did Montalembert's and Lacordaire's. Subsequently, therefore, he retracted his submission and cut himself away from the Church. Two years later, in 1834, the Pope condemned him by name in the encyclical *Singulari nos,* and Lamennais openly revolted from Rome. Montalembert and Lacordaire felt crushed, like Lamennais, but unlike him they both had the good sense and the humility to submit to Rome's decision in spirit as well as in form. There were still other crusades to go on. There was still much to be rescued from modern society, and when they could collect their wits they would go on fighting for the Church and for liberty – along lines that would be acceptable to Rome. They were crushed, but they were young – and life was still worth living. Nevertheless, Montalembert came back to Paris a depressed young man. His second crusade had been a total failure. He was too young to realize that he had won a victory by his submission, nor did he enjoy the gift of prophecy to enable him to see that most of his ideas would be adopted by future popes when the times had changed. Paris seemed insupportable just then. Moreover, the young nobleman could not take his seat in the House of Peers until he was twenty-five. So he traveled through the Germanies. There he gathered the material for his life of St. Elizabeth – his crusade with the pen was under way – and there he traversed the territory so well covered by the medieval monks about whom he was to write his monumental work after his forced retirement from French politics.

* * *

In 1835, Montalembert returned to Paris to take his seat in the House of Peers. Here he was now eligible to speak, though he could not vote for another five years. His career as a crusader for God and Liberty began seriously at this time, for his earlier ventures had been those of a romantic youth not yet arrived at full intellectual or psychological maturity. After 1835, it is true, Montalembert's crusading continued to be Quixotic for another thirteen years, but it had settled objectives and a fixed technique. Montalembert is no longer jousting with the wind. He knows what he wants to achieve, and he thinks he knows how to do it.

Throughout his political career he seeks to create a Catholic party – a party of Frenchmen who would be Catholic first and foremost, whatever else they might be afterward. Catholics must get into politics actively, he repeated time without end. He censored them for remaining aloof, for withdrawing haughtily and contemptuously from the political arena, as they had done, when the Bourbon monarchy was overthrown. "You possess half the soil of France," he told these Catholics; "by your numbers, by your faith, by your virtues, even by your wealth, you are invincible. How do you dare, then, to remain longer apart from the struggles which decide day by day the important interests of your country? While you await the time when you can expose your lives for France on the battlefield, why do you shirk the duties of peaceful and free citizens?" Catholics must therefore exercise their political rights and "descend into the political arena to defend the greatest of causes without reservation." They are to enter politics as Catholics, then, and to defend the interests of the Church on the basis of its constitutional rights within France.

Montalembert was vehement in his denunciation of Catholic conservatism. He insisted time and time again that the Church, an eternal institution, should not be more than accidentally united to monarchical government. The Church should adapt itself to any kind of society and find a way to live in it. But it should identify itself with none. Here he disagreed not only with older Catholics who considered monarchy the only good government, but also with Lacordaire, who wanted to commit the Church to democracy as the only valid kind of society. Montalembert wanted the Catholics of France to accept their existing government — a constitutional, limited monarchy like England's — as provided by the Charter of 1814, and to organize themselves into a powerful party on the basis of their Catholic interests.

To do this he had to rouse his fellow Catholics from their lethargy and from that "hateful indifference" which, he said, made the Catholic a foreigner in his own country. Montalembert's sarcasm rises to flood tide in the Chamber of Peers when he describes the Catholic group in passages like this: "The Catholics of our day have in France one predominating inclination and one function which belongs especially to them. It is sleep. To sleep well and softly, and to sleep long, and after waking for a moment to sleep again as soon as possible — such has been, up to the present moment, their policy, their philosophy, and, according to some, their greatest gift. . . . When an eloquent voice or a too significant fact has raised around the Catholic Frenchman commotion enough to trouble his peace, he half opens his eyes for a moment and turns a dull, astonished gaze upon the unequal fight which is going on over his head. . . . He yawns and grows impatient of the noise which disturbs him, and finally falls asleep again."

It was to overcome such indifference that Montalembert wrote thousands of letters and delivered hundreds of addresses throughout the country. He worked on the bishops, and as a result of his almost superhuman effort they did endorse a bill for freedom of education in France, eventually passed in 1850. He worked on Catholic laymen too, to make them *Catholique avant tout* instead Catholic after everything else. It was hard work, and, Montalembert complained, it took all his time because he had to do it alone. His was a one-man crusade to organize a Catholic party in France.

And it was not a success, because, whether he realized it or not, he was trying to work a double conversion in his native country. He was not only trying to organize a party of French Catholics; he was also trying to make it a political party in the English tradition. Though Frenchmen could conceivably become *Catholique avant tout,* they could never adopt the English system of politics and make it their own. Montalembert understood and admired the Anglo-American political system as few Frenchmen have ever done. He seems unconscious of the gulf between that system and the one of his native land – perhaps because he grew up knowing them both so well, politically bilingual as it were, and he did not realize how unique he was. Nor did he realize that, by and large, Frenchmen have somehow never really understood the English political system.

Montalembert did all he could to familiarize his countrymen with the idea of "loyal opposition," as that technique was used in the British Parliament. He was himself a one-man party of opposition to the Orleanist government. But he could not shake the mass of French politicians away from their traditional methods of opposing the government: conspiracy to overthrow it, or proud retirement into seclusion. Montalembert's first adventure into politics, when he and Lacordaire tested the legality of the government's monopoly of education, was typical of his whole political career. Such a test case was typically Anglo-American. It certainly was not French. It was even described at the time as being terribly "un-French," and though Montalembert and his associates succeeded in attracting much attention by their daring maneuver, still the purpose of their action was not generally understood in their native country.

Montalembert insisted that Catholics were morally obliged to exercise their political rights. They lived in a country, he pointed out, which had granted them "that political liberty by which we may hope to attain religious freedom." He went on to specify the means they ought to use: free speech and freedom of the press, continual publicity and organized party pressure, "these new and invaluable weapons" by which the cause of the Church should be protected. He insisted that Catholics were obliged to vote in every election. "Not to vote is at once a mistake and an act of treason. . . . Every soldier who is not in the ranks of his company on the battle-day [election day] is a deserter."

Montalembert did more than exhort Catholics to vote and to organize themselves into a party to defend the Church's interests. He also told them how to organize, how to guarantee the election of good deputies – and here he sounds like an American city politician, or a lobbyist operating out of Washington. Before the elections of 1844, for example, he instructed his fellow Catholics to insist that their candidates go on record as favoring their education bill. Do not commit yourselves to anyone, he advised, who will not explicitly pledge himself to vote for the education bill that the bishops and the Catholic party have before the Assembly. He even went so far as to draw up a three-point pledge which he urged his followers to force the candidates for election to sign before election day. This campaign was successful, for one hundred and thirty of the newly elected deputies were formally pledged to freedom of education when the new Chamber convened.

This was the closest Montalembert came to organizing a real party of Catholics. He believed for a while that he had achieved his purpose, but neither he nor anyone else in French politics has ever organized a party in the Anglo-American sense of the word. Whatever chance of success Montalembert had was ruined by the relatively radical Revolution of 1848 and the reaction into which almost all French Catholics blindly and foolishly rushed – Montalembert included.

If organizing Catholics into an active political party was Montalembert's first objective, his second was to vindicate liberty and to put the Catholics of France on record as favoring and supporting it. To him liberty was a pearl of great price, the one genuine jewel of the French Revolution, and he was anxious that it be preserved instead of cast aside with other of the Revolution's drosser products. He had declared for liberty before he was seventeen, as we have seen, and many years later he could defy his listeners in the House of Peers "to find a single word fallen from my pen or from my lips which has not been devoted to the cause of freedom." The challenge was not accepted.

Montalembert's devotion to liberty is not unqualified, despite his claim that he "has loved her too much, as one loves when one is young, without measure or restraint." Even as a boy of seventeen he wrote, with older wisdom, that "truth is more important to me than freedom." When he was twenty he saw what happens when liberty is exercised without restraint by those not mature enough to use it. He saw that liberty is like a sharp knife, which in the hands of a competent man is a tool of civilization, but which in the hands of an unscrupulous man is a dangerous weapon.

The Revolution of 1830, which he accepted as a "sublime victory" at first, had its less sublime side in its wanton destruction of property, especially in the looting of the Church of Saint Germain l'Auxerrois, where memorial services for the murdered Duc de Berry were being conducted, in despoiling the archbishop's palace, and in throwing its priceless library into the Seine. "Freedom never gains anything by such violent movements," the young peer wrote at once. "It lives by slow and successive conquests, by perseverance and by patience." Montalembert was sadly disillusioned, for he had dreamed of a "sublime alliance" between the Church and liberty, and now he saw the latter perverted to cover "the most revolting excesses." But he did not throw full blame on the street fighters of 1830. He blamed the reactionary Catholics above all. "It has been your doing," he told them. "You have fastened your *fleur-de-lis* [the symbol of the Bourbon monarchy] to a crucifix, and the people have protested against this union by a sacrilege."

Nevertheless, Montalembert continued to crusade eighteen more years for liberty, because he believed that the French were becoming mature enough to use it without abusing it. The revolution of 1848 disillusioned him even further, however, so that by then he concluded liberty was a name used all too frequently to cover license. In its name the most tyrannical of crimes were committed, for those who claimed they wanted liberty in 1848 wanted it only to deny it to their opponents. Just one month before the Revolution of 1848 broke out, in fact, Montalembert had distinguished between true liberty and false in a remarkable speech on Switzerland's civil war. "Liberty," he proclaimed, "is reasonable and voluntary toleration; radicalism [which claimed to be Liberalism, and was close to Socialism in 1848] is absolutely intolerant. Liberty imposes unusual sacrifices on none; radicalism cannot put up with a thought, a word, even a prayer, contrary to its will. Liberty consecrates the right of minorities; radicalism absorbs and annihilates them. Liberty is respect for mankind, whereas radicalism is scorn of mankind pushed to its highest degree. Never Muscovite despot, never Eastern tyrant has despised his fellows as they are despised by those radical clubs who gag their vanquished adversaries in the name of liberty and of equality."

Montalembert's attitude toward democracy was one of resignation. He did not like it, for he thought it a steppingstone to despotism — as it actually had been under Robespierre and Napoleon, and as it was soon to be again under Napoleon III. Nevertheless, he believed that democracy was the form of government for the future, and therefore that Catholics had to accept it, to find their place in it, to Christianize it. Because it was inevitable and because it was not vicious in itself, Montalembert believed that democracy must be accepted and must be made workable so that it would not degenerate into mere plebiscites and into the tyranny of a demagogue endorsed by the masses of voters. He called upon his followers to work in democracy so that it could never deny them or anyone else their rights as human beings by submerging them in the general will and "forcing them to be free," as the democratic theorist Rousseau had advocated. His great fear that democracy was the enemy of liberty was historically more valid for his time and place than we in England and America can realize.

It must be admitted, as Montalembert himself sadly complained, that he accomplished little in selling the Catholics of France his ideas on political Catholicism, on liberty, and on the acceptance of democracy. After 1848 he did secure the passage of a number of laws favorable to the Church. Moreover, concessions were made to the Catholics by Napoleon III after Montalembert's forced retirement from the political arena — and they were perhaps as much due to Montalembert's influence as to anything else. Catholics as a group backed the new despot after 1852, and they turned a deaf ear to Montalembert's pleas for freedom and for the English political system. Large numbers of them even refused to listen to Pope Leo XIII when, twenty years after Montalembert had died, he echoed the Catholic peer in telling French Catholics to accept the republican form of government. It is unfortunate not only for French Catholics, but for France herself, that the reactionary group triumphed and the Catholics repudiated their former leader. Not until the end of the century were his political ideas generally adopted by Catholics.

* * *

The Revolution of 1848 caught Montalembert off balance. Neither he nor anyone else expected this revolution which has been called "an effect without a cause." It came suddenly in February. King Louis Philippe fled the country hurriedly, and France was left in the hands of various groups contending for the government. One of the most formidable of these were the Socialists, led by such men as Blanqui and Louis Blanc. And though the Socialists of this day did not know Karl Marx, who was in this month finishing his *Communist Manifesto,* nevertheless they were extremist in both their political aspirations and their hatred for religion. They were the incarnation of that "radicalism" which a month earlier Montalembert had condemned as the perversion of true liberty.

Socialism, he therefore believed, was the enemy – the enemy which must be defeated at all costs. It was powerful, he maintained, because it was itself a religion. "It is man believing himself God." It is the "logical conclusion" of democracy, the result of "a wild, intolerant, unregulated, and hypocritical liberty," and it must be defeated even at the sacrifice of liberty or the independence of his hoped-for Catholic party. Montalembert therefore urged that all lovers of true freedom, his Catholic followers and all good Republicans, unite to wage war on Socialism, "war made loyally, frankly, energetically; legal war, by all the means which justice does not reprove and which the constitution permits."

One of these legal means was to restrict the suffrage in such a way as to eliminate Socialist voters. Montalembert therefore spoke in favor of and voted for a bill requiring a three-year residence qualification for voting – a move to cut about three million poorer and less stable persons from the electorate. Again in 1849 he favored a bill curtailing the freedom of the press. His first speech as a peer, back in 1835, had been against a similar bill, but fourteen years had disillusioned him and had made him believe that liberty must be limited to keep it from committing suicide. For by 1849 he had come to believe that full liberty, or license, meant the end of true liberty. About this time he adopted the slogan of "God and Society" to replace his former one of "God and Liberty." The security of the future, he now felt, rested upon the three props of religion, the family, and private property – the three props that Socialism would cut away as soon as it came to power.

So the threat of Socialism made Montalembert considerably more conservative after 1848 than he had been in the first part of his life. The man who had formerly gloried in constituting a one-man opposition to the government now looked for bases of combination on which an anti-Socialist bloc could be formed. The man who was formerly the orator without equal in France – and also without a single legislative victory – now became a mature politician who spoke in favor of bills that were made law by the Assembly. The man who formerly crusaded for ideals without winning a single victory now succeeded in winning one engagement after another. Montalembert is no longer the peerless knight of the Assembly jousting against all comers; he is rather the mature statesman accomplishing his objectives.

Most notable of these accomplishments was the passing of the education measure which he had agitated for futilely as a lad of twenty and had spoken for in vain from the time he entered the House of Peers. The passage of this bill, known as the *Loi Falloux* after the man who introduced it, was the fruit as much of Montalembert's long labors with the bishops and Catholic laymen of France as of his more recent maneuvers to win support from other sources. For a long time Montalembert had carried on the fight almost singlehanded – and he had not succeeded because he remained an uncompromising crusader instead of a mature politician. He had rejected various compromise bills proposed by the government of Louis Philippe after 1844, and he was indignant when the bishops of the Church in France and even Rome itself agreed to compromise measures – notably to the sacrifice of the Jesuits in return for freedom of education for the rest of the Catholics.

When the General of the Jesuits agreed to dissolve the order in France, Montalembert was so disgusted that he quoted St. Thomas of Canterbury's words: "I know not how it is, but at Rome men always prefer Barabbas to Christ." On paper the Jesuits were dispersed, but actually they remained in France and the way was cleared for obtaining freedom of education. Montalembert saw how this was a victory, but he was disgusted by the ignoble means used to achieve it, the backing down before the government of Louis Philippe and dispersing the Society of Jesus. Such maneuvers sickened the man who had insisted that he was a son of the crusaders and that he would never retreat before a son of Voltaire.

In 1850, however, it was different. He was willing now to compromise. And the bill which eventually became law in France was a compromise – aptly called by some French historians "a concordat between the Church and the University." Bishops were given a voice in setting standards and determining the curriculum for French schools; anyone was allowed to operate a private school if he met certain objective requirements; clerics were allowed to teach in the State schools. A situation very much like ours in the United States was therefore created, whereby private schools were allowed to exist side by side with State schools and their graduates were eligible to enter the University and the various professions on an equal footing with those from the French *lycées.*

The *Loi Falloux,* being a compromise measure, pleased no one, least of all the extremist Catholics who condemned Montalembert for his "radicalism" and for his leanings toward liberty. This success made Montalembert a man without a party, a leader without followers. For those who considered themselves *Catholique avant tout* thought that the bill had not gone far enough. They condemned it, with Louis Veuillot and *Univers,* as a compromise with paganism, a shameful thing. And the Liberals of France, of course, thought that the bill gave far too much power to the Church. They looked upon it as the first step toward the restoration of the Bourbon monarchy – and in some respects they were quite justified, for Montalembert's acceptance of the political order was not shared by Veuillot and his followers.

* * *

Montalembert's fear of Socialism caused him to make a serious political blunder – the same mistake that countless Catholics made in Italy in 1922 and in Germany in 1933, the mistake that Catholics have been all too inclined to make in many other countries in modern times. He helped bring a despot to power in France in 1852. Montalembert made this mistake because he was too much the orator and not enough the analyst. He saw things in black and white rather than in all the colors of the spectrum and all the shadings of the rainbow. He oversimplified the issue confronting the French people in 1851 by deciding that they were offered a choice between Napoleon III and Socialism. He chose the former as the lesser of two evils – and he lived both to regret and to repudiate his choice. Too late he saw that Catholics had other alternatives before them.

On the night of December 1, 1851, Louis Napoleon, then president of the French republic, dissolved the legislature – of which Montalembert was a member – and announced that he would ask the French nation, in a plebiscite, for permission to draw up a constitution on the basis of universal suffrage. Montalembert immediately was named to a commission to help the president draw up the new constitution – a commission which never met. The Catholics of France were in a quandary. Should they vote for this measure, or should they take the chance of throwing the country into confusion and chaos again? Thousands of them appealed to Montalembert for advice. So many inquiries did he receive that he decided to answer them all together in a public letter.

"I begin," he wrote, "by declaring that the act of December 2nd. [the president's *coup d'état*] has put to flight all the revolutionists, all the Socialists, all the bandits of France and Europe – and that alone is, in my opinion, a more than sufficient reason for all honest men to rejoice." Then he went on to examine the three alternatives the voter might take: to vote against Louis Napoleon, not to vote at all, or to vote for him. "To vote against Louis Napoleon," he concluded on the first alternative, "would be to sanction the socialist revolution, which for the present, at least, is the only one which can take the place of the existing government." The second alternative could not be taken by any honest man, for Montalembert continued to hold that one is duty bound to vote.

There remained the alternative of voting for Louis Napoleon. In the course of his letter Montalembert pointed out that he did not approve all Louis Napoleon had done, nor did he assert that his government was ideal. He only claimed that his vote would mean "we prefer a prince who has given proofs of resolution and ability to those who are at this moment giving their proofs of murder and pillage." He concluded, therefore: "My choice is made. I am for authority against revolt, for preservation against destruction, for society against Socialism, for the possible freedom of good against the certain liberty of evil; and in the mighty struggle between the two powers which divide the world, I believe that in acting thus, I am, as I ever have been, for Catholicism against revolution."

Whether Montalembert was right in painting the picture in black and white alone no one can ever say, for no one can know what would have happened in France had the people not voted to have the president draw up a new constitution. But at least we can be certain that Montalembert never suspected that this was a step toward making Louis Napoleon an emperor, for he had been completely taken in by this nephew of Napoleon whom he considered a man of principle and of sound ideas. At any rate, it was a serious mistake, and Montalembert soon came to realize it. He withdrew from the Consultive Commission a month later, and he severely criticized the constitution when it was published. He continued to criticize the Napoleonic regime from his seat in the Assembly — and his was almost the only voice raised in opposition to the new despotism.

Montalembert's political career was cut short in 1857 because of his critical opposition to the government. In that year he was defeated by the government's official candidate. His defeat cut him deeply because it was caused chiefly by the clergy of his district and by the rising "ultra-Catholic" group in France. "You will probably have seen by the papers," he wrote to a friend after the election, "that after twenty-six years of public service I have been set aside in the recent election, and for the first time since I came of age deprived of a vote in the councils of my country; and this thanks to the clergy of Franche Comté, half of whom voted against me, and the other half stayed home. Such has been the result of the influence of *Univers* [the Catholic paper edited by Louis Veuillot] and of its calumnies and denunciations for the last seven years." These are the words of a hurt man.

* * *

Montalembert lived thirteen more years. He lived the life of a good French nobleman — writing his voluminous and inspiring *Monks of the West*, advising young Catholic friends, corresponding with other Catholic leaders throughout Europe. His direct influence on French political life had been spent by 1850, for a newer and younger group had risen up in France, a group that was in the "old Catholic" tradition politically. They stood for religious absolutism; they were unwilling to meet modern society on any terms. They stood for an attitude toward the world utterly foreign to Montalembert's desire to create an alliance between God and liberty. Montalembert was too far ahead of his age to have moving, immediate influence. But eight years after his death a man was elected to the papal throne – Leo XIII – who with incomparably great authority and much greater wisdom carried on many lines of action advocated at a less propitious time and in less propitious circumstances by the crusading peer of France. For Montalembert advocated a program and proposed doctrines which the Church could adopt only when it was strong enough to assimilate them. Moreover, time and discussion were required to modify Montalembert's theories and to purify them so that their large measure of truth could be taken without their small admixture of error. This was accomplished by 1914, so that Montalembert's program has come to be generally validated in our own twentieth century.

Because Montalembert was at heart a humble man, he did not grow bitter in old age. His devotion to his Church had been sincere and selfless. He possessed rank and personal ability, wealth and influence, and all these he used in his crusade to bring about the "sublime alliance" between the Church and modern free society. This objective was not achieved by Montalembert himself, as we have seen, but others who have crusaded since his time have come closer to attaining it – and their success is due in part to his pioneering efforts. Successful or not, during his crusade, in the midst of disappointments and bitter disillusionment, Montalembert kept his heart pure and his mind high. "He was," in the words of the late Father Corrigan, "a paragon for the layman of any age." For this, too, he is important.

3. Ludwig Windthorst

The juxtaposition of man to man in time and place does strange things to the reputation of history's heroes. David, for example, is almost always remembered as a stripling with a slingshot weighing in for his seemingly unequal struggle against the heavyweight Goliath. It is not so often remembered that David was himself a mighty king, one of the greatest and most powerful the Jews ever had, or that he was the world's outstanding psalm writer.

Windthorst's reputation suffers in much the same way as David's. For Windthorst, whose body was dwarfish, was the only man in the German Empire who dared to challenge the giant creator of that giant state, Otto von Bismarck. The duel between diminutive Windthorst and gigantic Bismarck lasted twenty years, and in the end Bismarck was completely vanquished. The modern Goliath went into sullen retirement in 1890, whereas the modern David was toasted by all Europe in his old age. The European world looked to him as the century's foremost parliamentary debater, as the best party organizer and political leader in modern times, as the man who was the core of resistance to the encroachments of the modern Goliath on the German's right to be a responsible, free human being.

The European world tended to forget that this modern David had other claims to greatness. He was the outstanding Catholic leader of Germany. He was a social strategist, who with the immortal Leo XIII and Bishop von Ketteler, saw the necessity of preaching and practicing social justice both as insurance against Socialism and as the only way of doing right in the industrialized modern world. Windthorst was personally a good man. He supported charitable enterprises beyond his means. He gave unsparingly of his time and his energy in fighting for his Church. In the fight he made no personal enemies, for he never used foul tactics nor did he seek individual aggrandizement. These are things the world tends to forget about Windthorst when it looks on him as the conqueror of Bismarck.

Windthorst's career was cast along the same lines as O'Connell's and Montalembert's. He set out to accomplish essentially the same mission that they had ventured upon – to organize a party of Catholics who would protect the Church from State domination by forming themselves into a parliamentary bloc which would withhold its support from any group inimical to the Church. Windthorst's early career took much the same course as O'Connell's and Montalembert's – the fight against unequal odds, the seeming impossibility of victory, the little victories and the large defeats.

But Windthorst's struggle had a much happier ending than O'Connell's or Montalembert's. The Irish leader achieved only partial success, and then he wavered in the battle because the odds were impossibly strong against him. Montalembert likewise won some success, but he too failed to achieve his great objective of organizing a party of Catholics who would fight for God and for freedom. Windthorst, on the other hand, lived to see Bismarck defeated after twelve years of strategic retreat before the capably led Center Party. He lived to see his party become the largest one in the German Empire, a well-disciplined group that was the realization in Germany of the dream O'Connell had dreamed in Ireland, as Montalembert had in France.

Windthorst could achieve this success and bring his life story to a happy ending because he lived among the disciplined German people and because his age – two decades later than Montalembert's – was more favorable to his enterprise. Accidents of time and circumstance, then, worked, in Windthorst's favor, whereas they had conspired against O'Connell and Montalembert. Where the threat of Socialism had scared the French peer into the crushing arms of Napoleon III's dictatorship, in Germany it prompted Bismarck to meet Windthorst's demands. Where both O'Connell and Montalembert saw a radical young generation grow up to reject their leadership, the German Catholics loyally followed Windthorst until the day of his death. The intransigent Pius IX cut O'Connell and Montalembert off from any diplomatic or political help from Rome in their struggles against the State in England and in France, whereas Windthorst was aided in the years of his victory by the wise and conciliatory Leo XIII. These things, as much as his unquestioned personal ability, account for the unique success achieved by the mighty mite of Hanover in his fight for the Church against Bismarck.

* * *

Early in 1812, Ludwig von Windthorst was born at Keldenhof, near the city of Osnabrück in the kingdom of Hanover. His father was a doctor of civil and canon law who preferred the more peaceful and, for him, more profitable life of gentleman farmer. Young Windthorst was thus raised amid pastoral surroundings in the family of well-to-do and well-educated northern German stock. Ludwig's parents hoped that their son would become a priest, and with that end in view they sent him to the college of St. Charles at Osnabrück. There the young lad was a model German student — always receiving "perfect" in conduct, and either "excellent" or "very good" in his studies.

In 1830, when he was eighteen years old, young Windthorst decided that he did not have a vocation to the priesthood. Instead, he studied law at the universities of Göttingen and Heidelberg, where he might have met his future antagonist Bismarck who was then a hard-riding, hard-drinking Junker student at the latter university. Windthorst seems to have stood out in his university career as a professor's delight, the ideal student who works diligently, who is amenable to instruction but is still possessed of a vigorously independent spirit. One thing is certain: in this romantic age of loose morals — especially at the German universities — Windthorst remained an excellent practicing Catholic closely attached to his faith in personal practice and in intellectual conviction.

In 1836, Windthorst returned to Osnabrück with the intention of settling down in the community as a respectable lawyer. He was admitted to the bar that year and soon he developed an extensive, thriving practice. Two years later he married Julia Engeln — as the result, so the story goes, of his pertinacity and his *savoir-faire* in the face of adversity. The young lawyer had failed to find favor with his lady love. But instead of giving up he decided to use a different, desperate approach. He mastered the guitar, waited for an ideal moonlit night, and proceeded to serenade his Julia. Apparently his serenade was futile — until he stepped backward and fell into a brook. His splash into the water and his successful emergence from the waves broke the ice encrusting Julia's heart. Thus did Windthorst gain his first diplomatic triumph.

In these days before Bismarck had created the German Empire, Hanover was a small independent state in the northern part of the German land. Here the young lawyer soon attracted attention. In 1842 he was appointed president of the Catholic Board of Churches and Schools, a position which gave him insight into and experience in handling the delicate problem of relationship between Church and the State in the secularized society of the nineteenth century. But it was not until the year of revolution—1848—that Windthorst's political career really began.

King George V was forced by the revolution to re-establish the fairly liberal constitution of 1837, and in the first elections to the new Hanoverian parliament Windthorst was returned as a deputy. From the beginning, he stood out in this assembly both as an orator and as a parliamentary leader. As a liberal, and therefore as an opponent of centralization and State absolutism, Windthorst rose to leadership among those who opposed the trend toward a highly centralized German State. He was not an opponent of German unity as such, but he preferred a federal union which would have left to individual states like Hanover or Saxony full control of local affairs, such as education and religious matters. Early in 1851, Windthorst was elected president of the lower house in the Hanoverian parliament, and later that year he was given the portfolio of justice. In 1853 he resigned as a member of the government because he could not agree to its reactionary policies. The next ten years he served as a deputy in the House, and in 1862 he was again appointed Minister of Justice, a position he held until the Seven Weeks' War against Prussia. In this position Windthorst protected Catholic interests in the Protestant country of Hanover, even obtaining the government's consent to the creation of the diocese of Osnabrück.

As a result of this war, which was one of the steps of "blood and iron" whereby Bismarck united the German states under Prussia, Hanover lost its independence by being absorbed into the Prussian state. Windthorst was given the important but futile assignment of negotiating with the victorious Bismarck for his blind king. For the next three years Windthorst could do little but mark time, because in these years parliamentary doings were of small account. In 1871, Bismarck's wars of conquest were finished and the German Empire was created. There were still conquests to make at home, though, and to these Bismarck now turned his attention: Poles and Danes to be Germanized; Hanoverians, Bavarians, and all varieties of Germans attached to their former little states to be Prussianized; Catholics and Jews to be cut away from all non-German connections. Of all these "enemies" within his newly created German Empire, Bismarck feared the Catholic Church the most. Ten years earlier one of his associates had remarked that "now we have but one citadel to storm — that of Ultramontanism." Now that Bismarck had peace in 1871, he thought the time had come to storm that citadel and to detach Catholics from the Pope in Rome.

But there was a diminutive figure in the way, a little Hanoverian named Windthorst, who soon allied himself with prominent Catholics from various parts of Germany to form the Center Party and to contest each step of the Iron Chancellor's campaign against his bugbear of "Vaticanism."

* * *

What sort of person was this tiny nineteenth-century David who presumed to stand astride the path of the Goliath who had triumphed in successive wars over small Denmark, middle-sized Austria, and large, powerful France? What kind of man was this Windthorst who presumed to do what Napoleon III had so signally failed to do?

In 1890, the last year of Windthorst's life, Joseph Schroeder described him for American readers in the *American Catholic Quarterly Review:* "He is the accomplished statesman, the consummate orator, the party leader without equal, and besides all this, the Christian model." A year later the same author eulogized Windthorst in the same journal by calling him "the Christian Hero . . . the loving and beloved husband and father . . . the faithful servant . . . the great parliamentarian . . . the devoted Catholic . . . the party leader . . . the intrepid general." These are words of high praise written in the warmth of worship attendant upon a successful man's inspiring death — but they remain words which time has hardened as truth instead of eroding as eulogistic exaggeration.

Windthorst certainly did not look the part of a giant killer, Christian hero, or party leader. At best he looked like a faithful servant. He was a dwarfish figure, reaching up only to an ordinary man's shoulder, and on his shrunken body was perched an enormous head. There was nothing beautiful about that head, as Windthorst took a certain glee in observing, but it was nevertheless attractive with its prominent forehead, its wide mouth and its weak eyes peering out from behind thick glasses. Windthorst looked more like one of Walt Disney's seven dwarfs than anything else, out of which he was astute enough to make political capital.

This little man was one of the best politicians of his time – or any time in history. He knew how to stick to his principles until the bitter end, but at the same time he could yield on lesser matters and he always knew when he had pushed a point in politics to its limit. He never gave up the bird in his hand to grab the two in the bush – but at the same time he never quit trying to get one or both of the birds in the bush. Typical of his political judgment was his decision when Hanover became part of Prussia. He apparently had the choice of jumping on the Prussian bandwagon, as so many of his colleagues did, or of retiring in protest, as some few of them did. Windthorst did neither. He took his seat in the new Reichstag and continued to oppose Prussian centralization and domination of the new German Empire. This was the decision of one who had sound political judgment such as few continental Europeans possess.

Windthorst had no equal in the Prussian Landtag or in the German Reichstag, to both of which he belonged. He was excellent as a debater, for his tongue was quick, his repartee was telling, he had perfect control of his temper – a fact which exasperated the irascible Bismarck – and he had an uncanny ability to turn his opponent's words against him in rebuttal. Here Windthorst turned a weakness to advantage. Because his eyesight was so bad that he could not easily read, he had developed the ability to listen to a speech of two or three hours' length without taking a note and then to answer it perfectly point by point. He was particularly potent in summing up and answering tellingly the day's or week's debate on some issue under consideration.

But Windthorst was more than just a good politician and a good debater. He was a good man — an accomplishment more difficult of achievement in his world than might appear at first sight. His goodness and his lovableness were so apparent that he was never treated by the German people quite like a human being. They made way for him respectfully and helpfully, for example, as he walked from his flat in Berlin to the Reichstag. Even his opponents loved and respected him as a man — as he did them. It was frequently remarked of Windthorst in his old age that while he had countless political enemies he had not a single personal enemy. And when he died, his opponents were as lavish in their praise of his goodness and his worth as were his supporters.

As a man, Windthorst was possessed of those two virtues which it is so hard to find in the world's important people: real charity and a sense of humor. His hand was always open to the poor. With donations given to him and his wife on their golden wedding anniversary, he built a church to our Lady in his native Hanover. Because of his simple wants and his generous giving he managed to live well but frugally — and to die poor. At the time of death the *Berlin Tageblatt,* always hostile to Windthorst and his Center Party, observed that "outside his own family and the Center Party, those who suffer the greatest loss are the poor."

Windthorst also possessed that finer and more rarified charity of spirit, a generosity and a love which extended to his worst political enemies. When Bismarck was forced to retire in 1890, for example, Windthorst's was one of the few voices in Germany raised in his defense, for the leader of the Center Party could recall some good things, as well as the many mean things, that Bismarck had done during his career. Finally, Windthorst possessed a sense of humor which enabled him to see things in their right proportion, to weather many a storm when others were ready to give up the struggle, to understand how ridiculous some of the apparently ultra-serious matters of the day really were. This humor permeated his speeches and won him occasional neutral support — for he could turn a joke on himself as gleefully as he could direct it against a political opponent.

When the Center Party's great leader died, in 1891, the papers of the world paused to pay him their respects and heap on him their praise. Typical of the opinion in which he was held is the comment of a neutral observer, the German Jewish journalist Stern, who summed up his appraisal of Windthorst thus: "Windthorst is celebrated everywhere as a master of parliamentary strategy, and that is but simple justice. But his qualities as a politician, eminent as they were, do not give sufficient explanation of the universal and cordial sympathy manifested towards this fighter. . . . The respect shown towards Windthorst was directed in the first place toward the man of character, the man thoroughly good, noble and disinterested, the intrepid champion who forced men to esteem him because he fought from conviction."

Such was the man who dared to challenge Bismarck in 1871.

* * *

The political duel between Windthorst and Bismarck lasted twenty years. Throughout the two decades from 1871 until 1890, Bismarck was the "Iron Chancellor" of the German Empire, a large man, aggressive, imperious, imposing. Windthorst was an opposition leader, never a member of the government, never with a majority behind him, and still when the battle was done Windthorst could get almost any measure he wished written into German law, whereas Bismarck had been forced to resign his office and to go, unmourned, into retirement. Windthorst was successful in this long struggle largely because he fought for a matter of principle, whereas his opponent fought only for power. Windthorst fought for human freedom and human dignity, for those rights which the German people were guaranteed by the basic law of their land. Bismarck fought to deny those rights in the name of his omnipotent state. As he put it himself in a speech to the Reichstag, he "wished to be excused from listening to any more talk about the pretended rights of the people—mere reminiscences of days long vanished, and which merit no other designation than that of declamatory phrases." Time has a way of favoring those who stand for right principles, and time therefore favored Windthorst against Bismarck.

Except for the matter of physical size, Bismarck the Goliath was in every way a smaller man than Windthorst the David. He hated and feared Windthorst as he hated and feared no one else.

He subjected the leader of the Center Party to vicious personal attacks in the Reichstag, attacks which were always met with great dignity and by cool analysis on Windthorst's part – which, of course, exasperated Bismarck worse than ever. At one time the Chancellor went so far as to promise religious peace to the Center Party if they would sacrifice their diminutive "Pearl of Meppen," as he had come to be known from the constituency he represented for twenty-five years. In the things that count, Bismarck was small and Windthorst was big. But for many years it seemed that bigness of character or rightness of principle would play no part in deciding the issue between Bismarck and Windthorst. The former had power, prestige, numbers, the Emperor on his side; the latter had only a handful of valiant men possessed of heroic Germanic stubbornness and of sufficient good sense to band together to achieve their objective.

These were the men who became the core of the Center Party, which until Hitler's seizure of power in 1933 remained a decisive force in Germany's domestic policies. These men had, until 1871, belonged to various small German states – Hanover, Bavaria, Hesse-Darmstadt, Baden, Saxony, and so on up to thirty-nine. Suddenly they found themselves members of the most powerful nation on earth, a state which under Bismarck's direction had sprung like Minerva full-armed from the head of Zeus. What means could these individuals, who had so little in common, find to protect themselves from annihilation through their merging with Prussia in 1871?

That was their problem. It was difficult to solve because these men still thought as Hanoverians or Bavarians or Saxons instead of as Germans. They had to stick together closely, they had to form a compact, united party from distinctly heterogeneous elements. And that meant they had to find a strong leader who could weld them together, be their spokesman in the Imperial Reichstag, decide their general lines of strategy. Such a man they found in Windthorst.

* * *

By 1871, when the German Empire came into being, the political parties functioning in days gone by were either dead or antiquated. New parties had to be formed on a nationwide basis, and it was natural that they should form on the basis of opposition to Bismarck or support of him. Those who wanted to be *Catholique avant tout* — to carry Montalembert's phrase across the Rhine — therefore found themselves in a difficult situation. They could not logically join either the Conservatives who supported Bismarck or the Liberals who tended to oppose him. To join the Conservatives would have meant championing the claims of a powerful state that was reaching arms out in every direction, octopuslike, to pull more and more into its crushing embrace. To join the Liberals, on the other hand, would have meant combining with avowed enemies of the Church who, though their motives differed from Bismarck's, were willing to help him in his attack on the Church in Germany.

German Catholics were therefore forced to stand aloof from these two dominant political groups in order to form a party whose votes they could hold as currency for buying one or the other party's good will toward the Church. Though they never expected to be numerous, nevertheless German Catholic leaders thought they might achieve a balance of power between the two large parties. This they would use effectively to protect the Church from harmful legislation in the Reichstag. In January of 1871, therefore, a circular letter was addressed to German Catholic voters urging them to elect representatives who would join such a group. The letter was signed by five of the most prominent Catholic statesmen of the day: Mallinckrodt, Windthorst, Savigny, Reichensperger, and Prince Löwenstein.

Sixty-one Catholic deputies were returned that year to the Reichstag, where they banded themselves together. The leader of this group at the beginning was Mallinckrodt, a Westphalian of noble birth, who until his death in 1874 did an excellent job as party chieftain. During these three years, Windthorst played the role of party whip; and when Mallinckrodt died, the little Hanoverian was unanimously chosen by his associates as formal head of their band. The new party consisted mostly of Catholics, but its leaders insisted that it was not properly a Catholic sect nor one exclusively for Catholics. Protestants who subscribed to its platform and accepted its discipline were welcomed, and there always was a sprinkling of Protestants in the party.

Some members of the new group originally had wanted to call it the "Catholic Party," but Windthorst insisted that its objectives were wider than defending Catholic sectarian interests alone. Its aim, he claimed, was the defense of all constitutional liberties in the new German Empire – among which, of course, stood as pre-eminent freedom of religion both because it was so important and because it was so consistently under attack. The new party was therefore given the official formidable title of *Centrum-oder Verfassungs-Partei* – the Center or Constitutional Party – the first part of the name deriving from the fact that in general social policies it usually stood between the Conservatives and the Liberals, and the second deriving from its objective of defending all constitutionally granted rights. To save wear and tear on German tongues the party soon was called simply the *Centrum,* and under this name it continued to exist until 1933.

The Center chose for its slogan the vague, but in this case revealing, *Für Wahrheit, Freiheit, und Recht* – "For Truth, Liberty, and Right." It was a banner, the Centrists felt, which truly expressed their purpose, and at the same time it would attract all representatives in the Reichstag, Catholic or Protestant, who took the German constitution and its bill of rights seriously. In 1871, the Center Party published an official program in which it asserted that the German Empire was a confederacy and therefore that the central government had no right to interfere in local affairs. These, they claimed, were the concern of the individual states composing the Empire. They insisted, too, that "the moral and material good of the masses should be furthered, that the civil and religious freedom of the subjects, especially of religious bodies, be continuously protected from legislative greed."

This concern with religious freedom was not held by the Center Party for academic reasons. There was immediate, practical reason – Bismarck and his followers had begun their war on the Church. The Centrists therefore drew up their lines of defense by stating their position and then by going into the Reichstag to thwart Bismarck's proposals by speaking and voting against his measures. Through the next twenty years it was mostly on religious matters that Windthorst led the Center

Party into battle with Bismarck. Occasionally it is true, Windthorst and Bismarck crossed swords on a purely financial question or jousted on an unimportant political matter, but almost always the Center Party's opposition to the Iron Chancellor could be traced back ultimately to its defense of the religious citadel he was trying to take by storm.

* * *

It would be unfair to Bismarck – and perhaps naïve – to consider his attack on the Church simply a personal battle springing from a satanical hatred of Catholicism. His motives are to be found less in personal animosity than in what he considered reasons of state. Practically every country in Europe had its own peculiar equivalent of Bismarck's *Kulturkampf,* for it was the temper of the times in the latter nineteenth century to drive the Church off the street corner and out of the market place into the confines of the sacristy. Caesar was everywhere pushing back the fence between his yard and God's, claiming for himself everything except purely "spiritual" functions such as holding prayer meetings and encouraging people to go to heaven when they died. Cavour had already had his Piedmont-flavored *Kulturkampf* before Bismarck started his German "battle for culture" against the Church. Shortly after the Iron Chancellor admitted defeat, the Republicans in France inaugurated their peculiarly vicious French brand of antireligious legislation.

But there were more than general reasons, more than the *Zeitgeist,* or spirit of the age – to use the popular German expression of the time – which prompted Bismarck's action against the Church. There were reasons peculiar to Germany, and there were also convictions personal to the Chancellor as a pietistic Prussian Protestant. Bismarck was possessed of a phobia against Rome possible only in the heart of a Teuton in the latter part of the nineteenth century. He was convinced, as were so many Englishmen and Americans, that the so-called Latin sections of Europe were impossibly romantic and backward, that their days of supremacy were ended, and that they must therefore give way to the sensible, practical Teutonic nations. With France defeated in 1871, Bismarck was convinced that the last stronghold of Latin supremacy in Europe was the

Vatican. Storm that stronghold, he believed, and the last barrier to Teutonic supremacy and to material progress would be removed.

Bismarck also was motivated by narrower political considerations. The worst thorn in his side in the first years of his rule were the German Liberals. He hoped to win them to his side by sacrificing to them the Catholic Church which they so much hated. On his *Kulturkampf*, he knew, he had a broad basis of agreement with the Liberals. By securing their enthusiastic cooperation on this program he hoped to win them over to supporting his other measures for building a strong paternalistic state.

There was a broader political reason, too, for Bismarck's *Kulturkampf*. The German Empire was a rather loosely constructed confederacy which Bismarck hoped to weld into compact unity in a few decades. His measures were all in that direction: Germanization of the Poles and Danes, consolidation of the railroads and the telegraph system, Prussianization of the various smaller German states. Bismarck wanted all subjects of the German Empire made to the same mold — the image and likeness of the Protestant Prussian junker.

The Catholics were a relatively large group in Germany who, Bismarck feared, could never be fully Germanized unless they were cut loose from their allegiance to the Pope in Rome. Deceived by the German Catholic schismatics under Döllinger, who had rebelled against Rome after the declaration of papal infallibility, Bismarck thought that he could force German Catholics to create a national German church under the aegis of the government in Berlin. Finally, Bismarck saw a chance to win the gratitude and the support of the Freemasons of Germany, a large and influential body whose backing he would need to put over his far-reaching plans to build a compact, powerful German Empire in the future.

Preliminary skirmishes in the *Kulturkampf* took place in the first months of 1871 when Bismarck fired his first exploratory shots against the Church. He began by laying down a press barrage in which the world was told that the German government had determined to conquer her "foes within the country," those Catholics who by accepting the decrees of the Vatican

Council had "caused a lamentable division in the Catholic Church, and were thus endangering the peace of the Empire." The government had no intention of harming "real Catholics," those who had followed Döllinger out of the Church. It intended only to attack those "Jesuitical" Catholics who remained loyal to the Pope in Rome. The first overt act, after this press barrage had prepared the way, was the closing of the Catholic department in the Ministry of Worship on July 8, 1871 – a measure which meant, in effect, that the Catholics had been pushed outside the pale of governmental protection. In November a law was passed subjecting to imprisonment any priest who by his sermons should "disturb public tranquility."

As these first laws were debated in the Reichstag, Bismarck discovered that he had a disturbing and formidable opponent in Windthorst. So much did he come to fear the representative from Meppen that at this point he proposed a truce in his *Kulturkampf* to Mallinckrodt if the latter would disavow Windthorst. The Centrist leader, however, refused to part with his "Pearl of Meppen," and the battle went on. For the next few years Bismarck enjoyed a solid though diminishing majority. He therefore had no difficulty in obtaining the enactment of his series of laws against the Church which came to be known euphemistically as the *Kulturkampf*.

The laws were harsh, disturbingly harsh even to many Protestants who had no love for the Catholic Church but who feared such measures as destructive of the rights guaranteed to all Germans by their constitution. For Bismarck's laws suppressed religious orders in Germany, and gave the government control over the education of the clergy and the conduct of the bishops. They also gave the government arbitrary power over Catholic teaching in Germany, and removed ecclesiastical discipline from the bishops' hands by putting it in the government's domain. Such laws were clearly unconstitutional, but Bismarck relied on the anti-Catholic and the pro-Prussian forces in the Empire to back him blindly. And for a time they did. One of the representatives, Wirchow, said in the Reichstag that the laws passed in 1873 were "arbitrary in the extreme, and dangerous to liberty . . . but since we need not fear that the Center will soon attain power, and since these arbitrary laws injure the Catholic Church alone, we ought to adopt them."

Bismarck's laws were adopted exactly as he proposed them. For a time they seemed to accomplish his purpose. One of the Center leaders, Reichensperger, summed them up well when he complained: "Do you not perceive that Christianity is deprived of the right of existence, when the laws say that the Gospel cannot be preached without the permission of the civil authority, that no sacraments can be administered without the consent of the president of each province?" These laws seemed to accomplish their purpose for a time because they were rigorously enforced against the German bishops and priests who refused to obey them. One by one bishops were fined and deprived of their sees. Still they did not bend to Bismarck's will. Examples were made of several prominent bishops and archbishops who were imprisoned. One of them, the aged bishop of Treves, died in jail – an event which hurt Bismarck more than it did the Church. Parishes were without pastors and dioceses were without bishops. But though the Church's organization was disrupted, Catholics in Germany refused to back the government, as Bismarck had expected them to do. Only a few priests out of thousands obeyed the laws. Almost universally Catholic laymen voted for Christ instead of Caesar.

In the Reichstag, Windthorst breathed defiance at the majority passing Bismarck's bills. "You wish to make religion a police department," he told them, "you wish the power of the state to arrange and control all the acts of our lives from the cradle to the grave. . . . But just as the early Christians could not submit to the unlawful demands of paganism, so the Christians of today are bound to with-hold submission to unjust and conscience-violating laws." Again, in one of his most challenging speeches on the *Kulturkampf*, the intrepid Center leader asserted: "You have the power to torment us, to render our condition miserable indeed; you can wound our hearts, but you cannot take from us our faith. If you close all our churches, we will assemble in the forests, as the Catholics of France used to assemble, during the rule of the Jacobins. . . . You may thrust into prison a bishop who is armed only with the Gospel;

you may condemn him by your laws, but you cannot conquer him."

For seven years Bismarck laid siege to the Church in Germany. He thoroughly disrupted its life, but he failed to conquer it. Instead, he found the Center Party grown in size with each election and in prestige with each session of the Reichstag. Exactly when the Chancellor realized his *Kulturkampf* was not successful no one can say for sure. He was an intelligent pragmatist who could not understand how men could die for so nebulous a thing as the spirit — or even a mere idea, as the Socialists were soon to annoy him by doing. Though he could not understand these things, he saw that they thwarted him and doomed his campaign against the Church to failure. But Bismarck was a politician — and politicians cannot afford to lose face. He therefore waited for the time when he could begin a graceful retreat from his campaign against the Church. As long as Pope Pius IX was alive such retreat was impossible. Bismarck either had to stand firm or to confess himself routed by the blunt pontiff in Rome. Pope Pius IX died in 1878, however, after having occupied the papal throne almost 32 years — the longest pontificate in modern history. He was succeeded by the conciliatory Leo XIII, a man who knew how to make Bismarck's defeat as face-saving as possible.

Bismarck certainly knew by the time of Leo's election to the papal throne that it was high time for him to change his policy toward the Church in Germany. His attack had never been basically a matter of principle — as the defense of the Church was with the Center Party. It was mainly a question of power, and it had failed to increase his personal prestige or his government's power. It had rather increased the power and the prestige of the Center Party. In the first elections after the beginning of the *Kulturkampf*, those of 1873, the Catholics gained twenty-eight seats in the Reichstag, and by 1878 they constituted one of the largest parties in the Empire.

Windthorst, moreover, had been carrying on a running fight with Bismarck in the Reichstag — on such things as the tobacco monopoly, the alcohol monopoly, on the granting of Secret Service funds, and invariably on the laws dealing with religion. Bismarck had suffered a loss of face for, capable man that he was, he could not match Windthorst in the give-and-take of parliamentary debate. If the Iron Chancellor had any sense of human relations he must have realized how sympathy naturally turned more and more toward this little man from Hanover—and insensibly toward the things he championed. He could not fail to notice how Windthorst's continual opposition to his measures made it each year more and more difficult to get them passed. The Center Party, under Windthorst's leadership, had come to be a force that must be reckoned with in Germany.

Bismarck saw, then, that his policy of destroying "Vaticanism" among German Catholics had failed. He saw, too, that many who had enthusiastically supported his attack on the Church in the first few years of the battle had come to counsel retreat. His retreat was prompted, however, by a factor neither he nor Windthorst had reckoned with in 1871. This factor was Socialism. There had long been Socialists in Germany, but Bismarck did not fear them as a political force until 1875, when the followers of Marx and the disciples of Lasalle united to form the Social Democratic Party. The rapid industrialization taking place in Germany had given Socialism strong impetus, so that suddenly in 1878 it loomed as a menace which Bismarck feared as a vague, unwholesome thing he could neither understand nor extinguish. His clumsy attempts to kill the movement by force only gave it stronger vitality and additional converts. Different measures were necessary. Social legislation was needed, Bismarck finally realized, to steal the Socialist's thunder from them by providing such things as unemployment insurance and old-age pensions. But this could not be obtained without the cooperation of the Center Party.

Windthorst was quick to take advantage of Bismarck's difficult position, a position made most embarrassing when within a few weeks in 1878 two attempts were made by Socialists on the Emperor's life. That William held his chancellor at least partly responsible for these assassination attempts was made evident to Bismarck by the Emperor's complaint that they were probably due to the people's having lost their religion. This was the line of reasoning that Windthorst drove home in the Reichstag. When Bismarck asked the Center Party to vote for a bill outlawing Socialism, Windthorst shot back the query, "How can we extinguish the fire, when you are continually nourishing it?"

In more measured phrases he pressed home his point that religion alone could protect the German Empire from Socialism. "In those sections where the Church has full liberty to carry out its works," he observed in the Reichstag, "socialists in vain seek to propagate their theories. Thus in the Rhine Province, in Westphalia, and in Silesia [three sections where Catholics predominated] the theories of Herr Bebel and Herr Liebnecht have had no success. But if you leave parishes without pastors, if you chase religion from the schools, if you exile the religious orders, whose chief aims are to increase piety, to soften the misery of humanity, to instruct the children of the people, you must not be astonished if in these very provinces Socialism grows and flourishes."

Reluctantly, then, Bismarck set about obtaining the cooperation of the Center Party in his new war – this one against Socialism. Rather than approach Windthorst, something Bismarck was too proud and too small a man to do, he approached Rome in the hope that the Pope would command the Center Party to back Bismarck against the Socialists. In his attempts to end the *Kulturkampf* even more than in the reasons for his beginning it, Bismarck betrayed a lamentable ignorance of the Pope's relationship to Catholics on questions not involving morals or doctrine. His proposals to Rome for a compromise on the *Kulturkampf* were unavailing. With extreme reluctance, then, did Bismarck set about winning the support of the Center Party by securing the repeal of those laws which had been passed against the Church since 1871.

It was done slowly – so Bismarck could save face. In 1880 the first step was taken when the government surrendered its assumed right to depose ecclesiastics. Additional laws against the Church were repealed from year to year until, in 1890, practically nothing of the *Kulturkampf* remained on the statute books in Germany. That Bismarck did not stop his retreat after a feinting step or two was due almost entirely to Windthorst's political sagacity and his ability as a party leader. The Centrist chief found himself caught between two millstones, which Bismarck tried to push closer and closer together to crush him. The chancellor used the technique of working out an agreement with the Pope, through the papal nuncio, and then getting the Pope to ask the Center Party to stand back of the agreement. Often the terms were not as favorable as Windthorst knew they should be. On these questions of political procedure he sometimes followed the nuncio's advice – and he sometimes respectfully told the nuncio that the advice was given *in ignorantia* and must therefore be ignored. This was the case, for example, when Bismarck wanted to be given control of the Empire's revenues for seven years. The Pope suggested to Windthorst that the Center Party create no opposition to Bismarck's proposal, but Windthorst knew better than to give Bismarck a free hand with the revenue for so long a time – so he opposed the bill despite the Pope's advice, which, as a good Catholic and a German politician, he had a perfect right to do.

By the time Bismarck was removed from office, in 1890, when both he and Windthorst had reached old age, there was no doubt that in their twenty-year battle the little Hanoverian had won the decision. The *Kulturkampf* was dead, Bismarck was disgraced; Windthorst was acclaimed – almost venerated – by Catholics throughout the German Empire. Through the twenty years of fighting, moreover, he had showed himself the bigger and the nobler man. He could therefore feel doubly triumphant for his victory against the Goliath of the nineteenth century.

* * *

As David ruled a nation and wrote psalms, in addition to having slain Goliath, so Windthorst did much more than defeat Bismarck's *Kulturkampf*. He directed the Center Party's activity in the Reichstag and translated Catholic social teaching into workable legislation. He became unofficial ruler of the large Catholic population of Germany – "His Little Excellency" they correctly dubbed him. As a parliamentary tactician and a party leader, Windthorst was unexcelled in his own or any other time in modern German history. He willingly cooperated with the government in social legislation of which he and his Church approved. But his cooperation was always given from bill to bill. It never implied surrender of independence by the Center Party; much less did it imply that Centrists approved of anything more than the bill they endorsed at the time. The Center's cooperation with Bismarck after 1878, therefore, was always conditional upon his not renewing the *Kulturkampf*. And because the Center had grown large under Windthorst's leadership, Bismarck had to meet its conditions in order to secure its sorely needed cooperation.

Windthorst deserves a large share of credit for the wise social legislation which the Center Party advocated and which it passed into law in cooperation with Bismarck. In the field of social legislation, though perhaps not in social theory, Windthorst and his followers were pioneers. Largely because of them Germany was the first state in modern times to pass laws such as England adopted early in the twentieth century and this country in the New Deal, such laws as unemployment insurance, old-age pensions, and minimum-wage legislation. The Center's stand on such legislation was based upon the adaptation of Catholic moral teaching to the newly industrialized world, an adaptation worked out by such men as Bishop von Ketteler in Germany, Cardinal Manning in England, and best stated in Pope Leo XIII's famous *Rerum Novarum,* published within a few months of Windthorst's death. It was a program which covered the whole range of social and economic relationships, from credit cooperatives to sanitary working conditions and State aid for the organization of labor.

Windthorst was himself abreast of the latest developments in Catholic social thought. Moreover, he led the way in enacting that thought into law. Without his cooperation, there can be no doubt, the social legislation of the 1880's credited to Bismarck could never have become law. His cooperation, moreover, was salutary in making the legislation somewhat less paternalistic and somewhat more Catholic in its content. In 1883 a law was passed insuring workmen against sickness, and in the following year employers were forced to insure their employees against industrial accidents. The labor of women and children was drastically reduced in 1887; maximum hour laws, provisions for government regulation of factories and mines, and provision for Sunday as a day of rest were also provided in 1887. Two years later old-age pensions became law in Germany. All these things were part of the Center Party's platform, and it is largely because of this that they became law in Bismarck's Germany.

Under Windthorst's leadership, Centrists worked toward solving the social question outside the framework of the government. They fostered the unionization of workers and helped them fight for their rights. Windthorst insisted vehemently – against both the capitalists and the Marxists – that there was no inevitable struggle between employer and employee. "One of the greatest errors of our epoch," he said, "is the belief that masters and their workmen must necessarily be enemies. The true interests of the former can only be maintained when they agree with the real needs of the latter, and both can only have common interests when they are on friendly terms." Windthorst, like Montalembert, was a thoroughly liberal Catholic without falling into the heresy of Liberalism.

One of Windthorst's most important acts was his organization of the *Volksverein* – the "People's Union for Catholic Germany" – which he formed in order to educate the German citizen in social and economic questions. It was a union formed against the equally vicious extremes of Liberalism on the one hand and Marxism on the other. These are accomplishments of Windthorst's that do not loom so imposing as his victory over Bismarck in the *Kulturkampf*, but they are perhaps more important in the long run. For they made the Catholics of Germany the best informed Catholic group in the world on social questions, and the best trained, best disciplined political party in nineteenth-century Europe. Because Windthorst's work was solid and thorough, the Center Party remained a strong force in German social and political life until, in 1933, Adolph Hitler destroyed it as an obstacle to his totalitarian rule.

* * *

Windthorst was one of those few valiant men who are favored by Providence to see the full success of their struggles realized within their own lifetimes. For in the last years of his life, the little Hanoverian was politically the most important man in Germany. He was leader of the largest party in the Empire, a party whose members fifteen years before had been labeled *Reichsfeinde* – "enemies of the Empire" – but who in 1890 were hailed throughout the nation as Germany's truest patriots. Windthorst had become arbiter of the destiny of any bill proposed in the Reichstag. Whereas in 1873 he was powerless to prevent the passage of a single measure against the Church, in 1890 he could not only block any bill be disliked but even secure the enactment of almost any proposal he thought should become law.

Windthorst's death in 1891, exactly twenty years after the beginning of his struggle against Bismarck, was typical of his life. He worked energetically until he took to bed in his eightieth year with a severe cold. The infection grew worse. Within a few days Europe was waiting, some watching and some praying, as death closed in on the little leader of Catholic Germany. Spontaneous expressions of sympathy poured in from all sides, from all parties in Germany, from members of all religions. The Emperor came to his sickroom; the Pope sent his benediction. In his last hours Windthorst was delirious. And in these last hours he delivered a long, perfectly ordered speech – as though he were before the Reichstag – advocating the repeal of the last remnant of the *Kulturkampf* by allowing the Jesuits to return to the Empire. Such a speech was characteristic of the man's tenacity, for though he had cooperated with the government on social legislation through the 1880's, he never stopped erasing the last marks of the *Kulturkampf* one by one so as not to jeopardize the good work the Center was accomplishing in other respects after 1878.

The observation of an Irish author in the *Catholic World* made ten months before Windthorst died can stand today without modification: "Never . . . has there arisen a more valiant and successful advocate of Catholic rights than Ludwig von Windthorst." Certainly he was valiant; certainly he was successful. His valor was needed because through the twenty years of the *Kulturkampf* the Church was forced to rely almost exclusively on lay leadership. Bismarck's anticlerical legislation had driven the bishops and the priests into prison or exile. It had silenced the ordained men of God, so that only laymen could speak forth in defiance of the Iron Chancellor's attempt to exterminate the Church. This Windthorst did.

Under his adroit leadership the system of political Catholicism, striven for by O'Connell and Montalembert, was brought to successful fruition. For the short space of fifty years, at least,

Windthorst and the Center Party had found the answer to the never finally solved problem of how to protect the things of God from the encroachment of Caesar. Through the long struggles of three Catholic laymen, two of whom died before the battle was done, the campaign of adjusting the Church's relationship to the nineteenth-century constitutional state had achieved its objective. Catholic laymen had formulated a way of basing the Church's legal existence in modern society on the bill of rights found in every state's constitution, and they had perfected a means of protecting the Church's rights in the political party system which was universally respected in the nineteenth century.

4. García Moreno

Gabriel García Moreno is a striking contrast to the three men we have so far seen try to solve the political problem of the Church's place in the nineteenth century. He is a contrast both in himself and by reason of the setting in which he worked, for he is a unique individual in the nineteenth century, a statesman of the stature and the disposition and the mentality of St. Louis of France. Moreno lived in Ecuador, a Latin-American republic which was supposed to be almost exclusively Catholic in the mid-nineteenth century. In 1861 he was elected president, an office which he reluctantly accepted, and then only on his own terms, so he was in a position to reform the country pretty much as he wished. For a period of ten years, therefore, García Moreno had power such as O'Connell, Montalembert, and Windthorst never dreamed of obtaining. Whereas they sought to protect the Church from the secular State, Moreno was in a position to apply Catholic principles to the political and social life of his country. Whereas O'Connell and Windthorst, and even Montalembert, lived in countries where the governments were essentially non-Catholic, and frequently enough anti-Catholic, Moreno lived in a country that knew practically no other religion. The choice in Ecuador was between godless Liberalism,* the made-in-Paris variety, and Catholicism. Moreno was in a position to choose between the two.

Under him Ecuador became a testing ground on which the practicality of Catholic principles was tried. He is important for proving to a materialistic world that a Catholic can be modern and progressive, for showing that there is no antipathy

---

* The Latin-American variety of Liberalism in the nineteenth century should not be confused with the relatively moderate Liberalism of the Anglo-American world. The Liberalism we find in Ecuador was derived from French and Spanish sources, and it was bitterly anticlerical and even antireligious. It was a thoroughly doctrinaire thing that by its very nature could not tolerate Catholicism. Liberalism reached its most extreme form in Spain, where it was succinctly defined by Sarda y Salvani in the title of his book *Liberalismo es pecado*. This is the Liberalism with which García Moreno was confronted in Ecuador.

between the modernization of a state and the maintenance of the Catholic religion. He is important, too, for proving every day of his public life that a saintly man can be a good statesman. For although Moreno attended Mass daily and visited the Blessed Sacrament frequently, not even his bitterest enemies accused him of political naïveté or executive incompetency. He was equally at home at the altar rail and in the presidential chair. He was convinced that the best secular rule was that which successfully applied right moral and religious principles to political life. He is important, from the Church's apologetic point of view, because he was a success, because his truly Catholic rule brought to Ecuador unparalleled prosperity, a remarkable increase of cultural benefits, and a period of peace such as the country had not known since its birth earlier in the century. Even today, when things are bad in Ecuador, the newspapers and the people echo the refrain: "We need another García Moreno." For this saintly president is the outstanding individual in Ecuadorean history, perhaps the greatest man Latin America has yet produced.

Gabriel García Moreno was an almost unbelievable figure in the nineteenth century. In Catholic and conservative circles he was the most celebrated statesman of the century, with the possible exception of Windthorst. And when he was assassinated in 1875, he was extolled at Notre Dame Cathedral in Paris as "the just man of our century." He was similarly eulogized in Rome and London, in Brussels, in Dublin and New York. To his contemporaries, nevertheless, he must have seemed a man out of his time, a reincarnation in the nineteenth century of a medieval saint-king such as Louis of France or Canute of Denmark. He is important for showing that such a man with such "medieval" ideas could rule well and could confer on his country unprecedented prosperity. Thus he showed the world of the 1860's and the 1870's that the Catholic religion was not an obstacle to progress, that society did not have to deny or ignore God in order to have railroads and modern lighting systems. He showed that there was no connection between agnosticism and a balanced budget. García Moreno secured these material things and he promoted religion too. He has gone down in his country's history as a good statesman and a model Christian, as a martyr – which he came literally to be – for both his nation and his faith.

* * *

Historians treating of Latin America have a way of typing the characters they treat, making them *gauchos, caudillos,* and the like. They put García Moreno into the *caudillo* pigeonhole, treat his public career briefly, and then dismiss him with the rest of the men on horseback who came, who ruled, and who got shot to make way for another. García Moreno was not such a ruler. He was a reluctant president – "president in spite of himself" was his sobriquet – who enjoyed popular support in everything he did. He was universally mourned when an assassin's attack cut short his life the day after his election for a third term. The Ecuadorean senate and chamber met in joint session to proclaim him "Regenerator of his country, martyr of Catholic civilization"; pictures and statues, verses, plays, and biographies glorified his name, and, as the authority on Latin America, Rev. Eugene Shiels, S.J., puts it, "Today to all Hispanic America he is the symbol of good government, social justice and Christian culture, the epitome of their civilization."

Gabriel García Moreno was born of aristocratic parents on Christmas Eve, 1821, at the city of Guayaquil in Spanish territory that was soon to become Ecuador. Six months after Gabriel's birth, General Sucre defeated the Spanish forces outside the city of Quito in the decisive battle fought on the slopes of Mount Pichincha. The former presidency of Quito joined Bolivar's Greater Colombia. In 1830 it withdrew to become the independent state of Ecuador, but national independence did not give Ecuador domestic peace. Through the years when Gabriel was attending school the country was ruled by a former general, Juan José Flores, who became increasingly dictatorial and who, like most *caudillos,* ran the country in his own interests like a large personal estate. The year after young Moreno received his law degree, Flores was driven from the country and was replaced by another *caudillo,* Vincente Rocafuerte. From Spain, Flores tried to organize an invasion of Ecuador, hoping to receive aid from the Spanish Queen Regent Christina in return for his promise to install a Spanish prince on the throne of Ecuador. This was the hectic political setting into which García

Moreno was graduated as a lawyer and therefore almost inevitably an actor on the political stage of his native land.

Moreno's education had been solid, the kind that prepared energetic students for leadership among their fellows in the nineteenth century. And García Moreno was of the stuff to profit from such education. He was tutored by a priest until he was fifteen, when he enrolled at the University of Quito. There he took the usual courses, inasmuch as he intended to enter the priesthood, but his principal interests lay in the natural sciences. He followed his theological studies to the point of receiving minor orders and being tonsured, but the advice of his closest friends and his own inclinations convinced him that his vocation was in the world rather than in the cloister. So he turned his studies in a secular direction, acquired a fluent speaking knowledge of French, Italian, and English, besides his own Spanish, of course, and meanwhile pursued the course in law. Finally in 1844, at the age of twenty-three, he was graduated from the University of Quito and admitted to the bar.

His professors' reports reveal character traits which are more admired than liked by the common run of mankind: a strong sense of right and wrong, a rigid justice in dealing with his fellows, a strict obedience to all regulations, and an equally strict enforcement of them on his associates. As a monitor, for example, he performed his duties and reported on his charges as though he were dealing with complete strangers. As a student García Moreno revealed a strong clear mind and a desire to attain truth and to proclaim it at any cost. He is described as publicly correcting his professors on various occasions, not to show off among his fellows, but coldly and objectively, simply because they were wrong. His strength of character, combined with his firmness of will and his intellectual ability, made him a strong influence among his fellow students. He was admired by all his associates, but they were kept at a distance by this young man who formed no clique of close associates, who had neither the inclination nor the warmth to become "chummy" with anyone. He was a leader, even as a student, because his stature was objectively greater than his fellows' and because no one thought of questioning his integrity.

From the very beginning this young lawyer's services were in great demand. His biographers tell how he refused to take any case that he was not sure had justice on its side, and they relate several instances of important people of Quito vainly beseeching him to plead their cause, since it was understood in the courts of Quito that García Moreno took only cases which clearly deserved to win. Two years after graduation, he married a certain Rosa Arcasubi, described as "a young lady of large fortune" – a fortunate fact for both García Moreno and Ecuador, because this marriage freed him from financial worries and from the care of earning a living, and thus it gave him the leisure to continue his education and to enter the whirlpool of Ecuadorean politics.

* * *

When Moreno began to practice law, as we have seen, the factional fights against Flores were under way. And young Moreno entered the political arena not as a lawyer but as a writer, a hard-hitting journalist who stirred up the people of Ecuador – in time of all Latin America – against the dictatorial Flores. First in his weekly paper *El Zurriago* ("The Whip") he lashed out mercilessly at the venality and the corruption of the government, and later in *El Vengador* ("The Avenger") he attacked "the janissaries of Flores," who was at the time in Spain negotiating for an invasion of Ecuador. As a writer Moreno delivered many telling blows against the government. His accusations were damning and they were unanswerable. They aroused in the reading public disgust with their government and a sense of the danger in which they lived because of Flores' rather far-fetched plot to come back at the head of an invading army. But Moreno was not at his best as a writer. He convinced those enemies of the government who needed no convincing, and his biting satire did nothing to conciliate his enemies or to moderate their policies. He seems rather to have irritated them unnecessarily and to have driven them to even extremer measures.

Moreno still had much to learn before he was equipped to become his country's outstanding statesman. He took the first step in that direction late in 1849 when, wearied by his ineffective attacks on the government, he decided to visit

Europe. He stayed abroad for six months on this first visit, during which time he traveled through England, France, and Germany, broadening his practical knowledge of government by studying social and political conditions in the wake of the revolutions of 1848. His observations in these countries enabled him to fix more solidly and modify by the experience of others many ideas which he had acquired at the University of Quito. Paris was particularly helpful in this respect, for in 1849 and 1850, García Moreno saw a city in ferment with the radical ideas of men like Louis Blanc and Proudhon. He saw Ozanam's St. Vincent de Paul Society at work on the problems of poverty and social distress. In the same city he was able to compare and contrast the secular and the religious solutions to the pressing social problems of the time. In the same city he could see liberty employed with dignity by men like Montalembert and Lacordaire, who were working for the material and spiritual welfare of their fellow Frenchmen. At the same time he saw the name of liberty invoked to destroy Christian institutions and to deny men the very rights it was supposed to protect.

García Moreno returned from Europe a wiser and a more mature man. But maturity had not in any way diminished his determination, his energy, or his decisiveness. This was proved before he completed his trip homeward. On the dock at Panama he met a group of disconsolate, dispossessed-looking Jesuits who had just been expelled from the neighboring state of New Granada. They were on their way to England, where they hoped to carry on their educational and missionary work. Moreno persuaded them to come with him to Ecuador instead, and because the group was at loose ends, without commitments or assurances for the future, and because Moreno was so enthusiastic and apparently so sure of a friendly reception in Quito, the Jesuits accompanied him to his native land.

Moreno convinced President Noboa that he should welcome these missionaries and educators, for, he argued, they would be effective agents in civilizing the backward natives and in promoting culture in the urban areas. The Jesuits were re-established in the very church from which they had been driven eighty-three years before (and which had been vacant meanwhile), when the Spanish king, Charles III, had expelled them from all his lands. Moreover, they were given a vacant hotel to use as a college. The return of the Jesuits to Quito provoked another governmental crisis. The Liberals and the Masonic Lodges, of course, looked on them as the personification of tyranny and obscurantism, of royal despotism and religious authoritarianism. They accused Noboa of being an unwitting tool in the scheming Jesuits' hands – one more charge added to many they had already leveled at the president, but one which played a decisive part in his overthrow at this time.

The attacks on the Jesuits were both scurrilous and stupid. Moreno was not one to let them go unanswered, so within a short time he published his *Defensa de los Jesuitas,* called by some historians one of the best apologies ever written for the Jesuit Order. The central theme of his little booklet is that "war has been declared not on the Jesuits but on the priesthood and the Catholic faith." Moreno developed this theme by showing historically how enemies of the Church had almost always begun their attack by striking at the Jesuits first and then at the Church as a whole. We are told by local historians that the booklet created a sensation and for a time it silenced the attacks on the Jesuits. But Moreno soon found out that one booklet does not win a political war. Within two years a new government under Urbina came to power, the Jesuits were expelled, and Moreno was arrested for satirizing the new president.

The next few months were hectic. Moreno escaped from prison, was elected senator from Guayaquil, the second city of Ecuador, summarily arrested again, and deported to Peru. There he wrote an answer to the accusations concocted against him by the Urbina government. Then he settled down at Payta, where he led a leisurely life until the end of 1854, when he embarked for another and longer visit to Europe. This time he stayed in Paris, where he devoted himself to social and scientific studies and to his own spiritual improvement. He tells a friend how he studied sixteen hours a day and how "if the days were forty-eight hours long, I should spend forty of them in poring over my books." He studied physics and chemistry, bought a chemical laboratory for himself, worked with the agriculturist Boussingault, and learned all he could about social legislation in the European countries.

More important than these formal studies, perhaps, is the way in which García Moreno improved himself spiritually for the difficult tasks which lay ahead. During this stay in Paris he began his practice of hearing Mass daily and of reciting the Rosary every evening. As his spiritual life developed he came to understand more thoroughly the role that religion should play in social and political life. It can be said, without too much exaggeration, that the famous Ecuadorean constitution of 1869 took root in Moreno's mind while he studied and prayed in Paris, an exile from his native land. Louis Veuillot, a Parisian by adoption himself, grasps the importance of Moreno's visit to Paris and explains it to the reader of *Univers* thus: "In a foreign land, solitary and unknown, García Moreno made himself fit to rule. He learned all that was necessary for him to know in order to govern a nation, formerly Christian but now fast falling into an almost savage condition. . . . Paris, which is at once a Christian and a heathen city, is the very place where the lesson he needed could best be acquired, since the two opposing elements may there be seen engaged in perpetual conflict. Paris is a training school for priests and martyrs, it is also a manufactory of anti-Christs and assassins. The future president of Ecuador gazed upon the good and the evil, and when he set out for his home afar, his choice was made."

There is no doubt that when Moreno returned home, late in 1856, he came back a convinced enemy of Liberalism, a strong believer that the salvation of his people could be achieved only by the closer cooperation of the Church and the State, each working freely and independently in its own sphere. He returned to find his country governed by "the twins," Urbina and Roblez, whose rule was the worst in Ecuadorean history. Under them a war of extermination had been undertaken against the clergy; the people were exploited more systematically and more ruthlessly than in the days of Flores. Roblez, who was taking his turn at being president, granted Moreno permission to return to Quito. But the flattering reception given to this critic of the government must have caused Roblez to question the prudence of his generous impulse.

García Moreno was in politics at once. He was elected mayor of Quito and appointed president of the city's university. During the next year he divided his time between education and politics: he lectured on chemistry and gave public demonstrations with the apparatus he had brought back from Paris and which he now gave to the university; meanwhile he set about organizing a conservative party, establishing another paper with which to criticize the government, and rounding up his former conservative friends. In the fall of 1857, Moreno and a number of his associates were elected senators. In the national congress they became the party of opposition to the government, a party whose support throughout the country was so general that it could not be ignored.

Of course in Ecuador this meant revolution, a typical Latin-American revolution: struggle among the politicians, with the people sitting back, observing and waiting for a decision on the winner; some shooting and a good deal more speechifying; a good sense of the theatrical revealed by all the actors in the drama, especially by Urbina and Roblez with their third-act grand exit. The civil war had been typical for Latin-America, but its result was not—for this is the civil war which put García Moreno on the stage as president of his country, first provisionally and then by popular election early in 1861, the first president of Ecuador elected directly by universal manhood suffrage.

Moreno's first term lasted four years. About half this time he was busy first repelling the Colombian invasion undertaken by Mosquera "to liberate the brother democrats of Ecuador from the theocratic yoke of Professor Moreno," and then defeating Urbina's invasion attempt from the south. Moreno still found time to accomplish an amazing amount of reform work, the most important of which was his fixing the relationship between the Church and the State and his reform of the clergy. A good bit of work was done toward improving and extending education, and a beginning was made on road building and on the improvement of agriculture. Because the constitution forbade a president's succeeding himself, Moreno stepped aside in 1865 for Jerónimo Carrión, a faithful adherent of the "Moreno system." Carrión was weak, however, and he was overthrown by a Liberal revolt in 1867 when Moreno was in Europe on a diplomatic mission.

So García Moreno returned to Ecuador to find the accomplishments of his four years in office destroyed, the concordat abrogated, the clergy persecuted, the government again run in the interests of the small clique in power. He retired to his estate in the countryside until 1869, when he was triumphantly returned to office as president, this time, so it is reported, by all his associates, contrary to his own desire. He immediately secured the adoption of a new constitution which concentrated greater power in the executive's hands, and then he began his reform work all over again. In his second term of office, indeed, he refashioned the country according to the principles of government he had worked out during his second visit to Europe. He served six years this time, in accordance with the new constitution, and then he was elected for a third term. What he might have accomplished in the next years we shall never know, for he was assassinated before he could deliver the inaugural speech he had written and which he was on his way to read to the congress when he fell under the machetes and bullets of his enemies. Thus ended the career of the greatest Latin-American statesman of the nineteenth century, a man who, in the words of Father Peter Dunne, "was in all its history the nation's most remarkable man and may even be considered the strongest and most striking personality of all South America."

* * *

Louis Veuillot aptly describes García Moreno as "one who was at the same time a man of his own time and a man according to the Gospels." He can best be understood if one remembers that his parents came from Castile, that Castilian blood was therefore strong in his veins, and the Castilian outlook—a sixteenth-century attitude toward the world—was in his eye. García Moreno looked the part of a Castilian ruler. He was a tall, erect man in 1861, of commanding appearance, severe looking and stern, with piercing black eyes and snowy white hair. His bearing was dignified, his countenance revealed a consuming energy and an acute intelligence which caused men to respect him instinctively. Though he was respected even by his enemies and was admired by all who knew him well, still García Moreno does not seem to have been a likable man. He was too severe, too austere, too much the judge and too little the sympathetic juryman to form close attachments. These were qualities, of course, which made for a great statesman, since his very lack of human warmth enabled García Moreno to remain objective in his judgments and detached, in a proper way, from every question of policy he had to decide. It enabled him, too, to administer justice equitably, though severely, in every case brought before him. The moving force behind Moreno's every decision was his intense love of justice, which he looked upon as both ethically necessary and politically expedient. It is this sense of justice which accounts for his severity and for his cool detachment from those emotional, sentimental appeals which move the average politician more strongly than does abstract justice. With Moreno the criminal who deserved to die was executed – but one who deserved pardon, even if he were a bitter enemy, was pardoned. That is what made him an admirable rather than a likable man.

In his lifetime Moreno was subjected to bitter, vicious attacks by his Liberal opponents. He was accused of desiring tyranny when he insisted the president's power must be increased in the interest of peaceful government. He was accused of being a dupe of the Church who sought to ensnare everyone in the clergy's web, of trying to use the confessional, scapulars, and other such "tricks" to reduce Ecuadoreans to intellectual and political serfdom. His leading critic, the Liberal writer Montalvo, called him "an abominable monster, the scourge of humanity, the terror of the weak, the ruin of the courageous, the enemy of God and man who should be put to death with as much right as a tiger or a poison adder."

Such accusations were revolutionary ammunition, of course, and sensible people did not take them literally, but collectively they served to peg Moreno for foreign Liberal historians as a typical *caudillo*. The American consul to Quito, Charles Weile, who had no reason for passing biased judgment on Moreno, wrote: "These accusations cause a smile of pity and contempt on the part of all who have known García Moreno. Having resided in Ecuador very many years and being perfectly acquainted with all that has recently occurred there, I know well what I say; and I do not exaggerate when I declare that to me

García Moreno appears to be the most illustrious man that South America ever produced."

Finally, we should note that Moreno was an extremely pious and, to all appearances, a saintly man. He attended Mass daily, as we have seen, and in an age before frequent Communion was common he received every Sunday. Often he served Mass himself, and he could be found in one or another of Quito's churches two or three times a day making visits to the Blessed Sacrament. He belonged to the Sodality established by the Jesuits at Quito, being a member of the workers' section, and contemporaries tell how he never missed a meeting or a procession. These were religious practices that required a certain amount of courage in a Latin country in Moreno's day. He had courage in abundance. Moreover, because he was callously indifferent to public opinion on anything but affairs of state, he could not have had an ulterior political motive in his public profession of his religion—unless perhaps there was a note of defiance to the Liberals and the Masonic Lodges when he made a visit at the church across the plaza from the capital before going to his office.

* * *

When García Moreno became president he had clearly formulated his philosophy of government. For many years he had thought over the principles upon which he believed good government should rest. Moreover, he had gone on to work out in his own mind the ways and means whereby his principles could best be put into effect. His thinking was done before the backdrop of his country's hectic history. Ecuador had won its independence, Moreno once observed, but since that time it had accomplished nothing. He had seen *caudillos* come and go, he had heard promises made and seen them broken, he had watched cliques jockey for power while governments were too weak to preserve law and order. All these things led him to believe that his country could never have peace until it had an executive strong enough to enforce the laws on the statute books.

His visits to Europe also had influenced his political thinking. Each visit convinced him more firmly that the enemy was

Liberalism. By 1861 he was certain that even though the Liberals might mouth nice phrases about liberty and equality and fraternity, nevertheless their real purpose was to destroy the Church, to exploit the people in the interest of the business classes, and thus to use generous ideas as a façade behind which to operate for their own selfish aggrandizement. Moreno knew that many Liberals sincerely believed that their program would bring about a better world, but he insisted vehemently that such belief was based upon an erroneous concept of man and that Liberal rule could therefore bring nothing but chaos and disorder to his country. His two visits to Paris confirmed these beliefs, for there he saw the liberal party in action, there he tasted the fruit by which he judged the principles of Liberalism.

So Moreno concluded that his country's greatest need was a strong executive with power sufficient to effect necessary reforms and to assure the people thereafter that the constitution would be more than a piece of paper. The government must be strong, then, and it must be centralized, for only thus could the local officials be controlled. Moreno did not believe in dictatorship, however, for he conceived of the chief executive's power as limited in two ways. In the first place, it came from God and it was therefore limited to doing His will in society, caring for the welfare of the people and doing so in the way God required, which meant not violating human rights or divine prerogatives. In the second place, it was limited by the constitution under which it operated. García Moreno believed that the president was responsible not only to God but also, and very specifically, to the people. In his annual messages he gave the people of Ecuador a clear, exact account of his stewardship in the presidential office. He believed that he was the servant of the people, but at the same time he realized he must be more than that. "Government should direct public opinion," he used to say, "not follow it; it should lead the people, not follow them blindly." Though he considered himself a presidential professor, as it were, nevertheless the citizen-students remained sovereign, and when their will was clearly stated, in the proper way, then the president had the duty of conforming to it.

Moreno believed that social peace and an equitable prosperity could be achieved only by close cooperation between Church and

State, for experience had taught him that when the two did not work together harmoniously in his country they were bound to work at cross purposes, creating disturbances in the country. Union of Church and State was for him the ideal arrangement which could be put into practice in Ecuador.* He believed that the Church should be left completely free in its field and that the State should remain supreme in the secular field. Any conflict between the two, García Moreno insisted, resulted not from essential antagonism but instead from personal considerations or confused thinking. The State could not prosper without ecclesiastical cooperation, in his opinion, and the Church could not perform its mission completely without secular support.

García Moreno went so far as to insist that the State's first duty was the promotion and support of the Catholic religion — a logical but nonetheless shocking thing to say in the nineteenth century. "Let us do everything for the people through the Church," he said; "he who seeks first the Kingdom of God will have all things added to him." Such a statement must have sounded to his Liberal opponents, and even to many of his supporters, as though it were made by a simple lay brother in a religious order rather than by the president of the nation. Moreno acted out that statement literally — to the edification of his followers, to the consternation of his opponents, and with results that amazed them both, for all things were added to Ecuador in the decade of Moreno's rule.

* * *

Moreno accepted office when he was elected in 1861 only on

---

* Union of Church and State has had a definite meaning in European and Latin-American history that it does not possess in the United States. Union exists when Church law is enforced by State authorities, for example, when divorce is forbidden by secular authority. It almost always involves State support of Church schools and of the clergy, as well as Church support — in a positive way — of the existing government. Such an arrangement was almost universal in early modern times. Separation of Church and State came to be advocated, especially in the Latin countries, as a step toward abolishing the Church altogether.

Early in this century Cardinal Gasparri referred to "good separation" of Church and State, meaning the kind existing in the United States and England which is not aimed at killing the Church, and to "bad separation" — the kind advocated by Liberals in France and Spain and Italy and Latin America as a means for suppressing the Church.

condition that he be given a free hand in establishing a new set of relationships between the government and the Catholic Church, for he was convinced that this was the pivotal problem in his country and that, when it was solved, the other problems would be easily resolved. He was right in believing the religious arrangements in Ecuador needed drastic revision. The presidents of Ecuador had been holding intact all the rights granted by popes in days gone by to the Spanish kings. These rights, such as the *patronato* whereby the king nominated bishops, and the *exequatur* whereby no papal communication could be published without royal consent, were extensive enough to enable a hostile government to hamstring and eventually to destroy the Church within the country. Under Spanish kings these rights frequently were abused, but it was not until the nineteenth century that the successor states of the Spanish Empire used them in a consistent effort to destroy the Church. In Ecuador, for example, several bishoprics remained vacant for a quarter of a century while the diocesan incomes went to the government. Under these conditions the clergy had deteriorated sadly, and the Holy See could do nothing to raise ecclesiastical standards in Ecuador, for the bishops were government appointees who, even when they were good men, had to temporize to hold their positions.

García Moreno decided to change all this by giving the Church full control over its personnel and freedom of action within the religious field. He wanted, in this way, to fix responsibility for ecclesiastical conditions where it belonged: with the bishops and the pope. Even before he was elected president he had worked out a plan for effecting this drastic change through a concordat* between Ecuador and the papacy. So Moreno wrote to his ambassador at Rome that he wanted "complete liberty for the Church, and comprehensive reform of the diocesan and community clergy. I request the Sovereign Pontiff to send a nuncio invested with the necessary powers to effect this double

* A concordat is an agreement between the Holy See and a state governing the standing of the Church in the country involved. It has the status, under international law, of a treaty between two sovereign powers. Thus it cannot justly be abrogated unilaterally by either contracting party; its terms can be changed only by the mutual action of both the Holy See and the country concerned.

work." No difficulties arose during the negotiations, and within a few months Ambassador Ordóñez returned to Quito with a copy of the concordat for the signature of Moreno and the ratification of the congress.

Moreno surprised Pope Pius IX by refusing to sign the document. He was convinced that the mild method of reforming the clergy which the papacy proposed in the concordat would be ineffective and more thorough, truly drastic measures were required. "Return immediately to Rome," he ordered Ordóñez, "and tell the Pope that I accept all the articles of the concordat, but on condition that he also should *impose* the reform of the clergy. If he will not do this I cannot impose the concordat." The changes were made as Moreno requested. Later in the year (1862), an apostolic delegate arrived with the powers required to reform both the diocesan and the order clergy, and in the spring of 1863 the concordat was ratified with much pomp and splendor in the cathedral at Quito.

The concordat provided that Catholicism be the State religion, which, of course, was only a statement of the condition that had existed from colonial times. It required that a seminary be erected in each diocese, under the bishop's control, in order to provide a trained clergy for the country; it gave the bishops a large measure of control over education in the country; it surrendered the right of the government to prevent the publication of encyclicals, bulls, and other papal communications to the hierarchy and the faithful of Ecuador; and it gave the Church full freedom to hold diocesan councils. The government's right to nominate bishops was limited to a choice from among three nominees proposed by proper Church authorities. Provision was made for the creation of new dioceses and the realignment of old ones — a change much needed for administrative purposes in the Church. Other articles provided for the admission of new religious congregations, for equitable financial arrangements, and for other such administrative matters. These were all concessions by the State to the Church, but in return Moreno expected the Church to provide solid education and sound morality among the people. He was convinced that this boon to good government could be achieved only through the Church — and then only when it was rendered free to accomplish its work. Hence the generous concessions, for which he expected due return, with interest, in proper time.

By democratic standards the concordat was popular, for the large masses of people embraced it enthusiastically. But opposition was intense in Liberal circles and among many of the important citizens of Ecuador. It was ratified, nevertheless, by the Ecuadorean congress and duly worked into the law of the land. Its provisions for the reform of the clergy were taken seriously by the government and by the ecclesiastical authorities. A national council provided that the bishop was to oversee reform of the diocesan clergy in each see and establish a seminary to insure the right kind of priests in the future.

The religious communities presented a more difficult problem. García Moreno, working with the apostolic delegate, presented order priests, who for a long time had not lived by the rules of their respective orders, with the alternative of returning to their communities and living according to their regulations or else of joining a diocese and putting themselves under the jurisdiction of a bishop. Those who refused to do either were expelled from the country. To fill the places of these deported priests and to secure models for the native clergy, García Moreno imported a number of religious from various countries of Europe. By 1875 he could look with satisfaction on the improved condition of the Church in Ecuador, and, while due credit for this improvement must be given to the papacy, to the clergy of Ecuador, and to the zealous missionaries from Europe, nevertheless it was Moreno's idea and it could never have been accomplished without his persistent enforcing of its provisions.

In his second term of office, Moreno moved toward what his enemies called a "theocratic republic." The new constitution he urged upon the legislature in 1869 officially proclaimed Catholicism the State religion and required that all officeholders and voters be Catholic.* This constitution, which was the most

*Seen out of the full context of Ecuadorean history, which we cannot enter into here, this provision might seem arbitrary and unjust. It must be remembered that Liberals in Ecuador at this time were quite similar in their relation to the rest of society as Communists are in this country today. They were sworn to destroy the very culture of the people and to rule as a small minority in their own interests. They were incapable of cooperating with the government, for they were sworn to destroy it.

democratic Ecuador had yet enjoyed, was adopted by an overwhelming majority when it was submitted to the electors in a plebiscite. When Pope Pius IX proclaimed St. Joseph patron and protector of the universal Church, he suggested that he would declare March 19 a holyday in any country requesting it. Of all the countries in the world, Ecuador alone made such a request in reply to the Pope's invitation.

In 1873, again, Moreno had the legislature put Ecuador under the official protection of the Sacred Heart, and about the same time he suggested that the Congress vote a small sum toward the support of the Pope who had been driven out of Rome by the Italian king. He was, incidentally, the only ruler in the world to lodge official protest against Victor Emmanuel's violation of the Pope's sovereignty as a secular ruler when the Italian armies seized Rome in 1871. These were all minor matters of policy, but they indicated the direction García Moreno's government was taking, and the violent reaction to each of these measures indicated the temper of his Liberal opponents.

* * *

On other scores the Liberals had to content themselves with vague denunciations of Moreno's policies and with insinuations as to his ultimate objectives, for whereas the Liberals had always promised but never delivered prosperity — which for them was the alpha and omega of government — Moreno had talked relatively little about material accomplishments but he had produced them in surprising quantity. His first task, when he came to power in 1861, was to right the financial chaos into which the Liberal-supported *caudillos* had plunged Ecuador. The budget

---

Practically speaking, there seemed no alternative to excluding them from the electorate and from office. Ideally speaking, this is not a good thing — in the author's opinion — and no large body of Catholics advocate it anywhere in the Anglo-Saxon world. It is, at best, a measure defensible only under certain extreme conditions — which certainly seemed to exist in Ecuador.

It should be remembered, too, that there were no other religious denominations in Ecuador. There were only Catholics (constituting the vast majority) and the enemies of the Church (a small minority). This provision, therefore, was not directed against other religions, but against those of no religion.

had not been balanced in thirty years; the treasury was empty and the debt was heavy.

Moreno attacked the problem in two ways. First, he enforced stringent economy and the strictest honesty among public officials, and he abolished many unnecessary positions. Thus he reduced government expenditures considerably while actually increasing government services. Secondly, he improved the tax-collection machinery, seeing to it that the taxes did not leak into a string of pockets on the way to the treasury. Thus he managed to reduce taxes and still obtain a greater revenue than in days gone by. Within four years he built up a large surplus in the treasury. During that time he indemnified owners in full for the release of their slaves, and he undertook many new services without making use of such usual devices for balancing the budget as partially defaulting on the public debt or cutting down fixed obligations like pensions.

The army had been a source of trouble in Ecuador, as in other Latin-American countries, ever since it had won independence for the country. Moreno had announced that he would "reform the army or destroy it." He reformed it. Officers were sent abroad to study the latest developments in warfare, especially in Prussia, with a view to reorganizing the Ecuadorean army along modern lines. Classes were opened for those soldiers who were illiterate, which at the time meant almost all the nonofficer class; thus education was imposed on them, at least through the primary skills of reading, writing, and arithmetic.

Moreno also attempted moral reform throughout the country – but it is difficult to judge accurately how successful he was in this campaign. He closed many houses of prostitution and – against the bitter complaints of the Liberals – established a Good Shepherd convent at Quito. The police rounded up all men and women who had not bothered to get married though they lived together as man and wife – and it seems there were many such cases. They were given the choice of getting married or separating. These and other moral reforms along Catholic lines were enforced during Moreno's two terms of office, but, though there are no statistics on the matter, the historian has reason to believe that the habits of Ecuadoreans were not as completely changed as some of Moreno's enthusiastic biographers would have us believe. It takes more than ten years of reform rule to revolutionize a people's morality permanently.

There were other concrete accomplishments, however, about which historians do not disagree. Hospitals were established in the leading towns, for example, under the direction of the Sisters of Charity of St. Vincent de Paul. A railroad connecting the two principal cities of Quito and Guayaquil was built. Five national highways, each one an engineering feat through the Andes, were begun and almost finished by 1875. The postal service was developed, water systems improved, telegraph communications extended, city streets paved, banditry suppressed, and local tyrants eliminated. These were material benefits achieved within a short time because of the driving energy and the ruthless severity of this man who took his duties as president seriously, who was himself scrupulously honest, and who demanded of his subordinates honesty and competence.

Next to religious reform, Moreno looked upon the extension and improvement of education as his most important task. He improved the universities by securing and keeping competent professors; he established two polytechnical and agricultural colleges, as well as a military school, to train natives in the practical sciences of modern industry and modern warfare. In 1871, elementary State-supported education was made compulsory for all children. The number of primary schools increased from 200 when Moreno took office to 500 when he was assassinated; the number of students in these schools grew from 8,000 to 32,000. Because of the lack of qualified native teachers and because he was convinced that religious were the best teachers, García Moreno imported various orders from France and from Germany. Jesuits filled most of the university posts and they staffed the secondary schools for boys. The religious of the Sacred Heart took over the higher education of girls, while the Christian Brothers and various orders of Sisters worked on the primary level. Thus Ecuador profited from the anticlerical action of these two European countries.

* * *

All these measures, especially the concordat and the staffing of the schools with religious, provoked intense partisanship in

Ecuador. Moreno's supporters looked to him as "a Christian Hercules, a disciple of Charlemagne and St. Louis, a hero of Jesus Christ"; his enemies, such as Moncayo, claimed that "he avows himself a partisan of the *Syllabus,* in order to commit crimes at his convenience. Communicating and shooting; proscribing, scourging, and confiscating — such are the offerings which please the God of the Jesuits." The chasm cut in Ecuadorean society was too deep for even a Moreno to bridge in a single decade, for like France and Spain and the other Latin-American countries, Ecuador consisted of two hostile nations by the middle of the nineteenth century: on the one hand, the children of the French Revolution, a small minority who were implacable enemies of the Church and blind devotees of Progress, those Liberals who wished to destroy the Church as one of the last remnants of the Old Regime; on the other, the enemies of the French Revolution, loyal to the Church and hostile to the new civilization, conservatives by and large, whose faces were turned more to the past than to the future.

Moreno took his stand in the conservative camp, not blindly or stupidly, for he accepted many of the enemy's worthier ideas and he was willing to make concessions on neutral issues. But because he was Catholic, he was marked an irreconcilable enemy by the Liberals. Montalvo's exhortation that he "should be put to death with as much right as a tiger or a poison adder" was meant literally. And later, when it was so taken, Montalvo demanded that he be given due credit for promoting Moreno's murder. Moreno's election for a third term in 1875 was his death sentence — as he himself strongly suspected. He wrote a personal letter to Pope Pius IX informing him of his re-election and stating that, although he would send a formal letter of information as soon as he was inaugurated on August 30, still he wanted to waste no time in getting the Pope's blessing on his new term of office. "I wish to obtain your blessing before that day," he wrote, "so that I may have the strength and the light which I need so much in order to be unto the end a faithful son of our Redeemer, and a loyal and obedient servant of His Infallible Vicar. Now that the Masonic Lodges of the neighboring countries, instigated by Germany, are vomiting against me all sorts of atrocious insults and horrible calumnies, now that the Lodges are secretly arranging for my assassination, I have more need than ever of the divine protection so that I may live and die in defense of our holy religion and the beloved republic which I am called once more to rule."

Moreno had received several warnings that assassination plans were completed and that the time for his murder had been fixed. He took them seriously because he knew his opponents well, but at the same time he refused to take any unusual precautions. He kept his revolver oiled, of course, but this was as much a part of his attire as shirt or shoes. He declined a bodyguard and he refused to alter his daily routine. He seems, indeed, to have taken a close to fatalistic attitude toward this business of getting killed. "I prefer to trust myself to the keeping of God," he said to his friends who wanted him to secure a bodyguard, "and besides, what can a traveler desire more eagerly than to reach the end of his journey?"

He reached the end of his journey in the early afternoon of the First Friday of August in 1875. After finishing his midday meal, he went to the cathedral to make a visit on his way to address the Ecuadorean Congress. The conspirators collected outside the cathedral and, when Moreno remained at prayer within the church for a considerable time, one of them informed him that he was wanted outside on "a matter of immediate urgency." In front of the church he was cut down by revolver fire and machetes. Within a few minutes he was carried into the church and there, within twenty minutes, he died. In his pocket was the daily instruction he had penciled for himself for that day of his death, a note which accurately enough epitomizes his life: "Lord Jesus, grant me humility and a true love of Thee, and teach me what I am to do this day for Thy service."

Moreno was dead. With him died any chance Ecuador might have had of escaping the hectic, purposeless history of revolutions and *caudillos* that has been its story since 1875. The Liberals soon seized control of the government and turned their destructive guns on Moreno's work. Revolutions, conservatives, liberals, new constitutions, more assassinations have passed bewilderingly in kaleidoscopic fashion to make up the biography of a nation that produced only one really great man.

Before the reaction set in, however, Ecuador paused to pay

tribute to its great president, as did the rest of the civilized world. Even those who pleaded for his murder as a political necessity paused when he was dead to say, "This was truly a great man." Louis Veuillot saluted him as a man who "did honor to humanity . . . a noble figure, the most beautiful of modern times." Similar statements could be found in the journals and papers of almost all European countries. Father Kenelm Vaughn, brother of the famous Cardinal Vaughn, for example, wrote of him: "His true patriotism, his disinterestedness, his self-denial, his honorable actions, his zeal for the common good, gained him the affection of those even who until then had been his most bitter enemies."

The Ecuadorean Congress passed a resolution in which the legislators concluded that because "he has devoted his life and his rare genius to the regeneration and the grandeur of the republic by raising the social institutions on the sound foundations of Catholic principles," and because "he loved his religion and his fatherland so much as to suffer martyrdom for both," the people of Ecuador bestow on García Moreno "the title of Regenerator of the Fatherland and Martyr of Civilization." In similar words Pope Pius IX paid tribute to this man who suffered "the death of a martyr . . . a victim to his faith and Christian charity." With singular propriety, statues were erected to the memory of García Moreno in Rome and in Quito, the capitals of his Church and his country.

Moreno represents the high mark of civilization in Ecuador and, to a certain extent, in all Latin America. Francisco García Calderon sums up his importance to his country by concluding: "Union among his people, thirty years of battle against militarism, progress in material things, in religion and in morals, strong opposition to license, civil honor made a force against the sterile tradition of armies and warfare, true democracy combatting corrosive demagogy and raging anarchy." Moreno's public life was a protest against the secularist tendencies of the nineteenth century. He successfully applied sound Christian principles to the social and political life of his country. His success was proof that the price of justice and Christian decency was not, as the Liberals claimed, intellectual tyranny and material decadence. For under him Ecuadoreans grew bigger and better potatoes, erected larger schools with sounder curricula, built longer railroads and new highways, and secured something approaching social peace. Under him, paradoxical as it might seem to sincere Liberals, the meanest little Ecuadorean had rights equal to any *caudillo* or any Mason. Under him Ecuador approached closer to sound democracy than at any other time in her history. The franchise became wider than it had ever been in Ecuadorean history; real attempts were made to create an educated electorate; elections were made free.

Moreno was a conservative because he was opposed to Liberalism. But he was constructively progressive, whereas Latin Liberals never managed to get past the destructive stage of blowing up political and religious institutions to clear the ground for a "better society" for which they have not yet laid foundations. They were a selfish crowd who coined many liberal slogans but who never put them into practice when they controlled the government. Government for them was the rule of the many by the Liberal few in the interests of those few. Moreno did not hunger for power, nor did he use it for its own sake. He insisted that good government had to be strong government, but at the same time he scrupulously observed the requirements of the Constitution in his relationship with the Congress and with the electorate.

Thus Moreno proved that a statesman can be a Catholic to the marrow of his bones and still be a successful promoter of the commonweal. His plan of action, of course, was for Ecuador; O'Connell could never have applied it to England or even Ireland, nor could Montalembert or Windthorst have used it in France or Germany. His policies were applicable only in Catholic countries where the choice was a simple one between Catholicism and a hostile culture sworn to the Church's abolition. But his importance transcends Latin America because even today his rule stands as concrete proof that sound Christian principles are not medieval hang-overs which are ineffective in the world of the railroad and the assassin's revolver — and, by extension, the airplane and the various superbombs of our day.

II.

SOCIAL ADJUSTMENT

There was danger in the nineteenth century that charity might wither up and all but disappear from the face of the earth. At any time in history men without charity are social liabilities, but in the nineteenth century, when both charity of spirit and good works were needed as never before, men without charity threatened the very existence of the Christian society in which they lived and breathed and prospered. There was real danger that men would be reduced to mere units in society, nuts and bolts in the social machinery, that they would be completely dehumanized – both the workers, who were considered the raw material of labor, and the employers who had become human calculating machines.

This dehumanization of man in the nineteenth century accompanied the industrial revolution, which had been gathering momentum since the Napoleonic wars. Machines had been invented back in the eighteenth century, machines which at first lightened the load of man as he spun thread and wove cloth in the little shop attached to his home. Each machine made two or three others necessary, and the ingenuity of man produced the needed machines – which in turn made others necessary. Thus the craftsman became a tender of machinery. Then, when the problems of producing power from water and steam were solved, the machines were gathered under a single roof to be driven by power. Thus the factory was created.

As machines were gathered under one roof, so too were the laborers collected together, herded into the cities to live, cities where there was no clean air to breathe, no green grass or trees to see, no cow to furnish milk for the children, and, worst of all, no one who cared whether children saw trees or drank milk or starved to death. There was no one who even seemed to notice how the expression in the worker's eyes grew lifeless when his humanity was squeezed out of him in the factory. Whether his limbs still moved or not, death sat like a mask on his face. The light of human life had left his eyes; there was no smile on his face.

The worker had sufficient cause for becoming a living corpse. Things human had been stolen from him by the urban world into which he was thrown. Hours of labor were long, sixteen and fourteen a day; working conditions were unbelievably inhuman; and outside of working hours there was nothing for the laborer to do except to eat his bread and sleep in his hoval so that he could stay awake at his job the next day instead of falling asleep to his death in the machinery he tended – as his neighbor had done the week before. Decent family life was denied to these workers. They knew no recreation, except perhaps to escape temporarily from their miserable life with cheap liquor that carried them into a world of their own manufacture. For them to drink was to forget – for a bit. Their pay was not enough to keep a family in food, much less to clothe and educate the children.

So employers helped them by hiring their wives and their children, who at first worked fourteen or more hours a day under conditions not fit even for the animals they replaced. Little girls, for example, took the place of mules pulling coal-laden carts in the mines – because it cost more to cut a wide hole for a mule's passage than a narrow one for a small girl's. Human labor was cheap. The employer was careful of his prized machinery, because machines cost money and could be replaced only by an outlay of capital. But human beings cost nothing. They could be hired with no outlay at all, they could be driven until they wore out, and then they could be cast aside to make room for a fresh human unit of production.

It is difficult to exaggerate the inhuman conditions in which the worker lived and labored in the early nineteenth century. But the most terrifying thing of all is hardest to see or describe – what was happening in men's minds and hearts. For in this age the respectable people not only accepted this society as inevitable; they labeled it Christian and they considered it good.

Their outlook was not only un-Christian; it was inhuman. Men were reckoned as items of production, as were machines and money and raw material. They were units in an industrial army and they were given no more individuality or personality than ants carrying grains of wheat to an ant pile. Even when human instinct revolted, as it was bound to do, and created a sociology to deal with these conditions, it created a "science" that dealt with human beings as "cases." It was all handled scientifically, with human cases filed in metal drawers, with systematic records kept, with just another business created – this one dealing in the business of human misery, without knowing what it meant to be human or that misery was a condition of the human soul above all else. The infant science of sociology, in the nineteenth century, was as sick of soul as the world it sought to cure.

The worst feature of this nineteenth-century society, it must be emphasized, is that the people in control thought it good. They were a self-righteous crowd, the Liberal bourgeoisie of the age, who considered themselves God's chosen people. They had reasoned out their position, and they declared that they prospered because God wanted them to prosper, that they were wealthy because they were good. Their prosperity, they believed, was a reflection of God's glory on earth. So, in reverse, did the sufferings of the poor promote God's honor and glory, for the poor were the condemned of God, the reprobate whom God in His inscrutable wisdom had consigned to a life of misery on earth as a preparation to an eternity in hell. And who were the bourgeoisie to interfere with God's scheme of justice?

This is the mentality that must be understood if we are to know why an Anglican bishop could state publicly late in life that he had never given a cent to the poor. For it was generally believed that gifts to the unfortunate only aggravated their misery and interfered with the normal functioning of the divinely ordained scheme for running the world. That is why Malthus – himself a clergyman – tells the world that the only palliative he can propose for remedying the misery of the poor is "the total abolition of all the present forms of public charity and relief."

The nineteenth century was an age of rugged competition in which, it was believed, all things were regulated by deterministic laws of nature. One of these laws was Ricardo's Iron Law of

Wages, which told the workingman that he could receive in wages only enough to keep himself alive. With imposing arguments and even more imposing statistics, the workingman was shown how he was condemned by "the nature of things" to a subhuman level of existence. The workingman therefore lost hope of improving his lot. His resentment turned inward, growing like an irritating cancer deeper and deeper in his breast. He became sullen, a lost soul in a society of lost souls who watched the contrast between their own misery and the ostentatious luxury of their employers grow ever more marked as the century progressed. If the worker could not improve his condition, why should he not wreck the society that condemned him to this animal-like existence? Why should he not smash up the machinery that was prized over himself and his children? Why should he not smash up society itself – this society in which he had no place? Why should he not listen to one who told him he had nothing to lose but his chains?

In the latter half of the century competition was given a new "scientific" justification by Darwin's theory of struggle for existence and the survival of the fittest. His impersonal, "scientific laws" showed how all living things struggle for life, how some survive and some do not, how this struggle is neither moral nor immoral but is found in the very nature of things. It was Darwin more than anyone else who justified cutthroat competition for survival, who consecrated as a scientifically established law of nature internecine warfare among all living things. Those who were stupid or softhearted or overly considerate of their fellows, of course, did not survive; those who were sharp, hard, ruthless and clear sighted did survive and prosper. Consequently there was no room for that antiquated Christian idea of charity toward one's brothers in Christ. There was no room for either charity of spirit or works of mercy.

In still another way did the nineteenth century try to smother the flame of charity in men's hearts. Year by year the State took over more and more charitable functions formerly performed by individuals or by such organizations as the guild or the Church – never a healthy thing for the State to do unless all other agencies are incapable. Among these functions appropriated by the State were the care of the poor, the raising of orphans, the maintenance of hospitals and other charitable institutions. For various reasons these functions, formerly part of the apostolate of charity, were gathered in by that all-embracing octopus, the national State. Thus the care of the sick and the maimed, the education of orphans and the correction of delinquents, all these things were robbed of their soul – which is charity – and left only their corpse of material aid from the never charitable State. Those who needed help found themselves government wards.

For these reasons the flame of charity burned low in the nineteenth century. Those who realized how essential a part of Catholicism charity was, both the supernatural virtue of charity and the good works which flow from that divine gift, struggled to keep the flame alive and to fan it so that it could burn brightly again to warm human hearts in its glow. Catholic laymen played their part – a prominent part – in keeping charity alive in the nineteenth century in two different ways. First, they fired individuals with the spirit of charity and urged them to care for God's poor by giving freely and lovingly, for thus was Christian charity to be distinguished from philanthropy and from State aid. Such was the work of Frédéric Ozanam and Pauline Marie Jaricot. Second, they tried to work through government channels to see that laws helpful to the poor were passed, that abuses of the industrial revolution were ameliorated, that employees were treated as human beings instead of units of labor. Such was the work of Albert de Mun.

These Catholic laymen tried to accomplish a twofold objective, the realization of which was doubly difficult in the nineteenth century when class divisions grew sharper and class hatreds more intense. In this age of increasing selfishness and hatred Catholics like Marie Jaricot, Ozanam, and De Mun labored valiantly to make the wealthy charitable and the poor appreciative. They labored to show the rich that they were blessed by God not because of their own merit, that they were bound like good stewards to use their riches well; and they labored to show the poor that they were not condemned by any "natural law" to a life of poverty, but that they should accept their lot as long as God willed them to live in it. Meanwhile, of course, they should try to better their condition socially.

5. Pauline Marie Jaricot

Pauline Marie Jaricot is the only woman included in this study of outstanding Catholic laymen of the nineteenth century. She is one of two – Frédéric Ozanam is the other – whose cause has been presented at Rome for inclusion among the officially declared saints of the Church. Pauline Jaricot was feminine to her finger tips, and properly enough she remains something of a puzzle to the historian who wishes to assess her historical importance for the Church. In her own day two popes and several members of the hierarchy praised her without restraint. At the same time, other bishops and many priests labeled her a proud lady whose ambition led her to become a tool in swindlers' hands. It seems today that the accusations against this unusual French lady are baseless, and that some day she may be canonized. But until Rome finishes its exhaustive study of Mlle. Jaricot's life and hands down its decision, the historian must rely upon the evidence available to him and report the amazing things she did so easily as well as the long period of suffering and disgrace she endured because one of her charitable projects failed.

There is no doubt that Pauline Jaricot was important. She was foundress or cofoundress – the matter remains in dispute – of the Society of the Propagation of the Faith, sometimes called the "most important work of the Church in the nineteenth century." She is the undisputed foundress of the Association of the Living Rosary. Moreover, she advised and helped in the establishment of other Church institutions, such as the Marists and the Association of the Holy Childhood, and she poured out a steady stream of advice and encouragement to missioners at home and abroad, to lay people trying to do works of charity, and to religious trying to deepen their own spiritual life and to revive a languishing Church.

All these things Pauline Jaricot accomplished before she was forty. She was, until that time, a young lady of immense wealth and fervent piety upon whom God and the world apparently smiled. But in the last twenty years of her life God sent her much suffering, and the world came to frown on her and to turn away from her as it turns from those who are worldly failures. She bore this suffering without complaint. For twenty years she prayed and she suffered as she was tried by God – and she never rebelled. This was her greatest triumph. Those pleading her cause in Rome today, we feel sure, do not stress her great achievements nearly so much as they do her prayer and her suffering in the latter part of her life. It is by this that greater things are done than man can dream of, and the chances seem good today that in the future Pauline Marie Jaricot will be considered important in the Church principally because she lived a saintly life and because she prayed without ceasing. For, even more than the activity of men like Montalembert and Moreno, prayer and sacrifice are the means whereby the Church revived and grew strong again in the nineteenth century.

* * *

Pauline Marie Jaricot was born in 1799, a few months before the end of the eighteenth century, at a time when the Church was apparently at the nadir of its existence in modern times. Pope Pius VI was to die in exile within a month, and it seemed as if there would never be another pope. The Church had been expelled from France; it languished in the other parts of Europe. Those in France who remained loyal to the faith of their fathers had to hide priests in their attics and attend Mass secretly in their barns. Just a few months after Pauline was born, however, young Napoleon Bonaparte seized control of the government, and one of his first acts was to give the Catholic Church official recognition in France again, simply because there were so many people like the Jaricots who remained loyally and stubbornly Catholic. So Pauline grew up attending Church and practicing her faith openly, but she grew up a member of a Church which was trying to recover from an illness that had seemed nearly fatal. It was a Church, therefore, which in the days of Pauline's youth was still weak and timorous in Napoleon's France.

Pauline Jaricot was born in Lyons – an important fact, because Lyons was the Detroit of France, a city that even in 1800 was pretty much industrialized. Thus she grew up in the worst days of the industrial revolution, in a city where the workers lived wretchedly when they worked and literally starved when they did not. Pauline saw misery in the pinched faces of young girls who worked in her father's and her relatives' factories. She did not understand the economics of starvation wages, but she felt something must be done to help these wretched laborers, to help them both spiritually and physically, for they were sick of soul as well as of body. Pauline was distressed to find herself classed with the enemies of these poor people; she was perplexed in the days of her youth to find that only the Socialists talked of doing anything for the working class. The problem haunted her throughout her life, from the time she first went into her brother-in-law's factory to work among the girl employees down until the day of her death, when she was herself one of the poorest of the poor, one who held an official certificate of poverty and a license to beg on the streets of Lyons.

She saw street fighting between the workers and soldiers during the revolution of 1830. Most of the time through those crucial days she stayed in her chapel to pray; but when the soldiers returned to punish the rebellious Lyonnais workers, she and her associates scattered holy medals and prayer cards before the soldiers. Eventually the city was spared – and people cried out that it was a miracle. But the problem remained a deep-seated social cancer eating at the heart of Lyons. In 1834 troops came from Paris to shoot down workers again, and in 1848 there was rioting and civil war and barricades in the streets of Lyons. Even when there was no rioting or shooting in the streets, there was still hatred smoldering in the workers' hearts, and envy eating at their minds. Because Pauline Jaricot lived in Lyons, then, and because her father was a factory owner the social problem was not an academic one for this French girl. It was a terribly real, practical problem with which she grew up and which – typically – she set about solving singlehanded.

The Jaricots were one of Lyons' leading families. Antoine, head of the household, had done well even before his youngest child, Pauline, was born in 1799. In the years after her birth, however, he prospered greatly, and by the time the Napoleonic wars were over in 1815, Antoine Jaricot was a millionaire. He was a hardheaded businessman, practical, shrewd, a pusher who was able to take advantage of the favorable position in which he found himself with an expanding business during war years. In his way, however, he continued to be a charitable man, always willing to finance his youngest daughter's charities. And when he died in 1834, he left Pauline a wealthy woman in her own right, with a fortune of 800,000 francs to spend on the poor. Antoine Jaricot bestowed on his daughter something more than fatherly affection and an ever open wallet. Pauline inherited from him those gifts of a successful industrialist: great ability as an organizer, the drive to put things – even charity – on a paying basis, the energy and will and determination to build up associations to accomplish what one young lady in the nineteenth century could never do by herself. Thus, from her father Pauline obtained gifts which she applied to her Catholic Action work.

From her mother she received religious guidance and a spiritual balance which her father, in his worldly way, simply did not possess. Mme. Jaricot was a remarkable woman whose epitaph, written by Antoine, states that "forgetful of self, she thought only of God, her family, and the unfortunate." She had the leisure to supervise the early education of her two youngest children, Philéas and Pauline, and she never tired of pointing out the religious implications of a beautiful sunset or of crops ripening in the field.

Thus Pauline grew up a typical bourgeois girl of early nineteenth-century Lyons, in a wealthy Catholic family, under the supervision of a deeply religious mother. She was a joyful, carefree child, always singing – the "skylark of Paradise" her mother called her – whose principal fault was girlish imperiousness, a tendency toward pride. Antoine had high ambitions for his youngest daughter, whom he wished to marry off well and set up as a leader of the younger social set in Lyons. Nor was Pauline averse from such a life. Naturally gay, a cheerful young lady, she was popular with the members of her group. An attractive person, she set the fashions for her set in clothes, in conversation, and in all those little things which are so important for adolescents everywhere.

Arrangements were made by the Jaricots for Pauline to marry a suitable young man of the neighborhood. The young people were introduced, they found each other attractive, and preparations were begun to arrange for the formal announcement of their engagement. The ambitious father pushed the affair, hoping, in his businesslike way, to complete the transaction. But Pauline and her mother delayed from week to week because, womanlike, Pauline could not quite make up her mind to take the final step, and her mother intuitively understood that she was attracted by another vocation than marriage. While Pauline was in this state of hesitation, she fell from a high stool and suffered a severe back injury. For a long time she was seriously ill, suffering a series of heart attacks and then apparently a bad case of anemia.

Almost a year passed before she recovered enough to go about again. Meanwhile her mother had died, the engagement which had never been announced was canceled by default on Pauline's part, and the young lady was very much at sea, a girl of seventeen who had to get her bearings all over again. Providentially, she attended Mass one Sunday when a certain Abbé Würtz preached the sermon. Pauline was much impressed by this Lorrainer's simple, direct approach to spiritual problems, so she put herself under his guidance. Abbé Würtz realized that this was no ordinary girl who sought his direction. He therefore advised her to receive Holy Communion daily, an unusual thing one hundred years before Pope Pius X urged frequent Communion for all good Catholics. The abbé also ordered Pauline to trample underfoot all she had formerly sought after. Further, he advised her to forsake attachment to all worldly things, to give up all thought of secular love.

This was not easy advice for a young socialite to follow, but Pauline did as the abbé suggested—and more. She obtained permission from the Sisters at the neighboring hospital of Saint-Polycarp to work in the incurable ward. Soon the news buzzed through the social set of Lyons that Pauline Jaricot was working every day at the hospital—with the incurables! Perhaps her long illness had affected the poor girl's mind. Antoine Jaricot was not pleased with his daughter's exuberant charity. He wanted her to do works of mercy, of course, but in a manner and to the extent befitting a girl of good family. And when she continued to give her own things away with reckless abandon, her prudent father forbade her to give anything to charity except with his express permission.

What annoyed Antoine even more than his daughter's unrestrained charity was her new bizarre dress. In place of her former fine clothes, Pauline now wore the coarse clothing of a peasant, wooden shoes and all. When she appeared in this costume in the Jaricot pew at high Mass, the people of Lyons were convinced that she had lost her mind. As a matter of fact, Pauline later admitted that the clothes she wore were "ridiculous." But she explained her course of action this way: "I went to the extreme limit, for, if I had not broken off everything at the same time, I would never have gained anything. I was so overcome at appearing in public in the sorry purple dress that I trembled in every limb. A middle way would have been insufficient to make my resolution unshakable."

It must have been hard on a young lady of seventeen to give up her position of leadership in her set, to put aside her beautiful clothes, and to enter on a new way of life. It must have been particularly hard in Pauline's case, because instead of withdrawing into a convent where she would have had the company of similarly situated girls, she stayed in the world she was renouncing. But she surprised everyone by continuing her works of charity, by wearing her menial garb, by working among Lyons' most wretched paupers – and otherwise appearing quite sane. Abbé Würtz saved her from being a modern Martha all her life, however, for after the first year of Pauline's intensive charity work the abbé urged her to give less time to good works and more to prayer and meditation. Moreover, he ordered her to discontinue the excessive austerities in fasting she had been practicing and which were undermining her health. All these suggestions and commands Pauline obeyed.

* * *

Pauline Jaricot's first great gift to a reviving Church was the Society for the Propagation of the Faith, which she founded in 1819, before she was twenty-one. The beginnings of the Society can be traced back to 1818 when Pauline began to work among the girl employees of her brother-in-law's factory at Saint-Vallier. Her chief concern at this time was the girls' moral welfare, and she seems to have been eminently successful even at so early an age, for the girls came to her readily, talked freely, and poured forth their problems easily.

Pauline worked out a plan for the girls to have a short rest period at three in the afternoon, during which they said three Our Fathers and three Hail Marys. Then she brought her brother Philéas out to teach the girls their catechism. During the course of his instructions Philéas told about the desperate need of the missions for financial support. The young ladies in Pauline's group wanted to do something about this practical problem—a simple one, this need for money, which they fully understood. So they decided that each would give a *sou* a week to support the French missions of the Orient. By the time Pauline left Saint-Vallier to return to Lyons, the contributions were being faithfully collected each week by her group of factory girls, the "Reparatrices of the Heart of Jesus," whose main work was prayer of reparation for the sins of the world but whose secondary work of supporting the missions was the seed from which the Society for the Propagation of the Faith grew.

Another such group was soon formed among the female factory workers of Lyons under Pauline's leadership. To both groups she read letters on the missioner's need for help written by Philéas, who had gone to the seminary early in 1819 to become a missionary priest. Soon there were groups of Pauline's Reparatrices of the Heart of Jesus in other cities, at Nancy, Metz, Le Havre, Rennes, and other towns. Each group followed the same pattern of activity—prayer and the collection of modest sums for the missions. Each group, moreover, received from Pauline copies of Philéas' letters. Toward the end of her life, when the Central Council of the Society for the Propagation of the Faith repudiated Pauline Jaricot, she indignantly wrote to the Council: "Sirs, without lying I can add to my title of foundress that of nurse of the work; because for three years I stimulated the zeal of my associates by communicating to them the letters of my brother. . . . Those letters were like the first *Annals of the Propagation of the Faith.*"

But Pauline's really distinctive contribution, which gives her claim to the title of foundress of the Society, was the practical, businesslike step of organization taken in 1819. From the beginning she felt that the various sections of her Reparatrices were poorly organized. There was no central office; each local group was autonomous. Therefore no one could be certain whether the next week's collection would be gathered and sent to the missions. Pauline hit upon a plan for promoting and extending the work and at the same time organizing it under central control. It was a businesslike plan. Each member was to find nine others who would combine with the first into a group of ten. One of the ten would be responsible for collecting a *sou* a week from each member. Over every hundred groups was a chief collector, whose responsibility it was to bring or send the thousand *sous* to headquarters each week.

This was the distinctive feature of the Society for the Propagation of the Faith, which title was adopted by Pauline's groups at this time. She did not put her plan into operation, however, until she proposed it to Abbé Würtz and her brother for their criticisms. The abbé was delighted, and he urged her to carry it out. After Philéas talked the plan over with the priests at the seminary of Saint-Sulpice, he wrote back to Pauline that they all enthusiastically advocated her putting it into effect. So she did. And the plan was a success from the beginning. It both spread the work and systematized it.

Within a few months, however, Pauline Jaricot ran into a storm of abuse and opposition in clerical circles, the first of many such storms she was to encounter in her career. Her pastor ordered her to stop the work because, he said, it was controlled by a layman – a woman at that – and therefore it was illicit. Pauline appealed to the vicar-general of the diocese – there was no bishop in residence at the time – and offered to stop the work if the vicar-general thought her pastor right. He answered by telling her not to stop the work but rather to extend it.

Thus, with the permission and practically at the command of the proper ecclesiastical authority, she continued building the Society for the Propagation of the Faith. The very success of the work caused the opposition to grow more intense and bitter, most of it coming from the pulpit with priests saying that young women should say their prayers and leave other ecclesiastical matters in clerical hands. She was censured for her daring, for being proud, for proceeding without proper ecclesiastical permission. It was even hinted darkly that much of the money she collected went elsewhere than to the missions.

The work prospered, however, and it continued to spread rapidly through 1819. By the end of that year, the Society for the Propagation of the Faith was an established, prosperous institution giving valuable support to the French missions in Asia.

Three years later, in 1822, the Society was born a second time. The biggest difficulty to have arisen in the intervening three years was the question of the destination of the Society's funds. Pauline originally had intended to help only the Chinese missions, but there were others who were interested chiefly in America, and still others who thought the Society should help missions all over the world. The problem came to a head in 1822, when there arrived at Lyons a certain Abbé Inglesi, reportedly sent to Europe by Bishop DuBourg of New Orleans to get help for the American missions. The abbé, who proved in time to be a swindler who was repudiated by his bishop and who later apostatized, tried to take over Mlle. Jaricot's organization for the supposed support of the American missions.

In May of 1822, those interested in mission work met to draw up an organization for the support of missions throughout the entire world. Pauline did not attend the meeting herself, but she was represented by some of her associates. They drew up a constitution, took over the title, Society for the Propagation of the Faith, incorporated Pauline's system of the tens and the hundreds, adopted St. Francis Xavier as patron, and provided that each member should say an Our Father and a Hail Mary daily for the missions. It was Pauline's plan they adopted, and her groups were incorporated into the extended organization when she turned over to the Council her lists and her funds on hand. But in the proceedings which took place in May of 1822, Pauline Jaricot was not mentioned by name. Thus her name went into oblivion as far as the Society was concerned, for she remained only one of many heading a hundred groups — and thus thirty years later she was declared an impostor when, at the suggestion of the Bishop of La Rochelle, she laid claim to her title as foundress of the organization.

* * *

Pauline's second great accomplishment was another matter of organization. But this time she aimed at organizing prayers rather than coins, and her purpose was to deepen rather than extend Catholic life. The Living Rosary came about partly because Abbé Würtz realized that Pauline was one of those rare persons who excelled at both the active life and the contemplative. Because he believed that her intense activity in the Society for the Propagation of the Faith had caused her to neglect her contemplative development, the abbé ordered Pauline to discontinue her works of charity for three years and to concentrate on cultivating her own spiritual life. The young lady, as always, followed her spiritual director's orders, and thus she developed the Mary side of her nature as formerly she had developed the Martha side.

In 1825, Pope Leo XII issued an encyclical deploring the secular literature of the time and calling upon Catholics to read instead in the literature of their own great tradition. Pauline decided to organize a group of people to distribute good books and pamphlets in answer to the Pope's suggestion. But by 1825 she was more fully convinced than ever that good works without prayers are hollow and ineffective. So she planned to use the same organization to promote Christian reading and Catholic prayer throughout a pretty thoroughly pagan France. Her plan was to organize people into groups of fifteen, each one of whom would be pledged to say a decade of the rosary every day. In this way, by a businesslike division of labor she hoped to have France, the cradle of the rosary, saying its beads once more. "It will be an army of good," she wrote to Philéas, "and, besides, one minute of dwelling daily on the life of our Lord makes a half hour a month of meditation."

The whole thing was worked out in detail from the beginning. The Association, she decided, was to be called the Living Rosary. Each original member was to bring in five more, and each of these still another five. Each member was assigned one of the fifteen mysteries as his own decade to be recited daily. Each member, too, was to pay an annual dues varying from about fifteen cents to a dollar, depending upon his means. This money was to be used for the purchase and distribution of rosaries, holy medals, and Catholic literature.

This time Pauline was careful to get clerical approval from the very beginning. Three priests attended the first organization meeting at the Jaricot home, and they obtained approval of the plan from the archbishop of Lyons before the Association of the Living Rosary was first given life. Again, though, there were murmurings of disapproval among the clergy of Lyons, but this time they were not so loud and they were confined to those priests who did not like the new archbishop. These murmurings subsided when the papal nuncio to Paris, Cardinal Lambruschini, passed through Lyons in 1827, gave the Living Rosary his blessing, and agreed to take it under his official protection. They stopped altogether when Pope Leo XII gave the Association his official blessing.

As the movement spread it was brought to the attention of the Master General of the Dominicans – and for a few anxious weeks it seemed to Pauline that she might encounter difficulties with the Dominican Order. The Master General properly felt a responsibility toward the rosary, inasmuch as the Blessed Virgin had originally given it to St. Dominic with explicit instructions on how it should be said. He therefore wrote to Pauline for further information, since the reports he had received indicated that she had altered the rosary itself. Pauline answered by explaining her plan and telling the Master General that she "was convinced that the mere distribution of alms and pious books would produce no fruit unless it was accompanied by prayer, and it seemed to me that it would please God if we could have recourse to this ancient practice so long approved by the Church, since the distribution of books now gives us the opportunity of spreading it for the revival of faith among the people."

Her explanation satisfied the Dominican, and he wrote back a pleasant, kindly letter approving the work. Ten years later, incidentally, in 1836, the Living Rosary was affiliated to the Dominican Order. Meanwhile, though, it had spread rapidly through France, abroad into the other countries of Europe, and over the seas to the other continents of the world. Most French bishops were happy to have the Living Rosary in their dioceses, so by 1827 there were one hundred and fifty groups established in France. Within three more years it had spread into Italy, Belgium, and Switzerland; into England and parts of Germany; into Turkey, the countries of South America; into Canada and the mission territory of the United States.

As the movement spread it met a certain amount of underground clerical opposition which must have hurt Pauline, for it was all directed against her personally, and, being feminine through and through, her sensitive nature was not inured to such criticism. She was accused of presuming to do priestly work, and thus of violating both the letter of the New Testament and the spirit of the Church's tradition. It was hinted that Rome would never have approved of a lady twenty-seven years old directing such a work and sending spiritual advice to the members of the Association — if only the Pope knew what was going on. Again, she was accused of having a "racket" because of all the money that flowed into the Association's headquarters at her home.

To quiet this opposition, Pope Gregory XVI issued a brief solemnly approving the Association of the Living Rosary. The letter, however, never reached Pauline. Because Cardinal Lambruschini suspected that clerical politics were involved, he obtained a duplicate of the papal brief, sent it by special messenger to the French frontier, and had Pauline pick it up there. This time Pauline refused to recede into the background, as she had done with the Society for the Propagation of the Faith. She maintained control of the Association with headquarters at her home. She continued to send out letters of advice and spiritual guidance to the various units of the Living Rosary; and her home, which had a chapel with the Blessed Sacrament in it after 1833, became a sort of refuge where clergy and laity alike repaired for meditation and prayer, for advice and inspiration, and for material help. Among Pauline's visitors was the Curé of Ars, St. John Mary Vianney, who occasionally made the long trip on foot from Ars to Lyons to visit his friend and observe the results of her good work.

* * *

In 1830, Pauline's beloved brother Philéas died. She inherited from him a large house where he had established a community of unmarried women who helped him in his various charitable enterprises. Pauline took over the group, calling them "Daughters of Mary," and she became their "mother superior." The ladies wore no habit other than the simple peasant dress of the day. They attended Mass every morning, said the rosary and the stations of the cross daily, and spent an hour in adoration before the Blessed Sacrament. Their objectives — besides the general honor and glory of God — were specifically to effect the conversion of sinners by prayer and apostolic action, to maintain the Faith and to exalt the Church in France. Although "Mother Jaricot" seems to have intended to establish her Daughters of Mary as a regular religious community, nevertheless she never got around to officially organizing them and having them properly established at Rome. So in the last decade of her life, when she was no longer able to maintain her Daughters, Pauline advised them to join various established communities of nuns. Most of them followed her advice — and thus any dream Pauline may have had of establishing a religious community was dispelled in that dark night of her life when everything she touched seemed to turn to ashes in her hands.

For twelve years or more after she had founded the Association of the Living Rosary, however, Pauline seemed eminently successful. The Association continued to spread and to prosper. Mlle. Jaricot was wealthy. After she inherited almost a million francs of her father's estate in 1834, she was free to support almost any charitable enterprise that appealed to her. Meanwhile she happily contributed small sums to deserving priests who came to her home, Lorette, seeking her aid. The demands on this young woman's time, especially the hours on end she spent writing to the various units of the Association, took their heavy toll on her constitution.

By 1835 it seemed to all those at Lorette that "Mother Jaricot" — now thirty-five years old — could not live more than another few months. She had apparently always had a weak heart, and now she had an advanced case of heart disease. Only with great effort could she leave her bed to visit the chapel. Nevertheless, she announced to her Daughters one day that she was going to Rome to visit the Capital of Christendom and to ask the Holy Father for additional privileges for the Association of the Living Rosary! She set out with her faithful traveling companion, the young, healthful, and cheerful Marie Melquiond, who was well able to take care of Pauline as long as she could draw her own breath.

At length, after a wearisome voyage by carriage and ship, the two Frenchwomen arrived in Rome. At Mother Barat's request they stayed at the Sacred Heart Convent, but Pauline was too weak to visit the Holy Father as she had intended to do. Pope Gregory XVI therefore visited Pauline Jaricot. Accompanied by Cardinal Lambruschini and Mother Barat, the Holy Father personally thanked Pauline for her two great foundations, the Society for the Propagation of the Faith and the Association of the Living Rosary. Pauline informed the Pope that she intended to proceed to Mugnano, near Naples, the home of Blessed Philomena, to whom she was going to address her prayers for a miraculous cure. Both Pauline and the Curé of Ars were warmly attached to Philomena, whose cause for canonization was pending in Rome. Pope Gregory XVI is reported having promised Pauline he would officially authorize the cult of Philomena if she should return from Mugnano cured.

After resting in Rome for five weeks, Pauline declared she was ready for the journey southward. No one else believed she was strong enough to arrive at her destination alive, but she seems to have been convinced that she would not only arrive there but that she would walk away well. She was embarrassed when the Italian populace scolded their Philomena for failing to cure this poor French lady who had come from so far for help. That was on the first day. The next day was August 10 (it has since become St. Philomena's feast day) and on it Pauline was cured, apparently in miraculous fashion, while praying to the young Italian saint. She had been wheeled into the church, and she walked out – all the way to her lodgings.

For the next few days she had to submit to all sorts of tests and examinations and questions. She was forced to walk around the town several times, accompanied by a military escort and preceded by an Italian band. All this commotion was embarrassing, of course, but because it might further Philomena's cause Pauline submitted to it without complaint. She left her sick chair in Philomena's chapel and returned to Rome to report to the Pope and to hold him to his promise. Within a year the Holy Father authorized the cult of St. Philomena, officially declaring her a canonized saint on January 13, 1837.

For several years now, from 1836 until about 1844, the world smiled on Pauline. She was a beloved daughter of the Church, a wealthy French lady whose fortune was at the disposal of any charitable enterprise. She had met the Pope and secured his blessing on her work. She had the support and warm approval of such highly placed churchmen as Cardinal Lambruschini and Msgr. Villecourt, the bishop of La Rochelle. She was associated with that remarkable saint, the Curé of Ars. Her name was known in Rome, in England, and of course throughout France, where some called her the "Mother of the Missions" and others the "Mother of the Rosary." The Society had become an important institution in the Church; the Association had over 3,000,000 members. At this point in her life Pauline could be satisfied that she had done good work.

* * *

Nevertheless Pauline was not satisfied. There was still so much to do. One problem especially had been gnawing at Pauline's mind all those years when she was doing other things: the social problem of finding some way that working people could live like decent human beings. It was not a simple problem. Its aspects were both moral and economic – and it seemed that if anyone could solve it, then this saintly daughter of a self-made millionaire might be the person. "The question of a just wage is hardly considered," she wrote almost fifty years before Pope Leo XIII published his famous encyclical on the condition of the working class. "It is a problem that will not let me rest. I cannot do much, I know, but I feel I must do something to help in this regeneration of the workers." In 1838, when she visited Rome again for a series of audiences with Gregory XVI on the future of the Living Rosary, she had several discussions with Cardinal Lambruschini on the condition of the working class in France. They both felt the need for Catholic action on the problem, they both knew it was primarily a moral matter, and they both believed that somehow a morally just solution to the problem could also be economically sound. But neither had the specific, practicable answer of how industry could operate without dehumanizing the wage hands.

Pauline bided her time, turning the problem over in her mind, studying the "solution" of the problem preached on the streets of Lyons by Socialists, and finally concluding that the missing ingredient in the secular solution of the wage problem was the virtue of charity. She understood well how the workers needed something very concrete: higher wages with which to buy more food and clothing. But she understood equally well that increased wages alone would not solve the social problem created by the industrial revolution. What was needed, she concluded, was both an apostleship of love and higher wages. These would be the spirit and the body of her next great project. It would be an enterprise which somehow would restore the workers to a position of human dignity again – a position which the factory system denied them. She would teach the employee to take joy in his work, to see the dignity of labor, and she would teach the employer to pay his worker a wage commensurate with his dignity as a human being – a living wage.

In what concrete way was this to be done? That was the problem. Here Pauline took a page from the Socialist's handbook. Saint-Simon, Fourier, and the other early French Socialists, as well as Robert Owen in England, all proposed setting up model communities where their plans could be carried out freely. Now Pauline proposed to build a model industrial community which would have its own factory, its own civic, religious, and social life – all conducted according to Christian principles of justice and charity. It would be a Catholic utopia located somewhere in the industrial region of France. It would prosper, Pauline felt sure, and it would prove to the rest of the world that material goods could be produced out of something besides the blood and the souls of workers, as was the case everywhere in the 1830's and 1840's.

There remained one more problem, the financial one of raising sufficient capital to get such a project under way. Pauline worked out a scheme similar to the ones she had used so successfully twice before. She would establish a capital fund called the "Bank of Heaven" by obtaining 100,000 francs from each of fifteen wealthy persons. The money would be invested in a paying industry and thus a double advantage would be gained: the workers could be paid decent wages on which to lead a Christian life, and the profits could be used to finance good works by lending money, free of charge, to religious groups such as nuns needing a convent or bishops needing a new school or church.

To Pauline the plan seemed foolproof. It seemed sound financially; it seemed a businesslike approach to the moral side of the social problem. Pauline told her close friend, Abbé Villecourt, now bishop of La Rochelle, about her scheme, and from him she received enthusiastic support. "This design of yours," the bishop told her, "is not really an earthly enterprise. It is to open to the poor an honest means of making a livelihood; it will also be for them a place of peace and a school of virtue." But God, in His inscrutable wisdom, had decreed that this best laid plan of Pauline Jaricot should go awry to bring her nothing but suffering and disgrace down to the very hour of her death.

The human factors in the failure of this scheme were a bankrupt financier of shady reputation, a certain M. Allioud, and a scheming, dishonest associate of his named Gustave Perre. Pauline had heard of the Allioud family's plight from a friend; she offered them her hospitality until M. Allioud could get on his feet financially again. For two years the Alliouds lived at Pauline's house, and during that time M. Allioud talked more and more of his wonderful friend Perre, who always wanted to meet Mlle. Jaricot but could never get away from business long enough to make the trip. (The fact is that Gustave Perre was in prison those two years.)

At last the heralded "financier" arrived to talk with Pauline about the condition of the working classes, about various ways of helping the poor, about the missions, and all those other things in which she was interested. Allioud and Perre happened to mention a tract of productive mining property at Rustrel, in southern France, and some blast furnaces that were located near by. (Perre had purchased Rustrel for 18,000 francs in 1837, but he lost the property when he could not raise the required sum in eight months' time.) Cleverly these two associates took advantage of Pauline's eagerness to get her project under way. They pretended to share her desire to help the working class. To all appearances this was uppermost in their minds. They stressed the fact that there was a chapel on the property; they pointed out how a nearly self-sufficient, a truly utopian community could be erected on the location. Meanwhile, Gustave Perre was frequently seen in the chapel, and he had on hand an endless supply of pious, edifying stories.

Later on, Pauline wrote of Perre that "he had the gift of fascinating his victims, as a snake fascinates a bird." Most of the people around the Jaricot establishment at Fourvière distrusted him, so Pauline checked his references from southern France and when she received high recommendations for Perre from a certain Abbé Ricard she decided to invest in his scheme. Abbé Ricard had advised her to "give every encouragement to those who are prepared to provide funds and do business with M. Perre, for they have nothing to fear."

Perre and Allioud negotiated the purchase of the property, freely spending Mlle. Jaricot's money and carefully keeping all lawyers away from the transaction. They contracted to buy Rustrel for 452,000 francs, the entire sum being put up by their benefactress. A corporation was formed to operate the furnace as soon as the property was purchased in 1845 – the capital of 150,000 francs again being furnished by Pauline Jaricot. This corporation was called Notre Dame des Anges (Our Lady of the Angels), and Gustave Perre was named its manager. Pauline stayed at Lyons, waiting anxiously for the ideal community under Perre's direction to begin realizing some return on her large investments. Perre threw money in every direction, living luxuriously at Avignon, paying fabulous salaries to friends, purchasing some pieces of property for himself – and meanwhile failing to apply any of the money received from Pauline to the purchase of Rustrel.

A second corporation – La Société des Forges de Ste. Anne d'Apt – was formed to work the iron mine on the property at Rustrel. Again the funds came from Mlle. Jaricot and from her friends. Pauline had been convinced by Perre's clever letters that her ideal Catholic community was at the point of being realized. She was encouraged, too, by a development that was soon to cause her great grief: workers and small tradesmen, feeling that Pauline Jaricot was both a smart business lady and a holy woman, clamored to invest their savings in her project at Rustrel. So she accepted their funds because she thought she was not only promoting a great work but also because she was doing these people a favor by investing their money safely. Altogether, she turned over 180,000 francs of her own and her friends' money as capital for the second corporation.

Within a few months Pauline began to wonder when her property at Rustrel would produce a profit on her investment. One thing after another went wrong, and though it was obvious to many observers that Allioud and Perre knew nothing about blast furnaces or iron mines, still for some time they mollified Pauline's mounting suspicions by writing how they had the blast furnace blessed, how the workers were attending Mass, and other such things they knew would keep her satisfied from letter to letter. It became evident within six months, even to Pauline, that she was the victim of a gigantic swindle — and with her all those who had invested their savings in the project because of her reputation. In May, 1846, Perre was back in jail, the books were examined, and Pauline Jaricot found out how desperate her financial condition was. None of the money she gave Perre had ever been applied at Rustrel. There were 500 francs on hand, and she was in debt 895,000 francs. She assumed the full liabilities and full assets of Rustrel, partly because her partners were insolvent and partly because she still believed her Working Man's Mission could be realized on this piece of property.

She tried heroically to put the business back on its feet, and for a time she seemed at the point of being successful. Two of the four blast furnaces were put in operation, seven families were settled around them as an embryo community of Catholic workers, a capable manager was selected, and enough earnings flowed in to keep the creditors mollified for a time. There is no way of telling whether Pauline Jaricot's scheme could have worked out practically, for the revolution of 1848 cut the ground from under her. Creditors insisted on being paid — not only interest now but their capital loans as well. Business was disrupted by the revolution, and the debt was too big for Pauline to carry through those difficult years. She continued to meet one interest payment after another, but she could not reduce the debt.

* * *

It was at this point that the bishop of La Rochelle suggested that her only chance of saving Notre Dame des Anges was by begging. After all, he reasoned with Pauline, do not we support all Church organizations in this fashion? And do you want these poor people who trusted in you to lose their savings? So Pauline decided to beg. It must have been a heroic decision for this millionaire's daughter to make. Popes and kings can beg easily; bishops, nobles, and priests can do it without embarrassment, and so, too, can most of God's poor. But begging is hard on the bourgeoisie—and Pauline was thoroughly bourgeois in her upbringing.

Hard though it was, she agreed to beg throughout the length and breadth of France in order to meet her payments and save Rustrel. Bishop Villecourt told Pauline that her task would be made easier if she would get a letter from the Central Council of the Society for the Propagation of the Faith, a letter recognizing her as foundress of the Society and explaining why she needed contributions to sustain her work. The Central Council in Paris refused to give Pauline such a letter, for, it insisted, her claim to being foundress of the Society was preposterous. She was not even at the organization meeting in May of 1822. There was some justification for the Council's stand, because thirty years had elapsed since Pauline had been associated with the Society, and, as Pauline herself put it, "why should a match expect to be talked about?"

The Council remained obdurate when Pauline's friends tried to intercede for her. Frédéric Ozanam, a native of Lyons, wrote in some detail how Mlle. Jaricot had started the Society at Saint-Vallier and Lyons. Several others wrote in similar vein, but the Council refused to accept such testimony. It even went so far as to order local councils that were in favor of helping Pauline not to use the machinery of the Society to gather funds for her cause. Later on, when Pope Pius IX requested the Society to pay off Pauline's debt if it were possible—as a matter of justice, the Holy Father said—the Council sent back to the Pope the flat answer that it was impossible.

Rustrel was almost seized time after time, each time the quarterly interest payment fell due, it seemed; but Pauline managed for several years to scrape together enough to meet the interest payments. Finally, though, in 1852 she failed, and the property was sold for one third the sum she had paid for it six years before. She was left with a debt of 430,000 francs, and now her one worldly ambition was to pay off that debt before she died. So her begging continued through the last ten years of her life. Often she was cruelly humiliated as she went through Lyons, and then throughout France, a tired, shabby, elderly lady, who pinched *sous* and *centimes* now, trying desperately to add them up to 430,000 francs before she should die. She must have suffered a certain amount of disillusionment, too, in seeing how her businesslike approach to Church problems had this time produced nothing but material failure. Certainly she was disillusioned in her own middle class – a group in France which has always been prone to consider itself the salt of the earth.

Thus Pauline wrote to Count de Bremond, who with his wife did so much to help her in these dark days: "You must not expect anything of the rich, unless indeed they are poor in spirit. Count much more on the poor, the workingmen and women, the servants, the humble souls, who know how to deny themselves and give as the Gospel taught the early Christians." Again, in similar words she advised her associates to "count little on those rich in the goods of the world, to count greatly on the poor, the workers who know how to deprive themselves to give that charity which the Church had asked of the first Christians."

By one device and another Pauline cut down expenses at Lorette, dismissing her Daughters, living on little but bread and cheese, turning every *sou* she could obtain toward paying of the debt. One by one she paid off small investors, and then she drew a line through each one's name. But there were still many names, some with large amounts after them, when Pauline Jaricot died in her sixty-third year, on January 9, 1862. After her death Lorette was sold for 135,000 francs – she had long offered it on the market for the amount of her outstanding obligations – and the sum was applied to the debt she had worked so long to resolve. The remainder was paid off by her nephews.

This lady who had successfully applied the businesslike principles of her class to Church institutions thus passed from this earth a worldly failure. Her cause was introduced in Rome in 1930; and as this book is being written, reports of additional miracles connected with Pauline Jaricot appear in the papers. If she is someday canonized, she will likely enough become the patron saint of failures. From any but a worldly point of view, however, Pauline Jaricot was far from a failure. And her greatest success was the way she accepted the bitterness of her failure at Rustrel — a hard thing for any mortal to do, but especially hard and humiliating for Antoine Jaricot's daughter. The Curé of Ars observed of Pauline that "she knew how to accept the cross — the heaviest cross — with love." This was the most important thing about this remarkable and important French lady. Pope Leo XIII said that her work "brought her rebuff, blame, calumnies, contempt, and whatever could cast down the most steadfast soul. . . . By her faith, hope, fortitude, meekness and ready acceptance of every trial, she proved herself to be the true disciple of Christ."

Pauline Marie Jaricot is an important layman in the nineteenth century, for she founded the Society for the Propagation of the Faith, which shortly became an integral part of the Church Militant, and she established the Association of the Living Rosary, an important part of the Church Praying. But she is important too, perhaps even more — who knows? — because she prayed and suffered. In this way she made a personal offering to God as her contribution to a Church growing strong and healthy again during her lifetime.

6. Frédéric Ozanam

Not far from the Jaricot home, in the city of Lyons, at midnight on April 23, 1813, a son was born to Dr. and Mrs. Jean-Antoine Ozanam. They named him Antoine-Frédéric. It was fortunate for the Church and for the poor that this baby did not die, as had ten of the Ozanams' other children. It is fortunate because Frédéric Ozanam lived to breathe a spirit of love into relief work in the nineteenth century, a spirit which came like a cool breeze across a century that could find no place for charity in its scheme of life. Ozanam worked for the poor because he loved them as his brothers in Christ, and he did this in an age when his contemporaries considered the poor dirty and annoying, but necessary inconveniences to be handled with the least trouble and expense possible.

Ozanam loved even the enemies of his Church, for he understood them and he pitied them and he prayed for them — whereas most of his contemporaries sought to honor God by refuting the heretic with vinegar and vitriol. If Montalembert, Windthorst, and others who fought for Christ in the nineteenth century can properly be considered crusaders for God and liberty, then Ozanam can best be remembered as the Good Samaritan who went along on the crusade to care for the wounded, to minister to their material and spiritual needs, to comfort the suffering — both his crusaders and the enemies. Who knows — for there is good historical evidence to believe it — but that this Good Samaritan won more battles and captured more prisoners with his cup of water than his crusader friends did with their strong swords?

Providence put young Frédéric Ozanam in the right place at the right time. Lyons, we have seen, was an industrial town where the workers suffered and sweat, where they struck and rioted, where they were shot down in the streets by troops from the capital. Lyons was a town, above the others of France, which saw the ugly side of industrial life, the suffering and cynicism and hate which seemed by-products of the factory system. The Ozanams, however, were comfortably fixed, neither poor enough to suffer privation, like most of the people of Lyons, nor wealthy enough to have all they might want, as were the Jaricots. They were a family of remote Jewish ancestry, originally the Hosannams, who had been converted to the Catholic Faith in the seventh century. Since that time various members of the family had distinguished themselves as mathematicians, as religious, as professors. Frédéric's father was known through the city as much for his charitable work as for his professional excellence, and his mother was distinguished both for her cultural gifts and for her Christian goodness. Frédéric's home life was ideally suited to prepare him for his profession as teacher at the Sorbonne and for his apostolate of charity in Paris. He grew up in a cultured household, under the careful supervision of his parents, among good books and fine music, in morally and materially healthful surroundings.

Dr. Ozanam decided his second son should be a lawyer, and dutiful son that he was, Frédéric prepared to follow a career for which he had neither particular interest nor special talent. Besides the usual college courses of mathematics, rhetoric, and philosophy, he studied German, Latin, Greek, English, and Hebrew. These tongues, added to his native languages of French and Italian, put him in touch with most of the world's worthwhile literature. So at the age of seventeen he was graduated from the Royal College of Lyons with the usual classical schooling of the European who intended to study jurisprudence.

Then, because his father thought him too young to enter the University, Frédéric was apprenticed for a year to a local attorney. Here he discovered how little appetite he had for legal work. Here, too, he suffered a period of black doubt, a terrible few months which can be experienced only by bright boys whose early intellectual success tempts them to the sin of Lucifer himself — intellectual pride. Deftly guided by one of his teachers, the Abbé Noirot, young Ozanam came through this dark period to see the sun shining in the valley of faith on the other side. He had suffered more than most young men who doubt that there can be a God beyond themselves, a Truth and a Knowledge outside the ken of their own little minds. He had suffered more than usual because he was so sensitive a creature. Even this short period of doubt helped prepare Ozanam for his apostolate of charity, because it enabled him to understand sympathetically the tortured souls of those who railed against the Catholic Church. Largely because of this youthful temptation, Frédéric Ozanam could deal effectively with those enemies of the Faith whom other Catholics branded as hopeless outcasts, as agents of Satan attacking Christ's Church. That is why Lamartine observed of Ozanam that "one might differ from him, but one could never be polemical with him, for he had no bitterness in his nature. His tolerance was not a concession; it was a form of respect."

In those revolutionary years of 1830 and 1831, preachers of Saint-Simonianism came to Lyons. There they sought to sell their wares to the workers of the city, doctrines which appealed to the workingman in this age because Saint-Simonianism was a romantic form of Socialism directed against Church and State, and promising in their stead a scientifically organized Utopia. The Saint-Simonians' efforts in Lyons provoked an answer from the eighteen-year-old Ozanam in a hundred-page booklet, *Reflexions sur la doctrine de Saint-Simon.* It was a work which attracted the attention of the best minds of the day, men like Lamartine, Lamennais, Chateaubriand, and it drew from them high commendation.

Ozanam himself valued it for a different reason. "The reason why I like this little work," he wrote to his cousin, "is that in it I have planted the seeds of what is to occupy my life." At the age of eighteen he had dedicated himself to writing a many-volumed work which he had already entitled "The Demonstration of the Catholic Religion by the Antiquity and the Universality of the Beliefs and Traditions of the Human Race." It was a romantic thing to do, dedicating his future to writing The Great Work, but this was a romantic age, and young Ozanam was like a knight out of the popular storybook who had chosen his lady fair to defend from that day forever more. "My part is taken," he wrote to his friend Fortoul, "my task is traced for life."

* * *

But Dr. Ozanam's prosaic plans were hard reality intruding into Frédéric's romantic dream. For Dr. Ozanam had decided that his son should go to Paris to begin his legal studies at the university. So in the autumn of 1831, Frédéric Ozanam left Lyons for Paris. Here in this "capital of egotism," as he called it, young Ozanam felt terribly alone. The spirit of Voltaire hung over the city: churches were empty, except for older women; the "enlightened" people were skeptics; the university professors were almost all hostile to religion; faith was considered a superstition for women of weak intelligence. Ozanam was shocked to find only three other practicing Catholics in his classes. For a few long weeks this highly sensitive boy was friendless in a Paris that seemed the Enemy's capital. He had only his God to pray to and his mother to write to.

Before long, however, Frédéric found stimulating companionship with a few young men of like views. André-Marie Ampère, the saintly scientist, had offered Ozanam a room in his household, and here Frédéric met the leading figures in the early nineteenth-century Catholic revival: Chateaubriand, still the dean of the Catholic group in Paris; Lamennais, Lacordaire, and Montalembert of *L'Avenir;* Lamartine, the poet, who was still a leader in the Catholic circles he was soon to leave; Karl Friedrich von Savigny, later to be associated with Windhorst in the German Center Party; Eckstein, the Danish popularizer of De Maistre's traditionalism; Mickiewicz, the famed Polish poet; and many others. This was a group which for high and varied intellectual ability has perhaps not been surpassed in modern times. These were gifted individuals who lived in one of the exciting and productive periods of French intellectual history.

At the university young Ozanam soon found himself associated with a small group of select students who were intent on promoting a Catholic revival in religiously arid France. Properly enough, the university professors were their first target. Ozanam took the lead in challenging the professors' attacks upon the Church by sending his objections to the professors in writing. These objections often proved embarrassing for the teachers who were not accustomed to having to prove their often unfounded assertions, and sometimes weeks passed before the lecturer could prepare a suitable answer.

Ozanam and his associates also organized a history club. They felt that they could vindicate the Church to their contemporaries through history – for they saw how much bad history was used to support the irreligious professors' attacks on the Church, and they saw how splendidly the Church stood forth in European cultural and social history. The historical approach was part of the reaction, in France and the Germanies and England too, against the rationalism of the older thinkers. It was natural, then, for the young men of this romantic age to look to history for ammunition with which to defend their Church, as Görres and other German Catholics were then doing. The History Conference became an open forum where both sides of the burning questions of the day could be presented, because it was in this way that Ozanam's group thought they could attract and then convert students who belonged to the enemy camp.

Like college boys at all times, they put naïve trust in the persuasive power of truth. The debating society—for that is what it soon became—grew and prospered, but Ozanam was sorely disappointed in its results. He found that college boys love to argue far into the night, but he also found that they were not as hospitable as he had thought in entertaining truth in the parlors of their minds. He discovered what older men all know: that human beings enjoy wearing the intellectual blinders of prejudice, that it is the rare man indeed who does not lower the ken of his vision to the road at his feet. Something more was needed to convert these young men to the Faith. What that something was Ozanam, even with his keen mind and his perfect honesty, could not discover.

For a time he continued to put his trust in the power of argument. One day, when he heard the eloquent Lacordaire preach, he decided that this "is the man we want to confound Jouffroy [who was the most capable and influential enemy of the Church on the university faculty]." So Ozanam and his friends asked the archbishop of Paris to commission Lacordaire to preach a series of conferences at Notre Dame Cathedral. Here was a man, they respectfully informed Archbishop de Quelen, who possessed the reasoning power and the eloquence to convert thousands who remained in the dark because they had not seen the light of the truth. But the shadow of the *L'Avenir* episode still hung over Lacordaire in 1832, so the archbishop denied their request.

Two years later, early in 1834, Ozanam presented another petition to the archbishop, this one signed by two hundred young men, to have Lacordaire preach a series of Lenten sermons at Notre Dame Cathedral, sermons, the petition stated, "which would display Christianity in all its grandeur, and in harmony with the aspirations and necessities of man and society." This time the archbishop was moved by the young man's zeal for the Church – but, typical older ecclesiastic that he was, and therefore fearful of the "radical" Lacordaire, he selected seven "safer" men to preach the Lenten sermons. They were safe sermons, dull, uninspiring – and unattended. Meanwhile, Ozanam's crowd listened to Lacordaire at Saint-Stanislaus College, and they bemoaned the fact that Lacordaire's eloquence was cooped up in a chapel when most of the seats at the cathedral were empty.

A year later the college crowd was successful. For at last the archbishop commissioned Lacordaire to preach a series of six Lenten sermons. The cathedral was jammed for each sermon, and the thousands who heard Lacordaire were enthusiastic if they were Catholic, or at least deeply moved if they were not. Perhaps Ozanam's enthusiasm colored his comment when he wrote that "we seemed to be assisting not at the resurrection of Catholicity, for it never dies, but at the religious resurrection of society"; but the fact remains that his persistence with the archbishop of Paris had led to the establishing of the famous Notre Dame Conferences which have continued for more than a century to be bright lights in the history of the Church in France. Thus before he was twenty-one, Frédéric Ozanam had played a leading role in founding the Notre Dame Conferences and in bringing to light the most famous French preacher of the century.

Meanwhile, one of the Saint-Simonians who participated in the heated arguments of the history club had, quite by accident, told Ozanam what was needed in addition to good arguments in order to win converts. During the course of a debate on the benefits the Church had conferred upon Europe, this young man cut Ozanam short by saying: "In past centuries Christianity did marvellous things. But what is it doing for mankind now? And you, who pride yourself on being a Catholic, what are you doing for the poor? Where are those tangible results which alone will teach us the practical value of your faith? We await them, for it is through them that we shall be converted."

* * *

This was the challenge from which the St. Vincent de Paul Society took its origin. Ozanam was honest enough with himself to see how he and his group had been "put on the spot" by the Saint-Simonians. He had to put up good works, the college crowd would say today, or else shut up. As he thought the challenge over on his way home from the meeting, Ozanam decided that this practical activity, this concrete proving of the Church's mission by works of charity, was what converted men in modern times. It was by action more than by words that souls could be won for Christ. Had not He Himself said: "By their fruits you shall know them"? So this young man suddenly realized that up until then he had concentrated exclusively on good arguments. In the future he would concentrate rather on good works.

Ozanam therefore decided to go to the poor. And thus was founded the St. Vincent de Paul Society in the spring of 1833. One evening in May of that year, six students met in the office of Emmanuel Joseph Bailly, editor of *La Tribune Catholique.* There they banded together to serve the poor by bringing them both material gifts and spiritual help. Although Bailly presided at the meeting and was elected first president of the original St. Vincent de Paul conference, nevertheless, the true founder of the organization was young Frédéric Ozanam. The original members all agree in telling us that his was the dominant spirit, his was the guiding voice, his was the energy that quickened them, and his was the determination that rendered their conference a permanent organization. There has never been any question about Ozanam's being the founder of the St. Vincent de Paul Society, as there has been question about Pauline Marie Jaricot's rightful title as foundress of the Society for the Propagation of the Faith.

Thus at the age of twenty, Frédéric Ozanam had begun his greatest and most effective work in life. The new organization attracted attention because of its vigor, and soon the original seven were faced with the crucial decision of whether or not to admit new members. Here again Ozanam's was the decisive voice. He pleaded eloquently both for taking in the eighth member, Gustave de la Noue, and for a general policy of opening the door to all who desired admission. A year later, after the group had grown to an unwieldy collection of more than one hundred enthusiastic young men, there arose the question of splitting into several conferences or halting growth then and there. Argument grew warm, then it waxed hot, whereupon prudent "Papa" Bailly adjourned the meeting. In the next meeting, and the next, the question was heatedly debated – and there were excellent arguments on both sides. In the end, however, Ozanam had his way. A second conference was established. More important, a precedent was established from which thousands more would be founded in the years to come.

In those first years the St. Vincent de Paul Society grew amazingly. It grew so quickly, in fact, that its very size would have killed it – as has happened to other Catholic Action groups which have mushroomed up in the past – if it were not for the strong, truly charitable spirit of the original founders, a spirit which was caught up in the constitution and which has sustained all those St. Vincent de Paul conferences which have thrived in the past hundred years. It is a spirit which differentiates this Society from philanthropic organizations and "scientific" social work groups, for the latter are secular institutions moved by a worldly humanitarianism, whereas the soul of the true St. Vincent de Paul conference is the supernatural virtue of charity.

The Vincentian Rule was drawn up and adopted in 1836. It was "based on what the conferences have learned," Bailly reported to the first general conference, "not on theory." It is a rule whereby one may distinguish true charity from mere philanthropy. It breathes the spirit of love, and it therefore puts material gifts in their proper place as material things. But by infusing them with the spirit of charity, it gives them a value that merely material things, however costly, can never have. The giving of help by a St. Vincent de Paul group, when it is done according to the spirit of the constitution, benefits both the giver and the recipient. Nor can the recipient ever feel socially inferior to those who have aided him – as is the case when he receives formalized, institutionalized help from "the charities," after filling out many forms to prove that he is "a deserving case."

The first objective of the St. Vincent de Paul Society, as stated by the Rule, is to sustain its members "in the practice of a Christian life." Secondly, the members are "to visit the poor at their dwellings, to bring them succor in kind, to afford them, also, religious consolation." The Rule dwells on the spirit of charity as against the mere giving of aid to the poor. "We should be kind and obliging to one another," it reads, "and we should be equally so to the poor whom we visit. . . . It is a brotherly spirit which will make our Society of Charity become beneficial to its members and edifying to others. . . . Let us love one another." This is the spirit of Ozanam. This is the secret of his success through the society he founded. And it is, perhaps, the secret of its amazing growth. Within two years of his death in 1853 there were almost 3000 conferences spread throughout the world: in France and its dependencies, in the Germanies, in England and Ireland, in the countries of both North and South America, even in Africa and Asia.

By the time Frédéric Ozanam had reached the age of twenty-one, then, when one is supposed to leave the stage of being a child to become a man, he had accomplished his two greatest works of charity, which have grown and prospered down to the present day. He had established the Notre Dame Conferences to bring Truth to those who lived in Darkness – and this is the greatest charity of all. He had established the St. Vincent de Paul Society to succor the poor and to give practical proof to a skeptical world that the Catholic Church was the true Spouse of Christ. One should remember that both establishments were parts of a bigger purpose that young Ozanam had proposed to himself back at Lyons: the demonstration to the world that the claims of the Catholic Church were valid. Ozanam was first and foremost an apologist, one who understood and loved his brothers, one who therefore wanted to share with them the Truth he possessed. Both the Notre Dame Conferences and the St. Vincent de Paul Society had that for their purpose. Both were aimed at ultimately winning converts because Ozanam loved God and all His creatures as few men in modern times have loved.

* * *

It is not easy for an American or an Englishman to evaluate Ozanam's character and personality. There is no doubt that he was a saintly person – his cause for canonization has been introduced in Rome – and that he appeared to his contemporaries as the essence of goodness. Even his enemies respected his goodness and, in their various ways, they loved him. The typical Anglo-Saxon is likely, at first glance, to consider Ozanam effeminate. But closer acquaintance would convince even the roughest of Americans that this Frenchman was thoroughly masculine. Nevertheless, he was highly sensitive, almost too sensitive a soul to live long and to thrive in this rough modern world. He suffered acutely with those who suffered, he was most miserable with those in misery. Social injustice, material want, spiritual poverty all cut him to the quick when he came upon them, for Ozanam had never calloused himself to his brothers' suffering. His correspondence reveals that throughout his life he exhibited freely those qualities which most men hide in shame: a tenderness, an almost bashful modesty, a graciousness and a thoughtfulness which are too often associated with refined women and not enough with men. He was a kind friend to his young associates and later to his students, looking after them as an older member of a large family looks after the younger brothers and sisters.

But those who came to know Frédéric Ozanam well found that he was not at all effeminate. His position of leadership among his fellows is eloquent testimony to his true masculinity. He was respected by his associates and by his students for his courage, for his integrity, and for that manly toughness of character which they discovered beneath his tender exterior. It was because there was no question of his masculinity that he could afford to be tender – a seeming paradox, but something almost universally true, for those who are really masculine do not need to assume the so-called "manly" ways. And there was never any question of Ozanam's courage. As a student he possessed the moral courage to challenge his professors' assertions against his faith, to profess his religion publicly in the history club when it was smart to be antireligious, to address repeated petitions to the archbishop (something timorous students cannot do) that Lacordaire be commissioned to preach the Lenten sermons at Notre Dame Cathedral. These things required moral courage.

Ozanam possessed physical courage too. He joined the National Guard to help put down the revolution of 1848 because, though he was a democrat through and through and sympathized with the Parisian rioters, still he thought it was his duty to support the government. He stood long hours alone at his assigned corner in Paris, showing himself to be courageous in a quiet way, without display, without bravado. Although he was genuinely relieved not to have to shoot at anyone during the bloody June insurrection of 1848, still he stood at his post ready to shoot if duty should require it.

There were occasions when Frédéric Ozanam showed the highest kind of moral courage possible, that kind of courage which is a rare jewel in the modern world. Such an occasion occurred when one of his fellow professors at the Sorbonne became a Catholic. Charles Lenormant's students were incited by other professors to prevent the convert from lecturing at the university. They hissed and booed and made it impossible for Lenormant to begin his lecture – until Ozanam entered the classroom, risking his position at the University of Paris, to upbraid the students for their cowardly conduct and for violating the very principles of freedom of discussion they were allegedly defending. The students respected Ozanam for his unrequired display of courage and charity, and they allowed their professor to deliver his lecture. Again, Ozanam showed a reckless kind of courage by appearing in the classroom, when he heard it rumored that he was too lazy and too solicitous of his health, to deliver his appointed lecture even though his physicians and his wife forbade him to leave his sickbed. That was the last lecture Ozanam gave at the University of Paris, for in the next year he died without having regained his strength in the meantime.

Frédéric Ozanam was a man of high, acute intelligence. His booklet against the Socialists, written when he was eighteen, was no high school exercise. It was a solid, mature piece of work. His work as a student at the University of Paris was outstanding, and it was completed with a brilliant doctoral examination which Ozanam's friends and biographers report was one of the intellectual feats of the century. This man who seems at first glance to have been so busy with so many practical matters, then, was a brilliant student with an absorbing interest in cultural history. His insight into historical truth, his zeal in searching it out in the literature of the past and in long-forgotten documents, combined with his ability to present it engagingly, were qualities that might have made him a leading historian of the century if he had lived the professor's ordinary span of years. But Ozanam died when he was forty, thus closing his career as professor of modern romance languages at the University of Paris and bringing to an end a life that had been devoted to the service of his poorer brothers and, especially in the last years, to reaching the highest levels of holiness himself.

* * *

We have seen how Frédéric Ozanam had founded his two great works, the Notre Dame Conferences and the St. Vincent de Paul Society, before he finished school. But his lifework was far from done when he received his law degree, for in his remaining years he produced a number of scholarly studies, all of them parts of that Great Work he envisioned as a boy of eighteen, and he developed a body of advanced politico-social thought which was aimed at reconciling the new civilization with the old Catholicism. In both these fields, in historical scholarship and in reconciling God and liberty, Ozanam was the superior of Montalembert. Early in life he developed both a scholarly instinct and a feeling for social problems which Montalembert's social position prevented him from developing. Ozanam received a solid bourgeois schooling, a training which was exacting and systematic, whereas Montalembert's education was a hit-and-miss affair. Ozanam walked the slums of Paris and knew the poor by name, whereas Montalembert sympathized with them in an unknowing way because he had never been in their homes or talked with them when they were feverishly sick in bed.

In the last two decades of his life Ozanam advanced in holiness much as Pauline Jaricot was doing in the same years, though his life was serene and materially successful as compared with hers. He completed his legal studies in the spring of 1836, but he found law too sordid a business for his sensitive nature. "Fees come with difficulty," he complained, "and the relations with business people are so unpleasant, so humiliating, and so unjust that I cannot bring myself to develop them." So Frédéric Ozanam returned from Lyons to Paris to follow the career of professor of literature. There he obtained the chair of foreign literature at the Sorbonne, a position he discharged with brilliance in the last twelve years of his short life.

Ozanam had never given up his vocation of defending the

Church to "moderns" of his age. For a time he thought he could discharge this vocation best by becoming a priest, and at one point in his life he had almost made up his mind to join Lacordaire in the Dominican Order. His close adviser, Abbé Noirot, told him – and rightly, it would seem – that he was temperamentally unfitted for the cloister. This advice, coupled with his own experience of the Church's need for lay apostles, convinced him that he could best discharge his vocation by marrying, raising a family, and teaching young men in the university. These things he did with eminent success – and meanwhile he continued to promote the St. Vincent de Paul Society and to write articles in defense of the Church, both regarding its great role in the past and its place in nineteenth-century European civilization.

For the dozen years left to him, Frédéric Ozanam lectured at the Sorbonne and wrote learned treatises on various aspects of the history of literature. His lectures were brilliant contributions to the knowledge of literature as a telescope through which to view the past. They entailed a tremendous amount of work, for Professor Ozanam had to compile each lecture by culling through old manuscripts, reading and interpreting masterpieces of days gone by, and relating it all to the political and cultural history in which it was set. His writings were all directed toward showing the role of the Church in creating the culture of Europe in medieval and early modern times. Each of them, to borrow the simile of his biographer Hughes, was a fragment "of the great monument to the glory of God and of the Church which he had hoped some day to be able to build." Each was a "solid block of masonry which will resist the ravages of time, finished pieces of sculpture which charm the eye of the connoisseur." Ozanam's historical writings outrank those of Chateaubriand and Montalembert and have earned for him first place among the literary and historical students of the neo-Catholic movement in France during the first half of the century.

Ozanam's lectures and books should be viewed as chapters in the Great Work he dedicated his life to writing when he was a young man of eighteen at Lyons, for they are all apologetic in nature, aimed at showing the civilizing role the Church had played in European history. So evident was the apologetic content of his courses that one day there appeared on the door of his classroom the label "Cours de théologie." But Ozanam had no desire to twist historical truth in order to defend the Church. "We must learn to praise the majesty of cathedrals and the heroism of crusades," he wrote, "without condoning the horrors of an eternal war, the harshness of feudal institutions, the scandal of a perpetual strife of kings with the Holy See for their divorces and their simonies. We must see the evil as it was, that is, in its formidable aspect, precisely that we may better recognize the services of the Church, whose glory it was throughout those scantily studied ages not to have reigned, but to have struggled."

Ozanam's approach to those outside the faith differed noticeably from that of Montalembert and Veuillot – both of whom he admired for their daring and for their love for the Church. But Ozanam was more scrupulously honest, more fair-minded, more scientifically interested in truth than either Montalembert or Veuillot. "I am sometimes charged with excessive gentleness towards unbelievers," Ozanam wrote to his brother after Veuillot had accused him of deserting the Catholic cause. "When one has passed, as I have, through the crucible of doubt, it would indeed be cruelty and ingratitude to be harsh to those to whom God has not yet vouchsafed to give the priceless gift of faith." He therefore insisted that in apologetics "we must not compromise the holiness of the cause by the violence of the means. . . . Begin by pitying the unbeliever; he is already wretched enough. . . . It is never a question of mortifying but of convincing him."

It must be added that Ozanam's work has stood the test of time better than has Montalembert's or Veuillot's, for Ozanam was never so interested in winning an argument that he forgot to state the truth scrupulously and completely or to understand his opponent's point of view. Thus when the heat of controversy passed, Ozanam's works still stand as solid pieces of literary history – and they serve the purpose of pointing out to all who are not blinded by prejudice the civilizing influence of the Church and its essential role in creating that culture of which Europeans are still the heirs.

* * *

Frédéric Ozanam is also important for his social and political philosophy. Primarily a man of action, Ozanam never evolved a systematic body of social thought, as did De Maistre or Donoso Cortés or even Montalembert. He felt that Christianity was more than a sphere of thought and worship, that it was also a field of action and of conduct. "How much better actions are than words," he exclaimed, "and how ashamed I am of my role of scribbler, which I fill so badly." So Ozanam never separated his social theory from his social action. Indeed he arrived at the former through experience in the latter. "Knowledge of social well-being and of reform is to be learned in climbing the stairs of the poor man's garret, sitting by his bedside, feeling the same cold that pierces him, sharing the secret of his lonely heart and troubled mind. When the condition of the poor has been examined, in school, at work, in hospitals, in the city and the country, everywhere God has placed them, then it is and only then that we know the elements of that formidable social problem, only then can we begin to grasp it and have hopes of solving it."

Because Ozanam approached the problems of his age through the poor family's garret, he naturally arrived at a solution which seemed extremely liberal, even radical, to such other Catholics as Veuillot and Donoso Cortés. He was aware, he wrote to his friend Fortoul, "that the old order is collapsing, that the ancient foundations are shaken," and he therefore concluded his was an age of profound revolution out of which would come a new social order. With more penetrating insight than the other reformers of his age possessed, Ozanam realized that the great question of the day was not one of the suffrage or the organization of parliament. "It is a social question," he wrote to Lallier. "It is a struggle between those who have nothing and those who have too much, the violent clash of opulence and poverty which makes the ground tremble under our feet."

In 1837, more than a decade before Marx had written about class war between the rich and the poor, Ozanam described France as a nation living in two camps. "Here people are not divided by political opinions but by interests. On the one side is the camp of the rich, on the other side that of the poor. In the one selfishness wishes to keep all for itself, in the other selfishness wishes to seize all for itself. Between the two there is an irreconcilable hatred which threatens to cause a war that will be a struggle to extermination." The only solution Ozanam could see for this social problem lay in the full application of Christian principles of justice and especially charity. "Christians," he said, "must fling themselves between the two camps in the name of charity so that prejudices will be destroyed, the weapons of hate dropped, and the two camps brought together, not to fight but to be reconciled."

Ozanam therefore pleaded with Catholics, especially with the clergy and the rich bourgeoisie, to concern themselves with the problem of the poor, not so much the poor who begged as those who worked and still starved. He advocated a social arrangement which would put a limit on the amount of wealth any one person could acquire. "He who taught us to pray for our daily bread nowhere advises us to secure to ourselves ten years of luxury." The rich, therefore, should be less wealthy and the poor less poor. To many French Catholics, as to almost all the Liberals, this seemed radical indeed. That is why Ozanam warned his followers not to be "frightened when the wicked rich, irritated by your pleading, treat you as communists." He understood how essentially a Christian social program differed from the secularistic socialism of the Saint-Simonians, but because there were so few who knew the meaning of charity in his day, Ozanam's solution to the social question was not understood until after the publication of Leo XIII's *Rerum Novarum* in 1891.

The solution as Ozanam saw it, was simple – but hard to achieve. "Do away with misery," is the way he put it. "Christianize the people, and you will make an end of revolutions." The failure of Christians to do this very thing, especially the failure of the clergy, he wrote to his brother who was a priest, had brought on the revolution of 1848. As practical, immediate steps he suggested a "reform of morals through education rather than through legislation." He proposed night schools for the adults, schools for apprentices, libraries, and co-operative societies in which the laborers could learn to work together and to develop a sense of corporate living and of real brotherhood. Back of all these practical ideas lay Ozanam's insistence that without charity the problems created by industrialism could never be solved. These suggestions, made as they were in the early days of the industrial revolution, reveal Ozanam as a far-seeing social thinker who somehow felt his way toward the solution that was to be more fully worked out by Catholic sociologists of a later day. He was able to discern the outlines of the problem before others saw it was social and economic rather than political, and he was able to suggest the right solution because he was one of the few social thinkers who knew the poor personally. Whereas Marx poured over statistics in the London Museum and Montalembert sympathized with the poor without seeing the inside of their homes, Ozanam climbed the rickety back stairs to sit beside the sick wage earner's bed, thus to see how much misery was involved in one more case of unemployment. So when there were 267,000 unemployed in Paris in 1848, Ozanam understood what that meant as perhaps no one else of his age could understand it.

Politically Ozanam was a thorough democrat. And he was converted to democracy — strange as it might seem to modern Liberals — by Pope Pius IX. His visit to Rome took place in the days when the Holy Father was still the most liberal of all European rulers, some several months before the revolution of 1848 in Rome had disillusioned the Pope in the prospects of liberal reform. On his return to Paris, Ozanam gave a lecture in which he advocated "leaving the narrow camp of monarchs and statesmen, and going forward to the people, in order to draw them into the Church. . . . Conquer repugnance and dislike and turn to democracy," he urged them, "to the mass of the people to whom we are unknown. Appeal to them not merely by sermons but by benefits. Help them, not with alms which humiliate, but with social and ameliorative measures which will free and elevate them. Let us go over to the barbarians* and follow Pius IX."

Ozanam believed that democracy was the inevitable result of political progress and that "God leads the world thither." He

* This was an allusion to the way the Church survived the fall of the Roman Empire by "going over to the barbarians" and converting them, thus saving European society from complete barbarization. Ozanam saw the old social arrangements collapsing as the Roman Empire had done, and the proletariat coming to a position of control. Hence the allusion, which was not understood by his listeners to imply any contempt for the masses.

saw that the people would soon hold sovereignty in their own hands – and this, he insisted, would be a good thing if the people were sufficiently educated to use their power intelligently and sufficiently Christian to use it justly. "Must not a government elected by the vote of the people," he asked, "understand better the needs of the people and the duties of the State? Let us side with it, let us trust in it, let us work out the ideal of the Church under a new regime."

These were words with which Montalembert heartily agreed until the revolution of 1848 disillusioned the Count, as it did so many other formerly democratic Catholics. But Ozanam never lost faith in the people – even when he stood guard at his appointed post during the June days of 1848 ready to shoot. When the revolution was crushed, and when Montalembert and Veuillot backed Louis Napoleon as the alternative to communism, Ozanam and Abbé Lacordaire started a democratic paper *L'Ere Nouvelle* ("The New Age"), in order to reconcile Catholics with the short-lived Second Republic, to the mutual advantage of the Church and modern society. In his paper Ozanam warned his readers: "It is not enough to save France once or several times; a great country needs to be saved every day. You go and come now from one end of the city to the other in peace and security, but the danger which you flatter yourselves has disappeared from the streets is hid away in the garrets of the houses on either side. You have crushed insurrection; you must now deal with an enemy with which you are not acquainted, which you dislike hearing about, and on which we are determined to speak to you today – misery!" After peace seemed restored, Ozanam went on to advise Catholics that "it is time to prove that we can plead the cause of the proletariat, to pledge ourselves to the solace of suffering classes, to seek the abolition of poverty, without becoming an adherent to the doctrines which unchained the tempest of June and which are still spreading their dark clouds about us."

L'Ere Nouvelle was abreast of the times – but its thought was too far advanced for royalist Catholics like Veuillot and even for liberal Catholics like Montalembert. So when Ozanam and Lacordaire found that their paper divided Catholic forces in that critical period instead of converting them to their political views, they decided to cease publication. If Ozanam's view had prevailed instead of Veuillot's the history of the Church in France through the past century might have been a happier one — but that is one of those *ifs* about which speculation is idle, for it is also possible that a triumphant Liberalism and a victorious democracy would have driven the Church from France by the middle of the century. It is certain, however, that Ozanam's views were the ones eventually followed by the Church when it became possible a half century later to separate the wheat of democracy from the chaff of Liberalism.* His social and economic views can be found in *Rerum Novarum,* his political views in Leo XIII's *ralliement* policy.**

* * *

After the turmoil of revolution had subsided in the summer of 1848, Ozanam prepared to resume his classes at the Sorbonne at the beginning of the fall session. Only five more years were allotted to the young professor, and half of them were to be years of desperate illness. But he set about continuing his work of lecturing, writing, visiting the sick, and carrying on a voluminous correspondence with his friends. Against the advice of his relatives and his doctor he continued to lecture at the university, for, as he put it to his brother, "I am a worker and I must do my day's work." He delivered his last lecture in the spring of 1852, and in the summer he left Paris with his wife and daughter for a vacation trip to the South.

This turned out to be the last of Frédéric Ozanam's pilgrimages. It was in many respects much like the others he had made ever since he began to lecture at the Sorbonne. He always managed to find places which were supposed to be healthful, where there were sea breezes and warm sunshine, but where also there were manuscripts he could examine, saints' shrines to which he could retreat for prayer, and cities in which he could establish yet another St. Vincent de Paul conference. So it was on this last pilgrimage. He visited Spain and began there his *Pilgrimage Into the Land of the Cid,* and later, when he went to Italy,

* This point is discussed more fully in later chapters, especially in those on Donoso Cortés, Louis Veuillot, and Wilfrid Ward.

** A fuller explanation of this policy will be found in the following chapter, for it was in De Mun's lifetime that it was formulated by the Pope.

wrote his *Bible of the Sick*, an inspiring little book which has helped many of those "who labor and are heavy-laden" to whom he dedicated it. In Italy, where he spent the winter of 1852, he visited many conferences of the St. Vincent de Paul Society, and in Leghorn he delivered his last public address, fittingly enough to the Vincentians of that city.

Six weeks before he died, Frédéric Ozanam helped establish a conference of the Society in Siena, one of the few Italian cities not to have one by 1853. He found that the wealthy people of the city were unwilling to visit the poor in their homes, and he left Siena depressed by his failure. But he wrote one of his most moving – and one of his last – letters to Padre Pendola urging that priest to do all he could to establish a conference in his native Siena. "These young gentlemen [of Siena]," Ozanam wrote to Padre Pendola, "must learn to know what are hunger, thirst, and the destitution of a garret. They must look at wretched fellow-creatures, sick and noisy children. They must look at them and love them. Such a sight will pull at their heart-strings or this generation is lost." Such was the spirit of Ozanam and of the St. Vincent de Paul Society. Incidentally, Ozanam received a telegram on the feast of St. Vincent informing him that two conferences had been established at Siena, one at the college and the other in the city.

Eventually Ozanam grew too weak to leave his bed. He walked to church for the last time on the Feast of the Assumption, and three weeks later, on the Feast of Our Lady's Birthday, September 8, 1853, he died a peaceful death. Present were his younger brother Charles, a physician who could no longer give him professional aid, and his older brother Alphonse, a priest who could. Thus passed the remarkable Frenchman, still a young man of forty, who had accomplished so much good in his short span of life.

He is best known, as we have seen, as founder of the St. Vincent de Paul Society. It was important that he established the Society, but it was more important that he breathed into it his own spirit of burning charity. So it was with his other great establishment, the Notre Dame Conferences, which have continued to bring the truth to spiritually starved listeners this past century. But Ozanam did more than found these two societies which bring truth and charity to those in need. They, indeed, might be called his hobbies. His professional work consisted in presenting truth to his students through his lectures and to the world at large through his books. Both as a lecturer and as a writer he combined the erudition of a scholar with true brilliance of style. Thus Lacordaire could say: "One was as natural to him as the other. He was great when stirring up the dust about him with the miner's mattock, and great in the full light of day with the direct glance of the mind's eye. It was this that composed his moral nature—a mixture of solidity with young and ardent enthusiasm." In the last months of his life Ozanam summed up his career by observing: "I have never worked for the praise of men, but always for the service of truth." He illustrated this in his historical studies and in his social theorizing—both of which have stood the test of time better than has the work of his contemporaries.

In one other way Ozanam was important. He prayed and suffered, as did his fellow citizen of Lyons, Pauline Marie Jaricot. His saintliness impressed his friends and acquaintances as much as it has impressed posterity. His friend Montalembert, for example, appreciated the rare worth of this fellow crusader for Christ, and when he heard of Ozanam's untimely death he wrote to Frédéric's wife: "He leaves to us, as to you, Madame, the almost complete certainty of his immediate and eternal happiness. It is not for one like me to speak of God and heaven to a soul still flooded with the light which radiated from the deathbed of such a Christian as he. . . . When you pray for him, and with him, when you seek his soul in the serene regions in which it awaits yours, please, Madame, remember me at least once, offer him the pious grief of an old friend, of an old fellow-member of the Society of Saint Vincent de Paul, of an old soldier in the same cause, who will forget neither his instruction nor his example."

7. Albert de Mun

The first half of the nineteenth century was a romantic age, as we have seen, an age when men believed in the goodness and the reasonableness of mankind, when it was commonly thought that humanity could be saved by oratory and by properly devised constitutions. It was a time when Socialist thought was utopian, when reformers appealed to the decency of those in power and, like Ozanam, tried to use the personal approach in solving the problems of their day. By 1860, however, Romanticism was giving way to that harder attitude of mind commonly known as Realism. Bismarck epitomized the change well when he observed that great changes are effected by blood and iron rather than by words and good wishes. Socialism became "scientific," natural science replaced philosophy as the most important branch of studies, politics became hard, literature began to take on its "realistic" appearance.

Such a changed atmosphere was bound to influence Catholic social reformers who, after all, lived in the new climate and lived by breathing it. Thus we find Albert de Mun's approach to the social problem a different one from Ozanam's or Pauline Jaricot's. Where the latter two had asked the rich to help the poor and where they had tried to solve the social problem through the private action of individual people, De Mun tried to solve it through proper legislation. He was a pioneer in attempting to achieve social justice through State action. Where his predecessors had relied on man's good will, De Mun relied on the police power of the State. Nor was he wrong in doing so. For it was evident by 1860 that Ozanam's approach could not by itself solve the social problems created by the industrial revolution. His solution was good – but men of the nineteenth century were too hard of heart and too obstinate of mind to accept it. Something more in tune with the time was needed. And this is what De Mun proposed to supply.

Count Albert de Mun was a crusader like Montalembert. A professional soldier himself, he came from a family that had been in the military service of France since medieval times. One of his ancestors had served with St. Louis at Damietta, and all through the centuries of modern French history one De Mun or another was in his country's service. The family motto was *servir,* a motto which Albert de Mun kept before him throughout his life – when, as a young man, he was a cavalry officer, and later when he was an officer in another kind of army fighting another kind of war. De Mun's career really began when he left active army service in 1872 to take up the social work which he called his "vocation." The first phase of his career lasted for only three years, until 1875, during which time he devoted all his time and effort to organizing workers' clubs in order to promote the religious and social welfare of the laboring class. The second phase consisted of his long battle against the Liberals for social legislation, and the third part of his career was his unsuccessful fight against the Liberals for freedom of education and religion in France.

There is an epilogue to De Mun's career, too, a glorious epilogue for a soldier, when he came out of retirement in 1914 to become "the pulse of the nation's heartbeat" until overwork killed him less than one hundred days after the German army began its march toward Paris. With his pen De Mun did as much as anyone to stop that march on Paris, and when he died even his bitterest enemies willingly admitted that this Catholic lay leader was as loyal to France as he was to his Church.

Throughout his life De Mun battled for three causes: the poor workers of his native country, Frenchmen whom he considered the true descendants of Joan of Arc; the Catholic Church, without which he believed France could not be a healthy nation; and France, the land his fathers had served, the country to which he was loyally devoted. These three causes were inextricably bound together, as far as De Mun was concerned. He could not think of the one without thinking of the others; he could not promote the true welfare of any at the expense of the other two. "I love not only the earth I tread," he once proclaimed in the Chamber of Deputies, "but also the tower under whose shadow I was born, the altar where I said my first prayer, the tomb where those I love rest. These are marks God has left on my heart and on my country. I cannot defend the one without defending the other."

Thus he linked the welfare of his people, the glory of his country, and the prosperity of his Church.

* * *

Count Albert de Mun's early life was uneventful. Until he was thirty, when he discovered his "social vocation," he followed his family's tradition of military service in rather pedestrian fashion. He went to Saint-Cyr, the French West Point, where he proved to be a mediocre student. He failed to get his bachelor of arts degree, but after much difficulty he did manage to get an inferior degree in science. At length, in 1861, he was graduated from Saint-Cyr as a sublieutenant in the cavalry.

For the next ten years he lived the outward life of a typical young French officer, but mentally and spiritually he continued to grow. He served five years in Algeria, during which time he seems to have matured as a thinking man. These years in Africa taught him the value of discipline, both for the individual, who must order his time well, and for society, which can enjoy peace and order only when the individuals composing it subject themselves to some kind of discipline. The African service left officers most of their hours to use pretty much as they wished, and De Mun spent his years in that land of immense silences and vast spaces reading voraciously and thinking seriously. In those five years De Mun became thoroughly informed on French colonial problems, and he had dipped into social and political theory deeply enough to have developed an absorbing interest in current French affairs when he left Africa in 1867.

Back in France, young De Mun was assigned to garrison duty at Clermont-Ferrand. There he became interested in St. Vincent de Paul work, thus making his first close contacts with the poor and seeing something of their problems. For three years he continued to see more and more of the terrible social conditions around Paris; but when he was called to active service in the Franco-Prussian War in 1870, he does not seem to have had any inkling of the battle he would soon be waging to improve these conditions. His role in the war was heroic and glorious – like the role of a great halfback on a weak team playing against champions. For his heroic work on the field of Gravelot he was awarded the Legion of Honor, but with thousands of other soldiers in the Army of Metz he was captured by the German forces and sent as a prisoner of war to Aachen.

De Mun's four and a half months of internment became the first of two turning points in his career. During this time he had the provocation, the leisure, the correct reading, and the right companions all to converge toward sending him to his "social vocation." As an officer-prisoner he was treated well, given time to read and talk and think all day long and on into the night. He and a fellow officer prisoner, Count René de la Tour du Pin, later famous as a Catholic social theorist, began to reflect together on the causes of their country's ignominious defeat. Military men, officers in an army that was reputed to be the best in the world, they were predisposed to find their country's weakness in the social fabric of the nation rather than in the army. Nor were they far wrong.

A German Jesuit, Father Eck, who took part in their conversations, loaned them a copy of Emile Keller's provocative little book on the principles of the French Revolution as seen in the light of Pope Pius IX's encyclical *Quanta Cura.* Keller traced the social and political sores from which France suffered through the nineteenth century to the French Revolution. He claimed that the Revolution had inflicted serious wounds on the nation which had festered through the nineteenth century and were now undermining its very life. Moreover, he suggested that a reform of the mind and the morale of France, so deceived by the Revolution, should be the objective of patriotic Frenchmen. Still another influence on De Mun and La Tour du Pin was Doctor Lingens, later to be a prominent member of Windhorst's Center Party, whose home they visited and from whom they received a good briefing on the progress of Social Catholicism in Germany. Thus De Mun learned of Bishop von Ketteler's social program which, in time, became the basis of Pope Leo XIII's *Rerum Novarum.* Here it was in Germany, then, that he conceived his idea of a counterrevolution which was to be social rather than political and which was aimed at saving France by means of reform based on Catholic principles.

But Lieutenant De Mun was still a soldier with a military career before him. In March, 1871, he was again in Paris – just in time to witness the tragic confirmation of his social theories in the bloody Parisian insurrection. As a French soldier De Mun was obliged to help repress the insurrection. He saw the outrages committed by the Communards,* the profanation of altars and the brutal murder of hostages. He saw them die defiant and insolent, and the scene left an indelible impression on his memory. He looked upon the insurrection as a "monstrous crime," but at the same time he felt revulsion against the brutal reprisals visited upon the people of Paris. "Thiers [head of the government]," he wrote, "had no love for the people and his policy toward them was ungenerous."

De Mun was ordered to inquire from Parisian shopkeepers why the insurrection occurred. His investigations shocked him, for he found that the bourgeoisie, those Republicans who considered themselves heirs of the French Revolution and the champions of the people, were ignorant of and indifferent to the problems of the poor. In his report to the Parliamentary Commission he put the blame for the insurrection where it belonged by summing up the causes as being twofold: "the apathy of the bourgeoisie and the ferocious hatred of the masses." The government had done nothing, he charged, to alleviate the suffering of the poor, desperate suffering which drove them to acts of violence. The bourgeoisie were callous and indifferent. The poor despaired and took the only remedy they knew — armed rebellion.

The apprenticeship of this Catholic layman was almost finished. His study in Algeria, his work among the poor at Clermont-Ferrand, his study of De Maistre, De Bonald, Balmes, and Donoso Cortés, his contacts with the German Catholic reformers had been supplemented by the influence of advanced Catholic thinkers in France like La Tour du Pin, Le Play, and Veuillot, and by his personal experience in the Parisian rising of 1871. By this time De Mun had ideas and the determination to act. His plan was to effect a "revolution against the Revolution," but he had no idea of where to begin his campaign, nor did he

* The Parisian insurrection is known as the Paris Commune. Its leaders came from among the people of Paris. They were radical republicans, socialists, and some communists, who refused to recognize the new government that had made peace with Germany. The Parisian rebels are known as Communards — not to be confused with Communist.

know specifically what practical steps he could take to regenerate France socially and spiritually.

This was De Mun's state of mind when, in November of 1871, a Vincentian lay Brother, Maurice Maignen, came to his apartment with an invitation which decided the cavalry officer's future. His life will continue to be one of service, but Maignen's invitation caused De Mun to live up to his family motto *servir* in a new and different way. In his autobiography, *Ma vocation sociale,* De Mun gives a dramatic account of his first encounter with Maignen, who had come to ask his help for a "Club of Young Workers" that Maignen was promoting. De Mun was not impressed by his poorly dressed visitor, even though he saw beneath his rough exterior "the heart of a poet and the imagination of an artist." But when the young officer held aloof, the Vincentian Brother went to the heart of the social problem with simple, direct phrases that left no doubt in De Mun's mind about his social obligations.

As De Mun and his visitor stood at the window of the officer's apartment, looking across the courtyard at the ruins of the Tuileries while they talked, De Mun told Maignen that he could see only futility in workers' clubs. The Brother dramatically pointed to the charred ruins of the Tuileries, burned during the Parisian insurrection, and declared: "The persons truly responsible for the Commune are you, the rich, the great, the fortunate, who have amused yourselves within these ruined walls; you who pass by without seeing the people, without knowing them; you who know nothing of the soul, the needs, the sufferings of the people." Who had caused the bloody Commune? he asked again. "Not the people, not the real workers who toil and suffer." Maignen had lived close to the poor. He assured De Mun that they did not hate the rich; the rich were strangers whom they did not know. "Go to them with an open heart and an outstretched hand, and they will understand you."

For Albert de Mun this seemed the call of Providence. He promised the Brother that he would come to the club and address the members — and he kept his promise. This invitation, then, caused De Mun to become more important than several of his associates who were equally well intentioned and to all appearances better equipped intellectually than he to carry on the work of the social apostolate. De Mun was to become distinguished from such men as Le Play, La Tour du Pin, and Périn by his sense of realities and the practical. The others continued to be academic and, incidentally, to do excellent work in social theory. But De Mun contacted the workers, he came to know their problems concretely and intimately, he worked with actual conditions and not with abstract social theory. In this way, whether he realized it or not, he was following the advice of Ozanam in visiting the sick man in his own garret, shivering from his lack of coal, being uncomfortable on his broken straight chair.

* * *

A few weeks later the young officer stood on the speaker's platform before a group of workers, nervous by his own admission, in full uniform, and with his heart pounding against the medals on his breast. This was De Mun's first public speech. He had written it out and memorized it perfectly, but he found it hard to conquer his stage-fright. After a stumbling beginning, though, his tongue was loosened with an eloquence all France was to know and admire throughout the coming generation. De Mun was his own first convert. He tells us in his autobiography, written almost forty years later, how he felt he was pronouncing some solemn covenant that night dedicating himself irrevocably to a sacred cause. The conversion of Count Albert de Mun was complete.

Within two weeks he had gathered together a number of friends, including his brother Robert, Maignen, La Tour du Pin, and Emile Keller, and he induced them to form a "Committee for the Foundation of Catholic Workingmen's Clubs in Paris." The Committee's first act was to issue a manifesto of Catholic social action. This "Appeal to Men of Good Will," as they called their manifesto, asserted that "at the present hour the labor problem is no longer a problem for discussion. . . . It must be solved." The solution was to be found in Catholic Workingmen's Clubs, apparently to be founded and maintained by Catholics like De Mun and Keller and La Tour du Pin who were conscious of their social obligations. "The men of the privileged classes," the Appeal stated, "have duties to be fulfilled with regard to their brothers, the workingmen." "To subversive doctrines and dangerous teachings, we must oppose the holy teachings of the Gospel; to materialism, the notion of sacrifice; to the cosmopolitan spirit, the idea of country; to atheistic negation, Catholic affirmation." The Appeal was launched with an article in *Le Figaro* and, as De Mun puts it, there was tremendous excitement. Congratulations and contributions, threats and recriminations all poured into the Committee's office.

The Committee decided to begin its campaign by establishing its first club in Belleville, the worst of the proletarian areas of Paris, where hostages had been massacred and street fighting had been ferocious during the Commune of the previous year. It was a brash thing to do – but it worked. Albert de Mun and his brother, two young noblemen, entered the Belleville district unknown, unsuspected, alone. Somehow they managed to rent space for their club, recruit about twenty young workers as charter members, and obtain a Brother of St. Vincent de Paul as director. At the first meeting Lieutenant De Mun made a stirring speech and the workers sang a hastily composed club song – both the words and music of which, De Mun later admitted, were pretty flat. Socialist and communist eyebrows must have raised perplexedly on hearing the chorus from a meeting hall within shouting distance of where the archbishop of Paris had been murdered a short time before. "The hope of France," the words went, "you workers must Christians be!" Those inside, however, had the spirit and the enthusiasm necessary for success, a spirit which De Mun tells us caused them to leave the meeting hall and walk down the hill "drunk with victory."

For a while victory seemed theirs in this campaign to Christianize the workers. In the following month of May (1872) a club was established in the industrial part of Lyons; in June another club was founded in Paris, this one on the site of the bloody street battle of the previous year at Montmartre; in August another club was established in Lyons, in the Croix-Rousse section where forty years before workers had raised the desperate battle cry, "Live working or die fighting." A year later, in the summer of 1873, the clubs held their first pilgrimage. To it came workers from seven clubs in Paris, others from Lyons, Lille, Bethune, Roubaix, Maubeuge, Arras, Saint-Quentin, and other industrial towns of France. Two thousand men now sang

"You workers must Christians be!" When a general meeting was held two years later, 150 clubs were represented and they included 18,000 members.

This initial success made the committee feel, for a few years, that they would soon have a network of clubs throughout France, and that through these clubs they could effect their social reform according to Christian principles. But after the first few years of rapid growth expansion was slow and by the turn of the century the committee had a hard time holding the membership it had acquired. In 1884 there were 400 clubs with 50,000 members, but by 1900 there were only 60,000. The committee found that the workers did not like being patronized by benevolent aristocrats. The city workers were especially hostile to anything being done for them by these wealthy, privileged young men from France's fine old families. They were hostile, moreover, to religion – and this De Mun and his associates insisted was the very basis of their reforms. The workers wanted their pie here on earth, and they did not want it handed to them by the upper classes, nor did they want any spiritual meringue on it.

Workingmen's clubs, therefore, did not by themselves solve the social problem. So De Mun's first venture must be considered a failure – but not a complete failure, because the clubs spread Catholic social teaching and showed at least some of the labor leaders that Socialism was not the only solution to the problems created by the industrial revolution. Frequent congresses brought the workers together to listen to France's leading Catholic social thinkers and to exchange ideas. So, though their clubs operated on a small scale and did not renovate the social fabric of France, as De Mun and his friends hoped they would, nevertheless they did spread the reform ideas of Pope Leo XIII's *Rerum Novarum* even before the famous encyclical "On the Condition of Labor" was published. Important also was the fact that in their conferences the club leaders brought theory and practice together – to the benefit both of social thinkers and labor leaders.

An indirect but important result of the Catholic Workingmen's Clubs was De Mun's election to the French Chamber of Deputies, where for forty years he represented the poor people of France and the Catholic Church. De Mun had resigned his commission in the army in 1875 in order to give full time to his social apostolate. Then, when the elections of 1875 showed the country was unmistakably drifting toward anticlericalism and radical Liberalism, De Mun received repeated invitations to become a candidate for election on a conservative, clerical platform. As an orator who had discovered the power of speech he was not averse to entering political life. "The tribune [of the Chamber of Deputies]," he writes, "appeared to me as the theater where our ideas, being forcefully stated, could best arrest attention and bring conviction. Then, I saw the Catholic Church menaced, already attacked with violence by those whose reign was beginning, and I burned to defend it on the very battlefield where it might be attacked, with the weapon God had given me. Finally – why not admit it? – a certain amount of ambition urged me to employ in parliamentary battles the oratorical ardor I had hitherto expended in private meetings."

So De Mun ran for office in 1876. His platform was a concise summary of the principles and the objectives he was to spend the rest of his life defending. "The Revolution [of 1789] is today seeking to complete its work of destruction by giving the deathblow to the religion of our fathers, and everywhere those who speak in the name of the Revolution openly declare war on Catholicism. . . . It is therefore the part of Catholics to take in hand the defense of the social order, and, by protecting their religion in its rights and its liberty . . . to give France once more the peace and stability of which she stands so sorely in need."

Elected by the constituency of Pontivy, in Brittany, De Mun came to the Chamber of Deputies to discover that the Liberal group in power contested the validity of his election and refused to give him his seat. Henri Brisson, a high official in the Masonic Order – which De Mun had heatedly attacked as "the supreme effort of Satan against Jesus Christ" – demanded an investigation of De Mun's election because "this candidate of the Court of Rome" had received public support from the Catholic clergy. The committee of inquiry consisted entirely of Liberal Republicans, and naturally enough it reported unfavorably on the election and recommended that De Mun be refused his seat. He returned to Pontivy where he was immediately and overwhelmingly re-elected. This time the Chamber could not refuse to seat him.

The circumstances under which De Mun entered the Chamber of Deputies were unfortunate, inasmuch as he was more convinced than ever that Republicanism was necessarily opposed to Catholicism — his being Catholic and receiving Catholic support were the sole grounds of his rejection — and that if the Third Republic persisted in France the Catholic Church was doomed to destruction. Consequently, for many years, as we shall see, De Mun never thought of the possibility of reconciling republican government and the Church in France. When a republican deputy asserted in 1878 that "between the Catholic Church and the Republic no conciliation is possible," and when the Liberal leader Gambetta shouted, "clericalism is the enemy," De Mun accepted their declarations as statements of fact. "Very well," he answered in the Chamber, "so be it! It is true because you wish it to be so! Henceforth you must forget 'clericalism' and say frankly that the enemy is Catholicism. . . . It is not that I have said it, but I accept it thus, and in the future you will not be astonished at our lack of confidence in your Republic."

De Mun was elected again in 1878, and again he was rejected by the Liberal majority in the Chamber. Re-elected again, he held office continually, with the exception of one year (1893), until his death in 1914. During that time his social ideas underwent little or no modification. Neither did he modify his conviction that a return to Catholicism was the only sound basis for building a healthy France again. His political ideas, however, changed radically — though slowly — as he gave up his monarchist convictions and accepted the republican form of government with the hope of winning a majority over to his social and religious views.

* * *

Although De Mun was essentially a man of action rather than a theorist like Le Play or La Tour du Pin, nevertheless he worked out a set of social principles on which he based his work in the Chamber of Deputies and his activity with the Catholic Workingmen's Clubs. Like every Frenchman who has reflected in things social and religious in the past century and a half, De Mun took the Revolution of 1789 as his point of departure. He considered the Revolution not an event of the past but "a social-political doctrine that pretends to found society on the caprice of man, and not on the will of God," a doctrine which supplants divine law by weak human reason. "We must oppose the Declaration of the Rights of Man," he wrote, "which is the guiding light of the Revolution, with a Declaration of the Rights of God."

De Mun condemned the Revolution – which the Republicans of his day said they wanted to complete – because it did not give the nation the liberty or the equality or the fraternity which it had promised. In the Chamber he denounced it time and time again for having "destroyed the ancient organization of labor and replaced it with nothing but the fever of competition." In 1881 he made a memorable campaign speech in which he put his thought on the subject thus: "The people have been promised everything [by the heirs of the Revolution]: power, wealth, and independence! They have been given only the mask of a chimerical sovereignty, and behind that mask there is only a slave, a slave who carries on his shoulders the politicians whose fortunes he has made, a slave who belongs, body and soul, to the industrial furnace into which he is thrown like so much coal. All sorts of promises have been made to the workingman. But his leisure, his health, his old age, his home, his future, his professional interests – who cares about them? After ninety years they [the Liberals] have got around to discussing whether it is proper to restore to the workingman a part of the right of association of which the Revolution robbed him!"

The Revolution was evil, then, because it had been directed by the Liberal millionaire class against the workers, against the Church, against the nation of France. Its work must be undone, De Mun insisted, by another revolution, a counterrevolution, which would protect the workingman by guaranteeing him the right to form unions, by protecting him with industrial insurance, old-age benefits, and unemployment compensation. And this counterrevolution is to protect the Church from the Liberal attacks which aimed at destroying it.

De Mun spoke as a conservative – though a "revolutionary conservative" – in the Chamber, and he directed his speeches against the Liberals and the Socialists: against the Liberals for not being sufficiently liberal and revolutionary, against the Socialists for being the workingman's enemy instead of his friend. The Liberals, of course, had declared themselves De

Mun's personal enemy as well as opponents of his principles before he was ever allowed to speak in the Chamber. He took them at their word and carried on a spirited battle against them throughout his career as a deputy. He considered the Liberals, as they did themselves, the custodians of the Revolution's principles. "You are the Revolution [of 1789]," he told them, "and that is enough to explain why we are the Counter-Revolution."

He denounced the Liberals for their selfishness and for their utter disregard of the masses. Notoriously indifferent to the workingman's suffering, the Liberals ruled France in the interests of the capitalists – the class to which they belonged. De Mun condemned them for "considering labor a commodity instead of regarding it an act of human life, the noblest of all." He condemned them for their individualism, "the plague which infects our diseased society from top to bottom," for denying workers the right to unionize, for destroying all reciprocal duties between employers and employees. His speeches, then, were always on behalf of the worker against the wealthy employer. For many years De Mun was a thorn in the side of the exploiting industrial barons of France; for decades he kept honest grievances before the public in and out of the Chamber. He never let Frenchmen forget that there was a social problem and that the Liberals refused to admit its existence. In scathing language he told how the Liberal leader Gambetta had cavalierly denied that there was a social question; another time he asserted that the Liberal Thiers "had no love for the people." Thus repeatedly through the years De Mun drove home his point that the Liberals were not liberal at all, that they were a selfish crowd exploiting the masses, and that their fine phrases about liberty and equality were used to deceive the nation as to their real aims in controlling the country.

De Mun's indictment of the Liberals' capitalist regime sounded like an accusation from the Socialists' bench in the Chamber of Deputies. But De Mun had no use for Socialist reform. Socialism, he said, "is the most dangerous of chimeras and would lead to the worst of despotisms." He agreed with the Socialists in many of their criticisms of the Liberal Republicans, and at one time he even went so far as to say that far removed as he felt himself from Socialism, still he felt closer to it than to Liberalism. His frequent condemnations of the Socialists, however, followed the same pattern as had his indictment of the Republicans: Socialists, since they had come to power in 1898, had done nothing for the people. He berated them for preventing sound reform by focusing the workers' attention on some future, unrealizable Utopia which not even the Socialists could describe.

"With such doctrines [as class struggle and social revolution] do you know what you are doing? I say it with the accent of sorrowful conviction, you are delaying, you are retarding, perhaps you are rendering impossible the most just, most necessary, most urgent social reforms. . . . You have cruelly betrayed the cause of the people." De Mun's indictment of the French Socialist party, then, took an ironic twist—for he condemned them chiefly for their failure to pass social legislation. He pointed out, correctly enough, how a certain number of sound laws on trade unions, on the employment of women and children, on accidents and working conditions, had been passed before the Socialists came to power. Since then, however, "nothing has been done for the people; there have been inflammatory speeches, confused expositions of collectivist doctrines, but as for results, nothing except the Dreyfus Affair, the Associations Law [against the Church], the disorganization of the army, and the religious war, that is to say, the preparation for the social war." "That," he concluded, "is what the Socialists have given the people in five years. On the contrary, look across the border and see what is happening in Belgium. There the Catholics have been in power twenty years and no state in Europe today has a more advanced, a more constantly and boldly progressive social legislation."

So De Mun condemned Liberals and Socialists alike for not being revolutionary enough. He condemned them, too, for being equally hostile to religion. His own constructive thought, on the other hand, was both religious and revolutionary. It provided, indeed, for a social upheaval on Christian principles, for De Mun realized better than most of his contemporaries that nothing was quite so revolutionary in the nineteenth century as the concept of Christian justice. Its application was bound to shake society to its very foundations. "I have long been convinced," he told the Chamber in a debate on social legislation, "that underlying the demands of the people and in their vision of justice there is an unconscious groping toward that Christianity which they have forgotten." The most important revolutionary step, then, was to re-establish Christianity among the French people – and this meant Catholicism to De Mun. He insisted that "the Catholic faith is the sole indispensable basis of national laws and institutions, of social and political order . . . of securing the welfare of my country." So he concluded that to obtain social justice he must devote himself "unreservedly to the defense of religion."

His more specific social reforms centered around the guild system which he wished to adapt to an industrialized France. He believed that the guild was the answer to that individualism of the time which saw the employer bargain individually with each worker and thus hold them all at his mercy. Guild organization could readily be adapted to the factory system, he believed, by bringing together in the same society all persons engaged in production within a certain field. Employers and employees would sit around the same table discussing their common problems; they would benefit mutually from associating with each other in the same club. Capitalists opposed the system because it brought the workers together so that they present their grievances collectively; workers tended to oppose it because they suspected it was a device for preventing them from winning their battle against the capitalists.

Unfortunately, too, De Mun was an aristocrat, and even in his best utterances he betrayed his social position, inasmuch as he spoke of "helping" the workers in words that sounded patronizing – and the workingmen of France would rather see their children starve than accept condescending help. De Mun considered his social schemes a matter of justice, things to which the workers were entitled by right. But the workers frequently misunderstood him, as when he described "the Catholic guild, which is neither a trade union nor a tribunal of arbitration, but a center of Christian activity where the interest of the profession is superior to private interest, where antagonism between capitalist and workingman gives way to patronage [that is the word which hurt] exercized in a Christian spirit and freely accepted."

His plan was sound and his arguments were good – as recent

history tragically attests — but neither the worker nor the employer of his day was willing to listen. In the debate on a proposal to legalize trade unions in 1883, De Mun presented an amendment in favor of guild organization, and during the course of the debate he spoke so eloquently for his idea that he "created nothing less than a sensation" and emerged the outstanding orator in the Chamber on social questions. "What is lacking in the unions as you conceive them, unions of employers or of workingmen, isolated and separated from one another, is precisely what is the great want, the great social necessity of our time, and what existed at the basis of the old guild institutions, namely, personal contact, conciliation of interests, appeasement, which cannot be had except by the reconstruction of the industrial family." In prophetic fashion De Mun went on to tell what would happen if workers joined their own unions and employers formed their own associations. Capital and labor would be organizing for war, and "in this impious war, everybody will suffer: the workers first, because they are weaker; the masters, also, who little by little will be ruined; and finally the entire country." These are words which sound commonplace today as C.I.O. and A.F.L. battle Chambers of Commerce and N.A.M. — but they were not listened to in 1883 because few people appreciated De Mun's penetrating vision.

It is a social tragedy that De Mun's plan was not followed. He asked for unions composed of employers and employees sitting together, because, he maintained, such unions or guilds were best fitted to remove antagonisms between workers and owners, to improve the workingman's conditions, and to develop in both capitalists and laborers a sense of mutual rights and obligations. These unions, De Mun proposed, should administer social legislation passed by the government, laws providing for such things as accident insurance, old-age pensions, unemployment compensation, and those other security measures which have been commonly adopted since his day. Thus De Mun's proposal looked toward the workers' and the industrialists' welfare without creating the Welfare State. The government was merely to pass enabling legislation; the guilds were then to administer these social laws — so that the workers would take care of themselves through the guilds instead of becoming State wards, as the tendency has been in the past half century. De Mun's plan was defeated in the Chamber because, as one of his Liberal opponents put it, "Never has an enterprise of this kind been more eloquently defended . . . and more dangerous for society." It was dangerous, the Liberals believed, because it gave the workers a voice in the management of industry.

* * *

Although De Mun never managed to push his guild proposal through the French legislature, still he did enjoy some success in getting other of his measures enacted into law. This, indeed, is De Mun's most important practical work, his many proposals to the Chamber for sound social legislation and his occasional successes. For there were others who developed Catholic social theory more fully and more perfectly than he did—men like Bishop von Ketteler in Germany, La Tour du Pin and Le Play in France. But no one performed the practical political task of speaking for such measures as eloquently as De Mun did in the French Chamber of Deputies and getting some of them embodied in French national law.

For several decades De Mun kept one reform proposal after another before the Chamber of Deputies, proposals which added up, in Parker T. Moon's words, to "a remarkable constructive program of labor reform and social legislation, which was so sweeping and so radical that many conservatives branded it as socialist." He proposed his guild organization for industry in his first year in the Chamber (1876), and again he argued for it in 1883, as we have seen, when he amended the trade-union bill to make the unions consist of both employers and employees. In the following few years he adopted the better political technique of introducing social-reform bills one at a time, "very insufficient reforms" he called them: reduction of the working day to eleven hours; prohibition of labor on Sundays; total exclusion of children under twelve from industrial employment; restrictions on the use of women and girls in heavy labor; and other such provisions. He also presented bills for old-age pensions and compulsory sickness insurance for workers, for industrial accident insurance, for arbitration and conciliation boards to settle industrial disputes.

Some of these bills eventually found their way through the French legislature and became part of the law of the land. Usually they were modified in favor of the employer as they passed through the two French chambers, but in hesitating and fragmentary fashion they did give the workingmen some small part of what De Mun insisted was their just due. Accident compensation was provided for industrial workers in 1894, for agricultural workers in 1898, and for commercial employees in 1906. Old-age insurance was made compulsory in 1910, and a series of laws gradually reduced the working day and guaranteed the workers a day of rest on Sunday. These benefits were only a partial payment of the debt that De Mun insisted society owed the laboring class, but small as they were they did something to enable the worker to live like a human being again. De Mun was not the only person urging their adoption, but nevertheless he stands out above the others as the deputy who secured their passage into law.

* * *

Such was De Mun's contribution toward solving the social problem according to the formula of Catholic justice. That was one of his two big accomplishments in life. The second was his part in effecting a political revolution within French Catholic ranks — for De Mun played a leading role in converting Catholics from their obstinate though understandable monarchism to a sincere republicanism. His role in this revolution was hard, because he was a monarchist by tradition, by sympathy, by personal connections. But he was loyal enough to his duty, as he came in time to see it, to sacrifice his inclinations and sincerely support a form of government he found it difficult to like. The story of his conversion to republicanism is the story of a loyal Catholic Frenchman unselfishly sacrificing his personal feelings to the interests of his Church and his country.

De Mun's inclination toward monarchy had been strengthened by Republican opposition to his entry into the Chamber of Deputies in 1876 and again in 1878, since the tenor of remarks made against him by Republican leaders led him to identify republicanism with anti-Catholicism and with oppression of the workers. The Bourbon pretender to the throne, Count de Chambord, realized the political advantage of championing the Church and social reform. And when he assumed this role, he found De Mun his ardent supporter — a fact, it is worth remembering, which hurt De Mun's own political importance for many years. As time wore on, De Mun gradually came to realize that monarchism was a lost cause in France and that political expediency dictated his adapting himself and his program to a republican regime. This slowly growing conviction was hastened by several events, especially Chambord's death in 1883, the Boulanger episode,* and the Dreyfus affair.** These events convinced De Mun that continued alliance with monarchism was worse than futile; it threatened to become fatal for the Catholic cause and for social reform.

As early as 1885, De Mun proposed a "Catholic Union" party which was to include all Catholics, republican or monarchist, to form a united front in defense of the Church and in favor of social reform according to Catholic principles. The proposed party was to avoid taking a stand on the form of government and to concentrate on a platform of three planks: (1) liberty and security for the Church; (2) protection of the family, the sanctity of marriage, and the inviolability of religious education; (3) promotion of the social reform measures De Mun had long advocated. The party never materialized because Catholics could not agree to submerge their party differences; and when the papal nuncio, considering the scheme inopportune, advised De Mun to drop it, the Count formally renounced his project.

Seven years later, however, Pope Leo XIII wrote a letter "to the Archbishops, the Bishops, the Clergy, and all the Catholics of France" in which he stated his *ralliement* policy — a complete

* Boulanger was a general in the French Army who was appointed minister of war in 1886. Apparently moved by Napoleonic ambitions, he championed social reform and did all he could to endear himself to the French people. He grew increasingly popular until 1889, when his followers proposed he overthrow the government by a *coup d'état*. Boulanger tarried too long, and when the government ordered his arrest he fled ignominiously to Belgium. The failure of this affair hurt the opponents of the Republican government, especially the monarchists who backed Boulanger.

** Dreyfus was a Jewish officer in the French army who was wrongfully accused of selling military secrets. Dreyfus was convicted by a court-martial, but the case was reopened and it was proved that the criminal was a certain Major Esterhazy, an avowed royalist. During the trials republicans lined up behind Dreyfus, monarchists against him. His vindication was a severe blow to the monarchist cause.

vindication of what De Mun had attempted with his "Catholic Union" party of 1885. In his letter the Pope told French Catholics that while they "have full liberty to prefer one form of government to another" in the realm of speculative ideas, nevertheless as French citizens they owed obedience to the established Republic. He urged them to stop their ruinous factional struggles, to be loyal to the established form of government, and to unite in defense of their Church. De Mun had taken this stand seven years before the Pope spoke, and it was therefore with undisguised enthusiasm that he accepted Leo's advice and urged it upon his fellow French Catholics. Unfortunately for the Church and for De Mun's political success in the future, a large number of Catholics in France stubbornly refused to give up their monarchist leanings and reconcile themselves to the Republic.

For that reason De Mun's last twenty years in the Chamber of Deputies seemed futile. These were the years he called his "period of sorrow," years of defeat, when one measure after another was passed against the Church. De Mun watched his beloved France ruin itself as clericals and anticlericals locked in deadly struggle, wasting the nation's strength while the rest of France, the laboring class, continued to be ignored in its distress. He fought each government bill directed against the Church, first by his fiery speeches in the Chamber of Deputies and later, when his health broke, by equally fiery work with his pen. But it was to no avail. Religious orders were exiled from the country, the Concordat of 1801 was abrogated, the Church was driven from education, even from the ownership and control of church buildings. The work of destruction was almost complete when World War I broke out in 1914.

Bitterness filled De Mun's soul, but he never betrayed discouragement, nor did he sit idle amid the ruins of his country and the hopes of his youth. He continued to push his plans of social reform; he never stopped his defense of the Church. And again he tried to form a Catholic party which would reconcile Catholicism and French patriotism. He carried on the struggle through these hard years, then, and by doing so he left French Catholics a valuable legacy to be used in the twentieth century.

In 1899, De Mun combined with Jacques Piou, another Catholic leader in the Chamber of Deputies, to form the Popular

Liberal Party – De Mun's last and perhaps his most important single political achievement. Formed in protest to the government's anticlerical policies, the party accepted democracy in politics but rejected the government's anticlericalism and its Liberalism. The party's membership card stated that "it styles itself *Popular* because, on the one hand, it desires to derive its strength from the people by the number of its adherents; on the other hand, it is solicitous above all to defend the interests of the workingmen, which are constantly betrayed by those who promise everything before the elections and hold none of their promises afterwards." The party platform was a restatement of De Mun's aims in social reform: the formation of guilds – called the corporate system in 1899 after *Rerum Novarum* – the protection of workers against exploitation by means of proper legislation, the defense of the Church and the fostering of religion, constitutional reforms to make the government really democratic and to protect the masses from bourgeois exploitation.

Although De Mun was only one of several leaders in the Popular Liberal Party, nevertheless it was he who gave it its Catholic social character. This was the party that was destined to carry the program of Social Catholicism on after De Mun's death in 1914. It has well been called "the true bequest of nineteenth-century French Social Catholicism to the future," for it is the parent of the modern MRP group led by Bidault.

* * *

De Mun was not allowed to see the fruit of his labors, for, unlike Windhorst or Ozanam, he died without fully accomplishing his objectives. He had carried on a manly crusade for France, for the poor, and for the Catholic Church – but six months before his death it seemed that all three were at the point of ruin. Judged from the purely human, short-range point of view, therefore, it seemed that De Mun had been a failure. But the mysterious working of Providence and the strange turns of human conduct in history permitted this French Catholic layman to spend his last few months playing a glorious role in his nation's history – and to die one of France's best loved and most missed heroes.

Although De Mun was continually re-elected to the Chamber of Deputies until his death, he took a less prominent role in political affairs after the turn of the century. An increasingly dangerous heart condition confined him more and more to his home, and thus he was forced to work with his pen alone. But when World War I broke out late in the summer of 1914, De Mun insisted on coming out of his semiretirement, for beneath the robes of the old French Academician was the soldier whose family had for generations been dedicated to the service of France. De Mun was unable to offer his sword or even his power of oratory, as of old, but he did wield his powerful pen.

Every day in the first months of the war – when Paris was in such danger – De Mun contributed an article to *Echo de Paris*, articles which Paul Bourget called "the pulse of the nation's heart." Every day, too, he addressed the soldiers in the *Bulletin des armées*. His ringing appeals aroused the young men of France, and his messages to the civilian population earned him the title of "Consoler of Mothers." De Mun realized that this feverish activity was killing him, but when his friends tried to dissuade him from such strenuous exertion he characteristically replied: "If I cannot die on the field of battle, what more glorious death can an old soldier wish for than to die wielding the pen in his country's cause?"

De Mun never despaired, even in France's gloomiest hour, and when he died early in October the German drive on Paris had been halted and the war had settled down to a four-year stalemate on the Western front. Even his old enemies admired him and loved him for his patriotic work in these crucial days of French history, and all Frenchmen agreed with the epitaph pronounced over De Mun by one of France's leading journals: "Albert de Mun truly fell on the field of battle, having deliberately and voluntarily sacrificed his life for France." He was one of those millions of loyal French Catholics, clergy and laymen alike, who showed their government how unfounded was the Republican contention that good Catholics could not be good Frenchmen. He was one of those Catholics who by his activity and his death in World War I, secured tolerance for the Church once again in France.

* * *

Strange as it might seem to those whose thinking is done for them by handy, misleading terms like "Liberal" or "Reactionary," the conservative De Mun was a revolutionist through and through. He demanded a revolution on Christian principles. As a lay soldier of Christ, he fought to apply his Leader's laws to the society of his day — and the Liberals opposed him because Christian principles were really revolutionary. Laissez-faire Liberalism was in control of the Third Republic; De Mun tried to oust it in favor of a corporative system which would admit workers into the sphere of government and into the council rooms of industry. Even within Catholic circles, De Mun stands out as a revolutionist, for he broke from Gallican monarchism and advocated a sincere adherence to the established republican form of government.

Even though De Mun did not live to see his principles put into practice, still he did have the satisfaction of seeing the Pope's stamp of approval put on his two "revolutions," the economic revolution toward a guild or corporate system and the political revolution in favor of republicanism. *Rerum Novarum* was, in general, an endorsement from Rome of what De Mun had long been trying to accomplish in the French Chamber of Deputies; Leo XIII's *ralliement* policy was, again, essentially the same policy De Mun had advocated for seven years. On December 18, 1892, De Mun restated his revolutionary principles in the light of the two recent papal pronouncements in a famous speech made at Saint-Etienne. A few weeks later he received a letter from Leo XIII in which the Pope testified that De Mun had correctly interpreted the papal encyclicals. "The perusal of your speech," the Pope wrote, "was supremely agreeable. While We are pleased to bestow upon you the praise which you justly merit, We exhort you to pursue your generous enterprise. May there arise men who, with a devotion such as yours, and a large breadth of vision, will consecrate themselves entirely to the resurrection of France."

De Mun was a pioneer in trying to solve the problems of his day and ours by applying Christian principles to industrial society. He was a pioneer in evolving social reform along the lines that have become more or less official Catholic social philosophy in the famous encyclicals *Rerum Novarum* and

Quadragesimo Anno. Thus De Mun carried the work of Pauline Jaricot and Frédéric Ozanam a step further, since his reform was to be accomplished through appropriate legislation which would guarantee to the worker what justice rendered to him. Some of his reforms were adopted in his own day, more have been adopted since, but nowhere in the modern world has Catholic social reform been fully put into practice.

It would be a serious mistake to consider De Mun a failure simply because his reforms were not fully embodied in French law. For De Mun was the soul and the brain of the Catholic Workingmen's Clubs, a movement which accomplished much good for its members and did a great deal to spread a knowledge of Catholic social principles. In the Chamber of Deputies he spoke ringingly for the worker and for social justice – and his speeches did much to advertise their cause to all of France. Count Albert de Mun heroically fulfilled his family motto of *servir* – to his Church, his country, and the poor people of France whose cause he adopted in 1871. In serving faithfully he left a heritage to French Catholics, something that cannot be weighed or measured, like a law passed or a club founded, but something which has proved inspiring and invaluable to French Catholics of the twentieth century.

III.

INTELLECTUAL ACTION

Compared to preceding centuries, the nineteenth was an age of intellectual confusion. Before the French Revolution, the world had been relatively stable. Modes of thought and ways of doing things remained much the same throughout a man's lifetime. But in the nineteenth century nothing seemed constant except change. Thinking men therefore found it increasingly difficult to adjust their thought to the changing contingencies of life. They had to reconsider the basic assumptions they learned in school in order to find out whether the "eternal verities" of their boyhood were eternal enough to be valid twenty years later. A new set of principles was discovered each decade, it seemed, which the next decade proved worthless. All this change made for confusion of mind, partly because the face of the world was altered with the coming of railroads and factories, but mostly because the basic philosophies men lived by in the nineteenth century tilted and shifted and collapsed as though they had been built on sand.

The nineteenth century was one of revolution. True child of its parents, the Revolution of 1789 in France and the industrial revolution in England, it was itself a long revolution that fathered two world wars and various twentieth-century upheavals like Communism, Fascism, and Nazism. It was hard for people who lived in the nineteenth century to understand what was going on, for in many ways life seemed serene to the thinking and writing class, who lived comfortably; and unless one of them looked across the tracks, he was not likely to know how the whole world was turning upside down. And even if he did watch the old order disintegrate, he could hardly understand the pattern of movement and the direction of change, because the essence of revolution is disorder and confusion.

From our promontory of the mid-twentieth century, however, we can see that there was a single main note running through all the revolutions of the nineteenth century: the note of secularization. Each movement of the age – from the deism before the French Revolution, through the utilitarianism and materialism of the industrial revolution, to the atheism of preacher-scientists like Huxley and Haeckel – pushed God out of still another field of thought or action. These revolutions were directed against God and against His Church.

Catholics, therefore, were obliged to resist them, to point out what was heretical and false and dangerous in each of these intellectual revolutions as it made its appearance and sought to bend the mind of Europe before it. Catholic apologists tried to show that each new "discovery" discrediting Catholic teaching and practice was not the infallible, demonstrable truth its discoverers claimed. Sometimes Catholics completely rejected a doctrine, as the Liberal dogma of the immaculate conception of all men; sometimes they accepted part of a new theory, the legitimate part, and rejected the exaggerated claims of its exponents, as was the case with most claims of natural scientists in the latter part of the century; sometimes they modified or qualified a new theory so that it would be compatible with revealed truth, as was the case with Darwin's theory of evolution.

The better to understand the position of Catholic lay apologists in the nineteenth century, let us isolate and identify a few of the main strands that were woven into the confusing picture of this century's thought. There was, at the beginning, the rationalist heritage of the eighteenth century, the thought of the "Enlightenment," which was carried over into the nineteenth century as the basis of English utilitarianism and as the accepted thought of most Europeans who rejected the French Revolution. From his lonely retreat in Russia, De Maistre composed devastating attacks on eighteenth-century thinkers like Voltaire, Locke, and Rousseau. He vindicated the Church against the claims of rationalism; moreover, he met eighteenth-century rationalism with its own weapons and dealt it blows from which it never fully recovered. For De Maistre was read widely, and in proportion as his influence spread, the "Enlightenment" glowed less brightly.

By 1830 the "enlightened" movement had grown pretty dim. Liberalism had succeeded it as the dominant current of the age. It too enjoyed its day, until about 1870, when it gave way to other modes of thought. Liberalism, too, had its Catholic opponents whom time has proved essentially correct in their stand. Outstanding among these was Juan Donoso Cortés, who penetrated the essential viciousness of Liberalism and foresaw the direction in which it was leading Europe even before Marx wrote his heated denunciations of the Liberal regime. Louis Veuillot in France and Orestes Brownson in America also delivered telling blows in the name of truth against the Liberal doctrines of their day. We should repeat at this point – because Liberalism has a better connotation among American readers than it has among Europeans – that the Liberalism with which we are concerned in this book was that peculiar combination of doctrines condemned by Pope Pius IX in his *Syllabus of Errors.* It was an essentially selfish doctrine directed by the middle class against the aristocrats above them and the proletarians below. It was antidemocratic. It was secular. It was anticlerical, even antireligious in many respects.

Churches were places where Liberals appeared in the front pews for public-relation purposes, and where they hoped their employees would come to sit in the back pews to learn how to be honest, God fearing, and hard working. Liberals went to Church, and they even believed in their own kind of God – the divinity who drove a good hard bargain – but it was the stock exchange before which they tipped their hats, it was in the bank that they maintained a hushed, sacred silence. This is the Liberalism which could not tolerate Catholicism; this was the secular religion which Catholics rightly saw as the deadly enemy of the nineteenth century – an enemy, as Donoso Cortés showed so well, not only of Catholicism but of the Christian society which was Europe.

In the latter half of the century new currents of thought replaced Liberalism. The strongest and in time the most dangerous of these was Nationalism, that exaggerated worship of one's own nation and hatred of others which Pope Pius XI in the twentieth century called "by now a true form of apostasy." Catholic lay leaders did not take an active role against Nationalism in the nineteenth century, partly, we fear, because they were not perspicacious enough to see its evil essence, and partly because they were strategically in a poor position to resist nationalist pressure of the time. Always suspected and frequently accused of loyalty to Rome at the expense of the nation, Catholics were forced to guard against any word or action that might give credence to such accusations. Thus they tended, by reason of their position, to stress patriotism to such an extent that they sometimes bordered on an incipient Nationalism. Such was the case with Count Albert de Mun. When we remember the difficult position of Catholics throughout the nineteenth century, we must marvel at the sane, balanced patriotism most of them professed. Brownson, De Maistre, Donoso Cortés, Veuillot, Ward, and the others were all loyal to their respective nations – and this is the virtue of patriotism – but their sound sense of proportion, coming from a correct theology and a right philosophy, prevented them from perverting their virtue of patriotism into the vice of Nationalism, as was so generally the case with latter nineteenth-century thinkers.*

Other currents developed along with Nationalism, currents which attracted the attention of Catholic lay thinkers, which they analyzed critically and refuted successfully. Most prominent among these currents were three: the "scientific socialism" of Karl Marx and Friedrich Engels; the "survival of the fittest" theory of evolution propounded by Charles Darwin; and the "scientism" of the time, which was more an attitude of mind than anything else, an attitude which pulled the priest out of the pulpit and put the laboratory scientist in his place as the new infallible oracle of the world. A review of the claims made by these new systems of thought, Marxism, Darwinism, and Scientism, reveals how exaggerated they were; and a review of

* An exception to this statement must be made for the French royalist Catholics, who did fall into a full-blown Nationalism in the days of the Dreyfus affair and the Panama scandal. These royalist Catholics fell under the leadership of Charles Maurras and joined his *Action française*, which, incidentally, was condemned by the Pope just before the start of World War I. The condemnation was not published, however, until 1924.

Members of the *Action française* were Catholics "who did not believe in God or the Church." They used religion for nationalist ends.

Catholic writing against them shows how, generally speaking and allowing for occasional overzealous statements, the Catholic apologist did a good job of accepting the truth in each of these new doctrines while resolutely rejecting the error in each.

Catholic lay leaders who sought to justify Catholic teaching in the secular society of the nineteenth century were fighting for more than Catholic doctrine and Catholics' rights. They were defending the cause of truth against new aberrations. They were defending human dignity and human rights against novel doctrines which tried to deprive man of his soul, his free will, his intelligence, his property. For, it is well to remember, the new theories of the nineteenth century were robber doctrines. Darwinism tried to steal man's soul from him and reduce him to the same basic position as the lower animals. Marxism tried to steal his property from him and make him a cog in the communist social machinery. Scientism tried to steal everything spiritual from him: his mind, his soul, his free will, all those elements which are peculiarly human. Catholic lay leaders protected man from these robber theories by defending him as a human being in the light of long-accepted Christian teaching. The Church may have been particularly indebted to these Catholic lay thinkers, but at the same time Europeans and Americans of all faiths are also indebted to them for their having helped to preserve Christian society and hand it down to this century as something still worth saving. When the rest of the world was repudiating its precious heritage for cheap novelties, these Catholics held on to the real gems of Christian civilization.

Catholic lay leaders of the nineteenth century did not achieve unanimity on all points of political and social theory. Sometimes, indeed, they disagreed so vehemently as to scandalize those who do not understand how much intellectual freedom there is within the Church. Veuillot, for example, could write many vitriolic paragraphs against Ozanam and Montalembert for their political action in favor of a republic. Veuillot and Montalembert disagreed on almost everything social and political, but they were in perfect agreement on matters of faith and morals and on their loyalty to Rome and to France. And no one can say definitively who was the better Catholic, or that one helped promote the Church's revival more effectively than did the other. There was room for a Veuillot and a Montalembert in the Catholic Church – without either becoming a heretic – because the Church is truly Catholic, because in it there is room for loyal sons of many different political persuasions and various kinds of temperament.

Catholic lay leaders of the nineteenth century divided themselves pretty well into two groups, conservative and liberal, depending on their attitude toward the society of their age. Among the conservatives we should place De Maistre, Donoso Cortés, and Veuillot as outstanding thinkers. These were men who looked on their century as radically wrong. On the other hand were liberal thinkers, like Montalembert, Ozanam, Görres, and – in his individual way – Orestes Brownson. These were men who looked upon their society as basically sound, men who loved the new liberty and wanted to join it with Catholicism. The two groups were equally loyal to the Church. They differed on a question of policy, on which was the best way to achieve the end they both desired.

Even today it is impossible to say which side was closer to being right. For when we examine the writings of those Catholics carefully, we discover that the conservatives were not stupid in their conservatism nor the liberals naïve in their liberalism. Donoso Cortés and Brownson and Veuillot stressed the evils of the new Liberalism – and time has proved them right. Montalembert and Görres stressed the value to a reviving Church of the new freedoms – and time has also proved them right. This much can be said, however, for those who must choose sides: time and papal pronouncements have tended to vindicate the general stand of Montalembert and Ozanam and Görres, inasmuch as Leo XIII, Pius XI, and now Pius XII have issued a memorable list of documents in favor of democratic government giving to all classes their social and political due. The Church has tended to follow the line proposed by the Catholic liberal camp in the nineteenth century.

But to deny the conservative Catholic thinkers their due credit would be to see history through a peephole. For the warnings of Donoso Cortés and other critics of Liberalism have not been ignored by the Church in our own day. The Church in France needed a Veuillot as badly as it needed a Montalembert. Veuillot stood guard, like a divinely appointed watchdog, to see that Montalembert and Ozanam did not go too far in their efforts to compromise with the new society. And a barking watchdog was needed to keep eager, bighearted men like Montalembert on the track – else they might have overstepped the bounds and fallen into heresy, as clerics like Lamennais and Döllinger and Tyrrell did at various times in the century. Progressive thinkers like Ozanam and Görres were needed to push the Church's adaptation to the new society; conservative thinkers like Donoso Cortés were needed to see that adaptation was not so sudden and so extreme as to change the very constitution of the Church.

One can therefore hold, with propriety, that the Providential God who works through free human agents to accomplish His objectives in history, used the conservative and liberal elements in the Church to prod and to correct each other, since it was by this means that the Church revived remarkably in the nineteenth century, and that eventually it worked out its adjustment to the new society without losing any of its essential characteristics. It was by this means that the Church accomplished that kind of growth that another Catholic of the century, Cardinal Newman, so brilliantly analyzed in his *Essay on the Development of Christian Doctrine.*

The Church grew and prospered in the nineteenth century. Its prosperity and its revival in the climate of the century can be looked upon – if we may borrow the words of De Maistre – as "the greatest, the most manifest, and the most incontestable [miracle] of all . . . brought about in opposition to all the laws of human probability." De Maistre's dictum is true because the nineteenth century moved in a secular direction. Generally speaking, the Western World was considerably less religious in 1914 than it had been in 1815. Protestant religions had suffered, by and large; they had continued to break up into many divergent, discordant groups; most of them had given up doctrine as a bad job in order to concentrate on moral problems like prohibition and prostitution and on social problems like Y.M.C.A. clubs on university campuses. Generally speaking, too, religion was pushed out of more and more areas of life, out of family affairs, the education of children, social relief work, and so on.

But the Catholic Church revived and prospered in direct opposition to this secularist trend of the century. Ultimately, of course, its revival rested on divine support and guidance. But among the agencies used by God to accomplish this purpose were lay thinkers within the Church who by their vigorous writing and their straight thinking played their part in promoting and guiding this revival of the Church in the nineteenth century.

8. Joseph de Maistre

Joseph de Maistre's life can be told in paradoxes. An enthusiastic Freemason for fifteen years, he was nonetheless a good Catholic all his life, and in 1819 he published his famous book *Du Pape,* a work frequently called "the human preface to the Vatican Council," in which he argued daringly for papal infallibility and for papal supremacy over all the Catholic Church. The former Mason was more ultramontane* than the Jesuits or even the pope himself. Paradoxically, again, Joseph de Maistre spent fourteen years in Russia as ambassador at the world's most luxurious court – and he was so poor that he could not buy a fur coat for winter wear at St. Petersburg, nor afford better servants than a petty criminal he took in and, with his diplomatic immunity, protected from arrest. De Maistre represented the weak king of Savoy; nevertheless he was personally strong enough to become influential at the Russian court – though sometimes his country did not legally exist, and sometimes it was officially at war with Russia. De Maistre again is the man who wrote that "women have never done anything great," yet nothing "has ever been accomplished without them."

But there is danger in laboring the paradoxical in De Maistre's life, because he was a thoroughly consistent man. De Maistre the Freemason of 1780 and De Maistre the Ultramontane of 1819 are essentially the same. The loving father who wrote touching letters to a daughter he did not see until she was twenty is the same man who stoutly opposed the feminist movement of his day by insisting that women should aspire to be great women, not inadequate men. De Maistre was a consistent man in a changing, inconsistent world. He could logically be liberal as a young man and conservative in his maturity because he found that the promises of the Enlightenment were false expectations.

---

* Ultramontane, of course, is the adjective used in France — and later in Catholic circles elsewhere — to mean pro-papal or Roman. It stands in opposition to "Gallican" Catholicism which stresses the independence of the French bishops as much as possible. In the nineteenth century, French Catholics divided sharply into the two camps of ultramontanism and Gallicanism, a division that went down into the Vatican Council in 1870.

Judging the Enlightenment and the French Revolution by their fruits, he rejected them.

Hundreds of books have been written on De Maistre, and although biographers differ in their appraisal of the man, no one denies that he is a fascinating character, or that his life story is absorbingly interesting. He lived through sixty-three years (1753–1821) of critical European history, years that saw Louis XVI fail to reform the French government, years that saw that most important of all revolutions break out in 1789 and spread across the face of Europe, that saw Napoleon rise like a meteor out of the Mediterranean, flash across the European sky, and sink into the western ocean at Saint Helena in 1815. De Maistre saw all those things as a minor character on the scene. As he played his role he pondered the meaning of the drama and tried to penetrate through the stage props and the actors' lines to discover the purpose of Providence in history. He was intelligent enough – one of the few nobles who was – to see that he lived in a critical age when the world was turning a corner in history. He tried to play his part well to usher in the better age which he thought would result from the collapse of the old order and the purging effect of the French Revolution. "We are approaching the greatest of all religious epochs," he wrote, "in which every man is bound, if it be in his power, to bring a stone for the august edifice, the plans of which are obviously fixed by divine providence."

Those were apparently optimistic words for one who lived when the pope was a prisoner in Napoleon's hands, when the structure of the organized Catholic Church seemed about to collapse, and the Church ready to go into hiding. De Maistre did not ignore the difficulties which lay ahead. "A thousand causes," he admitted, "have weakened the priestly order." Priests and bishops were overworked in tending to their flocks. They who in the days gone by had been the natural defenders of the Church no longer had time for apologetic work. More than that, De Maistre argued, in his secular world "the priest who defends religion – appears to defend his own cause. . . . Unbelievers mistrust less the man of the world, and allow themselves to be approached by him, frequently enough, without the least repugnance."

So De Maistre issued a call for Catholic Action – the participation of Catholic laymen in the apologetic work of the clergy. "I see no reason," he wrote, "why men of the world, who from inclination have applied themselves to serious studies, should not number themselves among the defenders of the most holy of causes." This statement was a justification of his own work, for De Maistre was one of the first laymen of modern times to undertake apologetic action. This is his historic importance – an importance which no one denies, although, because he comes at the beginning of the Church's revival of the nineteenth century, it cannot easily be weighed or measured. Ten years ago Algernon Cecil did not hesitate to call him "the most influential layman since [St. Thomas More's] time." And T. L. Teeling wrote in 1895 that he was "the founder, with his fellow-writer and correspondent, De Bonald, of the great Catholic movement, the new Ultramontanism, of the present century."

* * *

It frequently has – and truly – been said that De Maistre's life was in perfect accord with his writing. So one can learn his principles almost as well from studying his life as from reading his works. Because his life and his writings illuminate each other, we shall follow him through his wanderings briefly, watch him endure hardship and privation without complaint, observe how his mind matured under the storm and stress of revolutionary whirlwinds that carried him from his native Savoy all the way to the capital of Russia.

Joseph de Maistre was born at Chambery, in the kingdom of Savoy, in 1753 or 1754. He was the first of ten children in a family of French nobility that had come to Savoy about a century before Joseph's birth. His father held various high offices in the Savoyard government, eventually becoming president of the Senate and codifier of the country's laws. The elder Count de Maistre was conservative, severe, and apparently somewhat distant with his family. But he preserved and passed on to his children the best qualities of eighteenth-century noble society: true parental affection on the part of the parents and filial devotion on the part of the children; a sense of obligation toward society; a life of service devoted to the interests of the crown and the altar; a concern for the welfare of the people living in the community, and a more general, less immediate, but nevertheless real interest in the welfare of Christendom as a whole.

According to the custom of the time, Joseph was destined to follow in his father's footsteps, thus to secure a comfortable, leisurely existence in government service. He was educated at the local Jesuit college at Chambery. There he obtained certain "Jesuit" traits which he manifested throughout life. He felt attached to the Jesuits and remained their advocate throughout the period of their suppression* because they exemplified those finer things of the old society which he admired. They were a manly group, as against the emasculated society of their age, and De Maistre was every inch a man. They opposed the rising fad of Voltairean cynicism in the days of De Maistre's youth, and De Maistre despised Voltaire as a dishonest sham. The Jesuits were attached closely to the Pope, strongly ultramontane in their long struggle against the Gallican element in the Church. So too was De Maistre. So he respected and loved the Jesuits, and when the occasion arose, after their re-establishment in 1814, De Maistre interceded for them at the Russian Court to obtain a better charter for their college at Potolsk.

After finishing his preliminary studies at Chambery, young Joseph went to the University of Turin to take his degree in law. From Turin, incidentally, he wrote to his parents for permission to read each new book he came upon — an indication of parental responsibility and family solidarity which made the old society the healthy organism it had once been. He returned to his native city in 1773 as an accredited lawyer. There he served as a magistrate and later as a senator, a typical eldest son of a leading family in the Old Regime. Like most younger magistrates of the latter eighteenth century, Joseph de Maistre was a proponent of liberal reform. Like his associ-

* The Jesuits were suppressed as an order from 1773 until 1814, largely because of the almost irresistible influence at Rome of the Bourbon rulers of France and Spain. Jesuits continued to work as individual priests and, with the tacit consent of Rome, as a teaching body in Russia, and for a time in Prussia. When Pope Pius VII re-established the Society in 1814, the general in Russia, Thaddeus Brzozowski, obtained universal jurisdiction over the remnants of the order.

ates, too, he was predisposed to accept anything new simply because it was not old. He acclaimed the American Revolution, for example, as the harbinger of a liberty he hoped to see cover the face of Europe. So young De Maistre was soon labeled a Liberal by the government, and he was described to the king as a "dangerous character, full of the new ideas."

This reputation for Liberalism came almost automatically to De Maistre with his membership in the local Masonic Lodge, because the Lodges were centers of Liberal, revolutionary thought all through Europe. He had joined the *Trois Mortiers* Lodge in 1774, when he was twenty-one, and four years later he passed over to *Parfaite Sincérité* of the Scottish Rite. Known to his brethren as *Josephus à Floribus*, he held a succession of titles which are all but meaningless to the uninitiated—but they do seem to indicate considerable activity and a certain amount of leadership within the order. He was Orator, Symbolic Master, Grand Professed, and finally Knight of the Beneficent Order of the Holy Spirit. As leader of the Chambery Lodge, he presented a memorial to the Duke of Brunswick, Grand Master of Masonry, urging him to lead a crusade for restoring religion throughout the world. Later that year, 1788, or early the next he broke completely with all Masonic organizations and activities.

De Maistre's biographers have attempted to explain this puzzle of an excellent Catholic being an enthusiastic Mason. Popes had condemned Freemasonry twice, Clement XII in 1738 and Benedict XIV in 1751, but Catholics of the eighteenth century seem to have exercised considerable freedom in "interpreting" papal condemnations. There were Masonic groups for the clergy, and it was not even unusual for a bishop to be a member. The Lodges ordinarily were looked upon as clubs of irresponsible professional and businessmen gathered together for drinking and arguing into the night. They were about like modern Rotarians or Lions. So it was apparently possible for a man to be sincerely Catholic and enthusiastically Masonic, if he did not know of the papal condemnations of the order or if he were elastic in interpreting them.

De Maistre was attracted to the Masonic order because of its quasimystic symbolism and because its membership list included most of the age's intellectually curious, liberal thinkers, the vanguard of the progressive European mind. In 1788, however, the king requested that the Lodge at Chambery discontinue its meetings, for by that time Freemasonry was suspected of harboring revolutionary designs. This was the time De Maistre chose for leaving the group. He seems not to have regretted his membership in the order or to have had qualms of conscience about it, but later in life he referred to Freemasonry as "foolishness, a kind of universal childishness on this side of the Alps [the Italian side]." He was invited to join a Masonic Lodge at St. Petersburg in 1810, when he was 57, but after toying with the idea for a bit he refused on the grounds that Masons were "a great and formidable sect long since sworn to overthrow all thrones." De Maistre had changed his mind about Freemasonry after the coming of the French Revolution and after traveling about Europe, especially through Switzerland, the Germanies, and Russia, where he observed Continental Masonry in operation.

De Maistre spent almost twenty years (1773–1791) living the comfortable, easy life of a man of position in his native Savoy. He was something of a social lion, one who impressed his fellow men with wide knowledge and a vigorous and direct masculine approach to all problems, one who was respectfully disdainful of womankind — and therefore much sought after and admired by the ladies of the town. He was the community's literary authority, the best read man in town who kept abreast of the latest works in French, Italian, Spanish, German, or English, all of which he read fluently. He was the one to whom people of Chambery turned when they wanted to locate a passage in the Bible or a quotation from Pindar or Seneca or Grotius. De Maistre seems to have read everything, and to have remembered everything he read.

But he found life at Chambery dull and flat. He had married at the age of 32 and settled down to a secure monotonous existence. This is the period of life he later referred to as *l'enorme poids du rien* — the dead weight of nothingness. Had the French Revolution not swept into Savoy, De Maistre would likely have lived an uneventful life, raised a family well, and perhaps written a book of reflections for his children to read as part of their education. Then he would have died and been forgotten. But Savoy lay in the path of the French Revolution, and when the revolutionary soldiers of France — missionaries with guns — poured into Savoy they wrecked all those comfortable, easy expectations which had been the normal thing in the Old Regime.

As a member of the established government, De Maistre was forced to flee before the advancing French forces, and thus in 1792 the course of his life changed abruptly. He left a life of security and ease at Chambery for a life of hardship and even want. The man who had seemed destined to help rule Savoy became an exile from his native land, a wanderer over the face of Europe. At first he fled with his family across the Alps to Aosta. After the French had annexed his homeland he returned to claim his property according to the new government's decree. His plan was to accept the new regime passively and to try to hold together his family and his estate. But when he found that he could obtain his property only by taking an oath of loyalty to the Revolution and by paying a special tax to support France's war of revolutionary imperialism he fled again, this time to Lausanne in Switzerland.

The next twenty-five years were hard. In time his wife and all children but the newborn baby Constance joined him at Lausanne. There he was in charge of the Savoyard exiles, and there he mingled with the intellectual lights of the age. The refugees at Lausanne spent most of their time chattering, dancing, conversing, killing time until the Revolution should collapse — as most of them naïvely thought it would — and they could return home from their enforced vacation. De Maistre was made of sterner stuff than the typical aristocrat of the Old Regime, however, and he was not content idling away his time in superficial entertainment. So he spent much of it reading and writing. "I read, I write, I study," he wrote to a friend, "for after all one must know something." At Lausanne he wrote his *Considerations on France*, a penetrating study of the French Revolution which was widely read and came to be known as "the Bible of the émigrés." He also published a number of minor things and worked on such other books as his *Study on Sovereignty*.

In 1797, after the king of Sardinia-Piedmont had made peace with Napoleon by ceding Savoy and Nice to France, De Maistre was recalled to Turin to take an active role in government again.

But his stay in Turin was short, for within a few months when Charles Emmanuel IV, the new king, fled from Turin, De Maistre accompanied him to Sardinia, the island part of his realm. There he stayed for only a short time before the king sent him to Venice. There for a year he and his family suffered real want and privation, lack of a decent place to live, of food and clothing, and the necessities of life. Again he was recalled to Sardinia, this time as governor of the island, a position which he held until late in 1802 when the king dispatched him to Russia as envoy extraordinary to Emperor Alexander's court.

De Maistre remained in St. Petersburg fourteen years. These were long, hard years of which he occasionally complained bitterly, especially for never having seen his "orphan daughter of a living father." Most of the time he was separated from his entire family, and all through those years he felt himself just marking time, wasting away his days performing his duty and accomplishing nothing. "I serve the king by wasting my time" is the way he described his work in Russia. "My life is very like . . . the motion of a clock: tick, tock, yesterday, today, tomorrow, and always." The story of De Maistre's service at the Russian court is an interesting study, the story of a man who represented a weak, poverty-stricken king at the most powerful and most luxurious court in the world. De Maistre had to practice humiliating economies – humiliating for an ambassador anyway – such as borrowing a coat for outdoor wear in Russia's winter, or not having domestic help at the embassy or even, at times, enough food.

These years of exile at Lausanne and Venice and St. Petersburg would have broken a weaker man's spirit. But they served only to make De Maistre sterner with himself, to give his outlook a certain firmness and inflexibility it might have otherwise not had. This kind of living broke decadent nobles, thousands of them, but because De Maistre was of that stronger, firmer stuff from which nobility had originally been cast, these privations tempered his strength. He bore them with good humor, maintaining his high personal integrity and developing a fineness of sensibility and perception which the easy life at Chambery could never have brought out.

When Napoleon and Alexander signed the Peace of Tilsit in

1807, De Maistre found himself ambassador at a hostile court with which his king had broken diplomatic relations. The Savoyard Count therefore became a Russian citizen and bided his time until Savoy and Russia should again be allies against France. Meanwhile he increased his influence with Alexander the Great until, in 1812, he became editor of the Emperor's rescripts and a minister of state. Meanwhile he kept up a steady diplomatic correspondence with his ruler — in cipher, which he knew the Russians could translate — intended not so much for his king's eyes as for Alexander's. In various ways, then, De Maistre served his native country well.

But the diplomacy did not take up much of the Savoyard diplomat's time during his fourteen years in Russia — a fortunate thing for him and for posterity. There remained much time, days on end, when he did not leave his rooms and when he devoted himself exclusively to reading, note-taking, writing, and meditating. During his stay at St. Petersburg, De Maistre wrote his most important works, especially *Du Pape,* and *Les Soirées de Saint Petersburg,* which occupies a high place in the history of French literature.

When the Napoleonic wars ended in 1815, De Maistre was anxious to return home. He was growing old, past sixty, and he wanted to enjoy that comfortable life he left at Chambery twenty years before. Moreover, Alexander was growing suspicious of this man who had once fascinated him. De Maistre was accused of making converts at the Russian court, and finally, when Alexander decided to suppress the Jesuits, an open rupture occurred between the Savoyard Catholic and the Orthodox Emperor. Alexander asked for De Maistre's recall, the ambassador demanded it in strong terms; so Victor Emmanuel I, who was then king of Piedmont, called him home in the summer of 1817. On the way back to his native land this man who wrote model French stepped on French soil for the first and last time in his life. With his family he visited Paris briefly, and then he settled down at Turin, where he served as minister of state and keeper of the great seal until his death in 1821.

* * *

De Maistre is the most difficult to describe of all the Catholic laymen treated in this book because the vocabulary of laudation has long since been exhausted by his panegyrists. And even though his critics disagree violently with his ideas, they are nevertheless willing to bestow lavish praise upon him as a man. In De Maistre they see one worthy representative of the Old Regime, "the mirror of all that was brilliant and profound" in the forces that opposed the French Revolution. His followers find no encomium too strong to bestow on him. He is called "a miracle of genius," "the greatest Father of the Church of this century [the nineteenth]," "the last of the great doctors," "a powerful logician, an incomparable herald and a superb champion." These panegyrics are from men like Hypolite Taine and Father Descotes who are not ordinarily given to lavish praise. Lecigne goes even further in asserting that "to exalt De Maistre is at least a sign of intelligence." And a presumably hostile critic, Paul Vulliaud, admits that those who resent De Maistre's attack on rationalism acknowledge "his honesty, courage, spirit, charm, courtesy, delicacy, amiability, his exquisite knowledge of the world and of human nature, his personal dignity, his vivid, incisive and penetrating irony, his ability to disentangle a sophism and turn it back on an enemy with blasting force."

These words of high praise are repeated by almost everyone who has made a study of De Maistre. Nor, as one comes to know him well, do they seem much exaggerated. For he possessed high integrity and keen ability. These qualities of character and mind he combined with selfless devotion to the causes he thought right and with an almost reckless courage in battling for the truth. Especially his integrity and his courage have won him the admiration of opponents and the worship of comrades in arms.

De Maistre is one of those few men in history who was both a student and a man of practical affairs, the St. Thomas More type who manages somehow to follow both scholarly and practical pursuits without allowing interest in the one to hurt the other. John Morley, the English biographer of Voltaire and specialist on eighteenth-century France, who later defended everything De Maistre had attacked, admitted of him that "few men knew so perfectly as he knew how to be touching without ceasing to be masculine, nor how to go down into the dark pits of human life without forgetting the broad sunlight, nor how to keep habitually close to visible and palpable fact while eagerly addicted to speculation." He believes that because De Maistre was "a student and a thinker and also a man of the world" he was able to "give a peculiar life, reality, and force to both scholarship and speculation." This point, which Morley makes condescendingly, is important for the reader of De Maistre's works to keep in mind — for his striking style sometimes screens the balance of speculative thought and experience which lies behind each of his statements.

De Maistre was a student. His mind, he says in one place, was "sunk since birth in study," and again he wrote to a friend that his brain "was a great bureau with numberless drawers, in which all sorts of information was stored up, to be drawn out at will." Here De Maistre is making offhand reference to the studious habits he followed throughout life. He had accumulated a large personal library — 2534 volumes — before he fled from Chambery. As he read he made copious notes which he took down in his copybook, and as each book was finished he carefully indexed it and put it away. Fortunately, when he became a wanderer he was able to bring along his trunkful of notebooks — which accounts for his works giving the reader the impression that they were written in the reference room of the British Museum instead of in De Maistre's barren study in Russia.

De Maistre was a vigorous but balanced thinker. He stated his conclusions so pungently and forcefully, however, that he is frequently considered an extreme opponent of anything new, a blind defender of State and Church alike. His striking, forthright style has earned him such titles as "the lone knight who stood fearless against the monster of Revolution." But we should not let his Voltairean phraseology blind us to the balance and the common sense of his thinking. For, as we shall see, he neither ignored nor defended the abuses of the Old Regime or the dangers of authoritarian government.

* * *

For about fifty years in the nineteenth century De Maistre was considered an uncritical defender of the Old Regime. He was so known because he was the authority quoted by almost everyone opposed to the new order of the nineteenth century, and he was the principal opponent whom the Liberals thought they had to refute. As time passed and as De Maistre's complete works were published, however, it was seen that his stand on political matters and on history was pretty much the same as Edmund Burke's. He was a traditionalist, like Burke, for experience had made him wary of things new or revolutionary. He had a rather low opinion of concrete human nature as it operates in this world. He was suspicious of institutions contrived out of thought alone. De Maistre was convinced that good constitutions, like good wine, are the work of time and of a natural fermentation process. They are the end result of a long series of events directed by Providence, and the man who would break into this development – the revolutionist – is bound to cause trouble.

Like Burke, De Maistre did not oppose change, but he wanted it slow, gradual, based upon the garnered experience of the past. This is the big point in De Maistre's political thinking, the acid test to which he would subject any proposal for reform; his appeal to experience, to history. His activity in politics and in diplomacy had put the mature De Maistre in close touch with the world of things and men about him. Thus he developed a prudential mind, almost a skeptical attitude toward changes which were concocted out of the thin air of rationalist theorizing, like the Rights of Man of the French Revolution or the Social Contract of Rousseau or Paine. De Maistre knew there was an impassable gulf between Rousseau's *Contrat social* and the reality of political life. This common-sense appeal to experience, this basic realism and this prudential approach to all political questions are themes running through all De Maistre's reflections on man in society and politics.

In this respect, we have said, he was very much like Burke. But he differed from the noted English statesman in holding a theology of history by which he explained historical events in the light of providential design. His view of history was therefore opposed to the "progress" theories of the time, which held that man got better age by age whether he tried or not. Whereas Condorcet had worked out a theory to show how man passed upward from one age to another, inevitably to future perfection, De Maistre thought that human nature is pretty much the same at all times. He stressed the role of Divine Providence in history and he tended to minimize the historical importance of single individuals. He considered men free in their human actions but unable by their free acts to change the divine plan. "We are all bound to the throne of the Supreme Being," is the way he put it, "by an elastic chain which holds us firmly but does not enslave us."

De Maistre applied this general view of history to his own age to conclude that the French Revolution was something more than a succession of turbulent events. "It is an epoch," he wrote in 1796, whose consequences are to be felt in all countries and in every domain of thought and action. The historian today does not think of history turning as sharp a corner as De Maistre sees it turning in the French Revolution, but he agrees with him that it did fundamentally change the face and the constitution of European society. De Maistre interpreted the Revolution in theological terms. "There is in the French Revolution a *satanic* character which distinguishes it from everything that has happened in the past or can occur in the future." He believes that it is essentially "a religious revolution. The rest, which seems immense, is no more than an appendix." It was prescribed by God as a scourge for sinful mankind, as the Deluge had been sent in Noe's day and Sodom and Gomorrha had been visited with death. Napoleon, like the Revolution before him, "is a great and terrible instrument in the hands of Providence." De Maistre sums up the meaning of the French Revolution as "a great sermon which Providence preached to mankind. It is in two parts: first, that revolutions are the result of abuses, and this part is directed to rulers; second, that the abuses are infinitely better than revolutions, and this second part is addressed to peoples."

This Savoyard Count was at heart an optimist. Although he refused to see progress accomplished by man alone, nevertheless he did look for a better age in the immediate future. This hope was based on his faith in Providence and on his conviction that the divine chastisement of the French Revolution would leave the world a better and a wiser society. This better society would be directed by the nobility of days gone by, De Maistre believed, since he was convinced that in his day they were only in "a well-deserved eclipse" from which they would emerge when the dark clouds of revolution passed. Most important, the future would be better because there would be a religious revival throughout Europe, and its principal note would be a return to Rome — by Protestants who had left the fold centuries before, and by Gallican Catholics who always stood on the porch with just a toe in the household of the Roman Catholic Church. De Maistre looked to the Anglican Church to begin the Protestant movement toward Rome, and he hoped to turn the French bishops from their Gallican sentiments to a Jesuit ultramontanism.

Unless such conversions were effected, there could be no good society in the future. De Maistre was convinced that there could be peace and security and order only when Europe was unified, and for him an essential element of any solid peace was the union of all European Christians in one religion. This could be effected only under the pope. So, as we shall see later, he looked to the pope as the guardian of the future, as he had been protector of the past. Among the nations of the world he looked on France as having a providential mission to perform in preserving and spreading the true Faith. Because she had been unfaithful to her high mission in the past, failing in her vocation and spreading the poison of Liberal heresy throughout Europe, she had been punished by revolution. De Maistre was hopeful that this great nation was learning her divinely taught lesson and would assume her proper role in the nineteenth century.

* * *

As we have indicated above, De Maistre's political thought was not a flat defense of the Old Regime nor just a well-reasoned case for authoritarian government. Realistic and prudent in his political thinking, De Maistre consciously tried to steer a middle course between the extremes of tyranny and anarchy. Time and time again in his correspondence as well as in his formal writings he stresses the need for reconciling authority and liberty. "It is necessary," he wrote, "to preach to the people incessantly the benefits of authority, and to kings the benefits of liberty."

De Maistre stressed the need of authority because he lived and wrote in an age when everyone seemed to reject authority of any kind. He insisted that no matter how much men railed against the authority of kings, the fact remained that in every society there must be a sovereign authority, even if it be the sovereignty of the mob with a rope, and therefore, he argued, it is well to recognize that legally and physically the sovereign authority of the government is unlimited. The only bounds to sovereignty, he held, are set by the good sense and the morality of the ruler himself. De Maistre was old fashioned enough to believe that the personal monarch was less likely to abuse the rights of sovereignty and to curtail the subject's freedom than any other kind of government.

So De Maistre advocated monarchy as the ideal form of government. "It is the best, the most natural, and the most durable form of government." But he did not defend the monarchy of the Old Regime, faults and all. He was a strong critic of those monarchies, including his own at Turin, which he said were too conservative, too stubbornly opposed to any change, and therefore became guilty of precipitating the revolutions of his age. For the fallen monarchs he had little sympathy, but for the revolutions which tumbled them from their thrones he had even less. Reform and change there should be, he frequently says, but such reforms should properly be inaugurated by the king.

In positing monarchy as the ideal form of government and in picturing strong authority as an essential note of good government, De Maistre did not sacrifice the individual to the government, as the French Revolution did in practice and Rousseau had done in theory. De Maistre endeavors to keep the individual a free person in society. But he believes that man's liberty is possible only in Christian society where there are strong moral sanctions on the bad use of liberty and where there are strong legal sanctions on wrongdoing. He appealed to history, in this argument, to show how governments had ruled only over free Christians on the one hand or non-Christian slaves on the other. He therefore concluded that unless the citizens are restrained from evil-doing by the sanctions of the Christian moral law, then the government must deny them their liberty in the interest of general security. This is the argument, incidentally, which De Maistre passed on to later Catholic lay apologists of the nineteenth century, an argument which Donoso Cortés developed against Liberalism in the next generation.

* * *

In *Les soirées de Saint-Petersburg,* De Maistre takes up that problem which has always baffled man, the problem of pain and evil in a world created by God, a problem particularly bothering to sensitive, acute minds, such as Voltaire in the generation before De Maistre and John Stuart Mill in the generation after him. Although his reflections on the subject do not solve the problem for all time, still they do throw much light on it and they do answer the objections against God's goodness brought up by the eighteenth-century rationalists. From his semiretreat in Russia, De Maistre penned his mature thoughts on this subject, turning it over and over in Socratic fashion, obtaining new views from various perspectives, and, all in all, saying some very wise things about God's Providence in the world, and saying them in very readable fashion.

The book is a series of conversations between a grave Russian senator, a spirited French knight, and *Le Comte,* who is De Maistre himself. The discussion begins when the senator questions "the prosperity of the wicked and the misery of the just." Before they are through the three have explored the whole range of God's action in relation to His creatures. They have raised the question of the utility of suffering, the problem of the justice of punishments meted out to the innocent, the question of the goodness of an all-powerful God. *The Count's* answers are taken from the shelves of standard Catholic theology, but they are presented in nontechnical fashion and they are interlaced with a pungent, sometimes flaying analysis of eighteenth-century thinkers like Voltaire and Rousseau, and, as Father Raymond Corrigan has put it, "The stature of the philosophes shrinks visibly under the withering criticism of De Maistre."

Throughout the *Soirées* run certain basic Catholic ideas which De Maistre put flatly before the world as an adequate explanation of the problem of evil. If the just man suffers it is not because he is just but because he is a man. Evil has entered the universe as the result of sin, and by suffering, he argues, man expiates sin, his own and that of the human race. In one of the conversations, De Maistre tells his friends how though a good father does not chastise the yardman for using coarse language, nevertheless he does punish his son for the same thing. He chastizes his son because he loves him and because he wants to raise him properly. In the same way, does God punish His children. Often enough, in the mysterious working of Providence, "there are just punishments of which the agents are most guilty" – as is the case in the French Revolution. So De Maistre goes on for two volumes justifying the ways of God to men of the early nineteenth century. His work was read widely because it was beautifully written, and it provided as adequate a popular answer as has been devised by man to the mysterious problem of pain.

This was a subject which interested De Maistre deeply because it is at the bottom a mystery. And all through life, from his early connection with the Masons until his death at the age of 68, De Maistre was attracted by the mysterious, the occult, the mystical. He was always possessed of a zeal for deeper knowledge than the merely rational. Sometimes, especially in his earlier years, he was extremely ill-advised in the ways along which he sought to penetrate the secrets of the heavens. As a young man he was attracted by the "Illuminism" of a certain Saint-Martin, *le Philosophe Inconnu,* whom his sister Thérèse characterized as "sublime, heretical, and absurd." Again, it seems to have been the mysteriousness of Masonry's symbolism more than anything else which attracted the twenty-one-year-old magistrate at Chambery.

As he grew older, however, De Maistre grew wiser and he became more cautious in seeking easy solutions for age-old mysteries. Throughout his life he maintained a sort of mystical straining toward that truth which lies beyond the ken of a merely rationalist philosophy, but in his maturity he confessed that youthful eagerness had led him naïvely astray along the paths of Illuminism and Masonry. By the time he had arrived at St. Petersburg he had repudiated any connection with the "Illuminati" of Germany, "a most criminal association organized to extinguish Christianity and sovereignty in Europe." And in time he came to repudiate Masonry for similar reasons.

De Maistre's straining toward a mystical higher truth is understandable as a reaction to the rationalism of Locke and Voltaire and Diderot, that narrow, shallow thinking which shriveled God and the universe in order to confine them within the bounds of the rationalist's little mind. The Savoyard Count may have gone too far in his reaction to rationalism, but certainly he was right in seeing God as unfathomable Being and in looking upon every theological truth as being ultimately a mystery—for each of them reaches back to God, who cannot be completely comprehended by the human mind. De Maistre believed that "religion is the mother of the sciences" and that each science ultimately ends up in a mystery, no matter how much of the preliminary ground can be explored and mapped out satisfactorily by human reason. Frequently he quoted St. Paul to the effect that "the world is a system of invisible things visibly manifested." He believed that human reason could explore the visible manifestation of these things, but he was himself always eager to know the "invisible things" which are revealed to man in their fullness only in the next life.

* * *

Although De Maistre's thought was always turned upward, straining to penetrate through the misty regions beyond the visible world, still he did not disdain to do battle with the rationalists in the world about him. More successfully perhaps than any other Catholic thinker of the nineteenth century, De Maistre engaged the great figures of rationalism by meeting them on their own grounds—very mundane grounds they were—and fighting them with their own weapons. His paragraphs on Voltaire read like Voltaire's paragraphs on Bossuet; they are witty, salty, epigrammatic, hard. Frequently enough De Maistre dismisses an eighteenth-century thinker with a withering retort or a clever epigram instead of a well-reasoned argument. That was the fashion of the time, it was the weapon of the rationalist, and it seems to have been more effective than hard thinking. He seemed to demolish men like Voltaire and Hume with a phrase—which you cannot really do—and even today his remarks are remembered and quoted, as they were all through the nineteenth century.

Throughout his writings De Maistre insists that the eighteenth century will form a shameful epoch in the history of the human mind. It is the age "that delivered you [his readers] from the faith of your fathers." It is an age whose leading thinkers posed as "infallible oracles" men whose lives and theories proved beyond doubt that "pride is the origin of all crime." It is an age that "destroyed the mysterious charm of government" and by doing so prepared men's minds for the French Revolution, the excesses of which proved conclusively how wrong rationalists were in making all their theories arid abstractions. This is the big point that De Maistre repeatedly makes against rationalism. "It was a singular absurdity of the last century to judge everything according to abstract rules, without any regard for experience."

Many pages could be filled with De Maistre's clever thrusts at rationalism as a method of thought and at those individual thinkers who were treated with a quasi-divine reverence by men of a little learning in De Maistre's day. Rationalist theories he likens in one place to counterfeit money "which is struck in the first instance by great criminals, and is afterwards passed on by honest folk who perpetuate the crime without knowing what they do." Although he is willing to see some good in men like Bacon and Locke, nevertheless he concludes that there is "not one of these men to whom the sacred title of honest man is quite suitable." They are all envious of those with position and authority, even God Himself who is their master; and for this reason, De Maistre believes, they rail against the authority of Church and State and of truth itself.

He refines this blanket denunciation of eighteenth-century rationalists by distinguishing the peculiar weaknesses of individual thinkers. Locke and Bacon he dismisses as mediocre philosophers at best, men who had mixed a measure of truth in their theories with a large part of error. Hume he thinks the most capable of them all, and therefore the one who has done the greatest amount of harm. Rousseau he considers the most dangerous, a writer to be taken seriously and to be argued with phrase by phrase. Thus he devotes the greater part of his *Study on Sovereignty* to a refutation of Rousseau's *Contrat social.* For Voltaire he has nothing but contempt, and he turns Voltaire's name-calling against him. "Voltaire's great crime," he says in the *Soirées*, "is the abuse of talent and the deliberate prostitution of a genius created to praise God and virtue. . . . Nothing absolves him. His corruption is of a kind which is peculiar to him alone; it takes root in the deepest fibers of his heart and it feeds itself on all the powers of his mind. . . . Paris has crowned him;

Sodom would have banished him." For such a man, De Maistre admits, he can feel nothing but "a kind of holy anger."

Better refutations of rationalism have been forged by Catholic apologists since De Maistre's day, but the fact remains that his withering blasts against eighteenth-century thinkers shriveled them down from the position of intellectual giants that they then held to the stature of the little men they really are. His was a daring attack, for it flew straight against the accepted opinions of the day. At a time when many members of the hierarchy were trying to accommodate themselves to rationalist thinking, De Maistre dared to cry out to the world that such thinking was shallow and selfish and false. Time has proved him right in his conclusions, though time has improved on his technique and his arguments – both of which were rightly gauged for the temper of his age.

* * *

De Maistre is known in Catholic circles mainly because of his vigorous defense of papal infallibility half a century before it was solemnly proclaimed by the Vatican Council in 1870. This, again, was a daring thing. De Maistre wrote when Gallican sentiment was strong, when he had to convince not only all non-Catholics but also most influential Catholics that the pope was really head of the Church and infallible guardian of Catholic doctrine. There is a paradox about De Maistre's stand on papal infallibility. His arguments are more curious than sound, and for the most part they were rejected by the Vatican Council – but they are arguments which lead to the right conclusion of infallibility. Moreover, De Maistre is important for standing at the threshold of the century directing Catholic thought Romeward – a most important thing for the reviving Church of the early nineteenth century.

De Maistre approaches the question of infallibility in unusual fashion. He is not concerned with infallibility as a matter of faith. To him the pope is not so much the guardian of true doctrine as he is the cornerstone of European morals and social institutions. His approach, therefore, is political rather than theological; he treats the pope as ruler of the Church universal, not as a doctor. The fact of infallibility, he claims, rests on the very structure of monarchical government, which, of course, the Church possesses. It rests on "the nature of things," and "by no means requires to be supported by theology." This argument for infallibility is not the traditional Catholic argument, the one adopted by the Fathers at the Vatican Council, but it was the most appealing approach for De Maistre's age. After the French Revolution and the Napoleonic wars, people were interested chiefly in political stability and social cohesiveness, and De Maistre adapted his apologetic to the common feeling of the time.

He states his argument succinctly in these words: "No human society can exist without government, nor government without sovereignty, nor sovereignty without infallibility. And this last privilege is so absolutely necessary that we are obliged to suppose infallibility, even in temporal sovereignties, where it is not, on pain of beholding society dissolved. The Church requires nothing more than other sovereignties, although it possesses an immense superiority over them, inasmuch as infallibility is on the one hand *humanly supposed*, and on the other *divinely promised*." Concentrating on the human argument, De Maistre develops the thesis that infallibility is a necessary note of sovereignty. "Infallibility," he says, "becomes a necessary consequence of supremacy, or, rather, it is absolutely the same thing under a different name." But by this he means only that the sovereign is the last court of appeal in the land, that there is no human agency capable of reversing his decision – else there is chaos and anarchy and revolution and therefore no sovereignty. In the same way, humanly speaking, the pope is the court of last appeal in the Church. De Maistre backs up his proof of papal infallibility from a wealth of historical evidence, from statements of ecumenical councils, from the general consensus of opinion throughout the history of the Church. He further strengthens his argument by pointing out that, as a matter of fact, the popes have never erred, "having never ceased, during eighteen centuries, to pronounce on all kinds of questions with prudence and accuracy truly miraculous."

De Maistre buttresses his claims for papal infallibility and sovereignty over the Church universal by developing the thesis that European society is built upon the cornerstone of the papacy and that loss of papal prestige would undermine Christian society — in Protestant countries as well as Catholic — so seriously that it might collapse like a house of cards. In the pages of *Du Pape* the Savoyard Catholic layman shows how the popes stood heroically in the face of the barbarian enemy when the rest of civilized Europe fled before the invading hordes, how the popes organized and developed European civilization by promoting and maintaining the priesthood, by fostering education, and by "softening and sweetening" the naturally tyrannical monarchs of Europe. "Imperceptibly," he tells us, "without threats, without law, without combats, without violence, and without resistance, the great European charter was proclaimed, not on perishable paper, not by the voice of public criers, but in all European hearts, at that time Catholic." This was the work of the popes.

Therefore, he holds, it is right to conclude that "the popes were the founders, the tutors, the saviors, and the real constituent minds of the social state of Europe." They ameliorated and eventually eliminated slavery, they raised the lot of women and gave them true Christian dignity, and most of all, by their influence on the monarchs of Europe they changed them from barbarian ruffians to civilized Christians. Thus did they humanize society and make it possible for men to enjoy a large measure of liberty, for "without Christianity, no general liberty" is possible. The choice before his age, De Maistre insists, is between Christianity and liberty on the one hand or secularism and slavery on the other. He allows mankind no other alternative.

We would say today that De Maistre hurt his case by trying to prove too much. (Pope Pius VII himself is said to have been embarrassed by the claims made on his behalf.) But we must concede that it was good tactics, apologetically, for his time. Men who read *Du Pape* remembered that the Pope had been imprisoned by Napoleon at Fontainbleau, even his fisherman's ring, his pen and paper taken away; they remembered that bishops frequently enough ignored Rome, going their respective ways pretty much as local ecclesiastical sovereigns. Now these men read that if the papacy is destroyed there will be no more civilization. Such a book appealed to thousands. And those who did not agree with it, Protestants and Gallican Catholics alike, were shaken by it, put on the defensive, and forced to try refuting it.

* * *

It is too much to call De Maistre "the preface to the Vatican Council" as his supporters have frequently done, simply because he defended papal infallibility in 1819, since his idea of infallibility and his arguments for it had little in common with those of the Council's theologians. But it is not too much to call him "the founder of the great Catholic movement, the new ultramontanism, of the present [nineteenth] century." De Maistre's historical importance was well summed up ten years ago by Father Corrigan when he wrote of *Du Pape:* "The book was smoke in the nostrils of a moribund Gallicanism. It gave heart to a rising Ultramontanism."

De Maistre made mistakes, sometimes serious ones, and curiously enough even his sound conclusions were often enough based on now insupportable lines of argument. He is nonetheless important, because he entered the breech early in the nineteenth century, a layman defending the Church in a day when the clergy were too overburdened with their priestly duties to enter into public debate on the claims of the Church. Moreover, De Maistre promoted the Catholic revival in those days by stressing essentially correct truths and thus directing the revival along the right path. He demolished the plaster statues of the great men of eighteenth-century rationalism, statues before which thinkers of his time bowed in unquestioning awe. He vindicated the Church against their attacks, and he showed how shallow intellectually were these intellects of the age of rationalism. He also directed Catholicism Romeward, an important thing in his day, for the Church was suffering from a centrifugal movement that had been going on for more than a century.

Finally, De Maistre is important because of the position time and Providence and circumstance assigned to him. He occupies a position that is not of benefit to his reputation, but one which has helped the Church. De Maistre lived during the French Revolution, and though he was perspicacious enough to see that it was a decisive turning point in history, still his very closeness to the event denied him the same perspective for judging it properly which was given to such later Catholic laymen as

Donoso Cortés and Louis Veuillot. The Church benefited from De Maistre's standing at the beginning of the century, both for what he did and for his influence on those Catholic lay leaders who followed him. Montalembert, Donoso Cortés, De Mun, Veuillot, all speak of "having been brought up at his feet." They all read De Maistre and were influenced by him in the formative time of their lives, when they were preparing to assume their respective roles as Catholic lay leaders in the two generations after their great Savoyard predecessor.

9. Joseph Görres

The revival of Catholic apologetics in the nineteenth century stems from two laymen. One of them is Joseph de Maistre, the other Johann Joseph Görres. We have seen how De Maistre tended toward conservatism, how he prized order and stability, how he opposed the French Revolution for making the good life impossible. Görres, on the other hand, tended temperamentally toward Liberalism. He loved liberty above all earthly things. A product of the rationalistic *Aufklärung,* he was at first the opponent of religious and secular authority, an ardent champion of the French Revolution, a battler for freedom of press and speech and education and action. For fifty years he pursued his twin ideals of freedom and truth, which he felt were inextricably intertwined, and he rejected one illusory solution after another until finally he found in the Catholic Church what he had sought so long.

Like De Maistre, then, in the last twenty-five years of his life he fought for the Church and for the papacy as the guarantors of truth and freedom in the modern world. Although he differed from De Maistre in emphasizing freedom rather than order, his enemies were the same: the French Revolution and its *enfant terrible,* Napoleon; the antireligious, secular dogma of Liberalism; the state of Prussia and its tendency to circumscribe its subjects' freedom by controlling their education, their means of expression, and their religion.

Görres agreed with De Maistre in essentials and differed from him in those incidental features which clothe a man's thought and his appearance. Whereas De Maistre was of the nobility and appeared every inch the proper gentleman of the eighteenth century, Görres was of the lower middle class of the early nineteenth century, and was therefore constitutionally predisposed against authority in any guise. The untidiest boy of his class, he was oblivious throughout life of his appearance, a tousle-haired individual, unfettered by the conventional accouterments of the society in which he moved so disruptively. Görres spent his life defying the law of averages. He was too busy learning ever to be a good student at school — but he became superintendent of instruction in the Rhineland provinces. He never took classes at a university — but he became the outstanding professor at the University of Munich. He was strongly anticlerical as a young man because he thought that the clergy hampered freedom of thought — but he became the German hierarchy's most powerful protector. So in the final analysis, Görres the liberal stood side by side with De Maistre the conservative, because, although they took different paths, both men arrived at the same goal of truth and freedom which they found within the wide compass of the Catholic Church. There they did great work defending the Church against the sapping attacks of late eighteenth-century rationalism and the frontal assault of secular forces unloosed by the French Revolution.

Görres is important for having defended the pope and the clergy of Germany at a time when the German hierarchy was still prostrate. He is important, as one of his students put it, for "teaching the Catholics of Germany to be proud of their faith." He was a philosopher, historian, and natural scientist who had earned the respect of German scholars and the fear of German statesmen — and therefore his arguments in favor of the Church could not be dismissed lightly. Thus he became the strongest, as well as the most gifted, champion of the Church in Germany, a voice that sounded loudly and continuously and earned for the Catholics of his land a hearing that they had long been denied. Moreover, for the last twenty-five years of his life he presided over the Catholic revival at Munich, from which developed in the next generation the solid Catholicism of Bishop von Ketteler's and Windthorst's day.

* * *

The remark Görres once made of his friend Clemens Brentano, that "the man himself is more interesting than his best book," can aptly be applied to Görres himself. For Görres was a good writer and a good teacher who wrote constantly and lectured frequently — but he stands forth a better man than his best book or his best lecture. He was a universal genius who cannot be contained in anything less than his own life story: journalist, pamphleteer, teacher, philosopher, historian, scientist, one whose intellectual interests embraced the whole realm of human knowledge. But he was primarily a man of action whose greatest importance lay in his unremitting fight for freedom and for the rights of the Church. Typical of his limitless interests and his wide enthusiasm in things of the mind was his translation of 60,000 couplets of the Persian epic *Shah Nameh* in which he had become interested – a truly Herculean task, since he had to learn Persian and make his translation from a badly written manuscript, and all this he did in two years!

Görres was possessed of a restless intellectual curiosity which prevented him from approaching his studies in that methodical, plodding fashion popularly associated with German scholars. He rushed from one field of interest to another – from politics to physiology, to Asiatic mythology, back to politics again, to mysticism, to a Romantic-Catholic philosophy of history. He cast the penetrating searchlight of his well-focused intellect on each subject he explored, and he seemed, for his time at least, to master each subject he approached. His detachment from mundane matters like food and clothing, his intellectual energy and his boundless curiosity, his love of free inquiry and liberty of speech gave him a Bohemianlike appearance, physically and mentally. His students at Munich, where he spent the last third of his life as a professor of history, describe him as a perpetually youthful, fresh, eager man whose lectures poured forth like a torrent of water spilling over a precipice. One of them tells how his "walk was swift, his pace short and precipitate," and how his mind behaved in exactly the same fashion, darting hither and thither through the fields of human knowledge, full of energy and zestful with the very joy of living in intimate association with the great minds of the past.

Diversified interests frequently lead to superficiality. But not with Görres. His acquaintances and his biographers all insist on his solid integrity. The most important Görres scholar in recent years, William Schellberg, describes him as "upright, honest, cheerful, fresh, plain and unassuming, solid even to excess, without a bit of fear, friendly and gentle with everyone, warm-hearted and understanding, free of any mark of selfishness." These high words of praise are used by all who met him and came to know him well. Father Corrigan summed up the general opinion held by scholars on Görres when he wrote: "His impatience with sham and pretence, with hypocrisy and time-serving was part of a character that never swerved from what he thought was right. He never sought personal gain; he never weighed the odds against him."

Görres is not important as an original thinker. Although he put together various ideas in the common stock of the Christian tradition to apply them in an original way to the problems of his time, nevertheless he did not make any lasting contribution to philosophical or theological knowledge. He is important rather as a journalist and a polemicist. Frequently he protested "I am no theologian," but the fact remains that he learned theology, as he learned physiology and history and government, from competent authorities – and his great work lay in popularizing this knowledge and in adapting it to the peculiar contingencies of his age. The effectiveness with which he did this work is witnessed by his contemporaries. Napoleon is said to have called *The Rhenish Mercury,* the newspaper which Görres edited in 1814, "a fifth power" joined to the alliance against him. And the Prussian Marshall Blücher said Görres' paper was worth four army corps. That is why historians generally refer to him as the "most important German publicist of the nineteenth century."

He was one of those comparatively rare persons – like St. Thomas More and De Maistre – who managed to combine theory and practice at all times. As a popularizer of the great truths found in the Catholic tradition, it was part of his very nature to apply those truths to the problems of his age. Thus he found the subject of Christian mysticism a very practical one, and he showed how theology and philosophy had a direct bearing on the problem of the persecution of the Catholic Church by the Prussian government in the 1830's. He was a teacher who was conversant with old manuscripts in the library but whose principal function was to bring truth to his students in understandable guise.

A word must be said about his style – for it presents serious difficulties to the scholar who would read him today. Görres belonged to the Romantic school of the early nineteenth century, a group that reacted to the dry rationalism of the preceding age and found truth and beauty, glory and nobility in the Catholic Church. He used typically Romantic language with which he built up beautiful, moving word pictures. He wrote in pictures rather than in syllogisms. German critics, indeed, all comment on the manner in which his tempestuous imagination colors his thought. His pages are something like the Gothic architecture the Romantics so admired: descriptive phrases, similes, and metaphors piled up diffusely to paint the picture he wished to show his reader. Such a style was most effective in the early part of the nineteenth century — but it makes for difficult reading today, and it defies accurate translation. His style reveals the manner of man Görres was, a volcanic sort of person who drives impetuously to the heart of a matter in the first paragraph of a book. He was a vigorous man with a vigorous style, a tempest of energy whose paragraphs and sentences lack orderliness and clarity. Such a defect did not hurt him in his own day; indeed it probably helped him in that age when thinking men reacted to the style as well as the thought of rationalism. But unfortunately it has "dated" him and cast him into the oblivion of history as part of an age now far behind us.

* * *

Görres spent his entire lifetime battling for freedom and truth. Paradoxically, he spent his first fifty years searching for true freedom and for the fullness of truth even while fighting in their defense. Suffering one disappointment after another as his various ideals proved false, he turned each time in another direction to continue his relentless search. At last, when he was about fifty, he found his goals in the Catholic Church — and there he remained for the rest of his life, fighting for three things in one: freedom, truth, and Catholicism. Because Görres always combined thought and action in intimate union and because his search for truth is so closely bound up with the exterior events of his life, it would be well to follow the most important happenings of his life in order to understand his writing more fully — and his importance as a lay defender of the Faith.

Görres was born in a year famous in the history of freedom, 1776, in the Rhineland city of Coblenz. This community was German in blood and language, but culturally and intellectually it was closely connected with France. The commercial class, to which the Görres family belonged, was especially associated with "enlightened" progress in affairs of the mind, all of which centered in Paris in those days. Young Görres therefore grew up in a city where rationalism was the vogue, where anyone who was awake intellectually was supposed to be cynical about religion and at least condescendingly anticlerical. It was a city where the dominant middle class, opposed to the twin authorities of State and Church, was eager to usher in an "enlightened" society patterned after the revolutionary thought of such men as Voltaire, Holbach, Montesquieu, and Rousseau.

Johann Joseph Görres was therefore exposed to an education colored and distorted by the rationalist *Aufklärung*. It is difficult to say how much his formal schooling influenced his development, because he was too independent a youngster to absorb classroom lessons passively. His report card shows he took such subjects as poetry, rhetoric, logic, physics and astronomy, and later on mathematics and chemistry and philosophy. But Görres was too busy educating himself to do well at school. When he was supposed to be memorizing poetry, he was devising experiments in his attic; when he was supposed to be learning Cicero, he was writing a manual of geography which the local printer considered worth publishing. Though Görres was condemned by his teachers for lack of industry he was no idler.

As a youth he revealed that intense intellectual curiosity which led him into so many fields of endeavor and eventually into the Church; he also possessed an ardent desire to do battle for the cause of truth. His biographers tell of an incident from his early boyhood which, apocryphal or not, is symbolic of how he was not content to be a hearer of the word only but also a fighter for good causes. One day the students of his school marched in procession through the streets of Coblenz dressed as angels. Young Görres was St. Michael; a less fortunate lad was Lucifer. In a flash, young St. Michael remembered he had better be about his Lord's business. So he layed into Lucifer with his wooden sword, breaking up the procession, and before hapless Lucifer knew what was up he had fallen under a rain of blows from St. Michael's avenging right arm. That impulse to action never left Joseph Görres. He was always anxious to deliver timely blows in the interest of truth and of freedom.

Joseph's formal schooling was completed when he left the local *Gymnasium* – at about the age of sixteen. Seeds of religious belief must have been planted in his mind, but the noxious weeds of the *Aufklärung* for a long time kept them from developing. Great dreams of a splendid new era in human history filled his imagination, for the utopian expectations of the French Revolution had reached the banks of the Rhine by the time Görres left school. He loathed the German petty princes who sold their subjects like cattle for service in foreign armies; he was disgusted with the corruption, the luxury, the cynicism of the French nobility who had fled to Coblenz. He therefore held the Old Regime in contempt and looked hopefully to the Revolution as the herald of truth and freedom for all mankind.

So Görres began his career an ardent Jacobin, a supporter of the French Revolution, a severe critic of the nobility, the clergy, and the monarchy. He expressed his youthful ideas in a pamphlet, *Universal Peace: An Ideal,* in which he displayed that intense hatred of tyranny which was to remain a part of his nature until the end. For a time he edited a radical little paper, *The Red Journal,* whose motto was "Eternal war to all scoundrels; the hand to the virtuous man." In 1799 the young Jacobin of twenty-four headed a deputation to Paris asking for the inclusion of the Rhineland as an integral part of France. In Paris, Görres "saw the actors undressed behind the scenes," as he put it on his return, and he found that they were made of the same sordid, selfish material as the rulers of the Old Regime. He found them as arrogant and tyrannical as the princes of Germany – and that was enough for Görres, because he could never tolerate shams. On his return to Germany he wrote of his Jacobin aspirations: "All these dreams are of the past, and I thank God that I have brought my love of science and art safely out of the storm."

Görres now turned to science, a field where political beliefs did not interfere with his quest for truth nor limit his freedom of thought. For the next six years he was professor of physics in the secondary school of Coblenz. During that time he wrote a number of scientific treatises and, more important, he became more and more interested in the German Romantic movement of the time. Through his friend Clemens Brentano he was introduced to a group of young men who looked to the past, when

German culture was healthy, to unearth principles and ideals on which a German revival could be based. This movement put Görres in touch with a more vital and virile Catholicism than he had formerly known. It brought him another step closer to the work which was to make him famous.

In 1806 he accepted an invitation to go to the University of Heidelberg, where the Romantics had gathered. Young men, they were attracted to Catholicism largely because it seemed old and still young, because it did not scorn incense or music or the appeal to the heart as well as to the intellect. They liked the Church for the same reasons the rationalists scorned and despised it. Görres was supposed to lecture on physiology at Heidelberg, but his students' letters, as well as his own temperament, lead us to suspect that his discussions ranged over the whole field of human knowledge. One of his listeners describes his lectures as "resembling a magnificent tempest at night, raging amid hidden precipices on the one side, and on the other revealing new, undreamed of landscapes, which were suddenly lit up, suggesting thoughts that influenced one's whole after-life." That does not sound like a lecture on bones and capillaries. It describes, instead, a typical Romanticist dipping into art, history, literature, mysticism, religion, and philosophy all at once.

An interfaculty war soon developed at Heidelberg: the older rationalist professors, who were Protestant, lining up against the young Romantics, who favored Catholicism as against Protestantism, whether they went to Church or not. The rationalists centered their attack on Görres. He, in turn, had little respect for pedagogues who, he said, "study the year through as though it were always Holy Week." The older professors, men like Paulus and Voss, objected both to the Romantics' glorification of things Catholic and to their lack of systematic, stultifying scholarship. And because the rationalists were the entrenched group, Görres had to leave Heidelberg in 1808. His two years as a university lecturer had not been wasted, however, for he had met many good friends who were to influence him and work with him in later years, and he had enkindled an enthusiasm for Catholicism which eventually would bring him to the Church.

Back at Coblenz, Görres was appointed director of the local *Gymnasium*. The publication of his *History of Asiatic Mythology* solidly established his reputation as a scholar, but he could not remain in the realm of scholarship when there was a call to action. So he entered the political scene again, working with Baron vom Stein, Goethe, and others, writing a series of political pamphlets urging the German people to take up arms against Napoleon in the War of Liberation. In 1814 he began to publish the famous *Rhenish Mercury,* called by a contemporary Englishman "the best journal ever edited in Germany." This is the journal, as we have seen, that Napoleon labeled "a fifth power," and which caused Marshall Blücher to remark: "We [Prussia] have four allies: England, Russia, Austria, and Görres."

With Napoleon defeated, Görres turned to the problem of German unification, championing the cause of the smaller powers against Prussia and advocating liberal constitutions for all the German states. This, of course, ran counter to the reactionary tendencies of the Prussian government, so in 1816 the *Mercury* was suppressed as dangerously radical. Typically, Görres replied with a counterblast, a little book called *The Reaction at Berlin,* which so antagonized the government that its author was deprived of his position as inspector of schools in the Rhineland. Görres answered with his famous *Germany and the Revolution,* a best seller even though – maybe because – it was ordered confiscated by the government. In it Görres denounced the practices of the German secret police, maintaining that such a group is unnecessary in any properly governed society. He asked again for constitutions which would give the people some share in the business of government, and he insisted on the inviolable rights and liberties of all German citizens.

At this point in the war of Görres *versus* Prussia, strategic retreat seemed in order for the smaller power. Görres might have had right on his side, but the Prussian government had the police – and it had ordered them to arrest its opponent. So in 1819 the fiery publicist fled to Strassburg where he settled down to eight years of reading and writing and thinking. The tyranny of Prussia and the blind conservatism of Metternich's Germany had shattered one more illusion. Görres had sought liberty in the French Revolution and then in the War of Liberation – and both times he had been bitterly disappointed.

* * *

At Strassburg he turned in a different direction in his quest for truth and freedom. His writings were more and more on religious subjects, many of his essays appearing in *The Catholic,* a journal founded in Mainz by Raess and Weiss and transferred to Strassburg in 1824. The best known of these was his study of "God's Troubador," St. Francis of Assisi, whom Görres looked upon as a model in his search for freedom and truth in this world. Throughout his stay at Strassburg he moved slowly but surely toward the Church. His faith in the secular dogma of Liberalism had been destroyed and he had no other faith to take its place. Contacts with Liberals at Strassburg, who enthusiastically welcomed him into their midst, showed Görres how far he had advanced from his Liberalism of twenty years before. He had abandoned one faith and had not yet found another. He described the unhappy condition of mind he suffered in those years in a letter written to his daughter after his "conversion" to the Church late in 1825. "It often came to me in the night," he wrote, "in the twilight between falling asleep and still being awake, that I lived like a tree pulled out of the ground, suspended in the air without support and without roots."

Alone at Strassburg, Görres revised his view of German history and with it the position of the Catholic Church in human events. He had formerly looked upon the Protestant Revolt as a step toward freedom; now he considered it an act of rebellion which had started the long fratricidal struggle leading to Germany's ruin. The Church loomed before him as the divine protector of a fallen human race, the guardian of truth and of that human freedom he so prized and jealously guarded. He saw the Church as a friend of the people, their protector against both the secular State and the errant thinker. He saw it as a supranational institution in no way subject to the State, the hard core, historically, of Christian civilization. At the same time his idea of true liberty became clearer. It was no longer merely the negative freedom from arbitrary restraint but also the positive freedom to cling to God and to the truth. Görres' long pilgrimage ended in November, 1825, when he attended a mission and entered the Church as an active, practicing Catholic.

Even before his "conversion" he had become an outstanding lay defender of the faith. For two years, until 1827, he edited

The Catholic, raising its prestige throughout Germany and using it as an organ for spreading a knowledge of Catholicism. In 1827 he was invited by King Ludwig I to occupy the chair of history at the new University of Munich which the Bavarian monarch had founded as a center of solid scholarship and vital Catholicism. Here at Munich, Görres served brilliantly as an enthusiastic professor of history and as head of the "Munich school," from which lay and clerical leaders of the next two generations were to come. This is the school the historian Dom Charles Poulet describes as "one of the greatest centers of Catholic action and scholarship, under the guidance of Joseph von Görres, who founded and presided over what was known as 'The Round Table.'"

Partly by chance and partly by reason of Görres' reputation and his attractive intellectual qualities, there came to Munich such future leaders of the Church's revival as Döllinger, Sepp, Windischmann, Brunner, Haneberg, Phillips, Moy, Möhler, and Streber. They studied under Görres and they all testified to his great teaching ability, his rounded intellectual accomplishments, and most of all to his inspirational leadership. To them he was more than the heart of the Munich school. He was the school itself until his death in 1848. Within a few years his reputation had spread throughout Europe and soon Catholics from other lands, like Brentano, Bohmer, Lamennais, Lacordaire, and Montalembert, visited Munich to receive inspiration and advice from the great Görres.

He was not a historian in the narrow sense of the term but rather a philosopher of history who soared above individual human events to survey them as the unified whole they are to the eye of God. He pleaded eloquently for a Christian view of history as contrasted to the mundane, plodding, nose-to-the-ground view then coming to be thought the only proper one for historians to take. And, as Father Corrigan has put it, "the spirit and elevation of thought that he put into the subject made his Munich sojourn . . . a bright chapter in the annals of Catholic Action." It is difficult – indeed impossible – to measure precisely the amount of influence that a man or a school has had in history. But it is generally agreed that the Munich school was the nursery which produced those titanic figures who promoted the glorious developments within the Church in Germany in the latter part of the century. The distinguished group of scholars gathered around Görres at Munich worked successfully for the renovation of spiritual life within the Church, for liberty of action for the Church in Germany, for all things of interest to the Catholic Faith.

This was Görres' most important contribution to the growth of the Church in the nineteenth century. In the last twenty years of his life, however, he continued to write incessantly, sometimes doing scholarly things like his four-volume work on Christian mysticism, sometimes rushing into print to defend the interests of the Church with such works as his famous *Athanasius*, more frequently publishing series of articles of an apologetic nature in which he described and defended Catholic beliefs and practices. In 1838 he founded the *Historisch-politische Blätter* to defend the rights of Catholics and to maintain an organ for the expression of scholarly Catholic thought. The journal was put under the editorship of Görres' son Guido, but for ten years its high reputation rested chiefly on the constant stream of contributions from the great Johann Joseph Görres himself. The Görres journal was commonly looked upon as "the official organ of Catholic opinion in Germany," although it expressed only the opinion of outstanding Catholics grouped around the Munich school. Certainly it was, as Pinson has recently written, "the most important organ of Catholic public opinion [in Germany]."

The four-volume work on *Christian Mysticism* is generally considered Görres' masterpiece. He wrote finer essays, better paragraphs, even better small books than anything in his long study of mysticism, but the total impact of this latter work was greater than anything else he wrote. Görres did this study, he tells us, "to reveal the glory of God in His saints" by explaining, illustrating, and classifying all the phenomena of the mystical life. The extent of erudition displayed by the author throughout these volumes, and the depth of reflection he occasionally revealed, enhanced his already solidly established reputation in Catholic circles. Even today it stands as a remarkable production. Its author lacked a good sense of historical criticism and he committed a number of theological and philosophical errors. How could it be otherwise in a subject ranging through the whole course of Christian history, taking in the compass of the heavens, probing into the spiritual depths of saintly souls, wrestling with the powers of evil and the mystery of grace, all done by a layman? But as Kirsch has well put it, the study "is a magnificent work [which] proved a strong stimulant to Christian faith and dealt a decisive blow to superficial rationalism in religious matters."

The work was directed against the rationalism of the preceding age, an attitude of mind which tended to reduce faith to philosophy and prayers to syllogisms. Görres turned to the Bible, to the early hermits of the Church, to the "mysticism of martyrdom," down through the Middle Ages to the great mystics of sixteenth-century Spain, in order to study this form of religious life which defies the rigidity of logic and soars directly to God. The importance of the work lay in its general influence—for it showed men of the nineteenth century that suffering, purification, and mental prayer have had an important place historically in the Church, that Catholicism is not circumscribed by philosophical proofs for the existence of God and the historical validity of the Church's claims to be His representative on earth, and that there is something more to religion than reasoning. The world needed to be reminded of these facts in the 1830's, and it is to Görres' credit that he did the job.

* * *

In 1838, Görres turned momentarily from his lecturing at Munich to dash off his most important book, the small volume entitled *Athanasius,* a ringing defense of the archbishop of Cologne, who had been thrown into prison for obeying the Pope rather than the Prussian government. This little book went through four editions within a few months and became "the great trumpet call for the political equality of Catholics and for the freedom of the Catholic Church." As one of Görres' students put it, he "roared like a lion" and the noise reverberated throughout Germany so resoundingly that the Prussian government could no longer pretend the lion was only a mouse. Görres had earned for Catholics the right to be heard.

The occasion for his roaring was the famous dispute over mixed marriages in Prussia. The main points of this complicated controversy can be outlined briefly in this way: in 1815 the predominantly Protestant state of Prussia had obtained provinces in the Rhineland with a heavy Catholic population. Back in 1803, Prussia had adopted a law whereby children of mixed marriages were to be raised in the father's religion. In 1825 the government ordered the Catholic clergy to follow Prussian law in the Rhineland, and the bishops agreed to submit to the practice. Some Catholic leaders felt, however, that this was a step toward the extinction of Catholicism purposely taken by the Prussian government, especially when there was a regular "invasion" of Protestant young men into the Rhineland with the apparent purpose of marrying local Catholic girls.

In 1837, Clement August von Droste-Vischering was appointed archbishop of Cologne. An old man by this time and one who had never displayed any kind of militant initiative, he was expected to submit passively to the government as his predecessor had done. But the new archbishop announced that he would carry out papal instructions on the matter of mixed marriages and that he would obey the government only insofar as its decrees did not violate canon law. At this point the government committed the tactical blunder of ordering Droste-Vischering to Berlin in 1837 and, when it could not browbeat him into submission, of throwing him into prison. To justify its action the government issued a paper denouncing the prelate as a traitor and accusing him of being a disobedient citizen.

Even listless Catholics were aroused by this brutal assault on the old archbishop. Catholic morale throughout Prussia, and in the other German states as well, stiffened noticeably. And Görres was more responsible than anyone else for the government's defeat in this matter, as well as for strengthening Catholic solidarity. His defense of the archbishop of Cologne, whose name he adds "to that honorable list of believers and martyrs who like Athanasius and Chrysostom resisted persecution," might sound exaggerated today, and the objective historian finds it necessary to tone down the pen picture drawn by the author of *Athanasius*. But the book still makes inspiring reading, its arguments are still essentially sound, the principles upon which they are based are forever correct — and there is a great wisdom to be garnered from its pages by those interested today in the problem of relations between Church and State.

Görres insists that the fundamental question is whether "force shall constantly prevail over justice or justice over force," since the government tried to solve the problem of the Catholic position on mixed marriages by putting the archbishop into prison. If Prussia is allowed to proceed in this manner, he argues, then Catholics – and other religious denominations too – will all be placed in "a most distressing situation." They will have "to accept the persecution befalling them as a beneficial disposition of God, strengthening them in their belief, and lodge their appeal with that Higher Power which punishes every crime in good time, slowly and late, but surely and inevitably." Moreover, Görres contends, persecution will always be an instrument in the hands of the State if force is to prevail over justice.

The rest of the book is an analysis of the stand of the archbishop as against the government, the archbishop being studied in his threefold capacity as a subject of the government, a prince of the Church, and a member of a Church whose rights and liberties are based on various guarantees made in the Prussian constitution and in the Federal Bill creating the German Confederation. The argument is a defense of a persecuted bishop against the "stupidity" of an absolutist government that placed itself above the laws of God. It is a call for the emancipation of the Church, even if martyrdom is the means for effecting it. It is an appeal to history to show the futility of attacks against the religion founded by Christ and protected by the Holy Spirit. Görres ends his case with a typical ringing exhortation to the Catholics of Germany: "Hold together with them [the Catholics of the Rhineland] solidly and closely, because you all have one and the same objective, and this objective is the complete and full realization of the solemnly guaranteed freedom of religion and the promised political and civil equality of religion to its full extent, without diminution or reservation. You will win this objective and so will they if you both insist on it with zeal and persistence."

The Catholics did win in the mixed marriage case. But more important in the long run, the battle brought them into close union and revealed to them the hitherto unsuspected strength they possessed. For this Görres was not solely responsible, but he deserves more credit than any other individual. That is why

German Catholics look upon his *Athanasius* as "the symbol of [their] battle for freedom," and Father Corrigan calls it "the dawn of a new day for German Catholics."

Görres continued the fight he had begun with *Athanasius* by founding a journal, as we have seen, and by putting together additional reflections on the subject in a book called *Church and State.* In this volume he develops his arguments along general lines, being less concerned with any single event than with the general policy of separation of Church and State advocated by the Liberals. Görres reminds them how novel their doctrine is and how, in time to come, it will have proved only a passing fad. "The theory of complete separation of Church and State, as it has been set up in modern times," he claims, "is a worthless, absurd, senseless and altogether unacceptable error; it is unacceptable in practice because, a product of political and religious revolutionaries, it leads to the ruin of both Church and State; it is unacceptable in theory because nowhere in existence is there absolute separation [of Church and State], for the two cannot exist completely isolated from each other." Görres ranges through history to show in what ways Church and State have helped each other and strengthened each other. He shows how their functions are supplementary rather than mutually exclusive or antagonistic. He indicates how, by tipping the delicate balance between the two established in the past, the modern State is forcing the Church to retreat on itself and become less extended but stronger, and how at the same time the power gained by the State from the Church will in the long run ruin the State itself. Christian society and individual Christians, of course, are the real victims of the struggle, since they find still another part of life, the religious, under the control of a State which has no interest in true doctrine nor in the religious welfare of its subjects. Thus Görres concludes his argument by insisting that separation of Church and State is a step toward tyranny rather than religious freedom.

* * *

We have already seen how the two watchwords of Görres were freedom and truth. He was convinced that the two lived in intimate union and that neither could be violated without hurting the other. In later life, however, he came to emphasize truth somewhat more than freedom, for much as he loved liberty he saw the need of regulating it in order to preserve it. In a testimonial to Görres his friends expressed their idea of his basic thought in the formula: "Truth, justice, and freedom regulated by law and by charity." In the name of liberty Görres delivered many telling blows in his fifty years of writing: against Napoleon, and the German princes as well, for arbitrarily restricting their subjects' legitimate freedom; against the French Revolution and Liberalism for offering sham liberty and denying people the real thing; against the tendency of states everywhere in the early nineteenth century to absorb more and more functions of life formerly reserved to the individual, the family, the local community, or other organizations like the guild or the Church.

Although Görres condemned the French Revolution as a step toward tyranny, he never made the mistake committed by Montalembert of turning to the authoritarian monarch as the sole alternative. He always denounced power for power's sake; he always condemned any kind of Machiavellism, even daring to censure Frederick the Great for disregarding justice and honesty when he was king of Prussia. Good government, he insisted, had no need of tyrannical measures, of secret police, or Machiavellian techniques. "The rulers are completely blind," he once complained, "because they do not acknowledge freedom as the basis of life."

Görres wrote a great deal on political matters. Much of what he had to say was important only at the time, since it dealt with immediate problems and practical contingencies which pass with the season. Some of his writing, however, is of perennial importance—and some of it is historically important because, tragically, it was never put into practice by legislators and statesmen and diplomats. Such, for example, was his plan for a united German state under the aegis of Austria. He advocated a federal government, like that of the United States, with a constitution for the federation and for each individual state. In this way he hoped to restrict government to its legitimate, necessary sphere of action and to protect the citizens with constitutionally guaranteed rights. If such a union had been accomplished in his lifetime the whole course of German history — therefore of world history — might have been different. There could have been no Bismarck to pound the various German states into a single empire on his anvil of blood and iron.

In mature life Görres consistently followed a middle-of-the-road policy in political matters. In this respect he stands alone among Catholic lay leaders of the first half of the century. He tipped neither in the direction of Liberalism, like Ozanam, nor in the direction of Conservatism, like De Maistre. He was liberal insofar as he advocated progressive reform and a diminution of State power; he was conservative insofar as he wished to build on the past rather than break from it. Görres wanted progress but he repudiated violent and abrupt change, and he never endorsed change simply for the sake of novelty. "Calmness and moderation are essential to government," he wrote; "avoiding every extreme, honestly satisfying every just claim of the age, repelling with firmness all injustice and violence, indulging in no reaction or abuse of power, executing only what is absolutely necessary, never anticipating the future, nor obstinately clinging to the past, it will succeed in promoting the re-establishment of good will by the re-establishment of confidence."

Görres came to prize the Church — as De Maistre had done a little before him — as the vessel in which the good things of the past were conserved for the present and the future. As a young man he had praised the Protestant Revolt for having destroyed the Catholic Church's monopoly on religion in Christendom. He had looked on Rome as the "the metropolis of the empire of stupidity." By the time he was thirty, however, he suspected that the revolt from Rome had led to tyranny rather than freedom; before he was forty he was convinced that the Protestant Revolt was one of Europe's greatest tragedies. He always remained tolerant of Protestants because he understood them. For a while he even hoped that a union of the churches in Germany could be worked out, but by the time he went to Munich he decided it was too late for such a reunion. Protestantism, he said, would remain as the "God-permitted antithesis to Catholicism as long as God should allow it." He insisted that liberty of conscience and freedom of worship should be granted to all forms of worship. "All of us," he wrote in 1842, "Catholics and Protestants, have sinned in our fathers and weave on the cloth of human error, one way or another; no one has the right arrogantly to think himself superior to the other, and God does not tolerate it in anyone, least of all in those who call themselves His friends."

For him the Catholic Church was more than the guardian of theological truth and the instrument of supernatural help to fallen mankind. It was also a civilizing force, a pole of stability and of sanity in a crazy, ever changing world. "She did not heed the objection," he said of the Church, "that since she was bound to the never-changing she would finally become rigid herself, for she well knew that ideas indeed excite to change but they themselves remain changeless. Amid all whirlings and upheavals of worldly events she has therefore remained constant, always the same Church. . . . Thus she has preserved for the benefit of the world her store of possessions undiminished, and thus has she emerged from this present crisis neither richer nor poorer than before."

Such was Görres' picture of the Church – an institution needing no human support because it had God's guarantee and the Holy Spirit's help for its continued existence. He dedicated himself to supporting and defending it, nevertheless, because it was the vessel in which he had found truth and freedom, those prize possessions for which he had searched so long and which he fought for selflessly and joyfully until his death.

* * *

In his own lifetime Görres frequently was referred to as "The O'Connell of the Rhineland," a title, incidentally, which tends to flatter O'Connell rather than Görres. He was great, like O'Connell, both for what he did and for the inspiring example he became to later generations. For about twenty-five years after his death, in 1848, Görres was more or less forgotten as German Catholics concentrated on the immediate problems facing them. But in the last quarter of the nineteenth century his importance was brought home to the German Catholic world. And with the founding of the Görres Association in 1876, he took on a legendary importance which made him remain a force in Catholic circles as an ideal and a model for imitation. In the Görres tradition, the association bearing his name was long a rallying point and a center of co-operation for Catholic scholarship in Germany.

Görres prized solid scholarship because he loved the truth, but he never made it an end in itself. He was too full and too fresh and too alive for that. He was the well-rounded man whose importance can easily be appreciated but not easily described. For Görres was not a man of one book — nor a man of books only. He was a man of action as well, a fighter, a publicist, a teacher, leader and inspirer of all those whom he met. *Defensor gloriosus Catholicae veritatis* is the title Catholics bestowed on him. He stands forth as the most important Catholic layman of Germany in the first half of the century because he did valiant service for the Church when the German hierarchy was still too weak and incompetent to shepherd their flocks well. He is important as a teacher because the Munich School, in Pinson's words, "marked the beginnings of organized Catholic political action in Germany." He is important as a writer because his pen scored many polemical triumphs, and especially because the several journals he founded set the pattern and the tone for a German Catholic press which presented the Catholic position fearlessly and effectively through the century. He is even more important as a man whose honesty and integrity set him forth in sharp relief as a lay defender of the faith who became the inspiration and the model for many other German laymen of succeeding generations.

10. Donoso Cortés

Juan Donoso Cortés, Marqués de Valdegamas, died in 1853 at the early age of forty-four. Five years later Louis Veuillot published a French translation of the Spanish nobleman's works, in the introduction of which he wrote: "The name of Donoso Cortés will not die. It will grow. His thought, far from falling into oblivion, will acquire greater influence in proportion as the symptoms which he foresaw manifest themselves." Louis Veuillot was wrong. Donoso Cortés disappeared into oblivion, except in Spanish anthologies, where his orations were always given prominent place — and there he remained until recently. This was the fate he foresaw for himself. When his classic work *Catholicism, Liberalism and Socialism* was published, he wrote to a friend that it had appeared before the Deluge it foretold and that it would not be popular until after the Deluge had inundated Europe.

The Deluge of which Donoso Cortés wrote came to Europe in two world wars, in Fascism, Nazism, Communism, and kindred forms of totalitarian rule — and Donoso's ghost was given a body again as scholars resurrected him as an acute prophet of our own disordered age. For more than fifty years, events had seemed to mock at Donoso's dire predictions of Europe's decline and eventual decease. Prosperity increased, revolution was checked, progress seemed assured. Then came world wars and revolutions, depressions and dictatorships — the very things that Donoso foresaw for European civilization a century ago. Time has proved him remarkably right in many of his forebodings. So his works were dusted off, his criticisms of Socialism and Liberalism are studied seriously, and he has come to be labeled the "prophet of our age."

Donoso Cortés could offer so acute a criticism of his age because he was so radically Catholic in his thinking. On the basis of the eternal truths he found in the Catholic tradition, he criticized the Liberalism and the Socialism* of his day and he

* The Socialism with which Donoso Cortés was concerned is much more like modern Communism than it is like the Socialism of Norman

prophesied the end to which they would come. He is important as a lay apologist for the Church who took the offensive in the great debate of the nineteenth century. He put Liberalism and Socialism on the defensive by insisting that their novel solutions to age-old problems were basically wrong, that their political, social, and economic errors flowed naturally from theological mistakes, that ultimately they must lead to anarchy and then to dictatorship. He asserted flatly that there was no choice except between tyranny and Catholicism, and that by turning its back on the Catholic tradition, Liberal Europe had started on the downhill plunge into the tyranny of totalitarian rule.

Because of a strange combination of historical accidents, then, Donoso Cortés is more important, more alive today than he was when he moved through Europe and wrote about its suicide. For the results of Liberalism and the working out of Socialism's erroneous solution to the problems posed by Liberalism have come to fruition in our own generation pretty much in the way he prophesied they would. In certain details, of course, he turned out to be wrong, for subsequent events are careless of prophets' sayings — but in other details, such as Russia's present role in European history, he proved to be remarkably right. And the general course of European history has been in the direction he insisted it would have to be. For that reason, Donoso Cortés has come to life again as a man to read and to ponder over in our own day.

* * *

Juan Donoso Cortés was born in 1809 of a noble Spanish family. A descendant on his mother's side of the more famous Hernando Cortés, Donoso was a typical Spanish gentleman: individualistic to the marrow of his bones, contemptuous of material things and the new secularist philosophy, devoted defender of his nation and his Church, a romantic intellectual crusader

---

Thomas. The Spanish nobleman wrote before the term Communism was in general use, it must be remembered, and the Socialists of his time were what today we would call Communists. Most important of these early Socialists were Robert Owen of England, Saint-Simon, Fourier, Cabet, and Proudhon of France. Proudhon, incidentally, was more of an anarchist than a Socialist, but Donoso looks upon him as the logical result of Liberal thought.

who was as just and as merciless to his opponents in the battle of ideas as his countrymen were on the field of war. His early education was under a tutor. At the age of twelve he was enrolled at the University of Salamanca. Later he went to the College of Caceres, and then to the University of Seville where he studied law. There he showed himself a brilliant, precocious youth who finished his prescribed studies so quickly that he was obliged to spend several terms waiting to attain the minimum age for receiving his law degree. During this time he developed an intense interest in history and literature, working under José Quintana, the outstanding Spanish Liberal of the time. From Quintana young Donoso received the typical Liberal outlook of the age: disdain for Spanish learning, an adulation for the French rationalists of the eighteenth century, a contempt for the past, and an uncritical faith in the future of humankind.

At the age of nineteen he was appointed to fill the chair of literature at the College of Caceres. His inaugural lecture was a sparkling demonstration in which the young Spaniard showed wide erudition and a facile, though not profound, knowledge. Even at this early age he exhibited striking oratorical ability and an independence of mind which enabled him to discard his rationalist heritage item by item in the years to come. Donoso is reported lecturing with Spanish enthusiasm and vehemence to his two students — some accounts allow him only one — as though they were a thousand. At any rate, from the age of nineteen he remained a fixture in Spanish and European intellectual life. A frequent contributor to various Spanish and French journals, a master of devastating logic and possessed of a gift for casting his thought in burning phrases, he could not be ignored by the Liberal thinkers of his day.

In his biographical sketch on Donoso, Louis Veuillot tells us that his friend's life "contains little in the way of events and is, in a way, only the history of his thoughts." His ideas are more important than his deeds, it is true, but Veuillot's belief that his political activity can be passed by quickly is not justified by the facts of Spanish history. Moreover, it does violence to Donoso's thought by wrenching it out of the social and political setting in which it was formulated. Donoso Cortés was a man of many parts — the ideal well-rounded gentleman pictured by Newman

– who was as much at home in diplomacy or in debates on a new tax bill as he was in philosophical or theological speculation.

At the age of twenty-three he plunged into the turbulent waters of Spanish politics with an essay on the vexing succession question. In proposing a solution to this problem of whether Ferdinand VII's daughter Isabel could succeed to the throne, Donoso displayed a wealth of information on Spanish history and constitutional law, as well as the ability to reason logically and persuasively and to appeal to his readers' hearts as strongly as to their minds. His essay attracted such favorable attention and so pleased the king that Donoso was given a place in the Spanish government as assistant to the Minister of Grace and Justice in 1833.

From this time until his death twenty-one years later, Donoso Cortés remained a prominent figure in Spanish politics. Many looked hopefully to him as the man capable of saving his country from the disastrous civil wars and the anarchy from which it suffered. For some reason – no one knows just why – he shied away from the highest places in political life and contented himself with less important positions. He was convinced that Spain was lost – "lost beyond all hope," he said – and it is therefore likely that he believed he could help his country and Christian civilization more by pointing out in his writings and his speeches the road back to sanity and salvation than by tending the helm of a sinking ship.

Meanwhile, though, he dutifully played the role of a Spanish nobleman in political affairs. Throughout the Carlist wars he remained loyal to Isabel's cause, which was a compromise between the extreme conservatism of the Carlists and the wild-eyed Liberalism of the republicans. He held a position in the government of Mendizabal, the reforming Liberal; and when the party split into extreme and moderate groups, Donoso joined the latter party. He went into exile with Queen Regent Christina when Espartero's revolt succeeded and the extreme Liberal regency of 1840 was established. Serving as the Queen Mother's secretary, he mingled in Parisian intellectual society and read such authors as De Maistre and De Bonald. Their writings, combined with his own independence of mind, did much to disabuse him of Liberal beliefs in these years.

Donoso played a prominent role in re-establishing a moderate Liberal government in 1843 and in having Queen Isabel declared of age and therefore competent to rule. In the last ten years of his life he served as a prominent member of the Cortes, the Spanish congress, where his speeches were attentively listened to and avidly discussed by Parisians, Berliners, and Romans, as well as by the citizens of Madrid and Barcelona. Between elections to the Cortes, Donoso served as ambassador to Berlin where he watched rioters intimidate Frederick William IV, and again as ambassador to Paris where he observed the disintegration of the Second Republic and the coming of Napoleon III's Empire in 1851 and 1852. These experiences in practical politics did much to change Donoso's opinion of Liberal rule and make him think that either Socialism or some form of dictatorship was the inevitable outcome of the revolutions he witnessed in three European capitals. Through these years Donoso found that his political experience and his philosophical reflections combined to lead him away from his earlier Liberal leanings in the direction of a Catholic "conservatism." Thus in his last few years this man, who had begun his intellectual and political career as a convinced Liberal, became one of Liberalism's severest critics. That is why he protested to the editor of the Madrid *Heraldo* that it was unjust to quote his early writings in favor of Liberalism. "Between your doctrines, which I myself professed when I still was quite young," he wrote, "and those which I now profess there is a radical contradiction and an invincible repugnance."

He went on to explain this "radical contradiction" in such a way as to summarize the differences between himself and the Liberal thinkers of the age. "You believe that rationalism is the means for arriving at the reasonable, that Liberalism in theory is the means for arriving at liberty in practice, that parliamentarianism is the means of creating good government, that discussion is the means of arriving at truth, and finally that kings are only the incarnation of human law. I believe, on the contrary, that human law does not exist, and that there is no law but divine law. In God is the law and the concentration of all rights; in man is obligation and the concentration of all duties. . . . As for parliamentarianism, Liberalism, and rationalism, I believe that the first is the negation of government, the second is the negation of liberty, and the third is the affirmation of folly." That put the contrast strongly, but it showed clearly where Donoso differed from Liberals on the leading questions of the day.

Donoso believed that his "repugnance" to Liberalism had developed as the result of his rather sudden "conversion" to Catholicism. He had been a typical "Latin Catholic" earlier in his life, one who took his religion as a matter of course and did not allow it to enter into his nonreligious activity. He continued to believe that the Catholic Church was the true Church, but at the same time it did not bother him to hold opinions contrary to Catholic teaching. Meanwhile, of course, he had not taken the practice of his faith seriously. Two things, Donoso believed, saved him from this secularist state of mind: "the delicate sentiment which I have always had of moral beauty, and a tenderness of heart which approaches weakness; the first caused me to admire Catholicism, the second caused me to love it."

His visits to France, as we have seen, had had a profound and salutary effect on his outlook. There he associated with some excellent Catholics whose virtuous lives, he tells us, convinced him of the reality and the efficacy of supernatural grace. There, too, he read De Maistre, whose style was much like his own and whose arguments seemed to pulverize his former idols into intellectual dust. This was the Paris of Ozanam and of revolutions that Donoso saw, a city of deep spiritual uneasiness and of great physical suffering, a city whose streets were frequently battlegrounds over which hatred hung like an electrically charged cloud. Donoso was appalled by the ugliness and the misery these revolutions had caused. "My conversion to good principles," he therefore wrote to Montalembert, "is due first of all to divine mercy and then to a profound study of revolutions." His brother's death, which he witnessed and which moved him deeply, proved to be the event which pushed him into the Catholic camp. And there he remained until his death, one of the foremost lay apologists of the Church.

A close examination of Donoso's writings and his speeches shows that his "conversion" away from Liberalism and toward the Catholic position was not at all the sudden transformation he thought it was. He moved slowly but surely in that direction from his inaugural address as a nineteen-year-old professor until 1847, when he was fully "converted" by his brother's death. His *Considerations on Diplomacy,* published in 1834 (when he was twenty-five), reveals an appreciation of the Church's role in history as a social institution. An article on "Religion, Freedom, and Intelligence" published three years later shows an even deeper appreciation of the Church as a historical agent working out the harmonious development of man's liberty, his intellect, and his religious faculty. In this article Donoso wrote a panegyric to the historical Christ as the only perfect man. By 1839, Donoso had definitely rejected Liberalism as a creed that offered solutions to all problems of life. Until that time he had tried to rescue items of Liberal belief from the shipwreck of rationalism, but one by one he discovered that they were not worth saving – so in 1839 he turned his back on Liberalism for good. From this time on he is a Catholic thinker. His "conversion" reveals no sharp change in his outward conduct or in his thinking. It was, most likely, a change deep within his soul which only he could appreciate. So for his last fourteen years Donoso Cortés is a strong defender of the Church and a foremost opponent of Liberalism and Socialism. As he attained greater assurance of his position after his "conversion," he stated his arguments more strongly, more starkly – but otherwise his thought is of a single piece after 1839.

* * *

Donoso Cortés is above all else an orator – "the greatest orator since antiquity" in Metternich's opinion. He is an orator of the romantic age, the age before Bismarck when men still believed that the great questions of the time could be settled by speeches rather than by blood and iron. We must remember this, for otherwise his oratory might impress us as florid rhetoric, when actually it was something more than this to his contemporaries. Donoso was never captivated by his own oratorical ability. Frequently he spoke of the vanity of orators and the futility of mere words, and on at least one occasion he used the example of eloquent Aaron and stuttering Moses to indicate the minor role of speech as compared with true leadership. Donoso was truly humble – a rare thing in the romantic period. The secret of his character is revealed in his appearing in full dignity as Spanish ambassador in the morning, and in the afternoon standing as godfather for a poverty-stricken baby, holding it for baptism in the dilapidated chapel of the Little Sisters of the Poor in Paris. Like Ozanam, he worked among the poor. Perhaps the two even passed each other on one of Paris' crooked little streets where the poor were huddled together. He was a devoted and generous patron of the Little Sisters of the Poor; he spent much time doing good works personally in the poor Mouffetard section of Paris.

But Donoso Cortés is important, above all else, as an orator — whether he addressed the Spanish Cortes or spoke with his burning pen in the various journals of Europe. He molded his thought in striking phrases, and, as almost always happens to the orator, Donoso's thought was affected, at least to some extent, by the rhetoric in which it was cast. Orators are not compromisers. The very surge of their rhetoric sweeps them on to an extreme position. So it was with Donoso Cortés. He was completely Catholic in his every utterance, unwilling to compromise with the nineteenth century in anything, strong and fierce in condemning the utilitarian and materialistic tendencies he detected in his age.

His speech is full of overstatements, of superlatives not to be found in the work of a philosopher or a theologian. He paints in deep colors, sweeping his big brush of generalization across the face of Europe and through the course of history much as the Italian Renaissance artists painted their masterpieces. And as the Renaissance painting is a faithful reproduction of reality when viewed from the proper distance, though it seems a chaos of color on close inspection, so Donoso's full speech or article presents his arguments accurately, although single sentences cannot stand up under microscopic examination. His was not the kind of work to be examined phrase by phrase. It was the total effect with which he was concerned. Thus was his thought understood in his own day. He was not taken to deny the Liberals free will, for example, when he told them that they were slaves, that true liberty was found only in the saints. Nor was he understood to have meant that a deist could not understand elementary mathematics when he wrote: "He who has no notion of the providence of God is in the most complete ignorance of all things." These are oratorical statements which are properly understood by the listener when kept in the context of the full speech.

Indeed, Donoso protested vehemently when his writing was picked apart — as it was sometimes by the liberal Catholics of France — when single phrases were wrenched out of context and used to prove that Donoso was a fatalist, or that he deprecated human reason or overestimated the effects of original sin. He protested that he was writing against the Liberals, that his book was not intended for use in the seminaries but in the parlors of the Liberals, that he was a popular writer instead of a theologian. "I am profoundly ignorant," he wrote to Louis Veuillot, "of the science of theology, which I have never studied. I am not a scholar." Veuillot, Catholic censors, and theologians all agreed that his theology was sound, even though it was written for popular consumption instead of for seminaries. It is generally agreed today, indeed, that Donoso did a masterful job of translating theological concepts into popular, even oratorical phraseology without doing injustice to the truth.

Donoso spoke, then, as a defense lawyer for his Church and as a prosecuting attorney against the secularist society in which he lived. Although he was a controversialist through and through, paradoxically he hated argument of any kind. "Discussion," he protested, "is the title under which Death travels when he seeks to avoid recognition and goes incognito." Again, he wrote that "polemics are dangerous and discussion is vain. . . . I have rarely let myself be drawn into a discussion and never into a dispute." Despite this aversion from discussion, he defended truth in the forum whenever he thought it needed his pleading. But he defended truth without condescending to argue with the Liberals and Socialists or to debate with them. He was a pulpit orator, not a platform debater. He simply stated his case against these two schools, ignoring all their counterarguments and their protests. His method was deductive — never quite fair, according to our Anglo-American notions of give-and-take debate — whereby he rigorously reduced his opponents' premises to their logical conclusions, whether they held such conclusions or not.

Such a method pointed up the contrast between Liberalism

and Catholicism, for it minimized what the two held in common, whereas Montalembert and Ozanam tried to find all points on which the two could agree. Donoso, therefore, cut an impassable chasm between Catholicism on the one hand and Liberalism on the other. He wanted to show how un-Catholic, even anti-Catholic, the society of his day had become. This seemed dangerous to many of his Catholic associates, for it denied Catholicism any credit for modern accomplishments. From the vantage point of the century that has since elapsed, however, it seems to have been good strategy because, following Donoso's method of reasoning, the calamities of modern times are to be laid at the door of Liberalism alone. No share of guilt for modern disasters attaches to the Church. Disaster, his method of argument ran, had come to Europe and it would continue to grow worse until the dark night of paganism covered the world, simply because the Liberals had turned their backs on Catholic truth.

* * *

It was Donoso's thought, then, which was important. And his thought was a constant criticism of his age, an age of crisis, he believed, from which Europe could not recover. In point of fact, he lived in days that must have disturbed anyone who thought seriously about the meaning of things. For years the Carlist wars had upset Spain socially and politically. Outbreaks occurred in the Italian states throughout the twenties. In 1830 there was revolution in most European countries. Finally, in 1848, revolution broke out everywhere. It began during February in Paris, where by summertime barricades had been thrown up in the streets, and college boys joined workingmen to contest bitterly each city block with the republican army. Revolt spread to Berlin and Vienna and Budapest, to Brussels, Naples, Milan, and Rome. The Hohenzollern king bowed ignominiously to the mob demonstrating in the streets of Berlin; the Hapsburg emperor beat a hasty retreat from Vienna to remote Innsbruck; the Pope was forced to flee Rome in disguise and retire to Gaeta. The old order seemed unable to stand on its feet in the face of mob action – and the mob leaders were unable to rule when they were suddenly thrust into positions of power.

Donoso Cortés, therefore, was not the only thinking man to

look upon his age as one of crisis. Others pointed out the same symptoms Donoso saw. But he was unique in his diagnosis—for Donoso Cortés believed the disease was a fatal one, and he was convinced that a new Europe could arise only on the dead ruins of Liberal civilization. Europe, he said, was on the eve of the "greatest catastrophe of history. For the moment, what I see most clearly is the barbarization of Europe and before long its depopulation." At the time he wrote, shortly after the revolutions of 1848, Donoso thought Europe was in a state of cold war between the rich and the poor. "The world stands between peace and war. It is not at peace, for its spirit is at war; it is not at war, for its arms are laid down. It is in a permanent state of discord and dispute, a peace unworthy of men, a truly feminine war."

The immediate future, he believed, would see the cold war become more intense until finally the Socialists would either triumph or be put down by an authoritarian government, like the Fascism or the Nazism of our own day. He described the coming day as "a period of anguish. All the symptoms indicate it: blindness of mind, animosity of spirit, arguments without object, battles without motive, but above all the furor of economic reform." Such would be the future because Europe had turned its back on God. It had cut itself loose from truth and had repudiated its earthly guardian, the Catholic Church. For such a world, Donoso insisted, there could be no social peace, no tranquil living in order.

The Liberals of his day had forgotten the purpose of life and they were beating the air in vain trying to be angels instead of men. They believed each man was sufficient unto himself, because they denied the fact of original sin and its deteriorating effects on human nature. They believed that man could live the good life without the help of grace and the sacraments, and the good life to them was one of material satisfactions. Donoso therefore condemned Liberal society for the same reasons that Liberals exalted it. "It is an age of utilitarian systems," he said contemptuously, "of great developments in commerce, of feverish activity in industry, an age characterized by the insolence of the rich and the impatience of the poor." It was an age which had overturned right order by giving first place to economic and social questions, which, Donoso insisted, were not of primary importance.

This social and economic upheaval had its counterpart in the political revolutions of his day. Donoso claimed that the Liberal governments of the early nineteenth century had resulted in political anarchy because rulers did not know how to rule and citizens no longer knew how to obey. "This middle class which today rules in Europe," he said, "completely lacks the two qualities which alone render government possible: they have neither the gift of commanding nor the virtue of obeying, and, not knowing how to command those who obey or how to obey those who command, they only confuse society. . . . All peoples over whom this class rules oscillate perpetually between dictatorship, the remedy of anarchy, and anarchy, the remedy of dictatorship."

From this confusion he saw coming inevitable dictatorship, either of the Socialist Party or of one man who would "save the nation" from Socialism. "The way is prepared for a gigantic tyrant," he told the Spanish Cortes in his famous speech on dictatorship, "a tyrant colossal, universal, immense. Note it well. There is no longer any physical resistance; the steamships and railroads have demolished frontiers, and the telegraph has demolished distance. There is no longer any moral resistance, all spirits are divided, all patriotism is dead." The choice for Donoso was no longer between dictatorship and liberty, for he thought that liberty was dead, that Europe had turned so completely against the truth that it could not recapture real Christian freedom. There remained only "a choice between dictatorship by insurrection and dictatorship by government."

Donoso based his pessimistic picture of his age on his own peculiar—and for his age unpopular—concept of history, whereby he centered all historical events around the two important facts of original sin and the redemption. By the first act, Adam and Eve had cut man away from the Source of life and truth. As a result, mankind's nature was impaired, his will was weakened, his intellect beclouded. His mind was naturally inclined to error, his will to evil. By the redemption, on the other hand, Christ had reunited mankind with God. Through grace man could again turn "supernaturally" to the truth and to the good. Without grace man could not be good.

* * *

Such was Donoso Cortés' opinion of the condition of mankind in his day. Because they were the children of Adam and because they refused to be children of Christ, they were naturally breakers of the law, they were naturally outlaws morally and legally. Donoso used the evidence of history to prove his contention that man needed strong authority to guide his weak intellect and to restrain his corrupted will. This authority, he pointed out, could be either interior or exterior, the moral authority of religion or the physical coercion of the State. In the past, whenever religious authority was weak physical authority became strong, and whenever religious restraints were strong physical power was limited.

From this observation Donoso deduced "a law of humanity, a law of history: they [the two kinds of sanctions] are of such a nature that when the religious thermometer rises the thermometer of repression falls, and, reciprocally, when the religious thermometer falls the political thermometer – political repression or tyranny – increases." Because men of his age recognized almost no religious sanction, State authority must become dictatorial. Donoso therefore concluded that Europe was faced with dictatorship everywhere, inasmuch as men had allowed the thermometer of religious restraint to fall to zero. Men must be ruled, he held, either by God or by Caesar, or by a combination of the two. God had been pushed completely out of the picture, and into the vacuum created by His absence Caesar was bound to rush.

Thus the Liberals, who until his time had likened the Church to an albatross hung around the neck of humanity, were thrown on the defensive by Donoso's insistence that Liberalism did not bring liberty, that it brought Socialism and tyranny instead. Before Donoso, apologists for the Church had to show that Catholicism did not stand in the way of progress and change; after Donoso, Liberals were forced to show that progress and change were for the betterment of mankind, as they had asserted but never proved before. They had to show, moreover, that their basic assumptions were valid. Donoso had, in effect, recovered the ball for Catholics and he had thereby put thinking Liberals on the defensive.

He accomplished this feat by approaching his contemporary civilization historically and by showing that Liberalism was the culmination of all previous error. He saw history as the dramatic struggle of good and evil, both within each man and in society at large. For him this struggle is the red thread of history. It is the story of man's natural inclination to evil and of God's saving him through the agency of grace. "There is my whole doctrine," he wrote: "the natural triumph of evil over good, and the supernatural triumph of God over evil. There is found the condemnation of all these systems of progress whereby modern philosophers, deceivers by profession, benumb the people, these children who will never emerge from their childhood." The cardinal events of history are two: the original sin of Adam and Eve, which accounts for the evil in the world; and the personal intervention of God in the redemption, which accounts for the grace whereby man and society can overcome evil.

The Liberals are condemned by Donoso for denying these two most important facts of history. By denying original sin they posit the immaculate conception of all men, the natural goodness of every member of the human race. They assert that men are good and that only environment is bad, and they therefore believe that heaven can be achieved here on earth by setting up an environment of birds and bees, flowers and perfumes, a heavenly paradise which will make crime impossible. To Donoso this is utter nonsense. Men are inclined to evil and to error, he insists vehemently, and only the Catholic doctrine of original sin explains this inclination, as only the Catholic sacramental system offers an effective cure for the evil of sin – which underlies all evil. The Liberals strive in vain, for they believe that by getting the right surroundings they will make it impossible for men to be unhappy or bad. By denying man's redemption by Christ on the cross they cut men away from the source of all life, from any chance of victory over evil, from any possibility of a satisfactory life here on earth.

Liberal solutions to the world's ills, Donoso holds, are therefore bound to be wrong. Each "solution," indeed, will only add to the confusion, because it will be based upon a fundamentally erroneous concept of man. The Liberals had lost contact with solid truth. They had lost all sense of values. Basing their thought on insupportable premises, they had built a new Tower of Babel out of bricks of error. Under the sway of Liberal philosophers and politicians, Donoso claimed, error was more prevalent than ever before in history. "It is in books, institutions and laws," he wrote, "in the journals and in discourses, in conversation, in the salon, the club, the home, and on the streetcorner, in whatever is said or done." Liberalism cannot correct these errors, in Donoso's opinion, because it looks for improvement in the wrong places. He insisted that economic reform, of itself, will correct nothing. Replacing one ministry by another will change nothing. The change must occur within man himself, since that is where evil finds its lodging place. Freedom of the press and of assembly, as Donoso saw it, could not bring social improvement because it only gives greater leeway to the propagation of evil. Freedom of trade, in similar fashion, only gives the strong more elbow room for pushing the little people of the world around. These Liberal "solutions" therefore are condemned by the Spanish orator as worse than the "evil" they propose to resolve.

Donoso boldly proposed a theory of history which was absolutely contradictory to the generally accepted progress theory of the Liberals. For, whereas the Liberals followed Turgot and Condorcet in asserting that mankind had progressed from a superstitious "theological" outlook through the abstract metaphysical stage to the final, rational scientific viewpoint, Donoso held that European civilization had reached its peak in the later Middle Ages, when all Europe was Catholic, and that it had declined steadily since the sixteenth century. As a result of the Protestant Revolt and the secularistic trend of thought in the eighteenth century, Donoso asserted, Europe had broken up into two distinct and irreconcilable civilizations: the rationalist civilization of the *philosophes* and Catholic civilization.

Donoso cut a sharper and more decisive line between Catholicism and the Liberal civilization than did any other writer of the century. His contrast between the two is typical of his thought — and it is, incidentally, too sharp a contrast, for it is drawn in black and white, without the suggestion of any truth whatsoever in Liberalism's body of thought. "Between these two civilizations," he wrote to Montalembert from Berlin, "there is a fathomless chasm, an absolute antagonism. . . . The one is error, the other is truth; the one is evil, the other is good. Between them one must make a supreme choice, and the choice having been made, he must proclaim the one and condemn the other without reserve in everything. . . . I believe that the Catholic civilization contains good without any mixture of evil, and that the rationalist civilization contains evil without any mixture of good." Thus Donoso accused the Liberals of embracing error pure and simple, and of building a political and social system on this error. He accused them of seeking evil, whether they realized it or not, and of weaving it into the framework of modern civilization by making it the object of man's activity.

* * *

Donoso could logically take so extreme a stand against Liberals in a day when most Catholics were trying to work out a synthesis between their faith and modern civilization because he insisted on pushing all social, political, and economic questions back to their theological premises. It was perhaps his greatest achievement that he raised the question of the theological basis of Liberalism and of Socialism. In this way he elevated the great questions of the day to a plane where essential differences could be clearly seen and where clean-cut decisions could be reached. Formerly Catholics, Liberals, and Socialists had argued about such things as wages and working conditions – and the result was always confusion. Donoso Cortés penetrated through these social and economic questions to the religious basis of all three systems, and he exposed the theological errors on which Liberalism and Socialism were built.

In doing this, of course, Donoso sailed against the generally accepted current of nineteenth-century thought. For the Liberals held that religion was a private affair, that what a man believed or felt about God had no connection with his earthly, social activity. And Catholics, by and large, were willing to accept that dictum in order to reconcile their Sunday religion with their weekly secular life by keeping the two distinct. So Donoso raised an issue which was unpopular with all Liberals and with most Catholics, but he made a point which was fundamentally sound in theory and, as thinking men realize today, one which has worked out logically in practice. Nazi concentration camps come logically from their worship of the master race, just as slums and poorhouses and the pinched faces of workers were the logical result of Liberalism's worship of Mammon.

In Donoso's thought, then, religion is not merely a private affair. It is the set of beliefs underlying a civilization. It is the essence of a culture. He spends many pages showing how European civilization was the product of the Catholic faith. Following closely on the lines laid down by De Maistre, Donoso argues in even more ruthless fashion that without Catholicism there could never have been a European civilization, and he concludes his argument by asserting that Europe is rushing into pagan barbarism by turning its back on the Church. That is how he interprets the revolutions of 1848, which, indeed, did drive the Pope out of Rome and did defile churches in various capitals of Europe.

Liberals try to erect the building of civilization without laying a foundation, Donoso holds, because they deny the immediacy of the supernatural and the providence of God. They hold a tenuous position midway between Catholicism and atheism in admitting the possibility of a Creative Force and in denying this Creator any personality or the right to participate in the doings of His creatures. This is an ambiguous position theologically which in time must lead to the atheism of the Socialists – unless it retrace its steps and recognize the God of the Catholics. This led Donoso to make still another and for him a damning accusation against Liberalism. It did not carry its beliefs to logical conclusions, and thus by the very nature of things it could be only a transitional society between the truly Christian state of days gone by and the Socialism which lay ahead. By finding evil in social institutions instead of man it prepared the way for Socialism's violent overthrow of society; by its agnosticism it prepared the way for Socialism's atheism; by its emphasis on things economic it created a new hierarchy of values which led inevitably to the economically determined state of the Socialists; by its individualism it prepared the way for Socialism's denial of private property; by its very anarchy it provoked the opposite extreme of the totalitarian Socialist State. "The Liberal school," Donoso concludes, "enemy at once of the darkness and of the light, has selected I know not what twilight between the luminous and dark regions, between the eternal shades and the divine aurora. . . . Its days are numbered."

Thus Donoso saw Socialism coming as the logical result of Liberalism. One could not accept the Liberal economic philosophy, he maintained, without arriving at the conclusions of such Socialists as Robert Owen and Saint-Simon. Donoso held that the two schools "differ not in ideas, but in daring." Socialists simply accepted the consequences of Liberal premises. Their system, he claimed, is as "surely the child of Liberalism as the cub is the offspring of the lioness." Although he considered Socialism the logical result of Liberalism – and therefore more vicious because it was error brought to its ultimate conclusion – nevertheless Donoso respected the Socialists for their daring and for their honesty in accepting frankly the results to which their thought led them. "They are not wanting a certain grandeur," he said of them, "in their manner of proposing the problems and solving them." This was a compliment he would never pay to the Liberal school, which he consistently regarded with contempt. "It knows nothing of the nature of good or evil; it has scarcely any notion of God, and it has no notion of man at all. Impotent for good because devoid of all dogmatic affirmations, and for evil because it is horrified by absolute negation, it is condemned, without knowing it, to embark on the ship which will carry it to the Catholic port or to the Socialist reefs."

Thus the Socialists are "far superior to Liberals just because they go straight to all the great problems and questions, and because they always propose a peremptory and decisive solution." Donoso respected the Socialists for their daring, but he refused to absolve them from inconsistencies too. Worst of all, to his mind, was the Socialist's denial of free will and his still talking of good and evil. "The absurd reaches the inconceivable and the monstrous," he wrote of Robert Owen, "when our author attempts to found a society and a government in connection with irresponsible human beings." Donoso goes on to accuse Owen of falling into "the inconceivable extravagance of recommending benevolence, justice, and charity to those who, not being responsible or free, cannot love, nor be just, nor be benevolent."

Of more immediate practical concern was the Socialist advocacy of absolute freedom in theory and its falling into an absolute despotism in practice. Donoso accuses the Socialists of secretly advocating totalitarian government at the very time they speak of doing away with the State. He accuses Proudhon, for example, "of proclaiming liberty and equality and setting up tyranny, of calling himself an anarchist and having a hunger and thirst for government." Socialist despotism might be idealistic, he conceded, but it is nonetheless a system which robs man of his freedom. He considered the various Socialist experiments of his day as comparable to large farms where all the pigs are gathered, animal-like, into perfectly arranged pens, fed well and scientifically, treated benevolently – but treated, after all, like pigs.

* * *

Logically enough, Donoso did not see any easy cure for the diseases of his age. His outlook was decidedly pessimistic. "Our nation is completely lost," he told the Spanish Cortes, "and what is true of our own country is true of the rest of Europe." He went on to explain his dire prediction in these words: "Individuals can save themselves, but society cannot save itself, not because there is no possibility of salvation but because it does not wish to save itself. There is no salvation for society because we do not wish to make ourselves children of Christ and because we are not now true Christians. There is no salvation for society because the Catholic spirit, the sole spirit of life, does not vivify everything, because it does not animate education, government, social institutions, the laws and our customs."

Donoso was pessimistic because he had a low opinion of fallen human nature. From man himself, unaided by supernatural grace, nothing could be expected. "I know of nothing under the sun," he wrote, "more vile and despicable than the human race outside the Catholic lines." And again: "I can say for myself, that if my God had not taken flesh in the womb of a woman, nor died on the cross for the whole human race, the reptile I tread on would be less despicable in my eyes than man. . . . To believe in the nobility of those stupid crowds, it was necessary for God to reveal it to me." Even when the reader allows for the orator's overstatement of fact against the Liberal insistence on man's immaculate nature, he must admit that Donoso put little trust in human nature's ability to solve autonomously the problems created by men in society.

He was firmly convinced that salvation for society, as well as for man, lay in the embrace of the Church alone. Outside of it not only was there no eternal salvation, but there was not even true civilization. Only in the Church could one find true order in the nineteenth century, he claimed, for only in the Church was God given His due place. Only in the Church, therefore, did political and economic and social problems hold their proper place and obtain their just proportion of attention. Only in the Church was there a proper hierarchy of values and a proper gradation of persons. Only in the Church could one find true liberty, the liberty of being at once God's lowly creature and master of the universe; only as sons of God and brothers of Christ could one find true equality and real fraternity. Donoso even went so far as to assert that the only true society in the nineteenth century was the Church, for he insisted that the various states had surrendered their claim to being real societies.

So Donoso offered the Liberals of his day the choice of coming humbly to the Church in order to save themselves and to preserve their European civilization, or else of remaining in their no man's land of error and perverted institutions — which would soon degenerate into animal life in the Socialist jungle. Donoso differed here from such Catholic Liberals as Montalembert and Ozanam. "I have never had any faith or confidence in the political action of these good Catholics," he wrote to a friend. "All their efforts to reform society by means of public institutions . . . will be perpetually futile." Donoso thought that those who proposed an alliance between the Church and the Liberal society of the nineteenth century, as Montalembert did, labored under the illusion that modern society knew true liberty. This Donoso flatly denied. He insisted that Catholic Liberals were asking from modern society what it could not give, what, ironically, they could find only in their own Church — and they did not know it. So Donoso concluded that there was no need of an alliance between modern society and the Church. Whatever truth and whatever good modern society possessed came from the Church, and on the other hand whatever admixture of error one might find among Catholics came from their being "modern." For Donoso, therefore, no compromise was possible between his Church and his age. One had to be either Catholic or else "modern" – which to him meant Liberal or Socialist.

Although this Spanish *marqués* was read avidly and discussed heatedly in European circles in his own day, his advice was not followed by any sizable group. For Donoso demanded of Liberals – and of Catholics too – more than one might well hope to expect of them. He demanded a full acceptance of Catholic teaching and a complete practice of Catholic virtue. He demanded that the poor suffer patiently and the rich give of their wealth in a true spirit of charity. Only thus, he said time and time again, will the perplexing question of the distribution of wealth be solved. Such a solution was too ethereal, too unworldly for the secularistic-minded men of his day. His was the age which laid the railroads and built telegraph lines – and he dared to tell his listeners that the only solution to their difficulties lay not in economic textbooks but in the New Testament! Naturally enough he was considered impractical and naïve. Wars and revolutions and concentration camps and dictatorships were needed to make practical-minded men realize that perhaps the Spanish "lay father of the Church" had reached the very core of a terribly practical problem and that he proposed the most practical solution of all – if men want to live together in human society.

* * *

The reader today can hardly appreciate how penetrating an analysis Donoso Cortés made of nineteenth-century society, unless he reminds himself that Donoso wrote in the middle of the century when Liberalism was just coming to maturity and when Socialism was only a vague theory. Marxism was just emerging, and no one had yet formulated a penetrating criticism of bourgeois life. When almost all but the disinherited of the world were convinced that mankind was moving on to a more perfect society according to the mysterious rules of Progress, Donoso Cortés had the vision and the courage to assert that "the dogma of indefinite perfectability is so far from being true that society is now in danger of falling into a new barbarism."

His insight was remarkable, for he diagnosed the disease of Liberalism when it was still young. He prognosticated the course the disease would follow, and he foresaw the ravages it would work in the body politic of Europe. Few men in his day could appreciate the accuracy of Donoso's diagnosis. One who could, Louis Veuillot, said of his Spanish friend that "no one in our day has taken so profound a view of the evil in society, nor has anyone shown so clearly the source and the measure of its extent." Today, however, Donoso has come into his own, for we are able to appreciate his vision and the depth of his argumentation. We are able to understand how right he was in the things he said. Thus Goetz Briefs has written: "Nobody could foresee the future reality of Liberalism and the coming strength of Socialism. It is Donoso's great achievement – in fact he is the first writer to be credited with it – to have measured both movements with the yardstick of Catholic doctrine and to have revealed their shortcomings, their destructive character, their incompatibility with man's nature and the nature of human society."

In almost all respects Donoso's criticism of Liberalism was more acute and more penetrating than Karl Marx's. Donoso saw the reality of class war as fully as Marx did. "There have always been rich and poor in the world," he wrote before Marx composed the *Communist Manifesto,* "but never until our own day has one been able to see war between the rich and the poor shattering society in all countries." He, too, saw how the middle class ran things in their own interest, how they oppressed the poor, how they rationalized their position, how they used the schools, the army, even religion when they could, to keep the poor in place. Donoso saw the symptoms Marx saw, but he surpassed Marx in recognizing that the symptoms pointed to a spiritual disease instead of merely a bad organization of the forces of production. Whereas Marx thought that all evil flowed from an iniquitous method of production, Donoso thought that it all came from iniquitous men; whereas Marx thought the crisis was basically economic in nature, and that all maladjustment was the result of the capitalistic system, Donoso thought the crisis was essentially spiritual and religious.

So the Spanish nobleman, who indicted his age as severely as Marx did, surpassed the latter in going to the roots of the trouble both saw. But Donoso made several mistakes which Marx committed in similar fashion at a later day. Like Marx, he mistakenly assumed that men would logically and rationally follow out in practice the theories which they held in the abstract. Thus, like Marx, he believed that the Liberal would be as selfish in his conduct as Ricardo's economic man was in theory. He believed that the Liberal society would work out its principles even while it brought the roof of revolution crashing down on its head.

He did not envision the contingency of reform within the Liberal system, reform brought on through pressure from the union movement and fear of revolution, reform which was a contradiction in Liberal society, but which came anyway. This is the sort of thing that kept Donoso's dire prophecies from being realized as soon as he thought they would. Finally, it must be admitted that time and the evidence of history have shown us that Donoso Cortés made the mistake, so common to reformers and orators, of painting his pictures in black and white. To him the Liberal and the Socialist were completely black. In denying them any redeeming qualities at all he did them a measure of injustice. Thus he oversimplified the picture of his age by refusing to credit it with anything good. His criticisms were essentially correct, but he failed to make those qualifications to his absolute statements which accuracy demanded. Nor did he see that Catholics could accept individual liberal ideas and practices – as Ozanam, and later Leo XIII, did, without succumbing to the heresy of Liberalism.

Donoso Cortés is important in the history of the Church for having carried on the thought of De Maistre and having applied it to mid-nineteenth-century society. The lengthened perspective afforded him by the passage of another fifty years gave Donoso a sounder historical view of modern trends than De Maistre could possibly have had. Donoso was able to see that the French Revolution had profoundly altered the face of European society and that it was impossible to get back to the old social arrangements. He was able to see that the nineteenth century was one of revolution and that civilization could be made safe for the future only by a Catholic counterrevolution. De Maistre still thought in terms of pulling up the weeds of rationalism, because he thought the flowers of Catholic civilization still grew healthily in the European flower bed. But Donoso understood that the flower bed itself had to be spaded up, refertilized, and prepared to nurture the flowers of newly planted Christian seeds.

This radical thought was passed on chiefly to the French school of Catholics. It is not too much to say – as we shall see in a later chapter – that Louis Veuillot rose from the level of mere journalism to the heights of true Catholic thought by climbing on the shoulders of Donoso Cortés. Veuillot's French edition of the Spaniard's collected works was important in "converting" several important French Catholics to a thorough and radical Catholicism. Thus Jules Barbey d'Aurevilly, and through him Péguy and Bloy, are indebted to Donoso, as in turn are those other more recent French Catholics as the Maritains.

In his own day Donoso Cortés was important as a balance to such relatively liberal Catholics as Montalembert and Ozanam. These two men were much impressed by the accomplishments and the apparent open-mindedness of the Liberal society in which they lived. They believed that the Church had to strain its every muscle to adapt itself to the new society. There was always the danger, humanly speaking, that they might strain too far and concede more than the Church could surrender without losing its independent character. Donoso's conservatism was a healthy corrective to the impulsive desires of the Montalembert group to effect a quick amalgamation with modern society. Donoso saw the implications of such a union, and he put Catholics on guard against Liberalism and Socialism by pointing out the theological consequences of their thought.

He was an independent thinker, Donoso Cortés was, as much an individualist in the field of speculation as his forebears had been on the field of battle. Like them, he was convinced of the rightness of his cause, even though he stood almost alone against the array of Liberals who in his day were in possession of the European mind. Donoso believed that time would prove him right. "I have faith in my ideas," he wrote to a friend shortly before he died, "but, as I have already said, my ideas will not triumph until after the Deluge, which should come but has not yet arrived." Recent events have treated Donoso Cortés more respectfully than they have his adversaries. In many respects he proved to be an accurate prophet of the tendencies inherent in the Liberal society. That is why he can still be profitably studied. The cure he proposed, of course, was as old as Christianity. But like Christianity, it is a cure never invalidated by the passing of the years. For that reason, too, his thought is still very much alive and very pertinent to our own civilization.

11. Orestes Brownson

On Good Friday of 1876, in the village of Detroit, Orestes Brownson called out from his room to his son Henry that he was too tired to continue the argument they had begun earlier in the day on the unforgivable sin. This was the first time in his seventy-three years that Orestes Brownson was not eager to finish the argument at a single sitting. So Henry knew that death must have already put its finger on his father's brow. Nor was Henry wrong. On Easter Sunday, Orestes Brownson received the last sacraments, and on Monday he sighed deeply and died. Brownson had a right to breathe that last long sigh, for his had been a rugged life, one of constant struggle. It was a typical American success story of the poor boy who by his own efforts educated himself, came to know all the important people of his age, won a reputation as America's most brilliant journalist, jousted with the best Protestant and the best Catholic minds of the day, and died leaving his imprint deep upon his age.

Brownson was a towering figure, both physically and intellectually. He was well over six feet tall, and after his conversion to Catholicism gave him his easy conscience – as he put it to his Protestant friends – he topped two hundred and fifty pounds. An equally imposing figure intellectually, he was, according to Theodore Maynard, "the greatest and most luminous mind that has so far appeared among Catholics in this country." The *Catholic Advocate* of Louisville went so far as to compare him with the leading members of the hierarchy, figures like Kenrick, Spalding, and Hughes, and to comment that "in the cause of what may be termed the higher education of the best Catholic intellect in the land, in the true relations of Catholics with non-Catholics, of the Church to the current State questions, Brownson has labored more than all these." Whether enthusiasm colored the *Advocate's* judgment is debatable, but certainly there can be no question that Brownson is the most important Catholic layman in the history of the Church in the United States.

His importance is due both to the circumstances in which he was thrust and to his own stature. He had reached a position of national importance in American religious and intellectual matters before he became a Catholic. He was respected as a thinker, feared as an adversary, welcomed as an ally. He was recognized as one of the flowers of American civilization: a Yankee, a Protestant, a solid thinker, and a fearless preacher, an honest, self-made man. In 1844 this Yankee Protestant became a Catholic. He joined a Church that was somehow suspected in those days of being un-American, a Church for poor and ignorant immigrants, a relic of the past whose days were numbered and whose claims were not seriously entertained by thinking men anywhere. Brownson's being a Catholic made Americans sit up and take stock of things all over again. After the first shock of his conversion had worn off and after men saw that he had not lost his mind, Brownson's friends—who were the important thinkers of the day—had to admit the possibility of one's being American, intelligent, and Catholic all at the same time. Ironic as it might seem, nevertheless it is a fact that this Yankee's entrance into the Catholic Church gave it an air of decency and respectability it had not possessed in the minds of Americans before that time.

Brownson spent the remaining thirty years of his life trying to show Protestants that Catholics could be good Americans and to convince Catholics that Americans could be good Catholics. He was an outstanding apologist whose arguments in defense of his adopted Church were never successfully contested by his former associates. Brownson could not be answered; his logic was airtight. Nor could he be ignored, for he roared like a lion. He does not seem to have convinced any large number of Protestants that they should take the step he had taken, but at least he did prove that it was a logical thing to do. Meanwhile, with his millions of written words he showed conclusively that there was nothing un-American about the Catholic Church, and he tried—without any great success—to reorient the approach of Catholic apologists to the American Protestant mind. Brownson worked these thirty years like a high-pressure steam engine, puffing, roaring, declaiming, debating, arguing for the spread of Catholicism in this country. That is why his biographer Father Virgil Michel claims that "his services to Catholicity are well-nigh inestimable," and Father John McCaffrey, Brownson's contemporary, compares him with Cardinal Newman and concludes that "each put Catholicity fifty years ahead."

* * *

Biographers commonly say of Brownson that he used an un-Catholic tone in arguing for the Catholic Church, while his Irish contemporaries were convinced he was not really a Catholic at all. To understand how such things can be said of this outstanding Catholic layman we must study his background, since a man past forty, which Orestes Brownson was when he entered the Church, cannot drop the mannerisms and the habits and the culture acquired through a lifetime. It is necessary, then, to see something about his New England setting, his puritan upbringing, his religious peregrinations in his individualistic quest of the truth.

Orestes Brownson was born in Vermont in 1803, and his mother's name was Relief. In a way, that tells the whole story of his pre-Catholic days. For the New England into which Brownson was born was still strongly puritan, possessed of the old virtues and the old prejudices generated by Calvin almost three centuries before. Brownson grew up in a deeply religious atmosphere, but one in which the "Scarlet Lady" of Rome was held in horror. He never saw a Catholic church, as a matter of fact, until he moved to Detroit some twenty years later. Certainly in his earnest quest for a true religion he never seriously entertained thoughts of becoming a Catholic until he was forty. Respectable people in New England did not think such thoughts.

From his earliest days Brownson was interested in religion. His father had died shortly after his birth, and his mother had found it necessary to distribute the children among neighbors. Young Orestes was placed with an elderly couple in Royalton, Vermont. There he grew up a lonely boy in gloomy, sad surroundings. The elderly couple were cold, austere, formidable. They had lost their religion, but they had kept the puritan's harsh way of life – a terrible thing to happen to anyone. Young Orestes was raised according to these forbidding standards. That is why he could complain when he was fifty that, "properly speaking, I had no childhood, and have more of the child in my feelings now than at eight or ten years of age. Brought up with old people, and debarred from all sports, plays and amusements of children, I had the manners, the tone, and tastes of an old man before I was a boy."

The lad was taught puritan virtues: not to steal, not to lie, always to work hard, to stay out of debt, and to save his money. He was also taught to read, and within a short time he had exhausted the meager libraries of the families in the neighborhood, reading the standard puritan literature of the day, and especially the Bible. So he grew up very much alone, a nonsociable little boy who, in his own words, "was rarely less alone than when alone." His chief diversion was solitary reading, and his reading was chiefly religious. So the young lad came naturally to wonder which of the religious groups in his neighborhood was the right one. About these things he thought a good deal, and thus by the time he was eight or nine he had selected for meditation and study most of the central ideas of faith. By nine, certainly, he was picking his way among religious truths, puzzling them over, and accepting or rejecting them as though he were a mature theologian. (One should remember Brownson's personal experience here in order to understand the charge of ontologism* made against him after his conversion to Catholicism.)

Young Orestes stayed at Royalton until 1817. In that year, when he was fourteen, he rejoined his mother and the rest of the family. Here it was, in Ballston Spa, New York, that Orestes went to school for a few months to receive the only formal education he obtained. Here he met lads of various religious groups, and others who had no religion at all. With them all Brownson insisted on talking religion. For five years, during which time he did not attend any church regularly, Orestes wrestled around in a state of intellectual confusion. Of one thing, however, he tells us he was certain: that God would not have given him a craving for belief if there was nothing to believe.

---

* Ontologism is a philosophy, stated at various times in modern history, which holds that the knowledge of God is intuitive. It was associated in the nineteenth century with the Italian patriot-priest and philosopher, Gioberti.

It was natural for Brownson to lean toward such a belief, inasmuch as he personally seems to have had knowledge of God from the time he began to read. Whether Brownson can properly be called an ontologist was debated in his own lifetime, and ever since by his biographers.

So this stubborn Yankee boy persisted in his search for truth. For a little while, when he was nineteen, he thought he had found it. One Sunday young Brownson happened to walk by a Presbyterian church just when the congregation was entering for services. Orestes walked in too. He stayed through the services, and came out feeling that he had "received the faith." So he presented himself to the minister, who duly baptized him and received him into the Presbyterian communion. Thus in 1822, Orestes Brownson entered the first of several religions in which he tried to find the truth.

* * *

But the Presbyterian faith was not for him. Its harsh, narrow spirit was uncongenial to his temperament. Moreover, its doctrines — at least as they were presented by the local minister — could not stand up under the corrosive action of Brownsonian logic. One of his biographers, Arthur M. Schlesinger, Jr., sums up the matter well by saying, "In his deep loneliness and ardent desire for salvation he had grasped too eagerly at a creed which could never become a part of him." Presbyterianism taught that man is sinful in the very depths of his heart. It taught a doctrine of predestination which consigned most people to hell and let a few, the Elect, into heaven by God's arbitrary choice. Its God was a severe, powerful tyrant who apparently enjoyed seeing people squirm and suffer here on earth and later in the fire of hell. All this Brownson would have accepted if it had been obviously true, if Presbyterianism could have defended its doctrine in the court of reason against the prosecuting attorney this young man set himself up to be.

Orestes particularly was annoyed by the tenet of predestination, because he thought it not only an ugly doctrine but also one which could not be squared with Holy Scripture. When he presented his objection to the minister, he was told not to worry about that particular item of faith, because, the minister said, the next assembly would probably change it. This was too much for Brownson — altering eternal truths of religion at each meeting! After having spent two miserable years in the Presbyterian communion, he walked out in indignant disgust.

Shortly after, Brownson went to the village of Detroit. Here he taught school. While he was recovering from a severe attack of malaria he read and pondered over the works of a certain Dr. Winchester, a man who, like Brownson himself, had left the Calvinist fold and who had embraced the opposite teaching of salvation for all mankind. Dr. Winchester had founded the Universalist Church of America, which was full of refugees from Calvinism, warmhearted, kindly people who liked to believe that a good God had arranged for all men to go to heaven. Universalism even went so far as to provide salvation for the fallen angels – and certainly the religious optimist can ask for no more.

At the time Universalism appeared most reasonable to Brownson, largely, it seems, because it had caught him "on the bounce" from the other extreme of Presbyterianism. So he adopted this new religion and applied to the Universalist Association for a preacher's license. In the following year (1826) he was ordained a Universalist minister in New Hampshire and licensed to preach. For a while Brownson did his best to defend Universalist doctrine, both in his sermons and in *The Gospel Advocate* which he edited. He found it impossible to arrive at the doctrine of universal salvation from the Bible, so he kept ferreting around intellectually, embarrassing his fellow Universalists with his questions and his merciless logic. He finally ended up skeptical of all things religious. Because he was an honest man and because he felt he wore a mask when he posed as a Universalist minister, he abjured his second faith to see if he could find the truth elsewhere. The Universalists, incidentally, were happy to see him leave, for there had been no peace in their household as long as Brownson was one of the family.

For two years now (1829–1831) Brownson was a Socialist and a World Reformer. Disillusioned with the two forms of supernatural religion he had thus far encountered, he decided to follow Robert Owen and Fanny Wright in their confused spiritual philanthropy. He preached against industrialism and he advocated the radical Socialist reforms proposed by Owen, but he discovered that good works without faith were not enough to reform the world. These were barren years religiously, the low point of Brownson's life, reached when he was twenty-seven and still fourteen years away from the Catholic Church. He later wrote that in 1830, "I was alone. There was no God in heaven, to whom I could go for succor; there was no spot on earth to which I could retire for a while, no sympathizing soul with whom I could talk over my plans, give utterance to the feelings which I must ordinarily suppress. . . . My philanthropy turned sour, and, I grieve to say, I ended by railing against mankind."

One thing, however, he did learn from his experiment with World Reform. By thinking Owen's scheme through, he came to the conclusion that Socialism demanded that people behave like soulless animals and that it was useless to attempt any such scheme for world reform without a religious faith on which it could be based. He was convinced, therefore, that religion was socially useful as well as personally necessary.

He therefore returned to religion again, this time to become a free-lance preacher at Ithaca, New York. In his first sermon, in 1831, he announced: "I belong to no party. I disclaim all sectarian names." But he went on to add that if he were to be anything he would be a Unitarian, "as that denomination approximates nearer, in my estimation, to the spirit of Christianity than any other." The Unitarians were a liberal sect, indeed, allowing each preacher to interpret Holy Scripture as he saw fit. This gave Brownson plenty of leeway—and all through his life Brownson, the rugged individualist, demanded lots of rhetorical breathing space and plenty of intellectual elbow room. At the same time, however, this lack of a definite, clearly defined doctrine involved Brownson and his fellow Unitarian preachers in difficulties. For Brownson was logical enough to see that when several Universalist preachers gave different interpretations of the same passage in Scripture, only one of them—if any—could be right. The others had to be wrong.

So he organized a committee of Unitarian Clergymen to arrive at a common method of teaching Christian truth and to establish a common creed. But he found that they could agree neither on the essentials of doctrine nor on the method of preaching. Annoyed at this disturber of the peace, Brownson's fellow ministers urged him to try his experiment elsewhere. He therefore moved to Boston where, in 1836, he launched his program for church unification. His aim was to combine articles of faith combed from the various religions and thus to concoct a formula that would unify worship in America. This involved him in a study of comparative religion, and now for the first time he seriously examined Catholicism in order to find what articles of faith he could extract from the Roman Church. He found elements in the Catholic Church which appealed to his logical, critical mind. As the years passed Brownson found himself more and more inclined to Catholic doctrine and morals – but at this time he had no idea of becoming a Catholic in order to get them. Until 1843 or 1844 his plan was to combine them with certain Protestant teachings, the synthesis of which would be his new religion.

Through these years Brownson was making a name for himself as a preacher and a writer. He edited *The Reformer* first, and then *The Boston Quarterly Review.* In these journals and in his sermons he appealed to the intellectuals of Boston, since his approach was always the thinker's, and his aim was always to test doctrine by human reason. That is why Isaac Hecker, one of Brownson's devoted followers, himself to be a convert to Catholicism and founder of the Paulist Order, tells us that Brownson's audience was composed of "thinkers rather than worshippers, persons with whom religion had run off into pure intellectuality. . . . There was more thinking in that congregation," Father Hecker wrote, "than in the rest of Boston."

What eventually brought Brownson into the Catholic Church was just this thinking – solid, steady, hard thinking by a man who was honest with himself and who sincerely wanted to find the truth, wherever it might be. He came closer and closer to the Church as he found its doctrines made sense and were not contradictory. But he did not rush in, for Brownson was a Yankee whose prejudice against Rome was deep in his soul. He tells us how he did all in his power "to find some middle ground on which I could be faithful to my Catholic tendencies without uniting myself with the present Roman Catholic Church."

Through 1843, Catholic journals mentioned Brownson's *Review* approvingly from time to time, and they quoted from it with increasing frequency. People listening to Archbishop Hughes of New York speak on morality and economics thought they were listening to one of Brownson's sermons on industrialism. There could be no doubt, early in 1844, that intellectually Brownson was practically a Catholic. In May of that year he took the final logical step of asking admission to the Church. He applied to

Bishop Fenwick, of Boston, whose straightforward answers to this preacher's questions evoked the latter's admiration. He took instructions from Coadjutor Bishop Fitzpatrick and was duly received into the Catholic Church.

Thus in 1844, at the age of 41, Brownson changed religion again. This proved to be his last "conversion," for this time Brownson found the truth for which he had been seeking since he was a boy. This time he suffered no disillusionment, found no doctrines which contradicted each other. This time, as he put it, he found a religion which succored and sustained him, whereas his former religions had required him to support them. Brownson's many changes in religion had not betrayed inconstancy on his part, as many persons believed, for he had been in constant search of that fullness of truth which would satisfy his demanding intellect. There were many who did not comprehend this, of course, and some of them wagered in 1844 that Brownson would not stay three years in the Church. These were men who understood neither Brownson nor the Catholic Church. They did not understand how the Catholic Church was catholic enough to contain even so energetic a man as Brownson, how he could find in it more breathing space and intellectual freedom than even he needed.

From a purely natural point of view, however, Schlesinger understands how Brownson reached home when he entered the Catholic Church. In a penetrating paragraph he says: "The pilgrim inevitably paused before the gates of Rome. To his inexorable honesty and his thirst for certainty, Brownson added a passionate and concrete belief in God and a deep need for a rich and logical theology. Such a man could not long continue within nineteenth-century Protestantism. If his vision of God had been less definite, he might have turned Transcendentalist. If his sense of logic had been less exacting, he might have stayed Universalist. If he had been less fervently honest, he might have remained a Unitarian, a Presbyterian or a socialist. If he had been content with anything short of absolute certainty, he might have continued forever a Protestant. But he tried Protestantism and found it wanting. Rome provided the only refuge. Entering the gates, he finally discovered a place to rest. . . . He found in the Catholic universe the security he had sought so long, and he rested joyously in the Catholic solutions of the central problems of life."*

Now for the first time he enjoyed peace of mind and the satisfaction of having solved that problem he had posed to himself when he was a little boy at Royalton: which of these various competing religions is the right one? And he enjoyed domestic peace — because fortunately for the tranquillity of the Brownson household, his entire family embraced Catholicism with him. But it was not for Brownson to settle down to a life of tranquil meditation.

* * *

Orestes Brownson went on as of old — arguing, preaching, writing, debating, only with more determination and vigor than ever, for now that he knew he possessed the truth he was anxious to share it with all the world, to impose it on all his friends. His entry into the Church had been a logical step, but it had not been an easy one. That is why, when he was later asked if his conversion had led him to a bed of roses, he answered, "No! a bed of spikes." Although a Yankee like Brownson probably felt more comfortable on spikes than roses, nevertheless his position was uncomfortable. Like St. Paul, who was accepted by neither Jews nor Christians after his conversion, Brownson found himself in a no man's land between Protestants and Catholics. By coming into the Church he had cut himself away from his prominent Protestant friends, but he had failed to gain new friends to compensate for the loss of the old. Although Catholics were happy to receive so important a convert, still they were suspicious of this man who changed religion so often. And they were temperamentally ill-suited, most of them, to accept so rugged an individualist as Orestes Brownson.

Brownson's desire was to bring into the Church hundreds, perhaps even thousands, of his Protestant friends. He believed that because of his prominence and through his *Review* he was in a position to start something like a mass movement of Protestants toward Catholicism, and he seemed more than ever convinced of this when he found how consistent and logically

---

* Arthur M. Schlesinger, Jr., *Orestes A. Brownson* (Boston: Little, Brown and Co.), p. 283, quoted by permission of the author.

irresistible were the articles of the Catholic Faith. His failure to start any such movement — which must have humbled as well as perplexed him — was due to two main reasons. In the first place, his Protestant friends were not as logical, nor as heroically courageous as he was. They were content to occupy the position which Brownson had found untenable because they were not bothered by that Brownsonian thirst for possession of the full truth. In the second place, the Catholic Church seemed socially and culturally a rather disreputable society when Brownson joined it. Respectable people might study it as an historic entity or they might examine it curiously as an alien organization identified with the excitable Latin races and with the unpredictable Irish. Certainly, though, respectable Americans never thought of the Roman Catholic Church as a society to which they might belong. To most of them it would apparently mean not only giving up Protestantism but also surrendering their Americanism, their intellectual freedom, their Anglo-Saxon heritage, their whole way of life.

Catholics were indeed a small and inconspicuous group in those days. In the bishopric of Boston, for example, which included almost all of New England, there were only twenty-seven priests. The Catholics of the diocese, moreover, were anxious to remain inconspicuous. Their leaders, by and large, were intellectually not able to stand on the same platform with the Protestant thinkers of the day. And the Catholic masses who filled the churches were ill-educated, poorer people, usually immigrants or their children who somehow did not seem to be Americans yet. These were Brownson's companions-in-faith. Not many of them were apt to read a man like Brownson. Nor were they large enough a group to make him important as their spokesman. Certainly, from a purely worldly point of view, Brownson had hurt himself by joining the Catholic Church. He was at the pinnacle of his fame in 1844. He was respected as a thinker. He was avidly read and admired as a cogent writer on religious, philosophical, economic, and political questions. Now he had become spokesman of an insignificantly small group, the Catholics, who were of even less importance than their numbers would indicate because of their poverty and their ignorance.

Nonetheless, Brownson thought that he could bring the best

Protestant minds over to the Church. His biographers maintain that he might have enjoyed greater success if his hands had not been tied by Bishop Fitzpatrick. The bishop, an intelligent but unsympathetic and unimaginative man, insisted that Brownson forego the kind of argument that had brought him into the Church in favor of the traditional Catholic apologetic. This tradition, of course, was foreign to Brownson. Thus he had to train himself in a method and a theology of which he was hitherto ignorant. Naturally enough, a large number of subscribers quit his *Review* when he made it a Catholic organ. For a time he thought of studying law and of entering politics for a livelihood, but at Bishop Fitzpatrick's request he changed the *Boston Quarterly Review* into *Brownson's Quarterly Review*, and he submitted his theological articles to the bishop's censorship.

The immediate aim of the newly named *Review*, Brownson told his readers, was not the conversion of Protestants. It was, instead, to encourage among Catholics "a firm and bold profession of their faith, and an independent and fearless, though quiet, assertion of their rights as Christians, as citizens, as men." The accomplishment of this objective was indeed very much needed. Characteristically, Brownson began his "firm and bold profession of faith" by turning his artillery on Protestantism. His defense of the Church always consisted of an offense against its opponents, so he set about attacking Protestantism by putting it on the defensive. His strategy was to destroy all the middle ground between Catholicism and atheism and thus to put his readers in the position of having to choose between the two. Put in other words, he tried to demolish all rational foundations for Protestantism.

Such an aim, from his fellow Catholic's point of view, was laudable enough. But Brownson did not use techniques which win friends and influence people. He had always been aggressive by nature, and now with absolute certainty that he was right, he assumed a tone and a manner that tended to repel even when it convinced his Protestant reader. As we have already indicated, Brownson could never understand why all people were not ruthlessly intellectual like himself. Thus when he was within the Catholic fold only five years he said of Protestants that "they have no sense of responsibleness, no loyalty to truth, no mental chastity, no intellectual sincerity." Such accusations may have applied fairly enough to some of Brownson's former associates, but it is hardly likely that all Protestants were as subjectively corrupt as he believed.

Sometimes his method of arguing took on an air that would have been almost comic were it not for his intense earnestness about this important matter of religion. On cold days, for example, he used to hold forth in a neighborhood drugstore where he took on all comers with his arguments against Protestantism. This sort of thing might have given Brownson many rounds in his intellectual bouts against Protestant apologists, but it does not seem to have given him any decisions. So it was when he picked up an acquaintance and threw him to the floor when the latter chided him for turning Catholic. So it was, too, when one Friday he complained loudly to the manager of a restaurant with only meat on the menu: "Why don't you have fish? No Christian eats meat on Friday." Brownson had apparently never heard the adage about sugar catching more flies than vinegar. It would not have mattered if he had, for Brownson was so constituted that to him truth was truth, and its flavor did not matter. He was of the school that gave children their castor oil straight.

Brownson's arguments against Protestantism were straight and simple. Protestants were wrong, he said, and that's all there was to it. Their religions were all man-made, and, as the name suggests, essentially negative. "For the three hundred years it has existed," he said of Protestantism, "it has proved itself powerful to destroy, but impotent to found; ready to begin, but never able to complete. Whatever it claims that is positive, abiding, it has inherited or borrowed from the ages and the lands of faith. Its own creations rise and vanish as soap-bubbles blown by our children in their sports." Brownson went so far as to assert that no one who thinks seriously at all could honestly be a Protestant, because "no man ever is or ever was strictly honest and sincere in the profession of a false doctrine." His argument was that no false doctrine could be so evidenced as to exclude doubt, and if you profess a false doctrine you therefore profess what, in some measure at least, you doubt.

What Brownson was doing in his attack on Protestantism, of

course, was reducing its doctrines with his devastating logic to conclusions never intended by its advocates – conclusions, however, which Brownson could fairly reach by showing the inner logic of Protestantism itself. He claimed that Protestants had rejected reason in the process of rejecting the Catholic faith and that they had therefore put themselves in a lower position than that of Aristotle and others who reasoned to a natural religion and morality before the coming of Christ. He claimed that the whole Protestant movement was anarchical, a "spirit of lawlessness which leads everyone to wish to have his own way," and that it must end up with as many churches as there were individuals. He concluded that because its essence was "mere vulgar pride, it is a moral disease rather than an intellectual aberration [and] it is evident that we are to treat it as a vice rather than as an error, and Protestants as sinners rather than as simply unbelievers or misbelievers."

On the surface at least, Brownson's logic was unanswerable, at least in that age when men still pretended to think logically and seriously. Most important, from the point of view of American Catholics, he put the Protestants on the defensive and made it no longer necessary for Catholics to justify holding their age-old doctrines. Protestants could not answer him and they could not very well avoid his conclusions by attacking logic itself, so they avoided meeting his line of argument at all, dismissing him as a "fallen-away" Protestant who had somehow got off the beaten American track and had fallen in with immigrant obscurantists.

Probably the most telling thrust Brownson made against Protestantism was his argument that its claim to religious liberty was a mockery, that it was indeed a despotic form of religion. "Spiritual despotism is that which subjects us, in spiritual matters, to a human authority, whether our own or that of others – for our own is as human as another's; and the only redemption from it is in having in them a divine authority. . . . Sectarianism is spiritual despotism." This sort of argument was aimed at making an impression on American minds. So it was with another line of argument Brownson developed more fully than any other American Catholic has ever done – that Protestantism's tendency was away from God and truth in the general direction of secularism and error, and that its destination therefore lay in complete secularism and full-blown atheism. Protestantism, he insisted, could not stop short in a respectable religion like Anglicanism or Presbyterianism; it had to go on, by the very logic of its system, "towards rationalism, Transcendentalism, and therefore towards pantheism, atheism, nihilism."

These Brownsonian arguments against the Protestants apparently helped increase the confidence of Catholics in their position, but they did little to convince Protestants that they should follow Brownson's road to Rome. So it was with the countless clever, quotable thrusts Brownson made in favor of his newly adopted Church. Such, for example, was the statement that "an infallible Church, the Church of God, needs no apologies; man's church or the synagogue of Satan, deserves none." Brownson's *Quarterly* bristled with clever phrases from one of America's most brilliant journalists – but the student of human nature knows that cleverness and brilliance often defeat the very cause in which they are enlisted. They seem to have done so with Brownson's campaign to turn Protestants into Catholics. But at the same time they furnished Catholics with a large store of ammunition on which they could draw for their own apologetic work in the future.

* * *

Brownson assumed the offensive in his apology for the Church by taking a line of argument that must have seemed daring for his age – a line of argument which Catholics almost all subscribe to in our own day, one which the sorry history of the past half century seems to validate. The year after his conversion, Brownson wrote an article on Catholicism and democracy in which he maintained the thesis "that without the Roman Catholic religion it is impossible to preserve a democratic government, and secure its free, orderly, and wholesome action. Infidelity, Protestantism, heathenism may institute a democracy, but only Catholicity can sustain it." It is hard for us to appreciate today the audacity, as well as the intellectual ruggedness, involved in a man's telling Americans that they could preserve their way of life only if the religion of an insignificant immigrant minority of Americans were to spread appreciably throughout the nation.

The line of argument Brownson used to sustain his thesis is a simple one: democracy is a form of government built upon the sovereignty of the people; these people are weak and fallible, and they stand in sore need of religious and moral guidance if they are to make wise decisions; such guidance can come only from the true religion – which, Brownson insisted of course, is Catholicism. Brownson found the first step in his argument the easiest to demonstrate: that the people are fallible, individually and collectively, that they are motivated by passion and by selfish interest more frequently than by public interest, and therefore that "the virtue and intelligence of the American people are not sufficient to secure the free, orderly, and wholesome action of the government." The second step was not as easy to prove, but Brownson insisted that Protestantism cannot guide the people because "it is itself subject to popular control, and must follow in all things the popular will, passion, interest, ignorance, prejudice, or caprice." What is needed is a religion which does not come from the people but from God, which will restrain popular passion, moderate greed for material things, teach men a true sense of justice, and guide them in their decisions by laying true principles down before them.

Thus Brownson offered Americans of the mid-century a choice between Catholicism and eventual anarchy or tyranny. Here he was following the same line of reasoning developed by Donoso Cortés in Spain, but he seems to have arrived at his conclusions before he read any of Donoso's works. He was satisfied, later in life, that he had proved that "without the Catholic religion it is impossible permanently to sustain popular institutions, or to secure their free and salutary operations. . . . Without Catholicity you can have, in principle at least, only despotism or anarchy." It is impossible today to see anything wrong with Brownson's argument as an argument. Things have not worked out exactly as he thought they would because men are not as simply logical in their action as he assumed they were. Brownson would have defined man as a rational animal, it is true, but he laid too much emphasis on the adjective and not enough on the noun. Protestants have been better persons than their doctrine, and Catholics have not been as good as their religion. Thus democracy has limped along in this country in a fashion Brownson did not foresee, not guided by Catholic principles alone or resulting in either pure anarchy or pure despotism – though there is reason to believe the drift has been in the general direction Brownson pointed out.

At bottom this Yankee convert was an optimist. He ranted against the shortcomings of his age and he condemned Protestants in the harshest of terms – but he was convinced, nonetheless, that his century was an improvement over the previous one and that the future would be even better than the present in which he lived. He accepted much more of the age than his critical articles on Protestantism would have led his readers to believe. There were good principles, as well as evil, at work in American society in the mid-part of the nineteenth century, Brownson told his readers, and he was convinced that Catholicism was ideally suited to be the "dominant principle of the nineteenth century, and of the most enlightened portion of mankind." This was true, he said, because Catholicism reinforced and promoted all the good trends of the age, such as "the improved tone of moral sentiment," the spirit of scientific investigation, the spirit of beneficence, the acceptance of man by reason of his integral worth rather than his social position. Moreover, it worked against the evil trends of the time, such as the spirit of rebellion, the denial of property rights, the looseness of the marriage bond, and the general advance of atheistic thought.

Thus Brownson did much more than show that there was no conflict between Catholicism and Americanism. He went on to claim that without Catholicism the American way of life could not permanently survive. In great detail, and in one article after another, he developed his thesis on the compatibility of the Catholic religion and American citizenship. This was a new line of argument and it was one which sorely needed development if Catholics were ever to live in the United States as citizens of worth and dignity like their Protestant neighbors.

• • •

Brownson did not get along much better with Catholics than he did with Protestants. His lack of social tact and his single-minded pursuit of the truth involved him in disputes with almost every important Catholic in America, and with many of them abroad. He clashed with Newman, for example, who was an equally brilliant, a more subtle, and a better trained mind than

Brownson; he clashed at one time or another with most of the American bishops. At other times and on other questions he agreed with them, as they agreed with him and respected him even when he annoyed them.

If the Catholic Church had been just another religious sect, Brownson would not have lasted the three years his former associates gave him. For it was not Catholics but rather the faith which kept him in the Church. From the beginning he had difficulties with Catholic leaders – and they with him. He was too much a Yankee for them, too independent a mind, too aggressive a writer. So there were conflicts. But never once did Brownson waver in his faith. Ten years after his conversion he could write bitterly, and truly, that Catholics "have so misrepresented and denounced me, and are so ready to seize every opportunity to blacken my character, that I do not feel that lively confidence in them that I did." Then he hastened to add: "I love the church more and more every day."

In the last number of his *Review*, published a half year before his death in 1876, Brownson took leave of his reading public with an article entitled "Valedictory," in which he professed: "I have and I desire to have no home out of the Catholic Church, with which I am more than satisfied, and which I love as the dearest, tenderest, and most affectionate mother. My only wish is to live and die in her communion." Brownson always felt that way about the Church, and had it not been for the Nativist controversy, in which he became embroiled, he might have felt that way about most Catholics too.

American Nativists attacked the Catholic Church, in the decades after Brownson's conversion, as an alien body in America, as an institution which was controlled by a foreigner, which forbade its members to become American. It was an institution, they therefore believed, which by the very nature of things was inimical to the American republic. As early as January, 1845, before he had been in the Church a year, Brownson wrote against "Native Americanism" as a threat to American institutions. He attacked Nativists not so much for being anti-Catholic as for being un-American – a telling line of argument for a Catholic to use. In a closely reasoned, hard-hitting article Brownson started out by showing that there was no need in America, still a land of opportunity, for excluding foreigners from immigration or for denying them citizenship when they arrived. On the contrary, he argued, there is every reason in the world why Americans should welcome immigrants. To exclude immigrants is to deny America the wealth of talent and the army of strong laborers which had done so much to develop the country in the first half of the nineteenth century.

Brownson went on to expose the facetious reasoning presented by Nativists against the Irish immigrant. "The political leaders of the Native American party," he showed, "are opposed to naturalized citizens solely on the ground that these citizens do not uniformly vote on their side." The followers in the party often oppose immigrants because they think these newcomers to America will compete for their jobs — a groundless fear, Brownson argued, and an un-American attitude toward getting ahead. But the basic reason for Nativism was the widespread hostility in America to the Catholic Church. "We know," Brownson boldly asserted, "it is a party formed for the suppression of the Catholic Church in our land." This is the point he labored in all his writing against Nativism. He developed this argument in two ways. First of all, he showed how contrary to the American spirit it was to exclude people from citizenship for religious reasons, because the true American spirit "places every man on his own two feet, and says to him: 'Be a man, and you shall be esteemed according to your worth as a man; you shall be commended only for your personal merits; you shall be made to suffer only for your personal demerits.'" Secondly, he showed how Nativism would undermine American institutions by destroying the only long-term "hope for our republic," the Catholic Church. "We look for our safety to the spread of Catholicity," he concluded. "And here, then, is our answer to those who tell us Catholicity is incompatible with free institutions. We tell them that they cannot maintain free institutions without it."

Unfortunately, Brownson incensed Catholics — especially the Irish — because in the course of his arguments against Nativism he said that there was a shred of truth to the Nativist complaint against American Catholics, insofar as many Catholics considered the terms Irish and Catholic interchangeable. Many did not try to become real Americans. But Americanism, he insisted, could lie as deep in the Catholic heart as in the Protestant, and it was a blunder for Catholics to identify their religion with any other nationality. He wanted Catholics to be catholic, not French or Italian or Irish.

Such writing brought Irish thunder down on Brownson's head. The archbishop of Baltimore asked him to remove the letter of approval which the bishops had given his *Review* five years before and which he had proudly published on the back page of each issue. In July and August of 1854 he was censured in at least nine Catholic journals. Newman was forced to write from Ireland asking if Brownson could postpone accepting his offer of a chair in the Irish university Newman was founding – all because of the vicious opposition of high-placed Irishmen whom Newman could not afford to antagonize. By rushing into the Nativist controversy, Brownson put himself between two fires – hot ones they were. As he complained, he was trying to defend against Americans his right to be a Catholic and against Catholics his right to be an American. He satisfied neither group, for as Van Wyck Brooks sums it up, "Brownson was too Catholic for the Yankees and too Yankee for the Catholics."

A century later the wisdom of Brownson's approach and the shortsightedness of the Irish stand have become evident.* For a century, however, down through the days of the Al Smith campaign of 1928 and into the Ku-Klux Klan movement, Nativist suspicion against the Church continued – largely because of the narrow-minded stupidity of the Nativist element in this country, but also partly because of the stand taken by that element within the Church which Brownson tried to convert to Americanism.** Brownson's line, if it had been generally followed at

---

* The Irish were not the only immigrant group to create a problem for the Church in America by identifying Catholicism with their homeland. Germans, Poles, Italians, almost every nationality did it at some time or other. It just happened that Brownson wrote at a time when the Irish were the only large Catholic group in America, and it was with them, therefore, that he ran into the most trouble.

** Americanism, as Brownson used the term, is not the same thing as the so-called Americanism dealt with in the Apostolic Letter of Leo XIII, *Testem Benevolentiae,* addressed to Cardinal Gibbons, January 22, 1899. Cf. *The Catholic Encyclopedia,* Vol. XIV, p. 537.

once, instead of haltingly and only by some Catholics, would have saved much suspicion and tension in the century to follow.

* * *

In 1857, Brownson moved to New York because he thought that there he could breathe in a more open-minded atmosphere than in tight, suspicious Boston. In New York, however, he had trouble with Archbishop Hughes – both were to blame – so he moved out of the archbishop's jurisdiction by going to Elizabeth, New Jersey, where he stayed until the last year of his life. Gradually he wrote less and less on theological subjects, partly because he never felt fully at ease with them, partly because of difficulties he had with ecclesiastical censors, and partly because he came to believe that other questions were of more immediate importance. He thought, in time, that his *Review* could do the most good by treating social, economic, and political subjects from a Catholic point of view.

Many of the *Review's* best pages – and they sparkle with journalistic brilliance no other journal of the time, Catholic or secular, possessed – are devoted to these social subjects. He condemned the secular trend in the public schools, for example, by insisting that any system of education which tried to make good citizens without reference to God's revelation of Himself was bound to defeat itself. Such a system of education, he claimed, "can never be beneficial either to the individual or to society." Secular education was typical of the society in which he lived, Brownson believed, a society which had deluded itself into thinking that man's sole end was happiness on this earth, a society therefore absorbed in things material and convinced that it was progressing toward absolute perfection. For the naïve beliefs of Liberalism, Brownson reserved some of his bitterest sarcasm and his heaviest scorn.

He was one of the early opponents of industrialism. His few years as an Owenite Socialist had equipped him with a penetrating insight into the evils of the factory system. His Catholic principles, added to his natural antipathy toward the materialistic emphasis of industrialists, made him both a keen and a harsh critic of the industrial system. He was willing to admit that industrial progress had changed the face of the earth and had vastly increased the power of production, but he seriously questioned whether it had "made it easier for a poor man to earn his living or added anything to the real happiness or well-being of the people." Today, when Christian thinkers all raise that question, it is difficult to appreciate how radical Brownson was in daring to suggest that industrial progress might not be essentially good. Even more daring was his attack on the Protestant religions for their close alliance with industrialism, an alliance which he saw symbolized in the churches of Boston renting their ground floors to business establishments so as not to have the square footage idle all week. "Oh, blessed thrift," Brownson could not restrain from commenting, "great art thou, and hast learned to coin thy God and to put him out at usury!"

His basic complaint about industrialism, however, was that it had divorced economic thinking from morality and it had created an abstract science which dealt with man as though he were a machine or a lump of coal. "The political economists consider man only as a producing, distributing, and consuming machine, and seek only to get the greatest possible supply with the greatest possible demand. . . . I look upon man as having a sentient, intellectual, and moral nature, and I seek for him the greatest possible sum of virtue and happiness. It is not likely, then, that the political economists and I should think alike." Nor did they. Brownson had no use for slavery, but he insisted that the relationship between slave and master was more human than that between employee and employer. His complaint against the impersonalism of the factory system and corporate ownership was summed up in a typical Brownsonian epigram: "The great feudal lords had souls, railroad corporations have none."

Brownson told his readers that there was no sense in idealizing the middle ages or in hoping to go back to a pre-industrial society. There was no point in flying from reality, or in sacrificing the material gains accomplished by this new method of production. The only solution lay in revoking the divorce between economics and politics on the one hand and religion and morality on the other. The initiative for reforming the industrial system, Brownson insisted, lay with the capitalists themselves. They must treat their workers as human beings who possess a soul as well as a body and who therefore have the same human dignity and rights as the capitalist himself. There was no solution outside religion, he showed, and both the industrialists and the economic theorists must admit this or they will find their vaunted industrial system collapsing about their heads.

There was nothing unusual about Brownson's analysis of the capitalistic system, for the same basic ideas were to find their way into the thinking of the popes and the hierarchy in time to come. The unusual thing is that Brownson penetrated to the heart of the matter so early in the nineteenth century and that he did it in a country where an economic and a geographic frontier prevented many of the system's evils from developing in acute form until after Brownson's death in 1876. Brownson's analysis of socialism, again, was surprisingly acute for an American who was not faced with any immediate danger of socialism, as Europeans were in 1848 and occasionally thereafter. His conclusions on this subject were essentially the same as those of Donoso Cortés. He saw Socialism as inevitable in time, for Socialist principles were inherent in capitalism, and "if we adopt the socialistic premises we must go on with the socialists in the career of destruction; nay, we shall be compelled to do so or strew the battlefield with our dead bodies." There is no escaping this course of development, Brownson argued, because whether we wish it or not the human race "tends invariably to reach the end implied in the principles it adopts or the impulse it has received, and that tendency is never self-arrested."

Why not go all the way to Socialism? Brownson's chief objection was that Socialism was a religion. Therefore, he concluded, it was a heresy and it imposed error on man's mind and limited his human freedom. It was a perversion of Catholic truths, such as the Catholic idea of equality based on the Fatherhood of God, the Catholic idea of brotherhood based on membership in Christ's Church, and the Catholic idea of liberty based on a knowledge of man's true nature. Socialism, by postulating happiness on this earth as man's sole end, enslaves man "to nature and society, and subjects us to all the fluctuations of time and sense." And no man can be free, he insisted time and time again, unless he can trample underfoot his animal nature and his attachment to the things of this world. Brownson's cure, therefore, was a simple but radical one: reject the principles of Liberalism, from which Socialism logically derives, and adopt instead Catholic principles which are the sole safeguard against Socialism's otherwise logical conclusions.

* * *

Brownson's biography is pretty much the story of his arguments, his debates, his quarrels. For this, Brownson himself is largely to blame. He was not a sociable man. He did not know how to get along with people, though he wanted to in the worst way. That is why he remains a somewhat pathetic figure, even in the day of his greatest success, for he was a charitable, humble man who loved humanity in the abstract and wanted to love them in the concrete and be loved in return. But he could never live down his boyhood and his youth. His Yankee heritage was unsociable. He was self-educated and self-made — and such persons are seldom the sort we lesser people find it easy to live with. They tend, unthinkingly, to be intolerant of us who are less aggressive and less successful. Brownson was such a man.

Most of all, though, it was Brownson's passionate love of truth which made it difficult for him to get along easily with his fellow human beings. He was not the sort to smile pleasingly and nod happily when his wife asked him whether he liked her hat. If he did not, he would have shouted "NO!" It was this relentless search for the truth, intense as a bloodhound after a scent, followed by his blunt, loud statement of it which is the key to his character. Only by remembering this can one understand both his virtues and his defects. His friend Father Hecker appreciated this point. "His predominant passion," he tells us, "was love of truth. This was all his glory and all his trouble; all his quarrels, friendships, aversions, perplexities, triumphs, labors." Again, Father Hecker explains that "without seeing clearly this passionate love of truth in him, it is, I think, hardly possible to understand him."

One must not expect to find Brownson everywhere in agreement with himself, however, because his search for truth was never ended and therefore he was constantly discarding theories which he had formerly believed true. This is particularly true of his political and social thought, for in these fields he did not find doctrines laid down by an infallible Church as he did in matters of faith and morals after his conversion in 1844. Thus we find him tending toward Liberalism in the 1850's, much in the Montalembert tradition, whereas later in life he is more in the conservative tradition of Donoso Cortés and Louis Veuillot. At any rate, he continued to change his stand on these prudential questions throughout life because, as he put it in 1865, "I have never been the slave of my own past, and truth has always been dearer to me than my own opinions." He always followed his thought to logical conclusions because, he insisted, "there is not a meaner sin than the sin of inconsequence – a sin which distinguishes us from the mere animal world." His change of position, both in religious matters early in life and in social matters later on, is testimony rather to his fidelity to truth than witness to his disregard for it.

Brownson is almost always taken to have been an extremist. Such was his own estimate of himself. "I always had," he wrote in 1854, "and I trust I always shall have the honor of being regarded by my friends and associates as impolitic, as rash, imprudent and impracticable. I was and am, in my natural disposition, frank, truthful, straightforward, and earnest, and, therefore, have had, and, I doubt not, shall carry to the grave with me, the reputation of being reckless, ultra, a well-meaning man, perhaps an able man, but so fond of paradoxes and extremes, that he cannot be relied on and is more likely to injure than serve the cause he espouses." Brownson wanted to be "an ultra." To him a compromiser was one who watered down the truth with error, one who had no respect for his God or for his own mind. Compromisers he contemned. "When there is work to be done," he wrote, "a cause to be advanced, the unsafest men in the world to confide it to are those who are usually termed safe men."

As a matter of fact, however, he was not really an extremist at all. He almost always found his truth somewhere between the extremes of error. He held to rather moderate positions on things political and social. He was a States-rights man, for example, and he vigorously backed Calhoun for the presidency in 1844; but when States rights meant rebellion and civil war, Brownson supported the Union and even voted for a Lincoln he did not respect. So it was in everything. His extremism lay not in the conclusion he reached, but in the manner in which he stated it. He was full voiced and dogmatic – and this made him seem to his contemporaries a true extremist.

The most impressive things about Brownson were his energetic activity and his vast erudition. He was built along dreadnought lines, and in his home he was surrounded by his friends and acquaintances – tugboats, sloops, cruisers, and such – all tooting and whistling about philosophy and religion and politics. But where the others tooted and whistled, Brownson blasted as became a battleship. When he was not busy arguing at home or writing for his *Review* he was on the road lecturing. Very much in demand in an age when platform speakers had to have strong lungs, Brownson lectured as far north as Montreal, as far west as St. Louis, as far south as New Orleans and Mobile. And he lectured on almost any current topic of the time.

In like manner, he wrote on everything. Brownson could do this without becoming shallow because he lived in an age when specialization had not yet advanced to the stage it has today, when even a brilliant man knows almost nothing about things outside the field of his competence. In Brownson's day an intelligent man who read well could keep abreast of both intellectual and practical things. Although Brownson tells us that "the only subjects I have really studied are English style, philosophy, the philosophy of history and of religion, or theology," nevertheless he read French, German, Italian, Greek, and Latin, besides his own English. He was well versed in history and politics and especially in the history of philosophy. He was a self-educated man, but he was nonetheless well educated.

* * *

"Every writer, whatever else he writes, writes himself." This dictum of Orestes Brownson probably applies to no one with greater truth than it does to himself. For Brownson's personality forces its way through every paragraph. The main notes of his prose style are its logic and its power. Brownson gives the reader the impression that he is being crushed by a heavy, powerful landslide of a man. His prose style is like his conversation, which Father Hecker aptly described thus: "What occupied his mind at the moment he would crowd upon yours. He would push his thought before your attention, and never be content until he had you full of his idea." Brownson makes the reader feel he is being crowded into a corner from which there is no escape.

This is partly due to the forcefulness of his language and partly to the rigor of his logic. For Brownson never went to a point indirectly, he never insinuated, he never used circumlocution. His logic was such as to frighten people. That is why one of his Protestant friends later observed that "the only safe way, in arguing with Brownson, was to deny everything. If you admitted anything . . . you were lost." Such a method, of course, enabled Brownson to defeat his opponents, but it did not help him convince them. Nevertheless, it was the only true style for him to use, for that was the way of Brownson's mind.

His writing is still looked upon as a model of journalistic style; it is still included in anthologies as an example of powerful editorial prose. Brownson excelled in use of the metaphor, in making abstruse subjects familiar to the reader, and in conducting him through difficult discussions with ease. His was the style of a preacher turned writer, a style which has been judged by competent authorities one of the best America has known. Often Brownson wrote hurriedly to meet deadlines, but he had studied rhetoric so thoroughly that he wrote much of his best prose while the printer waited to take the copy from him.

He was aware, too, like Belloc and Chesterton after him, that truly Catholic literature must be alive and healthy rather than sickly and pale. "Catholic literature," he wrote, "is robust and healthy, of a ruddy complexion, and full of life. It knows no sadness but sadness of sin, and it rejoices evermore. It eschews melancholy as the devil's best friend on earth, abhors the morbid sentimentality which feeds upon itself and grows by what it feeds upon. It may be grave, but it never mopes; tender, affectionate, but never weak or sickly. It washes its face, anoints its head, puts on its festive robes, goes forth into the fresh air, the bright sunshine, and when occasion requires rings out the merry laugh that does one's heart good to hear." How much better it would be if Brownson had been describing an actual fact regarding Catholic literature instead of stating a norm!

* * *

The Civil War occupied much of Brownson's time and attention in his declining years. He was almost sixty when it began. Almost sixty years of hard wear and tear on Brownson's big body had worn it down, and then the demands and the trials of the Civil War left him an unwell man. The war was hard on him in many different ways. He was misinformed that the Pope supported the South, and this caused him anguish; he lost two sons in the war, and this hurt him more than most people realized; his sight was failing, so he gave up the *Review* at the end of 1864. He had done his share for the North during the war, and now with victory achieved he was weary and worn and tired. He had labored twenty years for the Church, and it seemed in 1864 that he had earned only the indifference of Protestants and the animosity of Catholics.

Brownson therefore decided to retire and put in order his thoughts on political and philosophical matters. In these days of semiretirement he wrote his famous book *The American Republic,* and as his health improved for a while he contributed frequently to Father Hecker's *Catholic World* and to *Ave Maria.* One of his most notable contributions to right thinking in these days was the part he played in the religion-science controversy started by the publication of Darwin's *Origin of Species* in 1859. Brownson's stand was wise and calm. He advocated a free role for science – in its proper place. He advised Catholics that the best way to tame science was for them to become good scientists. Brownson condemned science only for not being scientific. He attacked those scientists who soared to metaphysical or theological conclusions on the basis of empirical evidence. "The greater part of what our advanced thinkers call science," he wrote in 1875, "consists not only of assumptions, but of assumptions hardly made before they are modified or rejected for others equally baseless, to be in their turn modified or rejected." This was hitting scientists with their own tools – and in a scientifically vulnerable spot. It left them without a rational answer.

Early in 1876 the *American Catholic Quarterly Review* was launched, and fittingly enough the first number contained an article by Dr. Brownson. The plan was for him to write a series on the philosophy of religion to help the review get started, but he was unable to finish the second article, and the third number of the *Review* carried instead a glowing "In Memoriam" tribute to its noted contributor. For Brownson had grown listless in the Lenten season of 1876. He started an article or two, but he could not finish them. On Good Friday, as we have seen, he became seriously ill, and on Easter Monday he died a worn out Yankee Catholic who had not spared himself in his thirty years of labor on behalf of the Church he had worked his way into without help from any man.

* * *

Orestes Brownson died an important figure in nineteenth-century American history, a man who had made a mark on his society. He was one of the instigators of the Brook Farm movement, which attracted some of the best minds of the country in those days. He associated with men like Henry Thoreau, Emerson, Alcott, and Parker. He influenced others like young Isaac Hecker, who entered the Church and in time founded the Paulist order. How much his influence was cut short by his entry into the Church one cannot definitely say, but it is certain that had he not entered the Church the chances are good that he would have become a more important figure in American culture than Emerson or Alcott or any of his other contemporaries. But enter the Church he did. Any prestige Brownson lost was gained by the Catholic Church, since it is not too much to say that Brownson found the Church in 1844 a small, inconspicuous organization in America, that by his conversion it gained a champion who commanded the respect of American intellectuals. Brownson felt free to shout from the roof tops, whereas Catholics before him had whispered in closets because they felt somehow that they were not at home in America.

Brownson was. He had become a Catholic without losing any of his Americanism. He was living proof that a man could be a Catholic, an American, and an independent, progressive thinker all at once. He was more than living proof of the fact. He was shouting proof as well. For he shouted that fact to America; he put it into print boldly and defiantly — and no one could say him no. That is why Daniel Sargeant felt free to say that Brownson found the Catholic press "in chains of timidity," and almost singlehanded emancipated it. His *Review* was denounced for not being sufficiently Irish, and it was condemned for being so much Brownsonian and so atypically Catholic. Catholics feared it because they never knew what the next issue might bring. They suspected it, too, because Brownson scoffed at the usual ineffective line of other Catholic journals, like counting the Catholics in Washington's army. He insisted on those elements in Catholicism which made it Catholic and distinguished it from the man-made Protestant sects. His Catholic contemporaries might not have appreciated the *Review* he enlisted in their support, but the fact remains that it stood head and shoulders above the other American Catholic journals of the nineteenth century. It was of high caliber intellectually, it had a way of getting to the core of problems, and it proceeded ruthlessly to logical conclusions. It made men think. Nor was it unappreciated by thinking men, Catholic and non-Catholic alike, even in Brownson's day. The *Nation,* for example, commented in 1873 that it was "a body of as good hard thinking on important topics as ever issued from the American press." Historians of American journalism have not found reason to change that estimate even today.

Much of Brownson's difficulties with Catholics, members of the hierarchy and laymen alike, came from his not having matured in the Catholic tradition. He was a rugged individualist, an independent thinker, who had arrived at the Church's door through his unaided reason and entered it through his own will power and the grace of God. He therefore knew the modern world of the nineteenth century as Catholics could never know it. By the same token, he could never acquire a full appreciation of the Catholic tradition. He was in a position, therefore, to free himself from the traditional Catholic apologetic and to formulate another peculiarly adapted to the Protestant climate in which he had lived.

Brownson summed up his position in this regard in the following words: "We certainly do not mean to undervalue the labors, the logic, or the services of the Scholastics. . . . There are few questions that they have not discussed, and well discussed; there are few truths in philosophy or in theology that they have not known, and, in one form or another, set forth and defended; and no man is, or can be, well qualified to engage in any of the controversies even of our day, who has not in some way availed himself of their labors. Still their methods will not answer our purpose now; for now we have to meet, not mere amateur foes, or reply simply to the objections of our own invention or statement. It is true that there is scarcely any objection urged at any time against our religion that we cannot find stated in its strongest form, and refuted by our Scholastic divines; but the objection is, for the most part, stated and refuted for the Catholic reader rather than for the non-Catholic mind. The Scholastics are, as controversialists, far more influential in keeping men who have the truth from going astray, than in recovering from error those who, unhappily, have yielded to its seductions."

Brownson's purpose, therefore, was to formulate a new apologetic. His plan was good, but unfortunately he was not temperamentally able to put it into effect in his own writings as thoroughly as Father Hecker's Paulists have done ever since their establishment. "My own conviction," he wrote to Father Hewit, one of Hecker's associates, "is that our true policy in dealing with the American mind is to study first to ascertain, not its errors, but the truth it still maintains, and to show that that truth can find its unity and integrity only in the Catholic Church." His aim was very much like Cardinal Newman's and Wilfrid Ward's: to accept all the good things in the age and to demonstrate how they were part of the Catholic tradition. But Brownson wanted to go on from there to show how his age was drifting further and further away from sound principles, how it could not remain where it was, in a state of transition, but had to drift on to anarchy and despotism or else come back to Catholic principles — which meant the Catholic Faith. In effect, therefore, Brownson offered his age a choice between Catholicism and chaos. He tried to show how the good things in American society could be preserved only by extending the Catholic Faith. He attacked Protestantism, not so much for being un-Catholic as for undermining the foundations of American society. Perhaps the alternatives were too simply drawn, but Brownson opened a new line of apologetics which enabled men like Cardinal Gibbons and Archbishop Ireland to demonstrate effectively how one could not be a good Catholic in the United States without being a good American.

By his life and by his arguments in favor of the Church, Brownson set an example for laymen of his and succeeding ages. This is the importance of Brownson, as the *American Catholic Quarterly Review* presented him in its post-mortem eulogy. The *Review* spoke of "the example he has left behind him. And it is precisely this example that should commend itself to the educated portion of our Catholic laity." The author of this tribute to Brownson went on, significantly, to issue to American laymen a call to Catholic Action. "The sphere in which the educated layman can cooperate with the Church is daily widening," he wrote, "and the value of his cooperation is daily growing in importance." As a pioneer in the work of Catholic Action, Brownson was important both for what he did and for the model he set for following generations.

12. Louis Veuillot

One of Donoso Cortés' closest friends was Louis Veuillot, editor of the great Catholic journal *Univers*. The Spanish nobleman and the French peasant loved and admired each other as comrades in arms fighting for the Church in the nineteenth century. Their attitude toward the century was identical — critical and hostile toward the new Liberalism and secularism. Their tactics were similar, for both of them put the Church's enemies on the defensive, making them justify themselves and their works to the world. Moreover, Donoso and Veuillot held similar positions within the Church's ranks, inasmuch as both opposed any compromise whatever with their age. They therefore looked upon liberals within the Church like Montalembert and Ozanam as well-meaning but dangerously confused Catholics.

Donoso Cortés' most powerful weapon was his tongue; Louis Veuillot's was his pen, an indefatigable pen with which he wrote more than sixty volumes of apologetic literature, in addition to his day-by-day editorial work on *Univers*. Veuillot edited this journal for forty years (1843–1883), and during that time he was the storm center around which raged almost every ecclesiastical tempest of these four decades. As a journalist, Veuillot took a definite stand on every issue that came up, a stand that set him off sharply not only from the Church's opponents but also from those in the Church with whom he disagreed. That is why *Univers* was suppressed three times by the French government, was interdicted from time to time by various French bishops, and became the most widely read and most frequently quoted of all European Catholic periodicals in its day.

A man who was "more Catholic than the pope" and "more ultramontane than the General of the Jesuit Order" was bound to excite lively opposition even within Catholic circles, just as he was bound to excite vehement and sometimes unthinkingly enthusiastic support. No Catholic apologist of modern times has been as strongly praised as Veuillot, and none as harshly condemned. When he died in 1883 he received almost ecstatic tribute from many Catholic journals, but from others there came a long sigh of relief and the charge that this man had hurt the Church by his violent opposition to any compromise with the age. In the first issue of *Commonweal*, which appeared in 1924, about forty years after Veuillot's death, Henry Longan Stuart asserted that "there never has been a writer who earned more abounding hatred, or who might be prouder of the hatred he earned."

Although such a statement can be applied justly enough to the freethinking Liberals against whom Veuillot waged a never ending war, it is not fair to liberal Catholics like Bishop Dupanloup or Montalembert, who rightly considered Veuillot their harshest critic. As we have already indicated, within the Church were two camps which differed in their attitude to the civilization of the nineteenth century. Both groups had thought their positions out well, both were sincerely convinced of the rightness of their conclusions, and both were partly right. Although they agreed on all essentials, like Liberals and Conservatives in nineteenth-century England or Democrats and Republicans in America today, they stressed their points of difference so strongly that they seemed at odds on everything. The two Catholic camps kept quiet on their points of agreement. They differed on tactics and techniques more than anything, and on these points they waged unrelenting, sometimes bitter conflict. There was room for both camps within the Church because the Church is Catholic and because the divisions were on questions of policy. In the providential plan, moreover, both camps made sound contributions toward the Church's revival in the nineteenth century. So no matter how harshly Veuillot's detractors may have dealt with him in his own lifetime, today there is fairly general agreement that he made important contributions to the welfare and the growth of the Church in the nineteenth century. Thus in his history of the Church in modern France, Lecanuet concludes that no matter what one thinks of Veuillot's policies and his extremism, "it is impossible to deny the marvellous and the truly powerful genius of Louis Veuillot, his absolute objectivity, his profound faith, and the real services which he rendered to religion in many ways." Of his genius and his importance there can be no doubt. To the keen French critic Jules Lemaitre, he is "the great Catholic layman of the nineteenth century." Those who will not agree with Lemaitre's superlative do agree in ranking Veuillot among the dozen most important Catholic laymen of the century.

He was important for waging a controversy on two fronts: against the secularist, anti-Catholic Liberals on the one hand, and on the other against Catholics who did not belong to the *Univers* camp. Veuillot expended most of his energy and he wrote most of his works against the Church's enemies, but he is remembered in Catholic circles more for his controversies with liberal Catholics than for his attacks on the Liberals. This accident of history is partly his own fault, because he employed as vigorous, vitriolic language against Gallican bishops as he used against a Guizot or a Lamartine. Especially after 1848, as we shall see, he tended to lump together as enemies of the Church all those who disagreed with him in any respect.

* * *

Louis Veuillot was born of poor parents in 1813 at Boynes, a village of the Gatinais. His father was a traveling cooper, his mother a peasant. When Louis was still a youngster the family moved to Paris. There he grew up in the streets of the city, without much formal education, without religious instruction except for what he received in cursory fashion in government schools hostile to the Church. He made his First Communion, the only time, it seems, he received the Sacrament before his "conversion" in 1838. As a boy, Louis Veuillot revealed a quick mind and a violent temper — and not much else. His biographers tell, for example, how he threw himself into a well when he was scolded, and how he tore up his school books when he memorized the lessons in order to show that he was through with them.

At the age of thirteen, the youngster left home to shift for himself. He entered a lawyer's office, where his employer's friends gathered to talk of politics and literature and where young Veuillot began his long process of self-education in letters and history. These were days that the mature Veuillot looked back on bitterly. The young men of Paris were a godless gang. From them and from the environs of Paris Veuillot obtained his education, his moral and intellectual habits, his avid desire for literary fame. "The streets of Paris formed the education of my mind," is the way he put it, "and some young men in whose company I had to live formed the education of my heart. When in my misery, in my isolation and solitude, I needed to learn a prayer, it was blasphemy that was taught me! It was blasphemy that I saw everywhere, that I heard in all speeches, that I read in all the books, blasphemy that I was called upon to admire in all the scenes that met my eyes!"

At the age of seventeen the young journalist was given an editorial position on *Echo de Rouen,* and a few years later he became editor of a paper at Perigord. In 1836 he returned to Paris where he worked on different papers, advancing in his chosen field of journalism, using a striking style and revealing a violent, irascible disposition which attracted attention if it did nothing else. Veuillot's journalistic adventures got him into innumerable scrapes, and at least three times his pen led him into duels from which he seems to have emerged unscathed. He was a physically powerful man, described by his brother as a *condottieri* of the pen who had no sense of right and wrong and who happily sold his services to anyone who would pay the price.

Such had been Louis Veuillot's progress at the age of twenty-four when one of his friends invited him to go on a journey to Constantinople. Veuillot accepted the invitation, and the two of them set out for the Turkish city by way of Italy. Veuillot never got past Rome, but, as he put it later, he went far past Constantinople — all the way into the Catholic Church. On Good Friday of 1838 he made a general confession and on Easter Sunday he made his second "First Communion." Violent journalist that he was, Veuillot now had a steady cause to defend. He was to find regular employment for the rest of his days as a Catholic journalist.

Veuillot's conversion, like everything else in his life, was a complete, even a violent thing. He felt that he had entered a new world, that he was living a new life which he was anxious to share with the rest of men. "Before my conversion," he wrote, "I was always tortured by *perhaps.* But now there is no darkness. . . . What was dead is now full of life; where I formerly saw nothing but the caprice of a blind power, I now see a clear witness of the existence and power of God. The most puzzling problems that used to baffle my ignorance are now vanishing like smoke; the iron doors everywhere shut against me are opening now of their own accord." So Louis Veuillot returned to Paris to continue in the only profession he knew, that of journalism, but now to write on behalf of the Roman Catholic Church.

For a time, however, he had to content himself with employment as a state functionary because there were no positions open except on the anti-Catholic papers with which he had formerly been associated. During this period he wrote a number of works demonstrating the beauties of the Catholic religion, such as *Rome and Loretto* and *The Holy Rosary*. There was only one Catholic paper in Paris in these years, the *Univers religieux* established in 1834 by "Papa" Bailly, one of Ozanam's associates in founding the St. Vincent de Paul Society. Veuillot contributed articles to this paper for about four years, during which time he began to appear as a leading figure in Parisian Catholic circles. In 1842 he became an active member of the Catholic Party which Montalembert was trying to organize in Paris. Montalembert was impressed with the young convert's enthusiasm and his ability. "This Veuillot enraptures me," the Count observed, "there is a man after my own heart." In the next year Veuillot was appointed editor of the *Univers* of which Montalembert was then the principal owner. Thus in 1843, shortly before he was thirty, Louis Veuillot entered upon the career that was to make him outstanding among the polemical editors of the mid-nineteenth century, an age known for the fire and the force of its editor-authors.

* * *

As editor of the *Univers*, Veuillot participated actively in all the controversies affecting Catholicism in the next forty years. He took the lead for seven years in fighting for freedom of education claimed by Catholics under the rule of Louis Philippe, and *Univers* played a considerable part in the ultimate victory of the Catholic group in 1850. Veuillot opposed the solution arrived at by the Falloux Law, a solution acceptable to Montalembert and Bishop Dupanloup, because he thought it a compromise with iniquity. But the fact remains that even this partial victory would have been less likely but for Veuillot's long campaign for complete liberty of teaching for Catholics.

Under the Second Empire (1852–1871) he battled freethinkers and those "Liberals" — Catholic as well as non-Catholic — who tried to reconcile religion with "modern thought." In these years Veuillot developed a strongly ultramontane tone which put him in bad with the Gallican-minded bishops of France and with the government of Napoleon III that was interfering with the Pope's temporal sovereignty in the Papal States. Preliminary work before the Vatican Council met in 1869 occupied much of Veuillot's attention, during which time he tried to build up a strong opinion in favor of the declaration of papal infallibility. He was also concerned with the general European conspiracy against the temporal possessions of the Holy See, with the visible decline of the imperial regime, and with the anticlerical policies of the Third Republic, as well as with the daily task of interpreting and explaining and defending the papal position on religious matters that came up from day to day. By doing all these things well Louis Veuillot made *Univers* the most influential Catholic journal of Europe, a paper with which both friends and enemies of the Church had to reckon seriously on all religious and social questions.

Veuillot took a rigidly ultramontane stand on all questions of domestic Church policies. Relying directly on Rome and being "the pope's man" at all times, he frequently found himself disparaging episcopal authority — though this was never his intention. Whenever a question of episcopal authority arose, Veuillot was careful to obey the letter of canon law, but his disposition to short-circuit the French bishops and to establish direct connections with the Bishop of Rome inevitably diminished the stature of the bishops as ecclesiastical authorities within their dioceses. Moreover, since many of the bishops opposed the claims of Pope Pius IX as unjustifiable or at best inopportunely made, this lay champion of the papacy was forced into many a dispute with them.

One can therefore easily see why the editor of *Univers* jealously guarded his paper from episcopal domination and even from the smallest degree of clerical control. *Univers* remained at all times a Catholic layman's journal, managed and edited by laymen in the interest of the Church universal — which for them meant the Church whose capital was Rome and whose earthly ruler was the pope. Fortunately, Veuillot was careful not to abuse his position, and whenever bishops interdicted *Univers* or found theological errors in his writings it turned out that their opposition was on a prudential question of policy — as whether the classics should be taught in Catholic schools — rather than on points of morality or doctrine. Whenever Veuillot's position became too difficult for him to hold alone, he succeeded in getting the Pope's backing against the French bishops. There is nothing scandalous in these quarrels; nor were they dangerous to the welfare of the Church as long as the opponents were men of real humility and of a strong sense of obedience, as was Louis Veuillot. Much heat was generated and much smoke arose, but *Univers* came out of these quarrels a better paper and the Church in France was helped rather than hurt by Veuillot's insistence that his journal remain in laymen's hands.

Univers was edited by a man from peasant stock, and it was read by the little people of France, the lower clergy in the parishes throughout the country, the villagers and the peasants who looked for it eagerly and followed its editorial opinion almost as though it were infallible. These masses of French Catholics were themselves ultramontane, ready always to support the Pope against the Gallican element in the Church. Veuillot's opposition, then, came from the wealthier and more influential minority of French Catholics, his support from the inarticulate masses whose thinking on religious matters he did for them. In this way *Univers* played an important role in keeping the rural element of France staunchly Catholic throughout the nineteenth century, whereas the upper classes and the city people tended to drift out of Catholic ranks into the Liberal camp.

Three times *Univers* was suspended by the government for its strong support of the Pope and its blistering attack on his enemies. The ax fell for the first time in 1860 when Veuillot twice dared to criticize the line of action taken by Napoleon III in supporting the Italian unification plans of Sardinia-Piedmont. Napoleon III had anonymously written a pamphlet suggesting that the Papal States should be reduced to the city of Rome and its environs. Pope Pius IX called the pamphlet "a signal monument of hypocrisy and an ignoble tissue of contradictions," and though Veuillot was warned that he had better not print the

Pope's address he did so without hesitation. Two weeks later he translated and published the Pope's encyclical *Nullis certe* condemning Napoleon's action. Nor was he ignorant of the consequences of this courageous act. "Our paper will be suppressed tomorrow," he told his staff.

It was suppressed on January 29, 1860, and it did not appear again until April 15, 1867. Meanwhile, Louis Veuillot and his brother Eugène put out a substitute paper, *Monde,* in which they continued their propapal policies in somewhat subdued fashion. Twice more *Univers* was suspended for shorter lengths of time. The first suspension was for two months, in 1874, at Bismarck's request when Veuillot published a papal message condemning the *Kulturkampf*. This time Veuillot was flooded with congratulatory messages, one of them from Pope Pius IX himself, who lauded this man "whose forces are faithfully applied to the propagation of good" and who fights "with a strong, confident and tranquil heart." During the course of his letter the Pope indirectly endorsed the general policies of *Univers* by condemning those who "try to conciliate darkness with light" and who "bow before the false wisdom of the century."

After two months' suspension *Univers* was allowed to appear again. It came out an unrepentant paper with its editor stating in the first number that "it has always seemed to us that *Univers* is destined to die a violent death," and that while he would do nothing to seek such an end, still he would do nothing to avoid it. Six months later the journal was suspended again, this time for about two weeks for having offended the Spanish government. Veuillot considered these suspensions a mark of honor, though an expensive one because of the fines and the loss of subscriptions involved each time. The editor did not fail to remind his readers that each time the government had acted without trial, without even an imputation of crime, and therefore its action was arbitrary and illegal. If Napoleon III's purpose was to intimidate the editor of *Univers* he failed signally, for each time that the paper reappeared Veuillot continued his editorial policy as though the journal had never missed an issue.

The most striking thing about *Univers* is the vehemently hostile tone it used in dealing with nineteenth-century civilization in general and with Liberalism in particular. Veuillot lived in a

France, where the Church was violently denounced and scurrilously attacked by the apparently learned men of the country. Quinet and Michelet were damning the Church with unscholarly attacks in the lecture halls of the College de France; Thiers was stating in the Chamber that it was time to "put the hand of Voltaire on these Catholics"; magazines, especially in Paris, were full of anticlerical propaganda; new editions of Voltaire and Rousseau appeared every year or so. Against this swarm of abuse Veuillot raised his head high. In a day when Catholics tended to hide until the storm of invective should blow over, Veuillot announced that he was proud of his faith and that he considered the Church's enemies abusive and ignorant men. Veuillot was viciously attacked by the freethinkers of the day, and through the columns of *Univers* he fought back savagely. He was more eloquent than they. He used their tactics of invective and violence and ridicule more effectively than they. And because he wrote in an age when such tactics were admired he was successful, whereas his more moderate allies attracted little attention.

Univers was therefore considered a "violent" paper, mostly because it used strong language. Veuillot, we must remember, was a poor boy who had been raised on the streets of Paris, and he never lost the hypersensitivity and vigorous language of the poor boy who had made good and who was always on the defensive in his new estate. His style is frequently likened to Voltaire's. Pierre de la Gorce, author of the definitive study of the Church in the Second Empire, tells how Voltaire had come – in the person of Veuillot – to haunt the sacristies. Voltaire, he says, had become an ultramontane defender of the papacy. Sainte-Beuve, outstanding critic of the century, insists that there is nothing finer in the French language than some of the pages from Veuillot, and Lemaitre claims he could have been in the French Academy and his work be included in all French anthologies if he would have given up his apologetics to conform to the secular standards of the time.

Veuillot was a journalist by profession and by temperament. He employed the tricks of his trade: paradox, striking statement, quick repartee, telling counterstatement, and all the rest. His paragraphs were full of well-directed thrusts, of ridicule and raillery. They revealed all shades of anger and derision, of contempt, of sarcasm and acid wit. Veuillot was merciless and scathing; he wrote, as he himself admitted, with vinegar instead of ink. Such a pungent style as Veuillot's was popular in a France where ridicule had long been the journalist's most effective weapon, and thus whereas the elevated, refined style of a Montalembert left large groups unmoved, Veuillot's trenchant prose captivated them and retained them. Perhaps many readers failed to penetrate through Veuillot's ridicule to the basic truths he defended as sacred, but there is no doubt that he effectively turned the weapon of ridicule against those enemies of the Church who had been using it freely and uncontestedly for so many decades.

Such a style can be misleading to those who read Veuillot today, because the opponents against whom he wrote have melted into oblivion, and therefore his sentences now stand without the evidence that then might have been available, and so as extremist statements hard to defend. Today it seems that Veuillot constantly overstates his case, but in his own day those sentences were always understood against the background of contrary overstatements by his enemies. But the power of his repartee can still be appreciated. His answer to Victor Hugo, who complained of Veuillot's sharp remark about his latest work, is typical: "What I gave you was a pin-prick. It is only because you are always scratching it that it has become infected." Or his pricking but accurate appraisal of Lamartine: "He is a skeptic under a covering of insipid religiosity."

This was the style that caused Veuillot to be read avidly, even by his enemies, and it breathed a life into *Univers* that made it the most powerful organ of Catholic opinion in all Europe.

* * *

Louis Veuillot was more than a clever writer with an agile pen. He was a solid, logical thinker, not a theologian or philosopher himself but an intelligent layman capable of understanding theological and philosophical speculation and of carrying it over into popular language. Veuillot was a powerful individual physically, a man of large body and big mind who enjoyed good food and wine almost as much as he enjoyed good argument. He was noted throughout France for his violent literary outbursts and for his irascible temper. He was almost bound, by the nature of things, to earn such a reputation because of his position as editor of a Catholic journal whose policy was announced as defense of the Church and opposition to the erroneous tendencies of the age. Necessarily then Veuillot was a fighter, and French journalism being what it was in the nineteenth century, he naturally came to be called such things as "the bulldog of Christ," or "the Catholic Bluebeard," or "the man who boasted of slaying at least one Philistine every morning before breakfast."

Such appellations are too strong, but they are not without some measure of truth. Veuillot considered moderation unseemly; he identified it with cowardice. Once when a friend suggested that moderation would advance his cause further than violence Veuillot gave him an answer which has become classic: "Do you remember the word of worthy Joinville [companion of St. Louis], who, watching the Saracens harry a Christian camp, although it was a Sunday, cried to a friend: 'Let us try what one charge on these Mussulman dogs will do!' And what were Mussulmans compared to this infamous gang for whom you ask quarter? No quarter! I swear it by God! I can feel the spurs sprouting at my very heels. My charger is neighing. My sword quivers in its sheath. Let us have at this pack!"

That was Veuillot. Intolerant of error at all times, and too often intolerant of the erring – though he never meant his intolerance to carry over to persons. With him it was a matter of principle to uphold the truth without compromise, without concession, without respect of persons. "I protest," he wrote of himself, "that I have neither enemies nor friends. In a matter of doctrine I would fight against my brother, and I would love my own murderer." Montalembert, Ozanam, Bishop Dupanloup, and others who had been closely associated with Veuillot before 1848 found out how literally he lived up to his claim that where truth was concerned he had neither friends nor enemies. Unfortunately, he never understood that in questions of ecclesiastical policy the answers are not always as simple as mathematical sums, that there was a sphere of activity where more than one solution could be right. So he always believed that anyone who disagreed with him was, to that extent, un-Catholic – even bishops and cardinals were suspect in his eyes for being insufficiently ultramontane, and therefore insufficiently Catholic.

Veuillot was irascible, hypersensitive, always on the defensive, as it were, for his own opinions and for the truth of Catholic doctrine – which for him were synonymous. Thus he was intolerant of Newman's approach to Catholic doctrine, and, like so many other Catholics born in the Church, he was suspicious of the English Cardinal's orthodoxy. He was even suspicious of Cardinal Manning's loyalty to Rome, perhaps the only man in the world who was. This was the one great fault in Veuillot's make-up, his edginess in controversy and his extreme rigidity in matters of doctrine. A partial explanation of this peevishness, we have suggested, is found in Veuillot's humble origin. "A Catholic and a child of the little people," he says of himself, "I am doubly their [the freethinkers'] enemy." Veuillot frequently asserts his peasant origin with the assertiveness of the poor boy who has made good but does not feel at ease in his new surroundings. He says, in effect, that he is a cooper's son – and do you want to make something of it?

Veuillot is hot-tempered only with important persons – state officials, bishops, counts, millionaires, and the like. With such people he could be downright impudent. His remark to a French count is typical: "I have risen from a cooper's family, Monsieur. From whom do you descend?" Sometimes he was more impish than impudent, as when he knew the police were intercepting his correspondence. "Vive l'Empereur, O police," he put in for their benefit, "vive l'Imperatrice, vive le Prince Imperial." But this man who was waspish with important people genuinely loved the little folk of France. He considered himself their champion, and it was in their name and in their defense that he frequently railed against the government of Louis Philippe as well as against the Second and Third Republics. He considered them all rich men's regimes exploiting the peasants and the proletariat of his native France. Veuillot had a strong, burning sense of justice, and because he saw Liberals use his people harshly and unjustly, he boiled them in the hot oil of Veuillotian sarcasm and ridicule. Thus he has the lawmakers say to the poor people of France: "If you revolt, we will kill you. If you steal, we will poison you. If you are ill, we can do nothing to help you. If you have no bread, you can go to the workhouse or die. It is none of our business which." Such passages as these, which abound in Veuillot's works, make Lemaitre exclaim: "What a revolutionary, had he not been a Catholic!"

Veuillot's rough exterior can be understood better against the background of his own severe personal life. Never quite destitute, he was never free from financial worries, never able to put away a month's salary in reserve. This does something to a man with a large family to support. Despite his continual flirtation with poverty, Veuillot refused more lucrative positions because he felt his vocation was to edit *Univers* and to fight for the Church. He accepted his poverty as a blessing – "without poverty I would have been lost" – but he was hardened by it. He became harder on himself and everyone else. "One should go to heaven with a stone in his shoe," he used to say. There were several stones in Veuillot's own shoes; Dupanloup and Montalembert and Ozanam, as well as Thiers and Victor Hugo and Lamartine, must have suspected him of slipping stones into theirs too.

Louis Veuillot loved his family dearly, and when he was still a young man his wife and four of his six daughters died within four months – a severe trial surely for any Catholic layman. He summed up his reaction to this tragedy simply by saying to a friend, "I am not beaten down because I am on my knees." Later in life his remaining daughters left him, one to become a nun, the other a wife, and Louis Veuillot remained a lonely man for the rest of his life. His family life, then, his own disposition, and his position as editor of *Univers* combined to make his life arduous. A rugged man strengthened by Faith, he bore up well under the demands of his profession and his family trials, which H. A. Jules-Bois says "catastrophically resembled the Greek tragedies of old." But occasionally Veuillot grew despondent, as when he complained: "I defend property, and have never saved a cent nor owned a single acre; aristocracy, and I have never met two aristocrats worthy of the name; royalty, in a world which will never have another true king. All these things I have defended from love of the people, and I am pilloried as their enemy."

Veuillot was temperamentally incapable of living the easy life. He was not exaggerating when he wrote: "I work like a pair of donkeys, without any regard for my aged head, but I am happy in my work." He often spoke, half jestingly and half endearingly, of being "married to *Univers*," of spending many precious hours with his "illegitimate spouse." Veuillot worked incessantly, as anyone who publishes sixty volumes would have to do. His labors, which would have wrecked a less rugged individual than himself, were the marvel of his friends, such as Donoso Cortés, who wrote that in a year he could not accomplish what his French friend did in a month.

Hard, irritable, violent man though he was, Veuillot was at bottom a humble and obedient child of his God and his Church. When his wife and four children died, he answered a friend who feared that in the shock of his tragic losses he might rebel against his Creator. "No," he wrote, "I am not crushed. I am only on my knees. God knows what He is doing. He is just, He is merciful. I have only to bless Him. The future before me is a gloomy one, but I know I am only a traveler, and the harder the voyage, the sweeter shall be the repose. Pray for me, not that my sorrow be allayed, but that I should bear it like a Christian. I feel that the plowshare which is tearing up my soul prepares the ground for the seeds of eternal life, for seeds of faith, hope, and love."

In the same way Veuillot was an obedient son of the Holy Father in Rome. Only once was his obedience tried severely – in 1872 when Pius IX rebuked him for lack of charity in dealing with his opponents. "The first moment [after getting the Pope's letter]," he says, "was very hard and full of terrible perplexities." But after a short time he resolved on humble, unquestioning obedience, much as he was convinced that he was not guilty of a lack of charity and that the Pope did not understand the caliber of his enemies. He accepted the rebuke because he believed that "the way to make great strides in progress is to get on one's knees," and because he saw that "this condemnation has been a blessing which entered my room by breaking the window."

• • •

From the time of his conversion in 1838, Louis Veuillot had no doubt about his vocation. He thoroughly appreciated the fullness of the new life given to him at Rome. "The Church has given me light and peace," he said. "I owe her my intellect and my heart.

It is through her that I know, that I admire, that I love, that I live." There was nothing halfway about Veuillot's conversion. Being a good Catholic was the most important thing in life, he believed, and he therefore concluded that he would "subordinate everything to my Catholic beliefs. The Church is my party and even my country." So Veuillot decided to devote full time to his vocation of being a lay apologist. To his brother Eugène, whom he soon converted and later made associate editor of *Univers*, he explained his new vocation in these words: "As far as I am concerned, I am fully resolved to give to this cause [working for the Church] my whole life, the best fruits of my intelligence, to make it the sole aim of my efforts and labors. I know I will have no position in the world, no bank account, but I will have my duty done, the manna of heaven for every day, the water of the torrent to drink from, and a few years less to spend here below. . . . All the wisdom of the world cannot change this fact: that I have to break away from the world and fight under the banner of God."

Fight is what Louis Veuillot did. As an apologist he won many an encounter because, as Monselet has put it, "he always had God and grammar on his side." Whether he convinced opponents is uncertain. Whether he even wanted to convince them is doubtful. He wanted to win arguments – and this he certainly did. He wanted to show how ridiculous, how absurd and petty and silly were the freethinking enemies of the Church. This, too, he succeeded in doing. As a champion of the Church crossing swords with its enemies, Veuillot won many a duel. During each encounter he was robustly cheered by the masses of French Catholics – but there is little evidence to suggest that Veuillot's apologetic work did more than restore confidence to these Catholics who saw for the first time how effectively a lay defender of the Church could use logic to undermine their enemies' position and make it untenable.

He attacked the freethinker because "he hated God and therefore, as a natural and foreseen consequence, he despises men." Veuillot defended the Church as incorporating "supreme justice"; he attacked its enemies for their "impiety, which is iniquity supreme, social iniquity." Objectively, the case Veuillot presented against the Liberals and the freethinkers of his day was a solid one. Perhaps he hurt his cause as much as he helped it – there is no way of knowing for certain – by the blunt and forceful way he phrased his arguments. His book against the freethinkers abounds with words like "hypocrite" and "blockhead" and "impostor," words which imply subjective guilt as well as objective error on the part of the Church's opponents. We must admire Veuillot's courage in presenting his case fearlessly and forcefully, but we shall never know whether his was the most prudent way to put it.

His arguments against the Liberals were as logical as they were hard hitting. They contained nothing substantially new, however, inasmuch as they were a restatement and a reapplication of traditional Catholic thought employed by those who belonged to the "conservative" group within the Church. Because we have examined these arguments as De Maistre employed them, and again as they were handled by Donoso Cortés, there is no need for us to repeat them here. It is enough to remember that, in general, Louis Veuillot popularized Donoso's thought for French readers, and that the columns of *Univers* were filled with Veuillot's running attack on all the beliefs and practices of contemporary Liberalism. He differed from his predecessors chiefly in his controversy against liberal Catholics whom he considered "fifth columnists" within the Church.

Unfortunately, as the years passed and Louis Veuillot grew more set in his belief that Liberalism was *the* enemy, he tended to lump together all those who had any strain of liberal feeling. This came to include many excellent, well-meaning, and intelligent Catholics, men like Ozanam and Montalembert and Bishop Dupanloup who were known in their day as liberal Catholics and who evolved a solution for reconciling the Church with modern civilization which, with modifications, has been utilized in more recent times. For a few years after he took over *Univers*, Veuillot worked closely with these liberal Catholics, but the Revolution of 1848 and the events growing out of it drove him further and further away from the liberal group. He thought he had given Liberalism its chance. He had found it vicious in its very essence, so about the middle of 1848 he rejected it with all its slogans and its aims. *Univers*, therefore, came to oppose any kind of compromise between the Church and the civilization of the age. For Veuillot compromise was sinful; it was consorting with Satan.

It was on these grounds that Veuillot opposed Ozanam. It was on these grounds that he completely missed the mark by underestimating the importance of the St. Vincent de Paul Society. For Veuillot, the good Catholic approached the world with fire in his nostrils rather than a cup of water in his hand. So though he admired Ozanam's obvious personal holiness he was contemptuous of his apologetics. Veuillot condemned Ozanam for wasting his talents with useless scholarly research instead of battling in the journals as he was himself. He reproached Ozanam for not siding with *Univers* against the Liberals but rather "coming to the window of his study and condemning us as strongly as the natural sweetness of his voice and his character permits." Veuillot was particularly annoyed when Ozanam was held up to him as the ideal Christian, as a model for him to imitate. "We find in the lives of the saints," he retorted, "all possible examples of Christian virtue and wisdom; we do not find any who advise us to abandon the truth."

That was the point on which Veuillot broke with the liberal Catholics. He thought they were sacrificing truth in order to work out a comfortable compromise with the age. Certain events made the rift grow wider. One of these was the Falloux Bill, which we have previously mentioned, giving the Church a voice in the French school system. Veuillot condemned it, whereas Montalembert and Dupanloup considered it a real victory for the Church, although it was not their concept of an ideal arrangement. Veuillot wanted the ideal or nothing – and he must have winced when Pope Pius IX expressed his gratitude to Montalembert for his long fight for freedom of education and his partial victory in the Falloux law.

Publication of the *Syllabus of Errors* in 1864 drove Veuillot and the liberal Catholics further apart. *Univers* was under government suppression at the time, but through the columns of *Monde*, Veuillot exulted in the *Syllabus* and interpreted it in as stringent a way as he possibly could. Bishop Dupanloup, on the other hand, an intelligent man and a well-trained theologian, was up in arms at Veuillot's interpretation. Dupanloup explained the *Syllabus* along more liberal lines – and even though semi-official Roman sources seemed to take a benevolent attitude toward the bishop's interpretation, Veuillot insisted that it was absolutely wrong. The two of them differed, again, on the famous question of Catholics using the classics of pagan antiquity. Veuillot insisted that it was not only unnecessary but also wrong to use them, especially in seminaries where they were included in the Greek and Latin curricula. Dupanloup maintained the traditional Catholic position on the propriety of using the pagan classics as rhetorical models without adopting their standards of conduct.

These differences, which were honest differences on matters of policy, could not be kept on the high plane of objective argument. Veuillot's forceful style and Dupanloup's imperious attitude toward laymen led, naturally enough, to personal attacks and severe strictures on each other's intelligence and even honesty. When Veuillot criticized Dupanloup's pastoral letter on the use of the classics, for example, the bishop forbade people in his diocese to read *Univers.* Both men were in good faith, but both were injudicious in the way they conducted their battle. The bishop wrote an anonymous pamphlet, *Univers jugé par lui-même,* which was libelous in its accusations; Veuillot was provoked by this and similar attacks to openly doubting the bishop's veracity and to asserting that Dupanloup had "cut himself off from the feeling of the Church universal" by his opposition to the declaration of papal infallibility. Even when Dupanloup died in 1878 and when Pope Leo XIII commented that the bishop's works were to the glory of the Church and the consolation of the Holy See, Veuillot refused to praise the bishop of Orleans. *Univers* dismissed his passing with the caustic comment: "He was in this life only one of the remarkable travellers who never arrived."

Such quarrels within Catholic circles scandalized many in the nineteenth century and caused many more to lament that the Church could not put up a united front to its Liberal opponents. But we can see today that the ultimate effect of these open differences of policy was good. It helped Catholics clarify their position on political and social questions, especially on that all-important question of how far the Church can go in compromising with the secular world. Dupanloup and Montalembert were ready to go far, maybe too far, and because Veuillot was stiffly against any compromise his influence in the long run was healthy. He was the conservative "watchdog" of the Pope and of the Church. He did not let the liberal Catholics shut their eyes to a fact they sometimes seemed anxious to forget: that Liberalism was essentially an enemy of religion and that its appealing qualities were only accidents of dress and make-up which quickly were changed when Liberals obtained control of the nation. He insisted that Catholics be true to their precious Christian heritage when the rest of the world was madly rejecting it for ephemeral "truths" discovered one day and discredited the next.

* * *

Veuillot was not nearly as reactionary in politics and in social thought as he is generally charged to have been. A reading of his collected works and a perusal of *Univers* through the years shows that he loyally endorsed any established government, whether it was republican, monarchical, or imperial, that he gave each new government the benefit of the doubt and tried to work with it until he was genuinely convinced that it was hostile to his Church. He had no direct concern with governmental policies personally. He consistently refused to ally himself with any party; instead he supported or opposed various parties and governments according to their attitude toward the Church. He refused to run for the legislature when his friends urged him to do so — for they thought he would be as eloquent in the Chamber with his tongue as he was with his pen in *Univers*. "I do not have the qualities which would fit me to represent Paris," he responded enigmatically to his friends' request, "nor Paris those she should possess to be represented by me."

One point on which he insisted vehemently against the Liberal press was that bishops had a perfect right to participate in politics. He upheld his contention by two lines of argument, both of which are still pertinent in the age-old argument on the separation of Church and State. He held, in the first place, that bishops were citizens like everyone else and that they therefore had a right to present their views, to engage in political discussion, and even to sit in the legislature. In the second place, he maintained rightly enough that political and moral questions melt into each other. Consequently bishops would neglect their moral duty if they maintained a deep silence on all political questions. Veuillot therefore rejected separation of Church and State on the terms with which the Liberals presented it.

Veuillot edited *Univers* under four different governments, each one ushered in by a revolution or a *coup d'état*. It is revealing – and upsetting as far as the general opinion on Veuillot is concerned – to see his attitude toward each of these governments. For the July Monarchy of Louis Philippe (1830–1848) he had no use. It epitomized all those attitudes and beliefs he associated with Liberalism and with freethinkers, but because it was the established government he tried to obey its regulations as far as he could. Nevertheless, he was sentenced to a month in jail and fined three thousand francs for taking the side of a priest who had written on the dangers of State monopoly of education by the University of Paris.

When the Revolution of 1848 overthrew the July Monarchy and ushered in the Second Republic, *Univers* wryly remarked that it had no cause for lamenting the monarchy's demise and that "there cannot be any better or more sincere Republicans than the French Catholics." The manifesto Veuillot published in his journal as soon as the revolution was completed shows how far he was from being blindly reactionary: "The dynasty of July has succumbed. The struggle was at an end on the third day. The revolution is accomplished, and it is one of the most surprising in history. . . . Today, as yesterday, nothing is possible unless through liberty; today, as yesterday, religion is the only possible basis of society. Religion is the aroma which keeps liberty from corruption. It is in Jesus Christ that men are brothers; it is in Him that they are free. Real liberty can save everything." Two days later *Univers* stated that it did not believe in the divine right of crowns "but, following Catholic theology, in the right of peoples."

Within a short time Veuillot grew bitterly critical of the Second Republic because he found it hostile to the Church and because he feared that it was degenerating into Socialism. Republican government, he held, had betrayed the French people by denying them real liberty and by violating their human right to practice their religion. Like Montalembert, then, he looked upon Louis Bonaparte as the champion of order against anarchy, and though he did not back Napoleon's nephew, still he did not condemn the *coup d'état* of 1851 by which he seized power. He expected better things of the Second Empire than were realized. He considered it an antirevolutionary government capable of preserving peace and order and of guaranteeing people the legitimate use of their liberty. But, as we have seen, Veuillot found Napoleon III less loyal to the Church and to justice than he had expected. *Univers* reserved its right to criticize the imperial regime freely, a right for which it paid with seven years of silence.

Thus when the Second Empire collapsed in 1870 and a Third Republic came into being, Veuillot insisted through the columns of *Univers* that Catholics accept the new government and back it loyally. "A Republic," he stated, "is compatible with liberty and justice, and it can bring forth other things than the violence and disorder which always give birth to dictatorship." He therefore called upon Catholics not to oppose the new government but rather to support it enthusiastically as it continued the war against Germany, then to guide it in the right way so that a just order and the blessings of liberty could be realized in the future.

Veuillot had hoped that the Third Republic would be a Christian state where the Church would be free to accomplish its work, but his hopes were soon blasted. He stayed in Paris through the days of the Commune, and thus he saw at firsthand the revolutionary government of the people when the archbishop was murdered as a hostage, when the churches were desecrated, when it must have seemed to Veuillot that this was the Reign of Terror all over again. He was therefore naturally inclined to sympathize with those who favored a monarchy instead of a republic in the years when the new constitution was being debated in Paris. He had insisted, back in 1848, that he favored democracy for a truly Christian people, but that it was an extremely dangerous form of government to put in the hands of "barbarian crowds."

As the years passed and the Third Republic consolidated itself, its generally anticlerical policies convinced Veuillot that the Liberals were right in asserting that betwen the Republic and the Church there could be no peace. So he kept a vigilant watch on the government's every action; he never stopped criticizing moves he considered hostile to the Church – as when the government appointed the liberal Catholic Augustin Cochin, who belonged to the Dupanloup school, representative to Rome. Veuillot therefore became an ardent champion of a royal restoration under Comte de Chambord. Like De Mun, the editor of *Univers* was taken in by Chambord's apparent love for the masses, his opposition to the Liberal element, and his promise to support the Church's social welfare program. Unlike De Mun, however, Veuillot came to back Chambord with unrestrained enthusiasm and to write in his favor in typically Veuillotian superlatives – even going so far once as to compare Chambord to Christ by developing a parallel between Christ's responses to the Devil and Chambord's to the Revolution. This incessant criticism of the Third Republic toward the end of Veuillot's life earned for him the reputation of being blindly set against democratic rule and against human freedom, though, as a matter of fact, he opposed the Third Republic only when he became convinced that it was the enemy of the Church and of the French people.

Veuillot, then, offered to support any form of government, republican or monarchical, as long as it respected human rights – the most important of which is man's right to worship God in the way He has directed. The editor of *Univers* found fault with all governments because he found none of them perfect and because he insisted on the citizen's right to criticize his government's policies and to protest against its unjust acts. But Veuillot was always enthusiastically loyal to his nation. The France he loved, he protested, was "the France that has been and will be again, not the France of the last century." When German journals referred to France as "the country of Veuillot," the editor of *Univers* used the opportunity to explain that "Veuillot and those who think like him are exiles within their country; they are the dispossessed." France, he held, should be Catholic; he could love it without reserve when it again became true to its inheritance.

Veuillot despised Liberalism and wrote incessantly against freethinkers because he maintained a deep and abiding respect for human liberty. About three weeks after the Revolution of 1848 took place in Paris, Veuillot published an article in *Univers* on "the Catholic line." In it he stated that the Church asked for nothing more than true liberty, that he "preferred liberty with its burdens and perils to the toils of [government] protection." Liberty, for Veuillot, was bound up with Christianity; contrariwise, "every illiberal principle is anti-Christian." He was convinced that "religion needs liberty and liberty needs religion, and between them they furnish the basis for a loyal alliance. This is the great fact of our century." Veuillot never lost his love of freedom, but in later years, after he had witnessed the excesses committed in the name of freedom, he insisted that liberty must be restrained in the interest of order and human rights. "I love liberty as much as a Catholic may," he wrote in 1865, "and that is very dearly; but I also reverence authority as much as a Catholic must. . . . The world has lost the secret of blending freedom and authority. The secret is at Rome."

* * *

Louis Veuillot's greatest satisfaction was the publication in *Univers* of a story from Rome: in ecumenical council the Church had solemnly proclaimed the Pope infallible when he spoke *ex cathedra* on a matter of faith or morals. Veuillot had carried on a long, intense, heated campaign in favor of the declaration before the Vatican Council met late in 1869. He had been invited by the Pope to Rome, where he set up headquarters while the Council was in session, acting as "the Pope's man" and knowing more about the inside workings of the Council than anyone except the members themselves. When, on June 28, 1868, Pope Pius IX called the Council to meet on December 8 of the following year, no mention was made of papal infallibility as an item on the Council's agenda. Nevertheless, it came to be included – basically because it was the will of God, but immediately because Providence worked through many bishops and laymen in the Church to have them request a statement on this important dogma. And the most insistent of these human agents was Louis Veuillot writing in the columns of *Univers*.

When the Council met there were three parties on the subject of papal infallibility: those who favored its being declared in no uncertain terms as an item of faith; those who opposed it as false on the grounds that infallibility did not reside in the pope but in the Church universal or in an ecumenical council duly assembled; and those who believed in papal infallibility but argued that the time was not propitious for its being publicly stated to an incredulous world. In the third party, as Veuillot argued vehemently and as the Pope well knew, were many who used the inopportunist plea to shelter their outright rejection of papal infallibility. *Univers* became an almost official exponent of the infallibility party, and during the seven months the Council was in session, Veuillot came to be known as "the journalist of the Pope and the majority."

It would be wrong to presume that Veuillot had any influence in the Council's decision, but he was doubtlessly influential in presenting to the public the arguments in favor of the decision and in preparing the way for its ready acceptance by answering the arguments of those opposed to the declaration. These latter included some of the best minds in France, Dupanloup and Montalembert among others, but they were men who, like Newman in England, were humble enough to accept the verdict when it was formulated by the Council. Although Veuillot's share of the credit for France, with its long Gallican tradition, accepting this "ultramontane" dogma cannot be measured, nevertheless the general feeling of time was that he played an important part in selling the doctrine to the country before it was formally announced by the Council.

* * *

The passage of the years has added to Louis Veuillot's stature as an important Catholic layman of the nineteenth century. When the editor of *Univers* died in 1883, Father William Loughnan wrote in *The Month* that "by his death France has lost one of her very greatest writers, the Church a valiant champion, and Catholic journalism a most formidable polemical writer." It is unlikely that anyone will contest Father Loughnan's statement, but for many years Catholics who followed in the Ozanam-Montalembert tradition felt that, important as he might be, Veuillot had done more harm for the Church than good. Typical of this perfectly understandable feeling is an article by William

Seton in the *Catholic World* in 1903, blaming the persecution the Church then suffered in France on Veuillot's refusal to work with the Third Republic after 1871. Seton believed that Veuillot and the clergy who followed his line of reasoning made the Liberals of the Republic anticlerical.

Opinion on this matter has changed in the past half century. The view held by Seton in 1903, and still held by some, is seen to be an oversimplification of a complex situation in French history going back to the Revolution of 1789 – and even before. To pretend that Veuillot made the Liberals anticlerical is to forget a century of history. It is possible that Veuillot's violent language made more enemies for his Church than friends – but even that is a doubtful matter. Certainly, as we have indicated previously, he made the Church's enemies sit up and take notice, whereas they paid less attention to the more moderate phraseology of a Montalembert or an Ozanam. Certainly, too, his forthright stand gave courage to many Catholics who needed someone to shout loudly that they were right and that the university professors, the scientists, the humanitarians, and the learned agnostics were all of them frightfully ignorant of the basic truths in life. Someone was needed to call the bluff of the freethinkers of the nineteenth century – and to call it in the same violent language with which it was made. Such a man was Veuillot.

His importance to the Church is attested by words of praise heaped upon him by successive popes – for who can judge better than the head of the Church how valuable this layman was in the battle against secularism and error? Pope Pius IX loved him as a brother. He frequently congratulated the rugged Frenchman for being his champion, as when he welcomed Veuillot to Rome in 1869 with the greeting: "You have done very well in this whole affair [the argument in France about papal infallibility], as you have in all others." Pope Leo XIII said that Veuillot "has always been a true Christian, a true servant of the Church." And Pope Pius X, a mild-mannered man himself, called the great French journalist "this great and good man, unconquerable defender of the rights of God and of the Church. . . . His pen was at once a trenchant sword and a luminous torch. With what upright and proud soul," Pius X continued, "with what unyielding courage, he spoke out on those fundamental questions, confessing Catholic truth without hesitation or attenuation, never consenting to distinguish between the divine rights which the modern world admits and those which it tries to proscribe! With what frank generosity he tore the mask off the Liberal theories, whose sophisms, misusing the name of liberty, dissimulate such deadly conclusions!"

Louis Veuillot performed a signal service for the Church – and for Christian civilization – by standing guard over the precious Christian heritage which lived on undiluted in the nineteenth century in the Catholic Church. There was danger that liberal Catholics, understandably anxious to reconcile the Church with the changing world, would unwittingly compromise their heritage away. There was real danger that they might twist true Christian liberty into modern illiberal Liberalism, or they might surrender the integrity of the family, the security of property rights, and other traditional Christian possessions to the encroaching secular state – all in the name of the new freedom. Veuillot stood guard against such unwitting compromise. That was his great value. Such a man was needed in the latter half of the century. Perhaps two Veuillots would have been too many – but one of them was just what was needed to keep men like Montalembert and Ozanam and Dupanloup on guard that in their adaptation of the Church to the nineteenth century they preserve intact the essential marks of Catholicism.

Veuillot was a fighter who suffered unpopularity because of the temper he displayed and because of the intensity with which he carried on his battle for God and His Church. But he always felt he fought fairly for what was right. So he could write, for his own funeral: "Place my pen at my side; put the crucifix, my pride, on my breast; lay this volume [*Ca et Là*] at my feet; then close my coffin in peace. . . . I trust in Jesus. Here on earth I have not been ashamed of His faith; and on the last day, when I stand before His Father, He will not be ashamed of me."

13. Wilfrid Ward

In the previous twelve chapters we have discussed a dozen different Catholic laymen who stood out prominently above their fellows for the work they did in promoting the Church's revival in the nineteenth century. There were included an Irishman, a Spaniard, a South American, a Savoyard, an American, five Frenchmen, and two Germans – but so far no Englishman has been treated. Several might be put on our select list: Frederick Lucas, editor of the *Tablet* for so many years and a member of Parliament; William George Ward, lay theologian and editor of *Dublin Review;* perhaps Lord Acton or the Duke of Norfolk; or any of several laymen in the Oxford Movement who eventually became Catholics. These Englishmen did a great work collectively, one that came to flower in the English Catholic literary revival of our own day, bringing into the Church such figures as Chesterton, Lunn, Knox, Bruce Marshall, and Evelyn Waugh. English Catholic laymen of high attainment and effective leadership are fairly numerous in the nineteenth century, then, but it is difficult to pick out one who stands high above the others, like a Windthorst in Germany or a Brownson in America.

Wilfrid Ward is perhaps the best figure to select. Some will argue that he was not as great a man as William George Ward, his father, and they are probably right as regards the comparative stature of the two men. But Wilfrid's work for the Church, we believe, was more effective and more lasting than his father's, partly because of the riper age in which he lived and partly because his talents were perfectly suited to the needs of the time. Wilfrid Ward is a convenient figure for us to study, moreover, since he serves as a connecting link between the great Catholics of the nineteenth century and those of our own day. As a young man he knew Wiseman and Vaughn and Manning and Newman, all great cardinals in the Church. Around him Belloc and Chesterton broke into print – and he recognized their genius. It was in the shadow of his figure that Dawson and other Catholic thinkers of the twentieth century began to write.

Ward is important in the Catholic revival first of all as a

man, a warm, human person around whom Catholics and non-Catholics enjoyed gathering in order to exchange their views. He was a liaison officer, as Sir Michael Sadler wrote to his widow upon his death, who served as a connecting link between Catholics and the rest of the world. He performed the same function within the Church as well, for he belonged to no party but was on good terms with them all, and it was through him that various groups within the Church exchanged their points of view to discover what they agreed upon and to move toward unity. Ward is important for promoting understanding and good will in religious circles as no one else could do it, for explaining the Church to the world and the world to Catholics. He won for the Church the respect of thinking Englishmen because he dispelled their ignorance and dissolved their prejudices by explaining the Church to them. He was effective in argument, paradoxically, because he did not argue. He explained. Moreover, because Wilfrid Ward possessed deep historical sense he was able to see just where on the path of history the Church stood toward the end of the nineteenth century. He was able, therefore, to point out the problems which had to be solved and to indicate which lines of action could safely be taken. Thus, as a man around whom Catholic thinkers and writers gathered, Ward was important.

As an author he did similar effective work for the Church. He employed his gift for lucid writing to present to the world in attractive garb the work of more recondite Catholic thinkers. By clear and accurate popularization of their thought he gave such thinkers as Newman a force in history they might not have otherwise had. His biographies of his father, of Cardinal Wiseman, and of Newman were more than pieces of good literature that brought their subjects to life; they were also revelations to countless non-Catholic readers of the inner working and the intimate thought of the Church. Finally, as editor of the *Dublin Review* from 1906 until his death ten years later, Wilfrid Ward brought together contributors from all parties within the Church, and he raised this review to a position of pre-eminence in English letters such as no other Catholic review has obtained in that country in the past century.

* * *

Wilfrid Ward grew up in the shadow of his father, William George Ward, a giant oak of a man whose overhanging presence did much to determine the sort of man Wilfrid Ward was eventually to be. W. G. Ward was one of those rare Englishmen who pushed ideas to logical conclusions. He breathed the air of pure theory; he suffocated in the atmosphere of the contingent and the possible. He had been the *enfant terrible* of the Oxford Movement, as his granddaughter Maisie puts it, until the inner logic of the movement drove him into the Catholic Church. He immediately joined the extreme "right wing": ultramontane, rigidly conservative in theology and politics, thoroughly anti-Liberal, completely at odds with his age. "There was a terrible truthfulness in him," Maisie Ward wrote of her grandfather. And there was a terrifying directness in the way he stated it. When Professor Sidgwick once asked him what the Catholic teaching was on a particular point of conduct, he is said to have answered: "There are two views, of which I, as usual, take the more bigoted." At any rate, William George Ward looked upon such liberal Catholics as Lord Acton and Cardinal Newman as more dangerous to the Church than atheists or bigoted Protestants. And he battled them with greater vehemence, pounding them relentlessly, mercilessly.

Wilfrid Ward grew up hearing how there were two sides to many Catholic questions of the day, "the right side," which was his father's, and "the wrong side," which was Newman's and Acton's and Montalembert's. The Ward family lived in an almost monastic atmosphere. The outside world was unknown to Wilfrid and his brothers and sisters except insofar as ideas about it filtered in through the lens of their father's opinion. Such a world, Wilfrid later observed, was too narrowly limited for a balanced education. The surroundings, he tells us, were "rigidly exclusive ecclesiastical." The children played at being priest or cardinal as other boys play at being policeman or fireman. The Church was the center of their lives, their studies, their recreation. In their family circle moved most of the Church's English dignitaries, such as Cardinal Wiseman, whom they never trusted as being quite Catholic because it was whispered he had a sneaking sympathy for Montalembert. More correct, from their viewpoint, were the two future cardinals, Manning and Vaughn, both of whom had considerable influence on the growing Ward children.

The Catholic Church, then, was Wilfrid Ward's one serious interest in boyhood, and it was taken for granted that he would be ordained and eventually become a bishop and perhaps even a cardinal. Had not Wiseman once put his biretta on Wilfrid's head and said, "You will be a cardinal" – a prophecy his father did not let him forget? Although Wilfrid later considered his boyhood too narrow and filled with "too many [obligatory] devotional practices," nevertheless he realized the advantages it bestowed on him when he went out into the world. He knew the fundamentals of his faith were right – and he understood them well. This gave him courage, for with the absolute assurance of being right, "one does not tremble lest to face a new fact may mean to dissolve one's faith." It armed him well for playing the sometimes dangerous role of liaison officer between the Church and the non-Catholic world.

Wilfrid's formal education was somewhat broader and certainly more varied than his education at home. His boyhood was spent in the shadow of St. Edmund's College, where his father lectured, and visitors to the household were mostly professors or authors. Wilfrid was tutored by one of the assistants from St. Edmund's until he was twelve, when a few boyish pranks on his part made his mother decide it was time for him to be in school. He was therefore sent to Downside in 1868 where, he tells us, he "was idle and not particularly good either at classics or at mathematics." He spent the next year at St. Edmund's. Here he stood at the head of his class, but his father "threw a douche of cold water" on Wilfrid's ambition by telling him he would rather have him fail, after having worked conscientiously, than take pleasure in success. Consequently, Wilfrid says, he spent the next five years "absolutely idle."

That seems a modest exaggeration, because he studied enough to pass the examinations for the bachelor of arts degree at London University. Meanwhile he had shown more than usual talent in dramatics and music. His successes at school, as he remembers them later in life, were at the piano or on the stage, and for a time he thought seriously of following a concert career. At the age of twenty-one Wilfrid Ward was like most young men: attracted to outdoor sports, fond of conversation, of music, and of genial horseplay—but suddenly he realized he must choose a vocation. Here his father was absolutely no help. William George Ward had never personally faced the problem of earning a living, since he had lived off the Ward family's holdings. As a second son, however, Wilfrid had to choose a career that would at least support him. He soon discovered that his father "was very slow to see the facts of life and to understand the workings of human nature." "Ideal" Ward could not suggest any career for his son, so Wilfrid went to his old friend Bishop (later Cardinal) Vaughn. The bishop was so "practical" as to be of no more help than William George Ward himself. He advised Wilfrid to become a merchant and make lots of money so he could be free to use his talents and wealth for the Church. When Wilfrid objected that he had no business sense, the bishop advised him to go to America, find a Catholic girl "with plenty of wool on her back . . . sing to her and she will marry you soon enough. Then you can come back here and go into Parliament or do anything else that you like."

Wilfrid felt that perhaps he had a vocation for teaching, but he found that there was no room for lay professors in English Catholic schools. And of course there was no room for Catholics anywhere else, because they could not attend either of *the* universities, Oxford or Cambridge.* While he was casting about this way, the confused young man decided that he had the vocation and the desire to become a priest. His father, of course, was overjoyed to hear of Wilfrid's decision. Plans were immediately completed for him to take his theology at the Gregorian University in Rome. He stayed there only nine months, when poor health forced him to return home. These were valuable months, Ward writes in his *Reminiscences,* in three different ways. First and foremost, his living among the monuments of Catholicism inspired him "with an ambition to work for the

* The Catholic emancipation act of 1829 had removed the Test-Act requirement for obtaining a degree at Oxford or Cambridge. The universities were willing to admit Catholic students, and Newman did all within his power to have this accomplished, but W. G. Ward and Manning took the lead in getting the English bishops to forbid Catholics' attendance at the two universities. Wilfrid Ward was especially hurt to know that it was largely his father's "garrison policy" (of which we shall speak later) that denied him an education at Oxford or Cambridge.

Church which instilled the ideal of doing great things and being part of a great and powerful organization." Secondly, though he found the lectures dry and turgid, he acquired a pretty good knowledge of scholastic philosophy. Finally, in his leisure he read the complete works of Newman, which his brother had given him as a going-away present, and this laid the foundation of his lifework.

In 1878, Ward returned to England where, at Ushaw, he continued his ecclesiastical studies for almost three more years. Early in 1881, however, he decided that he did not have a vocation to the priesthood, so he left Ushaw and began all over again to search for a career. His father continued to be of no help. For several years Wilfrid drifted about, taking law for a few months, thinking seriously about a stage career, trying his hand at writing, but mostly just reading, talking, and meeting people. It was providential fortune that he did "idle away" these years, for during them he met all kinds of people and thus he came to know the working of other men's minds in a very practical way. When Wilfrid Ward stumbled into his career of writing for the Church he was therefore equipped by experience to understand both the Church and the world. His own disposition, his experiences, and his reading of Newman had combined to make him a striking contrast to his father.

* * *

Wilfrid Ward moved in intellectual circles from the time he started crawling in his father's house until he put his last issue of the *Dublin Review* to bed shortly before he died in 1916. In the next issue of the *Review*, Chesterton wrote of Ward that "thinking was to him like breathing." Ward was a thinking man but he was not a philosopher. As he matured he became increasingly convinced that his father's work was good for training Catholic thinkers, but that it was otherwise practically valueless in the modern world. Moreover, Wilfrid seems never to have enjoyed abstract thought as an end in itself. He was more concerned with its practical application. Father Cuthbert explained his peculiar intellectual abilities this way: "He had not the temper of mind of the purely speculative thinker. He was really much more of a man of affairs than of pure thought, though the affairs which arrested his mind were mainly connected with intellectual speculation. He was more interested in thinkers than in thought itself. . . . He belonged, in fact, to that class of thinkers who may be described as the politicians of the world intellectual." And, it should be remembered, there was nothing the Church needed so sorely at the end of the nineteenth century as a "politician of the world intellectual" to bring the parties within the Church together in order to present a united front against encroaching secularism.

The secret of Ward's success as liaison man was his genuine interest in what other people thought. His daughter Maisie Ward claims that "the essence of his talent was an overmastering interest in the workings of other men's minds." And Chesterton remarked that "he was something better than disinterested; he was interested – interested even in his antagonist's case." So non-Catholics came to respect Ward because he respected them and thought their position deserving of careful examination; they came to respect the cause for which he stood because in holding it he never belittled their motives nor cavalierly dismissed their arguments. Because of this genuine interest in the position and the state of mind of those outside the Church, Ward was able to reach a large number of intelligent Englishmen who were concerned about religion.

Contemporaries had a habit of describing Ward by using and reusing three words: sympathy, understanding, honesty. These were the qualities which they saw him possess to a preeminent degree. What they probably did not realize is that he had developed them carefully, assiduously, knowingly from the days of his youth, because, we suspect, he saw the lack of these very qualities handicap his father and to some extent nullify the effectiveness of his great intellect. Wilfrid frequently insisted on De Maistre's famous slogan: "Truth can understand error, though error can never understand truth." In his first book, *The Wish to Believe,* he asserted: "It seems to me above all things important in these days to show that a Christian can fully realize the plausibleness of religious skepticism. None will have confidence in a remedy if it is plain that the disease is not understood by him who offers it." In contrast to his father and Donoso Cortés and Louis Veuillot, therefore, Ward endeavored to see in how many respects men of the nineteenth century were latently Catholic. He surprised the typical Englishman of the age, men like Balfour and Gladstone and Huxley, by showing them how many of their beliefs and attitudes were essentially Catholic.

In showing how much ground the Church and the age held in common, Ward did not minimize difficulties, nor did he try to effect a reconciliation by toning down the Church's doctrine or altering it ever so little in order to "modernize" it. His associates all speak of his absolute honesty and of his candor in analyzing the differences between Catholics and various non-Catholic groups. He showed how Catholic the Anglicans were, for example, but he was careful to point out that the differences between the two faiths were deeper than most Anglicans realized, that it was not merely a matter of episcopal succession but of a deep-seated difference of attitude toward the place of a Church in man's relations with God. So while Ward endeavored to show how much ground Catholics held in common with others, at the same time he insisted that the differences between the Church and the age were deeper than controversialists realized.

Ward did not perform the merely negative function of making contact between the Catholic and secular worlds — like a telephone operator connecting two parties for a conversation. He played a lively, sometimes vehement role as a controversialist. Maisie Ward describes this quality in her father's make-up by stating that "Wilfrid Ward was not pliable. He was vehement, rash, and excitable." He insisted at all times on telling the whole truth, in presenting his side of the case with all the forcefulness he could muster. Nor did his opponents take offense at this eagerness, for he was always willing to concede whatever measure of truth he saw in his opponent's argument. He could usually present an opponent's argument more forcefully than the opponent himself — but then he could answer it tellingly, for in presenting it he learned its weaknesses. Ward was therefore able to become an effective lay apologist for the Church who had earned the respect of non-Catholics without sacrificing any legitimate Catholic claims.

Ward moved about in intellectual circles, then, establishing contact between various groups and individuals who were interested in the religious aspect of the age's problems — and, as Belloc has pointed out so well, all problems — like all wars — are at bottom theological. As editor of *Dublin Review* from 1906 until 1916, Ward made that journal the focal point and the medium of expression for Catholic thought. The *Dublin* had fallen on bad days since its second revival under W. G. Ward thirty years before, and many Catholic thinkers felt that it should be allowed to die quietly. Father Tyrrell told Ward when the latter was invited to assume editorship of the *Review:* "You will have more worry over it than it is worth. I have seen death in its eyes for many a long day." But Wilfrid Ward used his special talents to nurse the journal back to vigorous life — its third within a century. Whereas his father had made the magazine a party organ, employing it against Newman and Acton and Simpson, Wilfrid Ward used it as a unifying force in Catholic life. Eschewing polemics, he made the *Review* an organ for a frank, friendly statement of the Catholic position on controversial issues of the day. He obtained contributors from all parties in the Church, and he opened its pages to non-Catholics for articles on literary and national subjects. Harmony with Catholic teaching, combined with literary excellence and solid worth, were the only criteria for acceptance of articles. Within ten years Wilfrid Ward not only revived the *Dublin Review* but carried it to a position of eminence in English letters it had never enjoyed before.

In his personal contacts, Ward also acted as liaison officer among persons of all faiths and all opinions. Father Cuthbert claims that he utilized his large circle of personal acquaintances to promote effectively the ideas he pleaded for as an author and editor. Ward was on friendly, intimate terms with people of every sort: Tennyson, Huxley, Martineau, Haldane, Balfour, Father Tyrrell, Manning, Vaughn, Newman — those who were skeptical of all religion, those who were "right wing" Catholics, those who were "left wingers," even those who apostatized in the Modernist controversy.* He showed Huxley that Catholics

* The Modernist controversy occupied chiefly the decade before 1907, when Modernism was defined and condemned by Pope Pius X in the encyclical *Pascendi dominici gregis.* The chief Modernists were the younger French clergy. The most notable among the English Modernists was the

could be intelligent and honest, and open-minded as well. He showed men like Gladstone and Balfour that there was nothing as tyrannical and reactionary about infallibility as they believed. He showed conservative Catholics that Newman belonged to the Church, and he showed liberal Catholics that there was some justification for the stand taken by men like his father and Cardinal Manning.

More or less symbolic of Ward's role in Catholic life toward the end of the nineteenth century was his joining with Balfour and Bishop Talbot in 1896 to establish the Synthetic Society. The three founding members believed that such an organization would effect some sort of unity among those who wished to preserve a rational foundation for a religion against the encroaching materialistic paganism of the times. "The thought of forming the Synthetic Society," Ward told members of the first meeting, "first occurred to a few persons differing from each other in theological opinion, and yet equally desirous of union in the effort to find a philosophical basis for religious belief." The group was always small, and frequently there was talk of discontinuing the sessions – but the Society continued to function and to invite into its ranks such later distinguished persons as G. K. Chesterton. There is no way of knowing how much effect the Synthetic Society had on the development of English religious thought, but at least it stands historically as a symbol of the work Ward had dedicated himself to and the way in which he tried to do it.

* * *

Ward's objective as a lay apologist for the Church, then, was to show that his contemporaries around the turn of the century differed from each other more than was necessary, that when they understood each other's position they would find how close together they were on many points. As early as 1885 he wrote an article on "The Healing Art of Philosophy," in which he suggested that Catholics should develop a new approach to the modern world, a radically different one from that used ever

---

expelled Jesuit, Father George Tyrrell, who had once been a close friend of Ward's but who steadily pulled away from him during the years of the controversy. A few more words about Modernism are said *infra*, pp. 344–347.

since the scholastic synthesis of the thirteenth century. Ward maintains in this essay that a normal philosophical education, which he defines as "a training in sound first principles and modes of thought," is useless in trying to convert men of the eighties because it is based on principles which are generally denied. What is needed is an approach which will "offer to those who are steeped in the unhealthy atmosphere of an age of intellectual disease a cure which shall be in some measure palatable and effectual."

The most effective approach to the non-Catholic, Ward claims, is to show him how Christian he is by a searching examination into the principles and the attitudes which he accepts. He believes that the writing of Herbert Spencer, for example, contains much more religious philosophy in embryo than anyone, even Spencer, realized. He thinks that arguments for the existence of God developed from conscience and from the consciousness of spiritual insight would be more effective in his day than the old arguments from causality or design. Ward knew the working of men's minds well enough to understand what his father could never comprehend: "A large Latin volume is regarded as a pill, and unless it be made palatable by surrounding jam it will do no good, simply because the age will refuse to swallow it, and not in any degree because of any defect in the medicinal properties of the pill." He therefore advised his readers to "dress their [the Scholastic] arguments in modern language, speak in the concrete rather than the abstract, help to render your meaning clear by analogy and illustrations." This was advice he followed himself, with the result that anyone who can read has no difficulty reading Wilfrid Ward.

* * *

Maisie Ward claims that her father's importance lies "in the analysis of the transition period [in which he lived] and of the possibilities and obligations it brought with it." This general observation can be particularized by stating that Wilfrid Ward's greatest importance lies in his masterful popularization of the century's greatest thinker – his father's *bête noir,* Cardinal Newman, a luminous mind whose brilliance is becoming annually more apparent to English and American thinkers. This is a point which Maisie Ward appreciates. "He asked nothing better," she wrote of her father, "than to continue to elaborate and explain the work of the great Cardinal," even preferring to be "a true disciple of Newman than a thinker in his own right." Ward's writing is permeated with Newman's thought — which became Ward's in the fullest sense possible, for Ward was not one merely to change the big bills of Newman's theory into intellectual nickels and dimes. His articles and his lectures center around various aspects of Newman's thought, his life of the Cardinal is the classic biographical study on Newman, his analysis of the age of transition and his plea for a new apologetic are a splendid application of Newman's theory of development applied to the problems of the time.

Ward presented Newman's vindication of the Catholic Church, showing how much the secular world owed it as an institution, for the Church, Newman had argued, preserved the fine things of European civilization from the attacks of individualism and rationalism. One might liken the Church to a lead vessel in which rested perishable treasures of Christian civilization — and this lead vessel proved the only container immune to the corrosive acids of individualism and rationalism which covered everything in the eighteenth and nineteenth centuries. As Ward put it, Newman's philosophy "vindicated the functions of tradition and of a visible organization in preserving religious truth." Weak individuals, he pointed out, are enabled to withstand the engulfing flood of skepticism and materialism when they are part of a corporate society. "A man who cannot hold to his faith in a world more and more infected by principles of unfaith, whose mind is poisoned by the atmosphere — secularist and sceptical — of a world which believes effectively only in the present life, may remain true to the unearthly principles of the Gospel if he is sustained by the atmosphere of the Church, its philosophy, its sanctity — even the beauty of its liturgy having its share in this work."

Thus the Church had performed a function in history which Protestantism, by its insistence on private judgment, could not perform. Only personal piety kept Protestants from yielding to the unbelief which surrounded them, Ward and Newman argued, because "they had discarded the bulwarks of a dogmatic system and a visible organization . . . which sheltered the weak individual from the assaults of rationalism." Ward rightly saw that Newman's genius lay in justifying the Church by practical arguments which his age could not ignore. The cardinal had turned the tables on an age that put reason and reform on one side, and on the other the blind force of custom and the pressure of ecclesiastical authority. He had reconciled philosophy and incense, so to speak, and he had shown that the Church system embodied a far deeper philosophy of religion and of life than did the religious individualists of the nineteenth century. He had rationally vindicated those practices in the Church which the rationalist considered superstitious; he had shown how the "weaknesses" in Catholicism had a firm foundation theologically, philosophically, and psychologically, and how they were one of the many reasons for the Church's unbroken continuity through eighteen centuries.

Wilfrid Ward explained Newman's vindication of the Church in terms that his contemporaries could both understand and appreciate. Moreover, he made Newman's thought his own and applied it to the age of transition in which he lived, an age of opportunity, he believed, for those Catholics who were intellectually and temperamentally adjusted to it. Where W. G. Ward had looked upon the Church as a garrison invested by the forces of secularism, skepticism, and materialism in the nineteenth century, Wilfrid considered it rather a school in the market place. Its atmosphere was not to be one of armed and hostile defense but rather one of openhanded, friendly help to those in search of truth. Protestantism was no longer the enemy to be feared; the real enemy was a new paganism which went under such names as Liberalism, Humanitarianism, Skepticism, Higher Criticism, Materialism. Its proponents did not attack the Church for representing God falsely, as the Protestants had done; they attacked it simply for representing God as a personal Being to whom man owed allegiance and worship. They denied a personal God altogether.

But Wilfrid Ward did not condemn non-Catholics wholesale, nor did he look on modern thought as entirely bad. As a matter of fact he was at bottom an optimist, since he believed that the nineteenth century was better than the eighteenth – and he looked for continued improvement into the twentieth. He was convinced that thinking men had turned in the right direction, that they were more open-minded, more favorably inclined to Catholicism, more religious basically than their forefathers had been one hundred years before. He showed, for example, how the eighteenth century was quick to reject authority of any kind, as the thirteenth had been quick to accept it; but the nineteenth century, he insisted, is slow either to accept authority or to reject it. "It has thrown a glory around doubt and suspense of judgment." He saw his age groping for a new synthesis of human thought, a system which he thought would find its unity in the scientific spirit, but which need not exclude religion.

Ward's big interest, therefore, was to show how there was no opposition between religion and science, how, as a matter of fact, the dogmas and the practices of the Catholic Church had a solid scientific foundation, how they could be approached through science as formerly they had been through philosophy. Ward realized that it would not be enough to prove that there was nothing unscientific about Catholic doctrine. The problem was deeper and more difficult than that. It involved Catholicism's assimilation of everything valid in modern thought. If Catholic theology were to survive and grow strong, Ward insisted with Newman, theologians must assimilate modern developments in the historical and critical sciences, as they had already begun to do with the physical sciences. Not to do so, Ward held, was really un-Catholic, for it is "in accordance with the Church's true genius that it should assimilate all that is worthy in the civilizations in which from time to time it finds itself."

"Assimilation" is the key word for understanding Ward's view of the problems of his age – and ours, for we are still in that age of transition which began in Wilfrid Ward's boyhood. He held that there had been two other such critical periods in Church history. The first was the patristic period, when the Fathers were faced with the choice of taking the Church out into the desert or of keeping it in the Graeco-Roman world by assimilating the good things of that culture. The second such age was the thirteenth century, when the scholastics affected that wonderful synthesis of Christian theology and pagan philosophy to produce the thought of the Thomist tradition. Such a synthesis served well for many centuries, Ward believed, and its fruit need never be lost. But much truth of many varieties had been discovered since the thirteenth century, especially in the historical and the physical sciences, and this truth must be incorporated into a new synthesis of human knowledge.

The Church, of course, is faced with the problem of assimilating new knowledge rather than compromising with it or being swamped by it. Here again, in analyzing this problem, Ward followed Newman closely in what will probably come to be recognized as Newman's most brilliant piece of work, his "Essay on the Development of Christian Doctrine." Newman listed seven points which are distinctive of genuine development,* points which are to serve as guides in adapting the Church to the age. He insisted that growth is necessary for any system that is to avoid stagnation and decay, that doctrines and practices which do not develop must disintegrate. Most important, because of the division of Catholics into conservative and liberal groups and their opposed stands on the Church's relationship to the secular world, Newman insisted that Catholics must take the calculated risk of intellectual intercourse with groups outside the Church. "But whatever be the risk of corruption from intercourse with the world around," he said, "such a risk must be encountered if a great idea is duly to be understood, and much more if it is to be fully exhibited. It is elicited and expanded by trial, and battles into perfection and supremacy."

Ward applied Newman's thought on growth and development most fully in an address on "The Conservative Genius of the Church" to the Catholic Conference of 1900. Following Newman, Ward had reasoned his way to a middle position between the conservative element as represented by Donoso Cortés and Veuillot, and the liberal element represented by Montalembert and Ozanam. There were even more extreme conservatives than Veuillot, of course, especially among the clergy, and there were liberals like Lamennais and Loisy who ended up in heresy. Ward tried to show both parties how much room there was in the

* The seven distinguishing points of genuine development, as contrasted to change, can be put this way: There must be (1) "preservation of its type," which depends upon (2) "continuity of its principles." It is also necessary that a movement proceed (3) "according to a logical sequence" if it is to have assimilative power, which is the fourth note of genuine development. The last three are "conservative action upon its past," "anticipation of its future," and "chronic vigor."

Church, how nothing was out of place in Catholicism except the two extremes: those who identified the Church with blind, stagnant conservatism, and those who wanted to cut loose from eighteen centuries of tradition in order to establish a "modern" liberal religion.

The Church has opposed every system of thought which tried to swallow it up, Ward told his listeners, but at the same time it has always ended up by assimilating the truth they contained. "She broke them in pieces," is the way Newman put it, "and she divided the spoils." So Ward advocates a policy of "true conservatism" which "involves constructive activity as well as resistance to destructive activity. . . . The aggressive movements of the times she has opposed. To yield to them would have been to identify herself with partly false, partly one-sided and exaggerated phases of thought, and lose her own authority and her own individual character. But each movement witnessed to a real advance of human thought, new truth amid new error, and to fresh developments of human activity. It supplied *material* for repairs and reconstruction within the Church although it was unacceptable as a whole."

Ward therefore advised that Catholic thinkers should sift through the tenets of the age, through the claims of Liberalism and the new sciences, and select piece by piece the elements which are undeniably good. This is the work of individual thinkers, in the providential process, and not of the authorities in Rome. Assimilation of new truth is done originally by individuals; resistance to change is provided by authority. And eventually the healthy synthesis of new truth and old is worked out. Ward used the example of Aristotle, relating how in 1215 Innocent III forbade the faithful to read the great pagan philosopher because the good points in his thought were set amid dangerous doctrines. Meanwhile, Albert the Great and St. Thomas Aquinas went quietly to work assimilating Aristotle into their great synthesis of scholasticism. So too in the nineteenth century, Ward believed, individual Catholics were working out a *modus vivendi* with modern secular thought – and signs of acceptance by Rome were already at hand with such a document as Leo XIII's *Rerum Novarum,* which accepted many points of the new social theory worked into Catholic thought by men like Bishop von Ketteler, but did not rush headlong into Socialism as the extreme Liberals would have had the Church do.

Ward's address on "The Conservative Genius of the Church" was an attempt to explain to Catholics how the machinery of the Church worked in the assimilation of new ideas. He presented the other side of the picture to non-Catholics in an essay on "The Rigidity of Rome." In this work Ward tries to show why the Church has been "rigidly conservative" in the past three hundred years, and how adaptability to the world is more natural to the Church than opposition to it. "The Catholic Church," he tells the non-Catholic, "has been exclusive, not from choice in time of peace, but from necessity in time of war." After telling about the assimilative activity of the Church in ancient and medieval times, he explains how the Protestant Revolt created a new set of circumstances. "Her work [the Church's] became primarily militant. Organized zeal and skillful debate were at a premium. The intellectual element, properly so called, was necessarily for a time sacrificed for the controversial and the devotional. . . . Besiegers and besieged, as time went on, became, in their separation, ignorant of each other's character; and the intellectual virtues of justice, candor, and even the Christian virtue of charitableness became less in place than the more military qualities of *esprit de corps,* skill in the war of words, prompt obedience to orders."

"Free speculation was safe among friends," Ward explained of the Church's liberality in medieval times, "but not when there were foes abroad." The state of war between Catholics and Protestants is ending, Ward tells his readers, and they can therefore look for a more liberal policy on the part of the Church in the future. The principle of authority within the Church is safe now, the old enemies are no longer abroad, and the time has arrived to begin an accommodation with the secular world. In the last years of his life Ward seemed to believe that the criticism Newman had made of Catholics was no longer valid. "Instead of aiming at being a world-wide power," Newman had complained in 1866, "we are shrinking into ourselves, narrowing the lines of communion, trembling at freedom of thought, and using the language of dismay and despair at the prospect before us, instead of, with the high spirit of the warrior, going out conquering and to conquer." By 1916, however, Wilfrid Ward thought that he saw increasing respect for the Church among thinking outsiders, and he believed that Catholics were beginning to realize that they were destined to be the final arbiters of intellectual and ethical religious problems of the modern world.

These things were coming about, he must have felt, because Newman's thought had begun to take effect among Catholics and well-disposed non-Catholics alike in the days just before World War I. It is difficult, however, to know just how widely Newman's influence had spread. Father Cuthbert wrote in 1916 that "if today non-Catholics regard the Catholic position more intelligently and sympathetically, it is in no small measure owing to his [Ward's] handling of the great cardinal's interpretation of the Church's genius. . . . It is not saying too much to assert that Wilfrid Ward brought Newman's theory of development out of the shadow into the light."

* * *

By 1900 Englishmen looked upon Wilfrid Ward as the more or less official spokesman for the Catholic Church in England. He was the Church's diplomatic representative to the thinkers and readers of the time, contact man between Catholic thought and that of the secular world. Ward was therefore called upon to analyze that ever recurring question of the union of all Christian churches to achieve their common objectives and to stand united against non-Christian forces in the Western World. He saw developing in his own lifetime a new paganism based upon the rejection of Christ and eventually the denial of a personal God. He considered this new paganism the real enemy, both to the Catholic Church and to the Christian society in which he lived, and as "a politician of the intellectual world" he mulled over the idea of united action by all Christians against it. "As time passed," his wife later wrote, "Wilfrid matured a view, born of his own character and experience, of common action among Christians against 'the revival of pagan ethics and the destruction of faith in the unseen.' "

A group interested in promoting union among Christians established the *Constructive Quarterly Review* to further their objective. In the first number of the *Review* Ward put forth the Catholic position in an article on "Union Among Christians."

With that candor for which he was so well known, he admitted that Catholics must appear terribly "exclusive" to the outside world and that their talk of cooperation must have a hollow ring in non-Catholic ears. Then he went on to vindicate the Catholic position and to show how effective cooperation could not be achieved by merging all churches into one – as some of the Protestant sects advocated – but only by each maintaining its own identity while all worked together for those objectives they held in common. If the religious groups would merge by surrendering all points of doctrine and practice on which they did not agree, Ward argued, the result would be a watered-down, flabby religion without spirit or vitality. Such a "reduced Christianity" would defeat the very purpose of merging – for it would end up an emasculated religion condemned at its very inception to early death. "Thus," he concluded, "the refusal to make cooperation depend on amalgamation in organization and in worship, or on the dismissal of what is distinctive of the several denominations and the retention only of what is common to all, may be grounded simply and solely on the interests of vitality in religion."

The real difficulty, as Ward saw it, was to get the various religions to refrain from attacking each other. Much of Protestantism's vitality comes from its denunciation of the papacy and of Catholic practices, and many Catholic devotions and traditions arose in an anti-Protestant setting. Nevertheless, Ward believed, "for Catholics a new foe is more dangerous than Protestantism, for Protestants the same new foe is more dangerous than Catholicism. . . . The ideal aim is that every group of Christians should preserve its *esprit de corps,* but should at the same time refrain from mutual hostility." Such cooperation, with each group maintaining its identity, would reveal more and more points held in common and would bring the various groups into closer understanding – for Ward insisted strongly that there were many "real but at present unsuspected points of agreement." He was firmly convinced that the force and energy of Christians could be concentrated in this new crusade – but the quarter of a century which has elapsed since Ward's death has proved him too generous and too optimistic in his estimate of his fellow Christians. He seems not to have realized how deeply tradition had set them against each other, nor how the very vitality of some Protestants and some Catholics seemed to depend on their attacking each other. At any rate, both Catholics and Protestants have fallen far short of Ward's expectations for a common crusade against the new enemy of neo-paganism. There have not been enough Christians of Ward's caliber.

* * *

Within the Church, Ward also performed the invaluable service of a "politician" by trying to bring about an understanding between the rulers of the Church and Catholic thinkers, those who stressed authority on the one hand and on the other those who stressed the element of liberty. There has always been — as there always will be — tension between those who command and those who obey, but in Ward's lifetime the tension became tautly critical. There was urgent need of bringing the parties together, getting them to understand each other's point of view, and having them make concessions to each other. That this has been accomplished in truly marvelous fashion is due partly to the efforts of Wilfrid Ward.

Ward condemned extreme radicals, those "comparative tyros in the theological arena" who refused to admit their ultimate obligation to obey proper ecclesiastical authority; he also condemned extreme conservatives, the "enemies of all change — including the changes which mark off the living being from the fossil." With these unassimilable elements removed from the picture, Ward believed he could effect understanding among the remaining proponents of authority and of liberty in the Church — and these included the vast majority of thinking Catholics. Liberals must realize that the intransigents perform a real service for the Church, because they hold up the assimilation of newly developed truths until they can be sifted and purified and thus made digestible. New "isms," Ward explained, are like "the advertisements of quack doctors." They are panaceas which claim too much and go too far, intellectual fads universally applied to all problems which, in time, prove to be concoctions of truth and error. And if there were not always the tight rein of authority to hold exuberant thinkers in check, the Church would always be rushing from one heresy to another.

On the other hand, those in authority must give sufficient freedom to the thinkers in the Church. "In an age which is preeminently one of transition – when new lights on matters scientific, historical, critical; new points of view and new overmastering impulses on matters social, political, philosophical are making their appearance year by year, it is only those few who have made these subjects specially their own, and who, at the same time, have the interests of the Church at heart, who can be, in the nature of the case, equal to the situation. They alone have the perception and knowledge needed to see how Catholic thought can deal with and assimilate what is sound or true, can effectively resist what is dangerous." Now if these thinkers are ignored, Ward held, and if authority continues to run in the same groove forever, "Catholicism may lose touch with the age, and forfeit much of its influence. And this may happen although the Church is not internally corrupt." He therefore concluded that a large measure of freedom should be allowed to individual thinkers, but that they, in turn, should readily admit their ultimate duty of obedience when the proper authorities speak. What Ward did, in effect, was to ask both sides to recognize the proper function of the other, to be generous to each other, and to refrain from overstepping the bounds respectively of freedom and of authority.

This problem became a personal one for Ward when the Modernist controversy came to a head with the publication of Pius X's masterly encyclical *Pascendi dominici gregis*. Modernists were few in number, "officers without an army" they have been called, who gradually worked away from the Catholic position and eventually denied the historical reality of a divine Christ, the objective fact of revelation, and the importance of doctrine. There was much confusion throughout the Modernist controversy, for some of the leaders were apparently in good faith and some were not, some went part of the way into heresy and some threw the whole Catholic tradition overboard.* Most, it

* It has been well said that Modernism did not have a creed until the pope gave it one by his excellent summary of Modernist teaching in his encyclical. Modernism consisted of tendencies and of doctrines. The tendencies were toward subjectivism and naturalism, away from revelation, the supernatural, objective doctrine. No two modernists held exactly the

would seem, did not know just what they believed – perhaps because they did not believe in believing. They put their religious chips on spiritual emotion and pious activity. At last, in 1907, Pope Pius X published his famous condemnation of Modernism, which he aptly described as "the synthesis of all heresy," and a few years later he required all clergy in charge of souls to take an anti-Modernist oath. The effect of this strong action by the Pope was healthy, for it cut modern developments in Catholic thinking loose from the smothering subjectivism which clothed all Modernist thought, and thus it cleared the air for the sound doctrinal development which occurred since that time. Moreover, by condemning Liberalism in religion, which is Modernism, the Pope made possible healthy progressive developments in the Church, both as regards its own constitution and doctrine, and in its attitude toward political and social developments in the outside world. For the Pope pointed out the heretical items in Modernism and thus, by implication, showed what developments were orthodox.

There was never any question in Ward's mind about not accepting the encyclical. The Pope had spoken, and Wilfrid Ward obeyed. But it was hard for him to see one friend after another condemned. It was difficult to know just how to interpret the papal document. It was especially hard in that, for a while, Ward did not know whether Newman's teaching was condemned. Modernists had made use of his ideas – though they had twisted his thought to suit their more extreme theories – and they all told Ward that the encyclical clearly condemned Newman's thought *in toto.** Ward was confused by the welter of conflicting opinions about what was condemned and what was not – as for a time everyone seemed to be – but within a few months he

---

same doctrine, but there was a similarity among them all. This is not the place to enter into a full study of this difficult subject. Translations of the syllabus *Lamentabili,* which states Modernist teaching in sixty-five condemned propositions, and of *Pascendi dominici gregis* are the best sources for studying this movement. Maisie Ward's *Insurrection versus Resurrection* contains several excellent chapters on the subject.

* No names were mentioned in the encyclical. Condemned doctrines were stated — in Latin, of course. Much of the difficulty therefore revolved around translation, and much more around application of the doctrines to the theories of various "suspect" individuals.

got his feet on the ground, received assurance from the outstanding theologians of the time that none of Newman's thought could be found in the articles condemned by *Pascendi*, and thus he felt relieved to know that he would not have to renounce his lifework or give up Newman's theories on development which he had made his own.

The Modernist controversy, as a matter of fact, proved a vindication of Ward's analysis of the problem of authority and freedom. For the Modernists, as extreme Liberals in the Church, would have given up Catholicism in order to keep up with the times. Authority had to pull the reins tight to save the Catholic position, and wait until the crisis passed before letting out the slack again. Ward was in no way condemned – though some of the Modernists, and some extreme intransigents too, told him he was – because his theory of development was essentially different from that of the Modernists. For a time it was difficult to know just where to draw the line between Ward and Modernists, but today it is easy to see the difference, as Rome saw it in 1907. Maisie Ward has illustrated the essential point of difference well with the metaphor of the lion and the rabbit. When the two animals meet, the lion will "assimilate" the rabbit. They cannot simultaneously eat each other. Now when the Church and the age try merging is the Church the lion or the rabbit? Modernists made it the rabbit. Newman's doctrine of development, with its seven points for testing genuine growth, made it the lion. And Ward remained faithful to Newman's idea of development.

* * *

Wilfrid Ward is important not so much for arguing on behalf of the Church as for explaining it to the world. (It is well to remember, however, that exposition is the first step in successful argument.) He maintained that ever since the Protestant Revolt, Catholics had retreated on themselves. They no longer knew the world, and the world no longer knew them. To get them reacquainted was the purpose of his articles in various leading English journals of the time; it was the indirect purpose of his popularizing Newman and of his biographical studies of his father, of Cardinal Wiseman, and of Cardinal Newman. Thus the *Fortnightly Review* commented on his life of Wiseman: "Those who would understand the position of the Church of Rome in this country . . . will do well to give careful consideration to this biography."

Ward wanted to be a teacher. He was keenly hurt to realize that a Catholic layman could not be a professor in England, but he probably never realized that his lifework turned out to be the realization of his vocation. Though his lecture platform was not in the classroom, nevertheless he explained the Church to all who would listen to him or read him. And this is the work of a teacher. Ward was a professor of apologetics at large, and he lectured in the market place. He was, Father Cuthbert wrote in 1916, "one of the ablest exponents of the Catholic position." This was a good and a great work for a layman to perform in an age when sincerity and sympathy and honesty such as Ward possessed could secure for him an audience that a priest could never quite reach. Thus Ward did the same sort of work at the end of the century which De Maistre performed at its beginning. He stepped into a breach which, from the nature of things in the nineteenth century, the priest could not man. Throughout the nineteenth century — and on into our own day — this has been the function and the vocation of the Catholic lay leader.

IV

CONCLUSION

It will be recalled how, when Pope Pius VI died in 1799, diplomats and "advanced" thinkers generally felt that there would be no more popes. It will be recalled, too, how only with great difficulty and after the delay of several months did the cardinals assemble in Venice to elect Pius VII. When Leo XIII died in 1903, by way of contrast, there was universal mourning – well expressed by John T. McCutcheon, noted cartoonist on one of America's large metropolitan dailies, with his sketch of the earth encircled by a band of crepe. Again, in contrast to a century before, there was no question in 1903 whether another pope would be elected. There was great interest in possible "candidates," for the nations of the world realized the tremendous power wielded by the Pope as ruler and head teacher of the Catholic Church at the beginning of the twentieth century.

In the ten decades between the death of Pius VI and the passing of Leo XIII, the Church had recovered its health, reorganized its resources, increased its activity and influence, and enhanced its prestige in the eyes of the world to an extent that still seems incredible. It is hard to realize that only seventy-five years after Pius VII had been a prisoner in Napoleon's hands, Leo XIII would be called upon by Bismarck to settle the Caroline Island dispute between Germany and Spain; or that whereas Pius IX was rudely ignored when he offered his services to avoid the Franco-Prussian War of 1870, Benedict XV would be listened to respectfully when he proposed mediation between the Central Powers and the Allies in 1917.

The Church was respected by the world at the end of the nineteenth century for a very worldly reason. It had proved that it was not senescent, condemned to wither away and pass into history as a once glorious but now archaic institution. On the contrary, it had proved itself very much alive. It had grown healthy and vigorous, and by 1914 it gave every sign of being in the prime of life all over again. It had entered one of those ever recurring springtimes of its life – and because it was strong the world respected it. The Church had grown healthy because it had shaken off the most serious diseases which had weakened it in days gone by, and it had withstood the assault of its two most powerful enemies from outside. The two most serious diseases weakening the Church's constitution in the past had been Gallicanism and Modernism; their counterparts in the outside world were Statism and Liberalism, two of the most powerful enemies with which the Church did battle throughout the century. There was also the general virus of secularism which sapped religion everywhere and which the Church had to withstand at all times. That the Catholic Church alone among the major religions of the world was able to swim against the tide of secularism is itself testimony to the remarkable revival it enjoyed in the nineteenth century.

The virus of Gallicanism had been cured by necessarily strong measures taken by the Vatican Council in 1870, the statement of papal infallibility coming as the climax of a long struggle between the ultramontane and Gallican groups in the Church. With the authority of Rome safely established, the Church could turn its attention to other pressing problems. Modernism was condemned in a way that to many seemed harsh – but the virus was insidious and the medicine was necessarily potent. And with religious Liberalism condemned, article by article, boundary lines were drawn marking off healthy accommodations with the age from those which were suicidal.

For the Church these were the two most dangerous doctrines of the century, Gallicanism and Modernism, subscribed to by many of its most intelligent children. Their condemnations drove a few of these persons – those consumed with pride, like Döllinger and Loisy and Tyrrell – out of the Church, but it left loyal Catholics free to develop their various studies within the bounds of orthodoxy now clearly delineated for them. By severe action taken after long deliberation, the Church lost no portion of that precious deposit of the Truth. Had not Providence decreed action when it did, only after a long period of discussion and of trial-and-error by individuals like Montalembert, the truths in Liberalism would likely have been cast away with the dross of its error. Time and the arguments of individuals like Ozanam and Görres, Donoso Cortés and Veuillot, crushed the system of Liberalism into its component pieces, as crude ore is crushed in the mill, so that by definition Rome could separate the precious metal of truth from the crasser materials with which it was mixed.

By the end of the century, the Church had shaken off the incubus of the Old Regime. Three centuries of intimate association between the Church and the monarchy had caused many high-placed churchmen to believe that monarchy was the only form of government in which the Church could subsist – and the anticlerical attitude of republicans seemed to validate such a belief. We can easily see today how a union of the Church and the new republicanism was both possible and salutary, but we can also see how that union could not be premature, nor could it be on the terms laid down by the Liberals. At length, when the issues were clear and when it became evident that monarchists were abusing the Church for their own political advantage, Pope Leo XIII ordered Catholics to be loyal to the republican government of France – and by implication wherever it was validly established.

It was evident by the end of the century that intelligent Catholics had sincerely and honestly cut loose from traditional loyalties to the Old Regime and had become active citizens in the various republics and limited monarchies of the time. And they expressed the mind of the Church in this respect, as is indicated in Rome's condemnation of the *Action française** group of Catholics who were ultranationalistic advocates of a restored monarchy for France. Here again, then, the Church adapted itself to the modern world by endorsing whatever was good

* The *Action française* was condemned before World War I, but because a publication of the condemnation of such a nationalist movement during the war would seem a partial act on the part of the papacy, the condemnation was not made known publicly until after the war was over. It was a movement which used Catholicism as an instrument for building up hatred against the Third Republic, against Germany, and in favor of a restoration of the Bourbon House in France.

and healthy in the new political arrangements and rejecting only what enslaved the free citizen – as full-blown Liberalism and totalitarian democracies do.

Although the Church did not succumb to the attacks of Liberals, nevertheless it was far from completely successful in vanquishing this enemy. Despite the work of men like Brownson and Ward, the suspicion remained among otherwise well-informed Englishmen and Americans that the Catholic Church was essentially inimical to human liberty, that any concessions it made were merely matters of expediency. In the Latin countries the Liberals continued to advocate State measures aimed at the destruction of the Church. Nineteenth-century Liberalism was disappearing in the Latin countries, as everywhere else, but its deadly hatred for the Church was part of the legacy it passed on to Socialism as the metamorphosis from Liberalism to Socialism proceeded pretty much as Donoso Cortés prophesied it would. At any rate, in ridding the Church of the internal viruses of Gallicanism and Modernism, as well as in fighting against Statism and Liberalism, Catholic lay leaders played an important and a laudatory role.

* * *

In the course of its revival, the Church disengaged itself from that nervous Romanticism of the first decades of the nineteenth century which seemed at first so favorable to religion in general and to Catholicism in particular. Had the Church hastily adopted such a movement as its own, it would have identified itself with the religious emotionalism of men like Chateaubriand. And emotion by itself is sandy foundation on which to build. The solid revival came later, and it was built on the hard rock of the scholastic tradition – in which the credentials of faith are established by reason instead of feeling, in which room is made for both philosophy and theology, for reason and faith, for the mind and the heart and the body too, for the written word as well as the traditional teaching authority of the Church. This was a revival which was solid and healthy, which made room for all facets of the truth, which found expression in the lives of saints like the Little Flower and the Curé of Ars, in missionary work unequaled in previous centuries, in the beginnings of a liturgical movement, the reinvigoration of scholastic philosophy, renewed interest in the Fathers of the Church, in a vigorous application of Catholic principles to social and economic life. These were good things which did not pass with the moment. They continued on through World War I down until our own day.

Although the Church lost much property throughout the century and although the Pope was a voluntary prisoner in the Vatican, his State taken from him by force, nevertheless the Church engaged in more extensive social activities than in the eighteenth century. Many of Europe's greatest universities were Catholic, staffed by various teaching orders, by diocesan clergy and by laymen; orphanages and hospitals, credit unions and unemployment agencies, libraries and old folks' homes were still maintained by the Church through a century when the State was ever assuming more and more of these social functions. Thus despite the secular drift of the hundred years between the French Revolution and World War I, Pope Benedict XV was able to perform charitable works during the latter war which Pius VII could not even have dreamed of in Napoleon's day.

Problems remained for the Church, of course, as there always have been and always will be problems which seem temporarily unsolvable. The basic problem was still to baptize non-Catholics and make Catholics better, more thoroughly Catholic. More specifically, there was the new enemy seen by Wilfrid Ward, the neopaganism of the twentieth century, seen in harshest fashion in the anticlerical legislation of formerly Catholic countries like France and Latin America, observed in a more patronizing form in countries like England and the United States. There was the growing strength of Communism, a false religion which could not tolerate the Church nor be tolerated by it. There was still the problem of a ruthless capitalism which refused to admit that workingmen were human beings created to the image and likeness of God. There was still that predisposition of most men to disassociate their activity in this world from their occasional acts of religious service. There was still the general trend of the world away from God, that secularism which creates a stifling atmosphere for those who are concerned with the things of the spirit. These remained as real problems.

These were problems, however, with which the Church was better able to contend than it had been since medieval times, for it had generally solved its internal difficulties and it was healthy, vigorous, able to grapple with secularism and Communism and all those agencies of the world with which it must ever battle. By the end of the century, it is true, Catholics were neither as numerous nor as powerful as they had been four centuries before. But though the Church might not be able to impose its truth upon the world, nevertheless it did not have to contend with internal divisions and weaknesses which had prostrated it at the beginning of the century and rendered it incapable of performing its mission of teaching the Gospel to all men.

* * *

The historian who would account for this revival, as we have indicated before, must invoke many factors. He must stress the great popes of the century, each one, it seems, playing a providentially assigned role, a nearly perfect instrument moved by the hand of God. He must tell of great princes of the Church, like Newman and Vaughn, of great bishops like Dupanloup and Hughes. He must include the thousands of priests who worked and prayed and invoked God daily by offering the Holy Sacrifice of the Mass and saying their Office. He must mention the nuns who taught and who worked in the hospitals, as well as those who withdrew from the world to pray incessantly for those in the world. Nor can he neglect the millions of ordinary people in the Church who by their example, their prayers and sacrifices and good works gave vigor to the recovering Church. Nor, if the story be an adequate account of the Church's revival, can the historian fail to mention the Holy Spirit who breathed life into the Church and guided the human agents through whom He accomplished His work.

Such an account of the history of the Church in the nineteenth century has not yet been written — nor is this an attempt to do it. The thirteen laymen we have followed in these pages, however, played their roles — small, perhaps, when seen as part of the whole movement, but nevertheless an important part — in promoting the welfare of the Church throughout the century. And no account of the Church's history would be complete unless it gave them due credit for the work they accomplished. In our discussions of these laymen we have seen the problems they encountered, the work that each performed, and the contribution he made to the welfare of the Church in the century. It would not be amiss, by way of conclusion, to call the roll of these thirteen laymen again in order to see how each one's work fit in providentially as a contribution to the general development of the Church in these years of its great revival. That, indeed, is why each is important.

Four of our laymen were born in the eighteenth century. They stand first in point of time, then, and their function consequently differs from that of later Catholics. Their job was primarily to throw off the incubus of the immediate past without rejecting the long-established Christian tradition, and secondarily to lay down lines of development that their successors could follow. De Maistre and Görres are important for discrediting the rationalism of the eighteenth century. This was a body of thought essentially destructive of organized religion, especially of Catholicism. Deist at best, agnostic quite frequently, atheist at worst, the rationalists of the late eighteenth century waged bitter war on a Catholicism they considered superstitious, an opium for the ignorant, a racket for the clergy. De Maistre and Görres demonstrated to thinking men how shallow, though sometimes sharp and clever, was the thought of a Voltaire or a Holbach or a Grimm. They went further than that: they demonstrated that straight, hard thinking led men to the door of the Church by vindicating its claims. More than demonstrating that there was no real opposition between faith and reason, they showed how reason led to faith if it were inexorably followed to its logical conclusion. This was a most important point, for it showed thinking men of the nineteenth century that they did not have to choose between faith and reason, as the rationalists had insisted. Indeed, they could not reject faith without impugning reason.

De Maistre and Görres surveyed a road of speculation which was decisive in the revitalization of the Church in the nineteenth century — the road which led straight to Rome, that "ultramontane" road which laymen followed faithfully throughout the century, more faithfully, at times, than even the bishops and the diocesan clergy. De Maistre dealt with the subject specifically, as we have seen, and his influence in developing an ultramontane mind was most important. Görres was quite as "Roman" as his Savoyard counterpart, but his influence was not as direct or as weighty on this point because he did not write on it as De Maistre had done. Moreover, both Görres and De Maistre pointed out that true freedom was found not in the Liberalism deriving from the French Revolution but in the carefully developed doctrines and traditions of the Catholic Church.

These two men stand at the springhead of the Catholic intellectual movement of the nineteenth century, providential figures, we can say, insofar as their theories were in the right direction, their choices were the correct ones, and they started Catholic thinkers down the right path. Görres was the intellectual father of those outstanding men who joined the "Munich School," and his influence can be seen consistently in the development of sound Catholic scholarship in the next two generations. His influence was confined pretty much to the Germanies, it is true, and only indirectly did it come to be felt west of the Rhine. De Maistre occupied much the same position in France, the focal country of Western Europe, and to some extent in the other countries along the Mediterranean and the Atlantic, including even the two Americas.

O'Connell is important for two things – and it is hard to tell even today which is the more important. He led the fight for the emancipation of Catholics in Great Britain. It is largely to his credit that his fellow churchmen received the vote when they did, as well as those other political rights which they continued to exercise from 1829 on. But O'Connell is also important for having caught the imagination of Catholics all through the world. He became the gallant crusader, the noble knight who joyously fought against insuperable odds for freedom and justice. Thus O'Connell became a great symbol – in Paris, in the Rhineland, in Boston, in Berlin, in Madrid, even in Rome itself, the warrior of the nineteenth century who carried on a fight for which laymen were particularly fitted. In this way O'Connell gave heart to Catholics battling in the *Reichstag* of Germany and the *Chambres* of France and the *Cortes* of Spain.

Pauline Marie Jaricot is a pioneer figure whose great foundations were the bases of two of the Church's most glorious accomplishments of the century, the missions and the apostleship of prayer. Mlle. Jaricot is also important, as we have shown, for her vision in seeing the social and economic problems created by the factory civilization of her age, and for having felt that religion cannot be disassociated from the solution of those problems, that justice and charity, men's souls as well as their bodies, the Church even more than the State, are all concerned with the mess that machines were making of human relationships. She is important for having seen that machines were not to blame, that if they were put to good use by good men they could bring blessings instead of misery to human beings. Thus Pauline Marie Jaricot's experiment was a tentative though unsuccessful approach to the problems taken up later on by laymen like De Mun, by bishops like Von Ketteler, by popes like Leo XIII.

Ozanam, Montalembert, and Donoso Cortés were born within the nineteenth century, but they all did their greatest work before 1850. Like Pauline Marie Jaricot, Ozanam established two great foundations which played not inconsiderable roles in promoting the welfare of the Church throughout the nineteenth century – and down into our own. The Notre Dame Conferences became famous apologetic institutions presenting Catholic truth to the world; the St. Vincent de Paul Society kept the flame of charity burning in men's hearts as its members brought both bread and grace to countless suffering victims of the inhumanity of their fellow men.

For these things Ozanam is well known, but in time historians may consider his stand on political and social questions more important than these organizations he founded while still an undergraduate. Ozanam went further than any important Catholic – even further than Montalembert – in endorsing liberty and democracy. He took his stand for two reasons. First, as an historian he saw the inevitability of these results of the French Revolution, and he perceived the general direction in which society was evolving; because liberty and democracy are both good in the abstract he advised the Church to adopt them and Christianize them at once. Second, Ozanam intimately knew the people who made up "the masses," and he felt that they were not essentially vicious. He felt that they had been misled, that when they were taught the truth they would make good use of their freedom and their sovereignty. (It is surprising how similar a tone there is in Pope Pius XII's Christmas Message of 1944 and Ozanam's various writings on this subject.)

Like Ozanam, Montalembert was anxious to assimilate the good results of the French Revolution. He was anxious to work out an accord between human liberty and the Catholic religion, between the general trends of his generation and the Church of the ages. For a few years, however, Montalembert gave up his faith in republicanism, whereas Ozanam's trust in the people never wavered; but after his retirement from active politics, the French peer continued to work for accommodation between freedom and religion. Montalembert and Ozanam offered essentially sound proposals, we can see today, but they presented them prematurely. The Liberals were like the lion who, to borrow Maisie Ward's analogy, would lie down peacefully with the lamb only after having thoroughly digested him. The Church was likewise willing to lie down with Liberalism only after having assimilated it into the body of Catholicism.* Montalembert and Ozanam erred in believing that Liberalism and Catholicism could somehow assimilate each other simultaneously and still each preserve its own identity. Their solutions could therefore be adopted only in the fullness of time, when the Church had become more of a lion again and Liberalism was no longer king of the nineteenth century.

Donoso Cortés is important for having seen the other side of the picture presented by Liberalism. He perceived the inner logic of the Liberal movement and he understood how it led logically to totalitarian Socialism. (Today we would say instead Communism.) Donoso courageously warned a society enamored

* The Church never opposed Liberalism for giving men liberty. The opposition was to certain doctrines assembled under the heading of Liberalism, such as the denial of original sin and the assertion of man's complete natural goodness, and the assertion that man's sole end is earthly happiness.

There cannot be any real conflict between true liberty and valid authority; the two are, in the abstract, complementary rather than contrary. It must be conceded, however, that in practice tension frequently arises between those in authority and the human beings over whom the authority is exercised. The question is always where the line between true liberty and license, or an abuse of liberty, is to be drawn.

with Liberalism that by turning its back on God and His Church it was heading inevitably into dictatorship, either of The People or of The Man. Secularism eventually means slavery, he said in effect, for without religion you cannot be free. This Spanish peer was a prophet of doom, perhaps, but his dire predictions made at the middle of the nineteenth century have come true in our time. Unlike Ozanam and Montalembert, Donoso Cortés drew a sharp line between Catholicism and secular Liberalism. He refused to admit of any reconciliation between the two. In this respect, of course, he was not entirely right — as subsequent history has shown. For his day, we believe, he was right in thinking that the Church and Liberalism were necessarily committed to extinguish each other. Right or wrong, though, he was a necessary counterbalance to proponents of liberal accommodation such as Montalembert.

* * *

Donoso's friend and admirer, Louis Veuillot, carried the fight against Liberalism into the second half of the century. Veuillot went too far, his denunciations were too inclusive, his stand was narrowly conservative. These are faults of the polemicist, faults which almost appear virtues when seen against the Liberals whom Veuillot condemned. Louis Veuillot was a thoroughly good man personally; his mistakes were made in good faith, and they should not obscure the invaluable work he did for the Church. He was the lay pallbearer of Gallicanism, as he was the lay sponsor of papal infallibility. Moreover, he was a valuable "reactionary" in a France where the heresy of liberal Modernism was taking form. Veuillot may have leaned too far over the right rail, but he helped balance the ecclesiastical ship in France at a time when most of the intelligent younger men leaned so far over the other rail that the ship was in danger of listing dangerously into Modernism.

A host of outstanding laymen helped the Church grow and thrive in Germany in the latter half of the century. Call the roll of Center Party representatives in the *Reichstag* and you have a list of German Catholic leaders — men like Mallinkrodt, Windthorst, the Reichenspergers. Most prominent among them, of course, was Windthorst, the party tactician who worked selflessly in the interests of his Church. It was Windthorst who welded the Center Party into a disciplined group and directed its measures in order to defeat Bismarck's *Kulturkampf;* it was Windthorst who pioneered in putting into law Catholic social principles developed by Bishop von Ketteler and other great German Catholic social philosophers. Across the Rhine, Count Alfred de Mun tried heroically to do the same thing for France. His aim was to achieve social justice through legislation based upon Catholic principles, and though his success was limited his efforts were not entirely wasted. In the little country of Ecuador another great Catholic lay leader had the power, as well as the desire, to bring his country's legislation and administration into harmony with Catholic social teaching. His efforts demonstrated concretely that railroads and factories could run, education could prosper, the nation's wealth could increase, and material progress could continue when these Catholic ideas were put into action. García Moreno robbed the Liberals of their most effective weapon when he showed that they had no exclusive copyright on prosperity and progress.

The outstanding Catholic layman of the United States was Orestes Brownson, a convert whose most important contribution to the Church's revival was his proof that Catholicism was not an "alien" faith reserved for Irishmen and Italians and Poles. Brownson showed by his conversion that a respectable American, a thinking man, could be a Catholic too. More than that, he went on to claim that a thinking man could not be anything else. Many took offense at his bluntness, but none could deny his ability in defending Catholic doctrine and in pointing out the errors of Liberalism, capitalism, and those other secularist trends of his day for which Protestants in America seemed to show an affinity.

Wilfrid Ward is important for blending together and justifying both groups within the Church, liberal and conservative, and for showing how each group performed a valuable service in the Church's assimilation of the good things in modern civilization. He is important, too, for his popularization of Newman's brilliant thought. It was this layman who established contact between Newman and the ordinary people of the world, Catholic and non-Catholic. He served as a transformer, breaking down

Newman's high-voltage thinking into a current that the average man could utilize profitably. Ward is also important as contact man between Catholics and those outside the Church. He did a great deal to establish mutual respect between the two. In an age before public relations became a specialized art, Ward served the Church well as a public relations man who explained Catholic doctrine and advertised it and sold it without ever embarrassing the Church.

* * *

Together these thirteen laymen we have discussed in these pages helped the Church adapt itself to modern society. This was a great and a delicate task, this work of adapting an institution as changeless as the Catholic Church to a constantly changing civilization. It required tact and patience, skill and humility — abilities and virtues which these thirteen laymen possessed. The adaptation was delicate because it had to be accomplished without the Church's losing any of its essential characteristics. Of necessity it had to be accomplished on the Church's terms, not on the world's. And the world could not understand why the Church would not lie down like the lamb and become part of the world. Adaptation came about, slowly at first, and then toward the end of the century more rapidly, so that by the time Wilfrid Ward died no well-informed person could believe that the Church was the enemy of democracy or of social progress or of science or education or any of those things considered "modern." These problems were not settled for once and for all in 1916, of course, because the work of adaptation goes on forever — but for the time it seemed that politically, socially, and intellectually the Church had assimilated most of the good things engendered by the civilization of the nineteenth century. And in this work laymen had done their considerable share.

These Catholic lay leaders, we have seen, were not all cut to the same pattern — for the Church is catholic and it employs all kinds of talent. In temperament, in intellectual acumen, in ability, in almost everything they differed considerably. This, though, they held in common: a love for the Church and a willingness to give their time and their energies to its service. They were united in trying to solve the basic problem of adapting the Church to modern society in such fashion as to secure freedom for the Church and at the same time to save modern society by bringing it into the Church's embrace. Their work, then, was apostolic, that "participation of the laity in the apostolate of the hierarchy," as Pope Pius XI put it in 1929, "which in its essence is as old as the Church itself, but has only come to be studied in its fullness in recent times."

Each of these Catholic laymen can now be seen as fitting into a providentially designed pattern. Each in his own way helped the Church. Each answered the call of the Church with his own talents, as Pius XI teaches all are bound to do, and therefore became a promoter of Catholic Action before the term was actually defined. Most important, and reflecting greatest credit on themselves as individuals, none of these men we have discussed in this book succumbed to the sin of intellectual pride. The temptations were great – for Montalembert and Brownson and several others – to rebel when they were misunderstood by the hierarchy or when their work seemed anathematized. Time, and the Church in the goodness of time, proved them right – and they were right because they submitted to ecclesiastical authority even when they could not understand the rationale of its decision. They were capable men, these thirteen who were "doers of the word and not hearers only," and they were basically humble men – which is the principal cause of their greatness.

BIBLIOGRAPHICAL NOTE

The following books are suggested for those interested in further study of the Catholic lay leaders treated in this book. The list, like the book itself, is made up not for professional scholars but for intelligent men-in-the-street and students who may profit from the titles and the comments below.

Certain specific principles govern the selection of the following books and the omission of others.

1. No attempt is made to pile title on title. Any capable college freshman can do that simply by collecting items from the several guides to periodical literature, the Union and Congressional card catalogues, various encyclopedias, and appropriate special bibliographies. The titles included below are mentioned because of their intrinsic worth or because they reveal some particular viewpoint on the subject under study. It should be understood that they are not the sole sources of information from which the author gathered material for the preceding pages.

2. No attempt is made to list general works necessary for understanding the background in which the various Catholic lay leaders moved and thought, since such a list would defeat our purpose by growing unwieldy and unnecessarily formidable. It should be remembered, nonetheless, that one cannot understand O'Connell's activity unless he has a good general picture of Irish and English problems in the early part of the nineteenth century. So it is with Windhorst in Germany, Donoso in Spain, García Moreno in Ecuador, and all the others.

3. Works in English are listed more extensively than those in French, German, Spanish, or Italian. This procedure is based on the practical belief that Americans, generally speaking, are not conversant with foreign languages. In some cases where there is almost nothing in English on the man – as notably with Görres and Donoso Cortés – care is taken to give everything the author has seen. In other cases where a great deal is available – as

notably with O'Connell and Ozanam — only samples are listed in this bibliography.

4. Original sources — the writings of the Catholic laymen themselves — are invariably included in the original language, but care is taken to list any translations into English with which the author is acquainted.

5. The "classic biography" of each individual is given, whether it is in English or in a foreign language. The classic biography is that written by a close friend, a widow, a son, or someone who had access to the subject's intimate thoughts, as well as to his private papers and letters. It is indispensable reading for all students of the subject and for all later biographers. An attempt has been made to list a few other important biographies, including, whenever possible, both the latest one and the one which this author considers the best.

6. Periodical literature is cited, as a rule, with an eye to its accessibility to the average reader. This principle rules out listing articles in foreign journals; these would have to be included in any scholarly, "definitive" work on any of the Catholic laymen treated above. We have used such journals as *Études, Razon y Fe,* and *Der Katolik* extensively, but they do not contain information either extensive enough or exclusive enough to justify their inclusion in this bibliography. Generally, an attempt is made to list some general articles on the layman concerned, some studies on special aspects of his activity, and some critical as well as some eulogistic appraisals of his worth.

1. O'Connell

Daniel O'Connell was primarily a political figure, not an author or philosopher. His works are therefore not as extensive or important, relative to his career, as is the case with men like Louis Veuillot or Donoso Cortés. His speeches can be found in various numbers of *Hansard's Parliamentary Debates* (Third Series) covering the period when he was in Parliament. Available as primary sources — O'Connell's own writings — are the following: *A Memoir on Ireland* (1834); *Correspondence of Daniel O'Connell, the Liberator,* edited by W. J. Fitzpatrick (1888); *The Select Speeches of Daniel O'Connell,* edited by John O'Connell (1860); *Personal Recollections of the late Daniel O'Connell,* by William J. O'Neill Daunt (1848). Between 1882 and 1887 the *Irish Monthly* published the "Diary of Daniel O'Connell and His Letters" in five installments.

Biographies of O'Connell are numerous. It is almost impossible to find a thoroughly objective story of this man's life, for his biographers grimly carried on the Irish struggle and they enlisted O'Connell to fight all over again within the pages of each successive biography. In 1845 – two years before O'Connell died – Thomas D. McGee published *O'Connell and His Friends.* Sister Mary Frances Cusack's *Life of Daniel O'Connell* appeared in 1872, and in 1906 Robert Dunlop published his *Daniel O'Connell.* In 1929, the centenary of Catholic Emancipation, a rash of articles and books on the Liberator appeared on the market. Notable among the biographies of this year were Denis Gwynn's *Daniel O'Connell, the Liberator,* and Michael MacDonaugh's *Daniel O'Connell and the Story of Catholic Emancipation.* The most recent and the best life story this author has seen is Seán O'Faoláin's *King of Beggars* (1938). O'Connell is given a chapter in John J. Horgan's *Great Catholic Laymen* (1905), in *The Irish Orators* by Claude G. Bowers (1916), and in Robert F. Walsh's *Memorial Volume to Charles Stewart Parnell* (1872).

Articles on O'Connell abound in Catholic periodicals. Most of them are uncritically eulogistic, many are of a general nature and therefore repetitious of each other. In 1929 articles commemorating O'Connell's role in Catholic Emancipation and his life in general appeared in almost every Catholic journal – and there is no need to list these articles separately here. Mention should be made, perhaps, of the April, 1929, issue of *Dublin Review* which was devoted to O'Connell. In it were such articles as "The Liberator," "O'Connell and the Ireland in Which He Lived," "O'Connell and the Repeal." In addition to articles of a general nature on O'Connell, one can also find those which develop some particular aspect of his career. Typical of these are: C. P. Curran's "O'Connell's Deistic Tendencies," in the *Catholic World* (June, 1929); T. S. J. Corcoran's "O'Connell and Kildare Place," in the *Irish Monthly* (August, 1932); and M. V. Ronan's "Catholic Rent of 1828," in the *Irish Ecclesiastical Records* (October and December, 1942).

2. Montalembert

Montalembert's works were published within his own lifetime (1860–1868) as *Oeuvres de Montalembert* (eight volumes). This collection is far from complete, for his *Monks of the West* was not much more than begun when he began publishing his collected works. (*The Monks* was never finished, altogether seven volumes appeared, the last of them being published posthumously.) Other important additions in French to the *Oeuvres* were three volumes of speeches, *Discours de Montalembert,* edited in 1892 by Camille de Meaux, and *Pages choisis avec lettres inédites,* edited in 1920 by V. Bucaille. There are many different volumes of Montalembert's correspondence in French. Only one volume, *Letters to a Schoolfellow, 1827–1830,* edited by C. F. Audley, has appeared in English. Fortunately for the English reader, however, the greater part of Montalembert's formally published works have been translated into English. *The Monks of the West* (seven volumes, 1861–1869), and a later edition of the same work in six volumes by Gasquet, present Montalembert's masterpiece to English readers. The *Life of Saint Elizabeth of Hungary* was translated into English in 1867. It is, incidentally, better historical writing than *The Monks.* A number of Montalembert's writings on current subjects were also translated into English: *On Vandalism and Catholicism in Art* (1839); *Catholic Interests in the Nineteenth Century* (1852); *The Political Future of England* (1856); *Constitutional Liberty* (1858); *Pius IX and France in 1849 and 1859* (1861); *Memoir of the Abbé Lacordaire* (1863); and *Pius IX and Lord Palmerston* (1863).

The classic biography of Montalembert appears in English. It is Mrs. Oliphant's two-volume *Memoir of Count de Montalembert,* published in 1882, and written by a lady who had access to his papers and enjoyed long visits with his widow, whom the author knew well. Other important studies by contemporaries are Craven's *Le Comte de Montalembert* (1873) and Faisset's *Le Comte de Montalembert* (1877). The best later study is perhaps Lecanuet's *Montalembert d'après ses papiers et sa correspondance* (three volumes, 1910). It must be remembered that although Lecanuet is a competent scholar who has written the best history of the Church under the Third Republic, nevertheless he is strongly prejudiced in Montalembert's favor and against Veuillot. There are chapters on Montalembert in W. J. Sparrow-Simpson's *French Catholics in the Nineteenth Century* (1938), in Horgan's *Great Catholic Laymen,* and in Reuben Parsons' *Studies in Church History* (Volume V).

There are innumerable articles on Montalembert in French; even in English there is a considerable number. Most frequently they are restricted to an evaluation of his *Monks* or to his relationship with some other figure in French history, such as Lamennais or Lacordaire or Napoleon III. A few of the more general articles in English appeared in the *Catholic World:* "A Son of the Crusaders" (January, 1873); "Montalembert and His Visit to O'Connell," by Joseph G. Daley (June, 1900); and "Montalembert and Lamennais," by William L. Sullivan (January, 1903). In the *Dublin Review* one can find several articles taking cognizance of Montalembert during his lifetime: an article in the March, 1853, issue on his "Catholic Interests"; one in June, 1856, on his "Political Future of England"; and two on *The Monks,* in February, 1861, and June, 1868.

3. Windthorst

Windthorst was a politician rather than a theorist or a writer. Not much in the way of "primary sources" is therefore available to the American student. Three volumes of his more important speeches have been selected and published under the title *Ausgewählte Reden 1851–1891,* and Otto Pfülf has published a volume of his letters, *Aus Windthorsts Korrespondenz.* There is no biography of Windthorst in English. The best known biographies in German include the following: Menzenbach's *Windthorst* (1892), a eulogistic study appearing shortly after his death; Knapp's *Windthorst* (1898), in the *Männer der Zeit* series; Edward Husgen's *Ludwig Windthorst* (1911); *Ludwig Windthorst, ein Lebensbild,* by J. Bachem (1912); and *Ludwig Windthorst,* by A. Reumont (1920). There is a good study in French by G. Bazin, *Windthorst, ses allies et ses adversaires* (1896). Indispensable for a knowledge of Windthorst's career are the seven volumes on the Center Party by Karl Bachem, *Vorgeschichte, Geschichte und Politik der deutschen Zentrumspartie* (1927–1932).

Horgan devotes a chapter of his *Great Catholic Laymen* to "Windthorst, the German Liberator," and Parsons has a chapter on "The Bismarckian So-Called 'War for Civilization,' " in the sixth volume of his *Studies in Church History.* Three scholarly articles on Windthorst appeared in the *American Catholic Quarterly Review:* "Bismarck's Conflict with the Catholic Church," by H. J. Heuser (April, 1884); "The Impregnable Fortress," by Joseph Schroeder (July, 1890); and "Windthorst," by the same author (July, 1891). Four briefer, but equally solid articles are to be found in the *Month:* "The Present Condition of the Church in Germany" (June, 1885); "Dr. Windthorst" (May, 1891); "Lessons from German Catholics," by F. Goldie (May, 1892); and "The German Center Party—Past and Present," by A. W. G. Randall (February, 1919). William Kelley published an article, "Ludwig Windthorst," in the May, 1890, issue of *Catholic World*, and in the May, 1897, number of the same journal Mary Mitchell wrote on "Windthorst and the Kulturkampf." Other articles in English include M. O'Riordan, "Dr. Windthorst: His Life and Work," *Irish Ecclesiastical Record* (June, 1891); Francis Curran, "Ludwig von Windthorst," *Historical Bulletin* (January, 1939); and Thomas P. Neill, "Catholic Lay Leaders: III, Ludwig von Windthorst," *Columbia* (July, 1949).

4. Moreno

Like Windthorst, García Moreno is more a man of action than of words. He did edit a series of fly-by-night newspapers during the turbulent times when he was criticizing the government, and he wrote such pamphlets as his "Defense of the Jesuits." The most important collection of his works is probably Manuel Palit Laso's *Escrits y Discursos de Gabriel Garcia Moreno* (1923). There are, in Spanish, several different collections of his letters to various friends or on such subjects as the concordat or the constitution.

An adequate study of Moreno's importance to the Church and to Ecuador can be made only by a general study of his country's history. The best work in this respect, which combines the advantages of a biography and a cultural history of the age, is Richard F. Pattee, *Gabriel García Moreno y El Ecuador de Su Tiempo* (1941). Unfortunately, this work is not translated into English. The best known full-length biography in English is the translation from the original French of P. A. Berthe's *García Moreno, President of Ecuador* (1889). The only other biography in English this author has found is M. M. Maxwell-Scott's *Gabriel García Moreno, Regenerator of Ecuador* (1908).

There are many studies in Spanish journals, both of a general biographical and of a more specialized nature, as well as a goodly number in French. In English there are several articles of solid worth. The best of these, perhaps, is Sister M. Loyola's "García Moreno of Ecuador," in *The Americas* (January, 1945). This work contains a good bibliography. Fairly good coverage of Moreno's life is given by the three articles of A. M. Clark in the *Month* for January, February, and March of 1888. A number of articles on Moreno appeared shortly after his assassination, such as R. Searle's "García Moreno" in the *Catholic World* (February, 1876), and "A Friend of the Sacred Heart and a Martyr to Duty," in *The Messenger of the Sacred Heart* (February, 1876).

Later, and therefore usually better balanced, studies of Moreno include: "Gabriel García Moreno," by W. Eugene Shiels, *Historical Bulletin* (May, 1939); "Freemasonry in Latin America — The Modern St. Louis — García Moreno," by Reuben Parsons, *American Catholic Quarterly Review* (October, 1898); "García Moreno's Efforts to Unite Ecuador and France," by George F. Howe, *Hispanic American Historical Review* (May, 1936); "San Francisco de Quito" and "Il Venti Settembre," by Francis Montgomery in the October and December, 1929, numbers of *Blackfriars;* and J. J. Griffin's "Model for Catholic Statesman" in *Ave Maria* (November 5, 1938). Horgan's *Great Catholic Laymen* devotes a chapter to Moreno, and Parson's *Studies* (Volume VI) contains a reprint of his article from the *American Catholic Quarterly Review.*

5. Jaricot

There is not a great deal of information available in English on Pauline Marie Jaricot. Her own writings consist of her personal letters and the circulars she sent out to chapters of the Living Rosary. So far as we know, they have not been published in any language. They were used extensively, however, by her follower Julia Maurin, who wrote the now indispensable biography *Pauline Marie Jaricot* in 1881. This work is translated in English. Also available in English is Elizabeth Sainte-Marie Perrin's *Pauline Jaricot,* translated in 1928. Colette Yver's *Marie-Pauline de Jesus-Christ, Mlle. Jaricot* (1937) is one of the latest French biographies. The best study in English is Katherine Burton's *Difficult Star* (1947). This life story synthesizes the previous work done on Mlle. Jaricot and presents a balanced, sympathetic account of her life.

About six or seven articles on Pauline Jaricot have appeared in English periodicals in the past twenty years. Father Corrigan published one called "Catholic Lay Leader" in the *Catholic World* (January, 1940); M. J. Moore wrote on "Pauline Jaricot: A Daughter of Lyons," in the *Irish Ecclesiastical Record* (February, 1942); H. F. Hall's "Pauline M. Jaricot" appeared in the January, 1929, number of *Truth;* F. Gilmore's "Patron Saint of Failures" was in the January 17, 1943, issue of *Ave Maria.* Notice was taken of her in *America* (November 1, 1930) in the

"With Scrip and Staff" column, and an abridgment of part of Katherine Burton's book appeared as "Propagation Foundress" in the *Catholic Mission Digest* (November, 1947).

Exhaustive study on this subject is undoubtedly being conducted in connection with the progress of her cause in Rome. Students can therefore expect more definitive treatment of the subject in the years ahead.

6. Ozanam

There are more books and articles in English on Frédéric Ozanam than on any other person treated in this book, with the possible exception of O'Connell. Americans and Englishmen have inadvertently given us a lopsided impression of the French layman, however, because they have been interested chiefly in his St. Vincent de Paul Society. It is necessary to read among the French students of Ozanam's life to get a well-rounded picture of this literary scholar, professor, charity worker, and perhaps saint.

In 1855, two years after Ozanam's death, his works were published with a notice by Lacordaire and a preface by Ampère. The *Oeuvres complètes de A. F. Ozanam* are in eight volumes, the first six being his historical and literary studies and the last two miscellaneous pieces. The "complete" works, incidentally, are far from complete. Three of the historical works have been translated into English: *Dante and Catholic Philosophy in the Thirteenth Century; The Franciscan Poets in Italy of the Thirteenth Century;* and *History of Civilization in the Fifth Century* (two volumes). Also available in English are the *Letters of Ozanam,* translated in 1886 by Ainslie Coates.

The classic biography, written by his close friend Lacordaire, appeared in 1856 under the title *Frédéric Ozanam.* There are many biographies in English, of which we shall mention a few of the more important. Among the older lives are *Frédéric Ozanam,* by Archibald Dunn (1877); *Frederick Ozanam, His Life and Works,* by Kathleen O'Meara (1878); and *Frédéric Ozanam,* by Gerard Power (1878). Among the more recent works are the following: *Ozanam in His Correspondence,* by Monsignor Baunard (1925); *Frédéric Ozanam,* by James Broderick, S.J. (1933); *Frédéric Ozanam,* by Henry Louis Hughes (1933); and *The Great Friend,* by Albert P. Schimberg (1946). Individual chapters are given to Ozanam by Horgan in his *Great Catholic Laymen,* by Selden P. Delany in his *Married Saints* (1935), and by Reuben Parson in his *Studies in Church History* (Volume V).

Articles on Ozanam are scattered through Catholic periodical literature, hardly a year passing since his death in which several good studies have not appeared. In 1913, the centenary of his birth, and especially in 1933, the centenary of the founding of the St. Vincent de Paul Society, there were innumerable articles in Catholic journals. Most notable, perhaps, are the following for 1913: a series of four articles in *America* (October 4, 11, 18, 25) by Rev. Joseph Husslein, S.J., on the general subject of Ozanam and the labor question; Michael Kenny, "Ozanam Centenary," *America* (April 26); and William Kitchin, "Centenary of Frederic Ozanam," *Catholic World* (September). Among the articles appearing in 1933 are the following: H. Kildany, "Centenary of Saint Vincent de Paul Society," *Blackfriars* (June); A. C. Klass, "Frederick Ozanam – Historian," *Historical Bulletin* (May, 1932); A. C. Klass, "Ozanam, Pioneer of Catholic Action," *America* (May 20, 1933); C. L. Souvay, "Ozanam as Historian," *Catholic Historical Review* (April); Ray Codwallacher, "Ozanam: Christian Teacher," *America* (June 24); and "Frederick Ozanam, Influences on His Character," *Catholic Charities Review* (May).

7. De Mun

The most important work in English for a knowledge of De Mun is Parker T. Moon's excellent scholarly treatise on *The Labor Problem and the Social Catholic Movement in France* (1921). This book is a study of the Social Catholic Movement as a whole, but it treats De Mun extensively. The best scholarly article in English on De Mun is Richard L. Porter's "Albert de Mun and Social Catholicism," in the *Historical Bulletin* (January, 1940). More popular articles are: James B. Milburn, "Albert de Mun," in the *Dublin Review* (July, 1917); P. W. Browne, "A Modern Crusader," the *Catholic World* (December, 1921); Eugene Davis, "Count de Mun: Leader of the Catholic Republican Deputies," *Catholic World* (December, 1894); and Father Corrigan's "Albert de Mun: Revolutionist," *Fleur de Lis* (May, 1938).

To obtain more than a sketchy picture of De Mun, however, one must use French sources. Most valuable is De Mun's own autobiography, *Ma vocation sociale* (1908). His other writings have been collected in *Discours et ecrits divers* (seven volumes, 1888–1904), and *Combats d'hier et d'aujourd'hui* (six volumes, 1910–1916). The July, 1907, issue of *Dublin Review* carried an article on "La Question Religieuse en France" by De Mun. The text of the article is in French.

There are two standard biographies in French, but both are uncritically laudatory: A. Saint-Pierre, *Le Comte Albert de Mun* (1915), and Victor Giraud, *Un grand Francais: Albert de Mun* (1918). Lecanuet gives him extensive treatment in *L'Eglise de France sous la Troisième Republique* (four volumes, 1931). The student who wishes to pursue the subject even further can find a number of articles in contemporary French journals, especially in *Études* and *Le Correspondant.*

8. De Maistre

De Maistre's *Oeuvres complètes* were published in fourteen volumes in 1884–1886, and republished in 1926. *Du Pape* is the best known volume; in it are found De Maistre's ultramontane arguments in their simplest form. *De l'eglise gallican* was originally intended as the fifth part of *Du Pape,* but it was published as a separate work. It applies De Maistre's ultramontane arguments directly to France. *Considérations sur la France,* originally published in 1796, consists chiefly of reflections on the French Revolution. Eighteenth-century thinkers are dealt with especially in the two volumes of *Les soirées de Saint-Petersbourg* and in the posthumously published *L'examen de la philosophie de Bacon.* Eight of the fourteen volumes of the *Oeuvres complètes* consist of De Maistre's immense correspondence which he carried on with important people throughout Europe. This correspondence reveals the maturity of his thought on political and social matters; the letters to his family and his intimate friends do much to modify the reader's picture of this urbane Savoyard count. Only one volume of these writings, *Du Pape,* is translated into English. It appeared in 1850 under the title *The Pope.*

Works in English on De Maistre are rather scarce. So far as this author knows, there is no book-length study on the man. A sound appraisal of De Maistre is offered in Father Corrigan's "De Maistre: Freemason and Ultramontane," in the *Historical Bulletin* (March, 1939). *Dublin Review* (July, 1938, and January, 1939) carries two good articles by Algernon Cecil. Entitled "De Maistre," they are substantially a reprint of Cecil's address to the Thomas More Society on March 4, 1938. Less recent treatments of De Maistre in English include Hugh McElrone's good article "Joseph de Maistre" in the *Catholic World* (May, 1881); A. J. Faust's "Count Joseph de Maistre" in the *American Catholic Quarterly Review* (January, 1882); and T. L. Teeling's "Joseph de Maistre" in the October, 1895, issue of the same review. There are a few other articles which are not particularly helpful. Giovanni Papini has a short chapter on De Maistre in his *Laborers in the Vineyard.* James Broderick has an article "Paradoxes of De Maistre" in the *Month* (August, 1937), and Mrs. George Norman has a short piece "Joseph de Maistre" in the February, 1940, number of the same magazine. Finally, John Morley offers a condescending critique in the second volume of his *Critical Miscellanies,* published in 1886.

Works in French are numerous; indeed, they run into the hundreds. A few of the more important biographies are: Georges Cogordan, *Joseph de Maistre avant la révolution* (1893), and the same author's *Joseph de Maistre pendant la révolution* (1895); Georges Goyau, *La pensée religieuse de Joseph de Maistre* (1921); Emile Dermenghem, *Joseph de Maistre mystique* (1923); Camille Latreille, *Joseph de Maistre et la papauté* (1906); Amedée de Margerie, *La Comte Joseph de Maistre* (1896); Eugène Grasset, *Joseph de Maistre: sa vie et son oeuvre* (1901); and Paul Vulliaud, *Joseph de Maistre, francmaçon* (1926).

9. Görres

The works of Joseph Görres were originally edited by his daughter: *Gesammelte Werke* (six volumes, 1854–1860), and *Gesammelte Briefe* (three volumes, 1858–1874). A more complete and more scholarly edition of his complete works appeared in 1928 under the title of Görres' *Gesammelte Schriften.* Among his writings *Athanasius* and *Kirche und Staat* are most important for handling the problem of relationships between Church and State; *Europa und die Revolution* is the best single volume containing his political views, which are also to be found scattered among his shorter works and his letters; *Die Christliche Mystik* contains most of his views on philosophical and spiritual subjects, in additional to a wealth of historical information; his *Mythengeschichte der Asiatischen Welt* is of no particular importance for understanding his role as a Catholic lay leader, though its learning impressed German scholars and established Görres' reputation.

Most of Görres' important articles can be found in *Der Rheinische Merkur* (1814–1816), *Der Katolik* (1824–1827), and *Historisch-Politische Blätter* (1838–1848), all of which are in various libraries in this country. German scholars have made it easy for the student to read the most important passages in

Görres by having compiled selections of his writings in various volumes. The best of these that we have seen is William Schellberg's *Joseph Görres: Eine Auswahl aus seinen Werken und Briefen* (1927), which contains about six hundred pages of carefully chosen and well-edited selections. A shorter set is to be found in *Katholisch-conservatives Erbgut* (1934), edited by Emil Ritter and containing forty-five pages of selections on Görres by Auguste Schorn. Hans Munster published a selection of his political writings under the title *Joseph Görres: Eine Auswahl aus seinen nationalen Schriften.*

Only one of Görres' works has been translated into English, *Europe and the Revolution,* done sometime before 1839 and now difficult to obtain. (I have not seen this translation.) His four volumes on Christian mysticism have been translated into French under the title *La mystique divine, naturelle et diabolique.*

Görres is the subject of innumerable studies in the German Catholic periodicals. Good biographies include the one by his student Sepp, *Görres und seine Zeitgenossen* (1877), and the shorter *Joseph von Görres* by Joseph Galland (1876), both published in connection with the centenary of his birth. William Schellberg published a good concise biography on the occasion of the 1926 celebration in Görres' honor, *Joseph von Görres,* and at the same time Robert Stein issued a popular life replete with illustrations under the simple title *Görres.*

There is almost nothing on Görres in English. The January, 1839, issue of *Dublin Review* contains an article on "The Life and Writings of Görres" (nine years before he died), which offers a short sketch of his earlier life and a review of three of his books. In the July, 1905, number of the same magazine J. M. Stone's "Joseph Görres: His Work and His Friends" presents a simple but accurate account of the exterior events of his life. The only other article in English that I have been able to find is the excellent analytical and interpretative study by Father Corrigan, "Görres – Battler for Liberty," in the *Historical Bulletin* (November, 1937).

10. Donoso Cortés

Donoso's works were collected by his follower and admirer, Gabino Tejado, and published in five volumes. Tejado wrote a long introduction to the *Obras* which stands as the classic biography on Donoso. There are several later editions of Donoso's works in Spanish, the most important being the four-volume edition by Juan Manuel Ortí y Lara (1903–1904), and the recent Biblioteca de Autores Cristianos two-volume edition, *Obras Completas de D. Juan Donoso Cortés* (1946). Louis Veuillot edited a three-volume translation of Donoso's works in French, *Oeuvres de Donoso Cortés* (1858), in which Veuillot wrote a sixty-four-page biographical sketch of his friend Donoso.

Donoso's masterpiece is his only book-length study, *Ensayo sobre el catolicismo, el liberalismo y el socialismo,* which contains all his major ideas. It has been translated into English twice, the first time in 1888 as *Essays on Catholicism, Liberalism, and Socialism,* and the second time in 1925 as *An Essay on Catholicism, Authority and Order.* To know Donoso's thought in its fullness it is necessary to read his speeches and his letters. The most important speeches are those given to the Spanish Cortes on dictatorship (January 4, 1849), on the condition of Spain (December 30, 1850), and on the condition of Europe (January 30, 1850).

There is very little on Donoso in English. In 1938, Goetz Briefs wrote a pamphlet *A Christian Statesman and Political Philosopher: Donoso Cortés.* There is a good article by Alfonso de Cossio, "Donoso Cortés," in the spring, 1947, *Dublin Review,* and an article entitled "Metternich and Donoso Cortés," by Bela Menczer, in the same journal, last quarter, 1948. Thomas P. Neill has an article, "Juan Donoso Cortés – Spanish Catholic Layman," in the May, 1949, *Historical Bulletin,* and "Juan Donoso Cortés" in the *Catholic World* (November, 1949). There is a good deal of work done in German on Donoso Cortés, especially by Edmund Schramm and Carl Schmitt. The most comprehensive single work is probably Schramm's *Donoso Cortés – Leben und Werk eines spanischen Antiliberalen* (1935).

11. Brownson

Brownson's *Works* were collected and published by his son Henry in twenty volumes. They are arranged topically rather than chronologically, and they are not complete. Anyone seriously interested in Brownson must read the flow of his essays and reviews in *Brownson's Quarterly Review,* and perhaps turn to the *Boston Quarterly Review* for some of his earlier essays. No exhaustive work can be done without using the collection of Brownson documents at the University of Notre Dame library. Various anthologies of Brownson's writings, ranging from paragraphs to complete essays, have been made for the convenience of those who are not interested in plowing through the twenty volumes of his collected works or through the *Review*. One of these collections was published in 1852 by Brownson himself as *Essays and Reviews*. His son Henry culled a volume of *Literary, Scientific, and Political Views of Orestes A. Brownson* from the twenty volumes he had previously published. In 1910 J. Scannel O'Neill published his *Watchwords from Dr. Brownson*, and in 1923 David Battle published *Gems of Composition and Criticism Compiled from the Writings of Orestes A. Brownson.*

Which of Brownson's works is most important depends on what the reader is looking for in him – his defense of the Church, his attack on Liberalism, his economic thought, his political philosophy, or any of a dozen other things. Brownson wrote an autobiography, *The Convert*, which is good for the author's early life. Published in 1857, however, it does not deal with his important contributions to the Church's life in America. The classic biography, to which all later studies of Brownson must refer, is the three-volume life written by Henry Brownson. These volumes deal respectively with Brownson's early, middle, and later life. Four or five more recent biographies are worth noting. Sidney Raemers' *America's Foremost Philosopher* (1931), and Sister Rose Gertrude Whalen's *Some Aspects of the Influence of Orestes A. Brownson on his Contemporaries* (1933), and her *Granite for God's House* (1941) are overly eulogistic studies by authors who fell under the magnetic spell of their subject – an easy thing to do when reading Brownson.

Better balanced, more detached biographies are Arthur M. Schlesinger, Jr., *Orestes A. Brownson: A Pilgrim's Progress* (1939), and Theodore Maynard, *Orestes Brownson, Yankee, Radical, Catholic* (1943). Daniel Sargent treats Brownson well in his *Four Independents* (1935). There are also specialized studies on one or another aspect of Brownson's writing and activity, such as Father Virgil Michel's *Critical Principles of Orestes A. Brownson* (1918), or Paul R. Conroy's *Orestes A. Brownson, American Political Philosopher* (1937).

Articles on Brownson are legion in American Catholic periodicals. During his lifetime he was the subject of many articles, such as the series in *Dublin Review* by W. G. Ward. At the time of his death a number of encomiums appeared, such as "In Memoriam. Orestes A. Brownson" in the July, 1876, issue of the *American Catholic Quarterly Review*, and "Dr. Brownson" in the June, 1876, number of *Catholic World*. The latter review has had studies on Brownson appearing more or less regularly through the years since his death. Articles of a general nature can also be found in *Commonweal, America, Ave Maria,* and almost every Catholic journal. Studies of a specialized nature have also appeared frequently. Typical are Schlesinger's "Orestes Brownson, an American Marxist before Marx," in the *Sewanee Review* (July, 1939); Ryan's "Brownson's Hints to Preachers," in the *Homiletic and Pastoral Review* (May, 1943); and Thomas T. McAvoy's "Brownson's Ontologism," in the *Catholic Historical Review* (October, 1942).

12. Veuillot

Louis Veuillot did not write any single masterpiece. To know his mind and to understand his role in the history of the Church in nineteenth-century France one must read through his collected works – for Veuillot dashed off letters and articles and editorials at the rate of over a hundred a month, and it is through these journalistic pieces that we must study the man. His works have been collected and published by his nephew, François Veuillot, as *Oeuvres complètes de Louis Veuillot* (thirty-nine volumes, 1925). Among the more important single volumes should be mentioned *La vie de Notre Seigneur Jesus Christ* (which stands in striking contrast to the lives of Christ by Renan and Strauss, Veuillot's agnostic contemporaries), *Les libres penseurs, Rome et Lorette, Le parfum de Rome,* and the companion volume *Les odeurs de Paris, Ça et là, Portraits de saints,* and *Rome pendant le concile.* Only one of these works has been translated into English, *The Life of Our Lord Jesus Christ.*

Most informative for a history of the Church during the forty years that Veuillot edited *Univers,* as well as for an understanding of Veuillot himself, are his shorter, miscellaneous works published as thirteen volumes of *Mélanges* in the 1925 edition of the *Oeuvres complètes.* This collection consists of short articles on important questions of the time, letters to friends and acquaintances, and significant selections from *Univers.*

There is no biography of Veuillot in English. The classic work in French is the four-volume biographical study *Louis Veuillot* made by his brother Eugène and completed by the latter's son François. An interesting work, arranged topically rather than chronologically, is Emmanuel Gautier's *Le vrai Louis Veuillot.* In it the author offers a psychological study of his subject, based mostly upon his correspondence. François Veuillot's more recent

Louis Veuillot: sa vie, son âme, son oeuvre is another authoritative biography of the great French journalist. Written in answer to Veuillot's detractors, however, it tends to praise the editor of *Univers* somewhat too uncritically.

A goodly number of articles in English have been written on Veuillot. He is included, in a short chapter each time, in S. R. Delany's *Married Saints,* and W. J. Sparrow-Simpson's *French Catholics in the Nineteenth Century.* At the time of his death in 1883, Veuillot was treated eulogistically in an article by William Loughnan, "Louis Veuillot," in the May issue of *Month.* E. Myers presented a critical analysis of Veuillot's work in the August, 1903, issue of *Catholic World;* and an even harsher criticism by William Seton, "A Puzzle Explained," appeared in the following issue. Ten years later F. Drouet wrote a favorable study of "the most striking Catholic personality of nineteenth century France" for the same journal. Called "Glimpses of A Great Catholic Soul – Louis Veuillot," the article is a "revelation" of Veuillot as found in his correspondence.

In connection with a Veuillot celebration held in France to commemorate the hundredth anniversary of the publication of the French journalist's first article in 1831, several studies favorable to Veuillot appeared in English and American Catholic journals. Benjamin L. Masse wrote on "The Significance of a Centenary" in the February 12, 1932, number of *America;* G. O'Neill did "A Note on Louis Veuillot" in the July, 1931, number of *Month,* in which he defended Veuillot against such people as Father Cuthbert who wanted to minimize the French editor's importance; and *Tablet* carried a sensible, understanding appraisal of Veuillot in its "Et Caetera" column on April 15, 1933.

Finally, four good articles favorable to Veuillot appeared in the American Catholic laymen's magazine *Commonweal.* The first two numbers of *Commonweal* (November 12 and 19, 1924) carried articles by Henry Longan Stuart entitled "Louis Veuillot." They are studies of the man and the writer. H. A. Jules-Bois contributed "Veuillot, Master of Obedience," to the April 1, 1938, number of *Commonweal,* and a week later his "Veuillot of *L'Univers*" appeared.

13. Ward

The classic life of Wilfrid Ward is the two-volume study by his daughter, Maisie Ward, *The Wilfrid Wards and the Transition* (1934) and *Insurrection versus Resurrection* (1937). Four chapters of the first volume are Wilfrid Ward's own "Reminiscences" which his daughter printed without alteration. He was writing them at the time of his death, apparently intending to use them in a future autobiography. Maisie Ward's study of her parents will remain *the* biography of Wilfrid Ward. The only reason for reading anything else about him is to find other estimates of his importance and to read other judgments on his place in history. His widow wrote a fairly long biographical introduction to his posthumously published *Last Lectures* (1918) which deserves to be coupled with Maisie Ward's longer study as the classic biography. G. K. Chesterton and Father Cuthbert wrote quasi-official appreciations of the recently deceased editor of *Dublin Review* in the July, 1916, issue of that magazine.

Wilfrid Ward wrote four biographies, three of which are classic studies on important Catholic leaders of nineteenth-century England: *The Life of John Henry, Cardinal Newman* (two volumes, 1912); *The Life and Times of Cardinal Wiseman* (two volumes, 1898); *William George Ward and the Oxford Movement* (1889), and *William George Ward and the Catholic Revival* (1893). These biographies, combined with his little study of *The Oxford Movement,* present a good history of Catholic affairs in nineteenth-century England. Ward was a frequent contributor to leading reviews of his day, particularly the *Edinburgh Quarterly,* and *Nineteenth Century,* in addition to his many articles in the *Dublin Review.* The articles he considered most important were collected and published in book form in three volumes: *Problems and Persons* (1902); *Ten Personal Studies* (1908); and *Men and Matters* (1914). Two of Ward's earliest works are interesting for the apologetic he develops on the basis of natural religion and the human tendency toward the worship of God. The first, *The Wish to Believe* (1882), attracted the favorable attention of leading English thinkers; the second, *Witnesses to the Unseen and Other Essays,* continued the same train of thought.

INDEX